Ritual and Violence: Natalie Zemon Davis and Early Modern France

*Edited by Graeme Murdock,
Penny Roberts, and Andrew Spicer*

1 Great Clarendon Street, Oxford OX2 6DP

Oxford University Press is a department of the University of Oxford.
It furthers the University's objective of excellence in research, scholarship,
and education by publishing worldwide in

Oxford New York

Athens Auckland Bangkok Bogotá Buenos Aires Cape Town
Chennai Dar es Salaam Delhi Florence Hong Kong Istanbul Karachi
Kolkata Kuala Lumpur Madrid Melbourne Mexico City Mumbai Nairobi
Paris São Paulo Shanghai Singapore Taipei Tokyo Toronto Warsaw

with associated companies in Berlin Ibadan

Oxford is a registered trade mark of Oxford University Press
in the UK and in certain other countries

Published in the United Kingdom
by Oxford University Press Inc., New York

© The Past and Present Society, 2012

The moral rights of the author have been asserted
Database right Oxford University Press (maker)

First published 2012

All rights reserved. No part of this publication may be reproduced,
stored in a retrieval system, or transmitted, in any form or by any means,
without the prior permission in writing of Oxford University Press,
or as expressly permitted by law, or under terms agreed with the appropriate
reprographics rights organization. Enquiries concerning reproduction
outside the scope of the above should be sent to the Rights Department,
Oxford University Press, at the address above

You must not circulate this book in any other binding or cover
and you must impose this same condition on any acquirer

A catalogue for this book is available from the British Library

Library of Congress Cataloging in Publication
Data (data available)

ISBN 0-19-965496-3
ISBN 978-0-19-965496-3

Subscription information for Past & Present is available
from:jnls.cust.serv@oup.com

Typeset by Glyph International, Bangalore, India
Printed by Bell and Bain Ltd, Glasgow, UK

Past and Present Supplements

Supplement 7, 2012

Ritual and Violence: Natalie Zemon Davis and Early Modern France
Edited by Graeme Murdock, Penny Roberts, and Andrew Spicer

President of the Past and Present Society
E. J. Hobsbawm

Vice-Presidents

J. H. Elliott	Joan Thirsk	Keith Thomas

Editorial Board

Paul Slack (Chairman) *Linacre College, Oxford*	Peter Coss *Cardiff University*	Janet L. Nelson *King's College, London*
David Cannadine (Vice-Chairman) *Princeton University*	Eric Foner *Columbia University*	Robin Osborne *King's College, Cambridge*
Judith Herrin (Vice-Chairman) *King's College, London*	Roy Foster *Hertford College, Oxford*	Judith Pollmann *Instituut voor Geschiedenis, Leiden*
Gadi Algazi *Tel Aviv University*	Ruth Harris *New College, Oxford*	Alice Rio *King's College, London*
C. A. Bayly *St Catharine's College, Cambridge*	Matthew Hilton *University of Birmingham*	Lyndal Roper *Balliol College, Oxford*
Anna Bayman	Joanna Innes *Somerville College, Oxford*	S. A. Smith *European University Institute, Florence*
	Colin Jones *Queen Mary University of London*	Megan Vaughan *King's College, Cambridge*
Paul Betts *University of Sussex*	Alan Knight *St Antony's College, Oxford*	Alexandra Walsham *Trinity College, Cambridge*
David Blackbourn *Harvard University*	Mark Mazower *Columbia University*	Evelyn Welch *Queen Mary University of London*
Michael Braddick *University of Sheffield*	Rana Mitter *St Cross College, Oxford*	Chris Wickham *All Souls College, Oxford*
Sebastian Conrad *Freie Universität Berlin*		

Editors	Supplement General Editor	Associate Editor	Supplement Sub-Editor
Lyndal Roper S. A. Smith	Alexandra Walsham	Anna Bayman	Catherine Macduff

Contributions and Communications (two copies), editorial correspondence, etc., should be addressed to The Editors, *Past and Present*, 103 Walton Street, Oxford, OX2 6EB, UK. Tel: +44 (0)1865 512318; Fax: +44 (0)1865 310080; E-mail: editors@pastandpresent.org.uk. Intending contributors should write for a copy of 'Notes for Contributors'.

© *World Copyright: The Past and Present Society, 2012.*

Photocopying and reprint permissions: single and multiple photocopies of extracts from this Journal may be made without charge in all public and educational institutions or as part of any non-profit educational activity, providing that full acknowledgement is made of the source. Requests to reprint in any publication for public sale should be addressed to Oxford University Press. This policy may be reviewed by the Past and Present Society from time to time. More information can be obtained from Rights and New Business Development, Journals Division, Oxford University Press, Great Clarendon Street, Oxford OX2 6DP, UK. Tel: +44 (0)1865 354490 or 353695; Fax: +44 (0)1865 353485; E-mail: journals.permission@oup.com, www.oxfordjournals.org/access_ purchase/rights_permissions.html

The Past and Present Society is a company limited by a guarantee registered in England under company number 2414260 and a registered charity under number 802281. Its registered office is at 9400 Garsington Road, Oxford.

Typeset by Glyph International, Bangalore, India, and printed by Bell and Bain Ltd, Glasgow, UK

Ritual and Violence: Natalie Zemon Davis and Early Modern France

CONTENTS

Preface, 7
Graeme Murdock, Penny Roberts and Andrew Spicer

1. Introduction
Writing 'The Rites of Violence' and Afterward, 8
Natalie Zemon Davis

2. Rites and Ritual
Rites of Repair: Restoring Community in the French Religious Wars, 30
Barbara B. Diefendorf

Religious Violence in Sixteenth-Century France: Moving Beyond Pollution and Purification, 52
Mack P. Holt

Peace, Ritual, and Sexual Violence during the Religious Wars, 75
Penny Roberts

3. Rights and Agency
Massacres during the French Wars of Religion, 100
Allan A. Tulchin

The Rights of Violence, 127
Stuart Carroll

Prophets in Arms? Ministers in War, Ministers on War: France, 1562–74, 163
Philip Benedict

4. Rites and Representation
Rites of Torture in Reformation Geneva, 197
Sara Beam

From Christ-like King to Antichristian Tyrant: A First Crisis of the Monarchical Image at the Time of Francis I, 220
Denis Crouzet (Translated by Philippa Woodcock)

Painting Power: Antoine Caron's *Massacres of the Triumvirate*, 241
Neil Cox and Mark Greengrass

5. Afterword, 275
Graeme Murdock and Andrew Spicer

List of Contributors, 287

Index, 289

List of Illustrations

Jean Perrissin and Jacques Tortorel, *The Massacre at Tours, July 1562*. (Bibliothèque Nationale de France, Paris), 95

Map of the Massacres, 117

Triumph of the Eucharist and the Catholic Faith (Copyright the Frick Collection), 137

Jean Perrissin and Jacques Tortorel, *The Massacre at Sens, Burgundy, April 1562*. (Bibliothèque Nationale de France, Paris), 143

Map of towns and villages near Fumel, 152

Anthoine Caron, *Les massacres du Triumvirat* (Réunion des musées nationaux, Agence Photographique), 243

Preface

Graeme Murdock, Penny Roberts and Andrew Spicer

This collection of essays has developed from a one-day conference—'Religion and Violence in Early Modern France: The Work of Natalie Zemon Davis'—which was held in June 2008 at the Shakespeare Institute, Stratford-upon-Avon. We would like to acknowledge the support of Professor Andrew Pettegree, the financial contributions made by the universities of Birmingham, Oxford Brookes, St Andrews, and Warwick as well as thank those who contributed to the programme and discussions. Five of the papers published here were initially delivered on that occasion, but the conference also sought to learn from the differing perspectives of violence outside sixteenth-century France. This concern is also reflected in this collection, which seeks to offer new insights and approaches to the relationship and significance of religion and violence as well as paying tribute to the immense contribution made in this field by the writings of Natalie Zemon Davis.

Writing 'The Rites of Violence' and Afterward*

Natalie Zemon Davis

I

The year 1972 was the three-hundredth anniversary of the massacre of Saint Bartholomew's day, and French historians in many lands marked its bloodshed and cruelty by conferences and scholarly papers. Alfred Soman invited me to present a paper at a colloquium on the massacre in Chicago. I accepted with alacrity, partly because I was impelled toward the subject of violence for several reasons at once. Both the scholarly stakes and the political stakes seemed high.

In the years just before 1972, I was figuring out how to combine classic social history with the descriptive and semiotic approaches I was learning from reading cultural anthropology, ethnography, and literary criticism. Essays I wrote in the tradition of classic social history were, for example, 'Strikes and Salvation' and 'A Trade Union in Sixteenth-Century France' on the printing workers of Lyon; 'Poor Relief, Humanism, and Heresy' on welfare reform in Lyon; and 'City Women and Religious Change' on women and the Protestant Reformation.[1] Within structures of power and property, I was attentive to the social, geographical and gender origin of the actors, and to what they said or wrote or did in the form of resistance or reform or

---

* This essay is dedicated to the memory of Robert M. Kingdon (1927–2010) and Thierry Wanegffelen (1965–2009), whose writings brought us deep insight into the history of religion, religious conflict, and the possibilities for coexistence in the sixteenth century. I am grateful for friendship and shared learning with Robert Kingdon over many decades and with Thierry Wanegffelen until he was snatched away before his time.

[1] Natalie Zemon Davis, 'Strikes and Salvation in Lyon', *Archiv für Reformationsgeschichte*, 56 (1965), 48–64, reprinted in Natalie Zemon Davis, *Society and Culture in Early Modern France* (Stanford, CA, 1975), ch. 1; 'A Trade Union in Sixteenth-Century France', *Economic History Review*, 19 (1966), 48–69; 'Poor Relief, Humanism and Heresy: The Case of Lyon', *Studies in Medieval and Renaissance History*, 5 (1968), 217–75, reprinted in Davis, *Society and Culture*, ch. 2; 'City Women and Religious Change', in Dorothy McGuigan (ed.), *A Sampler of Women's Studies* (Ann Arbor, 1973), 17–45, reprinted in Davis, *Society and Culture*, ch. 3.

domination. I sought connections between patterns of experience and the adoption of social identities, aspirations, and religious beliefs. To account for choices, I talked about how people perceived their socio-economic interest, and also about their sense of worth and their hopes for community. I tried to give reason to behaviour through the ideas people had about themselves and their interests, ideas inherited or newly introduced, read about or heard.

At least some of the violence initiated by these sixteenth-century people could be understood in this fashion. The grain-rioters in the Grande Rebeine of Lyon in 1529 targeted grain merchants and hoarders; their actions were among the elements that pushed the city notables into welfare reform a few years later. The journeymen printers in their Company of the Griffarins beat up men they called Forfants, who refused to join the *compagnonnage* and were willing to work for 'beggar's pay'; the Griffarins even cut the Forfants' hamstrings, which incapacitated them from working at the press.

In these social history essays, I did little with the meaning of symbol systems or the character of performance. Rather I reflected on the consequences or functions of symbolic action. So the psalm-singing of the printing workers as they marched through the streets of Lyon drew them together in solidarity and pitted them against the pretensions of the canon-counts of the Cathedral of Saint Jean. So the Protestant attack on the Catholic 'god of paste' and the replacement of the Mass by the Lord's Supper were ways to unseat the Catholic priests and their claims to religious monopoly and elevate the lay community.

Yet all along, there were puzzles in the events I was uncovering, patterns of behaviour that in their full detail were baffling. What was going on in the elaborate ritual by which a printer's journeyman was initiated as a Griffarin? Surely this signified more than secrecy and comradeship. What was going on when the Seigneur de la Coquille—that is, the Lord of Misprint—led other artisans in a charivari, a noisy demonstration when a man was led backward on a donkey because he had been beaten by his wife? Surely this involved more than artisans simply enjoying themselves. What was a Lord of Misprint anyway, besides a witty title? What really was a charivari?

In pursuit of some answers, I turned during 1968–9 in a new direction: to the ethnography of Arnold Van Gennep, his great *Manuel de folklore français*, organized around the life cycle and around the seasons of the year.[2] There I found context and some meaning for the charivaris and the *Abbayes de Maugouvert*, the Abbeys of Misrule, cropping up in village after village, often associated with marriages where there was a gross disparity in age

---

[2] Arnold Van Gennep, *Manuel de folklore français contemporain* (Paris, 1946–72), vol. I in 7 parts.

between the partners. By the time I had explored sixteenth-century sources across France, I was reading about rites of passage in Victor Turner's *Ritual Process* and the carnivalesque in Mikhail Bakhtin's *Rabelais and His World*.[3] Now I began to take seriously social groups and symbolic actions usually ignored by historians at that time: youth groups and urban vocational or neighbourhood groups, with festive and local jurisdiction; and costumed and noise-making performance, in which social or community criticism was legitimated under the licence of the world-turned-upside-down. Ordinarily these festive activities ended in restored community, the rupture repaired; sometimes they tipped beyond truth-telling and mockery into violence, as when a target was chased out of town or even killed, and into actual uprisings against the city fathers, as in the Carnival of Romans at Mardi Gras, 1580. But, to use the title I gave to my essay, there were always 'Reasons' to the Misrule: protecting the local marriage pool or the hierarchical arrangements in marriage, targeting royal officers for corruption and oppression, and the like.[4]

But religious violence posed more of a problem. George Rudé, Eric Hobsbawm, and Edward P. Thompson and others had written about popular riots and uprisings with economic or social goals.[5] The hydra-headed mob became a crowd with actions organized towards a goal; rebels, though sorted into 'primitive' or pre-political and political, had some rationale to their violence. Thompson's 'Moral Economy of the English Crowd in the Eighteenth Century', published in 1971, expanded on that rationale: the belief that the people should rightly have bread to eat was shared by governors and subjects, and when the hungry rose up against hoarders of grain, they saw themselves as taking on the role that magistrates should properly be filling.[6] But these important interpretations stopped short when the bread involved

---

[3] Mikhail Bakhtin, *Rabelais and His World*, trans. H. Iswolsky (Cambridge, MA, 1968); Victor W. Turner, *The Ritual Process. Structure and Anti-Structure* (Chicago, 1968).

[4] Natalie Zemon Davis, 'The Reasons of Misrule: Youth Groups and Charivaris in Sixteenth-Century France', *Past and Present*, 50 (1971), 41–75, reprinted in Davis, *Society and Culture*, ch. 4. I tried to present a general picture of the classic social approach and the anthropological/cultural approach to a historical question, and the need to combine both methods, in 'Anthropology and History in the 1980s: The Possibilities of the Past', *Journal of Interdisciplinary History*, 12 (1981), 267–75, and 'The Shapes of Social History', *Storia della Storiografia*, 17 (1990), 28–34.

[5] George F. E. Rudé, *The Crowd in History. A Study of Popular Disturbances in France and England, 1730–1848* (New York, 1964); Eric J. Hobsbawm, *Primitive Rebels, Studies in Archaic Forms of Social Movements in the 19th and 20th Centuries* (Manchester, 1959); Charles Tilly and James B. Rule, *Measuring Political Upheaval* (Princeton, NJ, 1965).

[6] Edward P. Thompson, 'The Moral Economy of the English Crowd in the Eighteenth Century', *Past and Present*, 50 (1971), 76–113.

was, say, the holy wafer of the Mass or the Lord's Supper. If popular violence against religious targets had a rationale, it was reduced to a socio-economic one such as the poor against the rich. At best, the religious indignation of crowds was misguided, and could not be read in its own terms. At worst, religious violence remained a supreme example of passionate disorder, an irrational lashing out against a terrible other.

My hope in 1972 was to explicate the religious violence of sixteenth-century French crowds in the decades leading up to Saint Bartholomew's day both in social terms, familiar to me, and in cultural terms, some of which I had to invent. Through 'social' interpretation, I would be attentive to the origins of the actors—who they were, and what they did and where they came from—and consider how their experience and relations might inform their understanding of the world. Through 'cultural' interpretation, I would read the violent actions of crowds as guided at least in part by religious beliefs and sensibilities and the prescriptions of ritual performance. What were the stakes that rioters invested in their violence? What meaning did they give to their actions and how did they legitimate their conduct?

More generally, I wanted to deepen my understanding of Protestantism and Catholicism as systems of meaning, sensibility, and performance, sometimes overlapping systems and similar to each other, sometimes sharply different. (I am using Clifford Geertz's language here, even though I did not read his 'Religion as a Cultural System' until it appeared in his *Interpretation of Cultures* in 1973.[7] I surely posed the question more haltingly to myself in 1972). It seemed to me that the sharp confrontation called forth in popular religious violence might make it a privileged setting for examining these systems.

II

Popular protest and violence were also part of my own political world in the late 1960s and early 1970s, both contemporary and remembered. Resistance movements against the Vietnam War were widespread, and I participated in marches and demonstrations in Toronto and Berkeley. I stood with other demonstrators while young men burned their draft cards in front of the army induction centre in Oakland; I shouted slogans along with many other marchers in the streets of Berkeley, while unexpected violence cropped up around the edges: a car overturned by demonstrators, gun-fire from somewhere against the marchers, and finally the smell of tear-gas in the air and the sound of us all running away. In Toronto, I was one of the many witnesses to a

---

[7] Clifford Geertz, 'Religion as a Cultural System', in *The Interpretation of Cultures* (New York, 1973), ch. 4.

form of 'non-violent resistance': professors (my husband among them) and students standing in front of a University of Toronto building so as to prevent interviews with recruiters from American companies manufacturing napalm. Counter-demonstrators supported the war against Communism and did not want trouble-makers interfering with their chances to apply for a good job.

My closest encounter with disruptive action was during the day-care sit-in at the University of Toronto in March 1970. For several years I had been close to a small group of graduate students and faculty women who were trying to get university support from an indifferent, even hostile administration for a day-care centre for their young children. (My own children were by then in school). We were pleased when all of a sudden a group of undergraduate activists took up our cause on their own and organized a campus protest meeting. To my surprise, one of the speakers called for the occupation of the administration building, and many in the crowd poured through its doors, moving up the stairs and into the Senate chamber.

I followed with a sinking heart: on the one hand, I cared deeply about means to increase and facilitate the presence of women in the university (women were still a small number in the graduate school and a very small presence on the faculty); on the other hand, I found the breach of order, the transgressive act, quite frightening. I also found it fascinating. The august Senate chamber became the scene for carnivalesque reversal; students took turns relaxing triumphantly in the 'throne chair'. Was my 'Reasons of Misrule', penned the year before, coming to life? I left after a time, and the next day turned to a role I found more congenial: arguing before the president's council, together with another woman professor, for university support for day-care facilities. A moderate sum was allocated for building repairs, and the sit-in ended (though it would take three more years and the appointment of a woman vice-president before proper support was established).[8] This experience and the anti-war demonstrations intensified my hunger to understand the performance of protest, especially when it went in seemingly unexpected, disruptive or violent directions.

Along with these lived experiences, there was a ghost of violence from the past which had haunted me for years: the Holocaust. How had this come

---

[8] A brief description of the day-care centre sit-in is given in Martin L. Friedland, *The University of Toronto. A History* (Toronto, 2002), 535–7. Though not appearing in print until 1971, I wrote 'The Reasons of Misrule' in the spring of 1969. As Vice-President, Internal Affairs, of the University of Toronto from 1973 to 1975, Jill Ker Conway confirmed the university's commitment to the day-care centre that students had worked to create.

about, from the smallest acts of exclusion to the massive project of extermination? What could fuel such hatred, what could lead to cruelty on such a scale and with so much popular fervour behind it, to the invention of such seemingly unthinkable means of mass murder? I asked myself these questions as a historian, but even more as a woman who, if she had grown up Jewish in Europe rather than in Detroit, Michigan might well have ended up on a transport train to Auschwitz. I also asked them as a person who wished to view human behaviour as historically conditioned and, thus, susceptible to at least a tiny nudge toward the better. For the Holocaust itself, I could read during the 1960s Raul Hilberg's deeply researched *Destruction of the European Jews* (1961) and Hannah Arendt's provocative *Eichmann in Jerusalem: A Report on the Banality of Evil* (1963) among other works.[9] But 'The Rites of Violence' of 1972 was my effort to address 'the holocaust problem': by giving shape to extreme violence and seeing how it was understood and legitimated by popular crowds in the sixteenth century, I was presenting an example of how murderous and destructive actions were historically and culturally conditioned, not the simple expression of timeless demonic force.

To be sure, the religious violence of the sixteenth century could not be read as a replica of the racial extermination of the twentieth: the 'race' of hateful heretics was not an enduring biological category of persons who must be exterminated (the word 'race' had a different meaning in the early modern period), but a socio-religious category which must be effaced and from which one could escape by converting back to Catholicism.[10] But the sixteenth-century example might still suggest additional ways to reflect on, say, Kristallnacht and the murder of Jews by some of their neighbours in various eastern European towns during Nazi times.

---

[9] Raul Hilberg, *The Destruction of the European Jews* (Chicago, 1961); Hannah Arendt, *Eichmann in Jerusalem. A Report on the Banality of Evil* (New York, 1963); Saul Friedländer, *Pius XII and the Third Reich. A Documentation*, trans. Charles Fullman (London and New York, 1966).

[10] I was here taking issue with Janine Estèbe, whose important book on the Saint Bartholomew's Day massacre, *Tocsin pour un massacre. La saison des Saint-Barthélemy* (Paris, 1968), included many valuable insights. On concepts of 'race' in early modern France, see Arlette Jouanna, *L'idée du race en France au XVIe et au début du XVIIe siècle, 1498–1614* (Lille, 1975, rev. ed. Montpellier, 1981). For our exchange in regard to my essay, see Janine Estèbe and Natalie Zemon Davis, 'Debate. The Rites of Violence: Religious Riot in Sixteenth-Century France', *Past and Present*, 67 (1975), 127–35.

III

Let me sum up for current readers the principal features of the essay.[11] Though I used some archival materials from Lyon, my sources were Protestant and Catholic accounts of crowd violence, circulated and printed at the time. I was especially hungry for concrete details on what was shouted and done, and when and where. Though I took it seriously when Catholic and Protestant accounts of a violent event converged, as an indication of 'what actually happened', even a single unpaired description could provide evidence for how contemporaries interpreted and legitimated their actions.

In tracking religious violence, I sought crowds and rioters acting independently of official and governmental orders and independently of military command. (I was in dialogue in this essay with the literature on popular resistance and on the nature of social violence as much if not more than with the literature on the French Religious Wars). Under the rubric of 'violence' I included the wide range of behaviour so defined by sixteenth-century people, from disrupting the flow of a sermon to desecrating and destroying religious objects—a deeply wounding act for those who believed in their holiness and even miraculous power—to the public mockery of persons, to murder and the mutilation of corpses.

I found you could subsume these popular actions under three forms of defence of what was believed to be sacred. One was the affirmation of true doctrine and the refutation of falsehood by dramatic tests against, say, the Catholic holy wafer and relics in one direction or against the Calvinist French Bible in the other. A second defence was to cleanse the community of the pollution of heresy or vile religious practice: the lascivious and sinister practice of the Huguenots in one direction or the diabolic magic and debauchery of Catholic clerics in the other. Failing such purification would bring down the wrath of God. (Mary Douglas's *Purity and Danger* alerted me to the importance of the language about filth and defilement in the riots).[12]

In such defence of the sacred, rioters were enacting in symbolic and violent expression the roles of preachers and priests. In a third form of action, they were imitating magistrates. Here was a version of the mentality that Edward Thompson had found for the English grain riot: when the magistrates had not

---

[11] Natalie Zemon Davis, 'The Rites of Violence: Religious Riot in Sixteenth-Century France', *Past and Present*, 59 (1973), reprinted in Alfred Soman (ed.), *The Masscre of St. Bartholomew: Reappraisals and Documents* (The Hague, 1974), 203–42, and in Davis, *Society and Culture*, ch. 6. All further references to this essay will refer to the page numbers in the version in *Society and Culture*.

[12] Mary Douglas, *Purity and Danger. An Analysis of Concepts of Pollution and Taboo* (London, 1966).

done their duty, the people must do it for them. So the crowds rang the tocsin to assemble people. Protestants had mock trials of their captives and in some instances bore them off to prison 'bound like galley slaves'. Catholics killed their victims at the official places of execution in other instances.

Among the forms of legitimation drawn upon by crowds to take matters into their own hands were the sermons of a zealous priest or pastor, who cited appropriate verses from Deuteronomy. And much of the religious violence was timed to and clustered around ritual events: a Protestant baptism or funeral or psalm-singing procession, a Catholic Mass or Corpus Christi day procession or feast-day celebration—these stimulated a response from opponents and fights ensued.

Though the violence of Catholic and Protestant crowds was fed by a perceived deep cleavage in belief, there were some overall similarities in their conduct and goals, as just suggested. These groups were drawing on a shared repertory of actions derived from Scripture and popular folk justice, and the presence of women and young men and teenage boys in both Catholic and Protestant riots guaranteed their access to certain forms of opposition, resistance, and techniques of humiliation.

But there were contrasts, too, and the ones that seemed to me most significant were those linked to differences in ritual sensibility and the location of the sacred and the polluting. Especially, I noted the heightened targeting of heretical persons and bodies by Catholic rioters and the heightened targeting of defiling objects by Protestant rioters. The contrast was by no means absolute, and I gave examples of overlapping conduct: Protestant crowds broke religious statues on Lyon churches; a Catholic crowd demolished the newly built Reformed Temple of Le Paradis in the same town; Catholics tore French Bibles to shreds, Protestants disposed of Catholic missals. Both Catholic and Protestant crowds left dead opponents in their wake.

But overall, the privileged actions of the Catholic and Protestant rioters (and I stressed that I was talking about riots and crowds, not military battles and soldiers) differed somewhat, not just in number, but more importantly, in significance. For Protestants, relics, statues of saints, sacramental wafers, chalices, priestly vestments, and church buildings were embodiments of pollution. Cleansing here was a godly ritual. And when Protestant crowds assaulted, mocked, or killed persons, the preferred targets were priests as the essential producers of defilement, all the worse for their spurious claims to purity. For Catholics, with a different sense of the body social and religious and its internal links, all heretics were contaminating in their persons, rebels against God, a scandal in his eyes. Effacing their presence was a godly act. Telling evidence for this contrast were the targets favoured for extravagant rites of cleansing, the Protestants multiplying ways to show their contempt for Catholic holy objects (rubbing boots with baptismal oil; shitting in holy-water basins), the Catholics to show their contempt for the dead bodies of heretics, by mutilation and ghoulish display.

In this specific contrast, I was to some extent doing a version of Weberian 'ideal types'. Not only were there overlaps and similarities in behaviour, as I noted, but also any individual Protestant or Catholic participant might have distinctive sentiments or grudges of his or her own. This is inevitably the case in describing group behaviour. But two of my goals in 'The Rites of Violence' called for such description: to take as seriously as sixteenth-century Catholics and Protestants did their differing locations of and relations to the sacred, and to see how this played out in their violent conduct; and (using a phrase from a sociological study of contemporary violence) to show the 'conditions for guilt-free massacre'. A key transformation effected through these rituals and beliefs was the dehumanizing of victims, at least for a time: they were 'vermin' to be stamped out, 'devils' to be destroyed. These dehumanizing mechanisms, found in some form in both Catholic and Protestant moments of violence, were among the most important insights I acquired from the whole quest.

I concluded my essay insisting that 'the rites of violence are not the rights of violence in any absolute sense'.[13] Giving mindedness and shape to extreme violence incorporates it more readily into the range of human behaviour and offers us a chance to understand it and think what to do about it.

IV

'The Rites of Violence' was first published in *Past and Present* in 1973, and in the next years I read with great absorption studies—including some by contributors to this volume—which took the story of violence and response to religious cleavage in important new directions. Here I will point briefly to three approaches, two giving different structure and frame to the question of violence, the third asking a different question.

Denis Crouzet's magisterial *Les Guerriers de Dieu. La violence au temps des troubles de religion (vers 1525–vers 1610)*, published in 1990, made violence the central thread in his narrative of religious innovation and conflict in sixteenth-century France.[14] Considering religious violence and religious/political violence in all its forms, from the street riot to military operation to assassination, the book follows the changes in mood, religious thought, and

---

[13] Davis, 'The Rites of Violence', in *Society and Culture*, 187.
[14] Denis Crouzet, *Les Guerriers de Dieu. La violence au temps des troubles de religion (vers 1525–vers 1610)*, 2 vols, (Paris, 1990). See also his later book *Dieu en ses royaumes. Une histoire des Guerres de Religion* (Paris, 2008).

action of Catholics and Protestants throughout the century. Among many contributions, the picture of mood and mentality emerging from *Les Guerriers de Dieu* is especially illuminating: the society breathes in and out with expectation and fear of the Last Days, of which the prophetic signs are everywhere. Transformative hope alternates with penitential guilt depending on the advance or retreat of the Protestant or Catholic cause. Crouzet contrasts the desacralizing iconoclastic violence of the Protestants with the assaults of Catholics, inflated with mystical sentiment, on heretical bodies; but he also shows that eschatological excitement cuts across religious lines. It is not just the property of radical religious groups, but can grip a whole society.

David Nirenberg's *Communities of Violence. Persecution of Minorities in the Middle Ages* (1996) reframed persuasively the long-term history of 'tolerance' and 'intolerance' in Christian Aragon and southern France through closely observed events of violence, which he compared in their targets (Jews, Muslims, lepers, prostitutes), geographical location, and timing.[15] The interests and beliefs invested in different episodes were surprisingly varied and complex. Local politics generated factions supporting violence and factions opposing it; both must be examined. The systemic character of violence emerged dramatically in the yearly Holy Week stoning of the Jewish quarter by young clerics and students. With an ancient ritual structure, timed to follow the celebration of the Passion of Christ, the violence was a condition for the coexistence of Christians and Jews: it reaffirmed the boundary between the two groups, reminding everyone of the sufferance and dangers under which the Jewish minority must live in a Christian land.[16]

If wide frames and comparisons brought new insight into the moods, meaning, and social dynamics of violence, studies focused on one locality also deepened understanding. Barbara Diefendorf's 'Prologue to a Massacre: Popular Unrest in Paris, 1557–1572' asked what could have led the Catholic majority of Paris to fall upon the Protestant minority within its walls in 'a citywide orgy of violence' at Saint Bartholomew's day, 1572.[17] She answered this question with a sensitively chosen sequence of events over a fifteen-year period, which enhanced in waves the feelings of religious hatred and fear and a Catholic desire for vengeance. This explosive emotional economy was

---

[15] David Nirenberg, *Communities of Violence: Persecution of Minorities in the Middle Ages* (Princeton, NJ, 1996).

[16] Nirenberg, *Communities*, ch. 7.

[17] Barbara B. Diefendorf, 'Prologue to a Massacre: Popular Unrest in Paris, 1557–1572', *American Historical Review*, 90 (1985), 1067–91. Diefendorf has carried the story farther in her important book *Beneath the Cross: Catholics and Protestants in Sixteenth-Century Paris* (New York and Oxford, 1991).

centrally fed by religious events: Protestant desecration at the church of Saint Médard or even permitted preaching in a private house enraged Catholics at a given moment. Short-lived royal edicts of pacification and efforts of the city authorities to protect Protestants from mob violence and thus to keep order in the town were regarded as betrayal by the Catholic populace. (Nirenberg found similar crowd hostility toward Catholic authorities trying to put a stop to the Holy Week stoning of Jews in Girona; in both instances we see the kind of situation in which crowds believe the magistrate has failed them and they must righteously take action). Along the way 'the climate of fear' in Paris was darkened by other events, such as the high price of grain in 1565–6.

Diefendorf's sequential narrative builds to late 1571, to the disorders around the authorities' removal of the cross of Gastines, which had been erected by Catholics on the site of the demolished house of an executed Huguenot to symbolize the destruction of heresy. The removal incited attacks on the authorities' agents and Catholic stoning, pillaging and burning of Protestant houses. Eight months later, 'tensions rose to a fever pitch' with anger at the forthcoming marriage of the Protestant prince Henry of Navarre and the Catholic princess Marguerite, and with the fear of Protestant revenge for the murder of Admiral Coligny. Diefendorf concludes with a wise remark about royal responsibility for the mass murders of August 1572. Whatever was hatched at the late-night meeting of Catherine de Medici, Charles IX, and the *Prévôt des marchands* on Saint Bartholomew's eve, 'we can . . . scarcely avoid the conclusion that anyone in a position of responsibility at the moment would have known, or should have known, that the sound of the tocsin in the night would touch off massacre'.[18]

Narrative sequence, effect, and political interests also played a role in Allan Tulchin's account of the Michelade of Nîmes in 1567, which brought other valuable perspectives as well.[19] Unlike Paris, the Protestant movement of Nîmes was large and powerful and had won control of that city from late 1561 to 1563 by political means and without an armed uprising. Most of the city councillors and royal judicial officers had converted to the Reformed religion, and with support from the *menu peuple* had been able to rid Nîmes of the Mass. Then in 1564 to 1567, through royal intervention, the minority Catholic party was gradually restored to power, the clergy returned, and the Mass was performed once again in the churches that had for a time resounded with Protestant psalms. At the end of September 1567, as part of a planned uprising of Protestants throughout France on St. Michael's day, the Reformed

---

[18] Diefendorf, 'Prologue to a Massacre', 1091.
[19] Allan A. Tulchin, 'The Michelade in Nîmes, 1567', *French Historical Studies*, 29 (2006), 1–35.

leaders of Nîmes formed 'a provisional governing committee', known as *les Messieurs*, and organized companies of the city's faithful to march through the streets and round up and imprison Catholic suspects. During the night of 30 September, *les Messieurs* ordered their soldiers to take more than a hundred of the prisoners to the courtyard of the bishop's palace, murder them, and dump their bodies down a well.[20]

'The Michelade shows', says Tulchin, 'that Protestants could be just as violent as Catholics'; in this regard he sees it as a counter-example to 'The Rites of Violence', whose argument in his view (though not in mine) is 'that sixteenth-century French Protestants were less violent or practiced different forms of violence than Catholics'.[21] In fact, various forms of ritual violence were described in Tulchin's richly documented study, all of them ordered by *les Messieurs*: every Catholic church in the town was razed, except one saved as a site for making gunpowder; every scrap of church furnishing burned. The

---

[20] Tulchin, 'Michelade', 14, 20–4.

[21] Tulchin, 'Michelade', 2, 34. 'The Rites of Violence' was not about 'French Protestants' and 'Catholics' in general, but about the behaviour of Protestant and Catholic *crowds* during riots; there might well be wider implications for my findings for other settings, but I explicitly tried to exclude the behaviour of soldiers or militias acting under command and formally government-sponsored assault because I wanted to explore issues of popular legitimation. The essay's purpose was not primarily quantitative—to assess more violence here, less violence there, but was rather to find semiotic typologies, characteristic performances in the religious violence of crowds, and, as suggested in my summary here, some of these were similar in the two religious groups, some different. Tulchin says 'Davis's interpretation cautiously endorses the Calvinist *Histoire ecclésiastique,* whose authors wrote that "those of the Reformed Religion made war only on images and altars, which do not bleed, while those of the Roman religion spilled blood with every kind of cruelty" ' (33). I did, indeed, cite that quotation, but immediately added, 'Though there is some truth in this distinction, Protestant rioters did in fact kill and injure people, and not merely in self-defense; and Catholic rioters did destroy religious property'. After explicating the Protestant attention to religious objects because of the danger of defilement, I turned to a contrast between the victims of Protestant and Catholic crowds, pointing out that Protestant targets were most often priests, monks, and friars 'usually unarmed . . . [but that] did not make them any less harmful in Protestant eyes, or any more immune from the wrath of God'. I went on to say that 'lay people were sometimes attacked by Protestant crowds' and gave examples of stoning and murder of lay people, then concluded 'there is nothing that quite resembles the style and extent of the slaughter of the 1572 massacres'. 'The Rites of Violence', in *Society and Culture,* 173–5.

Authors must give leeway to their readers, but my comment here is intended to discourage a simple social science reading of my essay ('Protestants smash, Catholics kill') and encourage an anthropological and semiotic one.

murdered Catholics were not just dumped in the streets, but thrown in the water of the bishop's own well.

In particular, Tulchin's analysis of the Michelade offered new understanding of Protestants as killers. Murders by Protestant crowds had figured in my 'The Rites of Violence', if not as frequent a form of violence as with Catholic crowds, but I had been able to assign meaning only to the privileged Protestant attacks on and killing of priests.[22] In the Michelade, half the known victims slain were clerics, and half were laymen. The killings were done not at the initiative of a street crowd, but at the order of *les Messieurs*, and thus reveal an important feature of Protestant mentality in a situation of power. One Protestant captain of Nîmes saw the killings as revenge, 'because the papists did the same thing throughout the kingdom of France', but Tulchin finds a deeper explanation in a sense of political entitlement among the Nîmes Protestant elite. The conviction that they should rule came not only from their desire for religious restoration, but from their linking of political and religious reform in the remarkable *cahier de doléances* they had submitted to the Estates-General in 1561 and from their previous leadership in the city. 'The Protestants of Nîmes felt deprived of what they saw as their right to rule' and they resented, indeed hated the pretensions of Catholic usurpers. Catholicism must not be allowed to revive: its leaders must be slain, its buildings demolished. In the words of one of the Messieurs, 'The nests must be destroyed, so that the birds will not return'.

The Nîmes example thus shows the entwining of religious and political 'motives' (as Tulchin says) in religious massacre, or as we might also put it, a chilling fear both of pollution and of powerlessness.[23] The Michelade yields not a generalization about power and mass murder, but a case whose detailed configuration provides important questions to ask about analogous seizures of power.

V

Another way of approaching religious violence is to turn the subject upside down and ask what people do to avoid it: what were the practices that early modern Catholics and Protestants sometimes undertook so as to live side by side during the precarious regime of the Edict of Nantes and even during the Wars of Religion that preceded it? Among my moving memories here is of the late Elisabeth Labrousse telling me of Protestants and Catholics in early

---

[22] Tulchin, 'Michelade', 29–33. Tulchin devotes a very enlightening chapter to the 1561 *cahier de doléances* of the Nîmes Protestants in his important new book, *That Men Would Praise the Lord. The Triumph of Protestantism in Nîmes, 1530–1570* (Oxford, 2010), ch. 5.

[23] Tulchin, 'Michelade', 14, 29–33.

seventeenth-century Languedoc who accommodated to the differing rhythms of their ceremonial lives in a neighbourly fashion. Then in 1994, I heard Penny Roberts's electrifying talk, '*Huguenottes* and *bigottes*. Women and Confessional Identity in Sixteenth-Century France', in which she gave examples of strategies of coexistence and called for their further study.[24] Not long before, Gregory Hanlon had published an ethnographic study of coexistence in Layrac, a small Gascon town whose Protestant majority gradually dwindled over the course of the seventeenth century. Local identity was more important than confessional loyalty, and the townspeople crafted institutions to assure balance in the town's political life, and served as godparents for each other's children across religious lines. Intermarriage was not uncommon, and if the wife converted to her spouse's religion for the event, she was able to return as a widow to her own faith.[25] Recent doctoral dissertations on Saumur and Loudun have searched the archives for evidence on coexistence: economic life was found to be an area for open transaction, for instance, while intermarriage was charged and infrequent.[26]

Keith Luria has given important new perspective to these social histories by his use of the symbolic notion of boundaries.[27] Religious identities in France were partly formed and changed by relations across boundaries: some were porous, permeable, as in trade or neighbourly exchange; some were negotiated, as in agreements about the use of space and time for religious worship; some were sharp, clear (the kind I link with fears of pollution), initiated perhaps internally by both confessions for better self-definition, but in seventeenth-century France increasingly used by the Catholic monarchy

---

[24] Penny Roberts's paper was delivered at the Women's History Workshop held at the University of Warwick in October 1994 and will be published in the volume of *Hommages* in memory of Thierry Wanegffelen. The late Thierry Wanegffelen himself made important contributions to the study of strategies of coexistence, as in his book *Ni Rome ni Genève: des fidèles entre deux chaires en France au XVIe siècle* (Paris, 1997).

[25] Gregory Hanlon, *Confession and Community in 17th Century France. Catholic and Protestant Coexistence in Aquitaine* (Philadelphia, 1993).

[26] Scott Marr, 'The Practices of Religious Coexistence: The Catholic and Protestant Population of Saumur, France, 1589–1665', unpublished Ph.D. thesis, Boston University, 2010. Marr presented material from his thesis at a talk at the meeting of the Society for French Historical Studies, Rutgers University, 5 April 2008. Edwin Bezzina, 'After the Wars of Religion: Protestant-Catholic Accommodation in the French Town of Loudun, 1598–1665', unpublished Ph.D. thesis, University of Toronto, 2004.

[27] Keith P. Luria, *Sacred Boundaries. Religious Coexistence and Conflict in Early Modern Europe* (Washington, DC, 2005).

and clergy to exclude Protestants. The historical anthropology of Luria's *Sacred Boundaries* revealed the possibilities of and constraints on coexistence.

Benjamin Kaplan has now extended the geographical range of this story of accommodation across Europe. Local populations found ingenious ways to get around, say, the Religious Peace of Augsburg, which permitted only one confession in a polity: churches were built just across a political boundary, on-the-spot authorities looking the other way as their citizens walked to worship. Catholic services in private dwellings or in embassy chapels in the Protestant Netherlands were another arrangement. Kaplan insists that such practices, 'limited, tension-ridden, and discriminatory' though they were, are as much a part of the history of tolerance as the philosophical arguments of the Enlightenment.[28] Indeed, Stuart Schwartz has found in the Iberian world on both sides of the Atlantic a folk philosophy of tolerance, extending beyond Christians to Jews and Muslims. In the words of a peasant woman of Aranda in 1488, 'the good Jew would be saved and the good Moor, in his law, and why else had God made them?'[29] To be sure, Schwartz found these affirmations in the records of the Spanish and Portuguese Inquisitions, which indicates how the road to tolerance is strewn with land-mines.

VI

In the years just after publishing 'The Rites of Violence', I tried to fulfil the anthropological programme behind that essay in regard to the location of the sacred—though here drawing implications for city life and commerce rather than for violence. In 'The Sacred and the Body Social in Sixteenth-Century Lyon' (1981), I conceived of Protestantism and Catholicism as two 'languages', sharing some vocabulary and metaphors, differing strongly in others, yet both adequate to certain needs of urban life.[30] Catholic sacred space had hot spots and enclosures, marked by processions, relics, and holy ritual: the bounds of the city and the parishes, church buildings, special places on or along the Rhône and Saône. Protestant urban space was more uniform and made holy by the usage to which it was put: any place was available for holy action, so long as the believers attended it. Sacred or liturgical time—the rhythm of festivals and holy days—contrasted in a similar way. Both

---

[28] Benjamin J. Kaplan, *Divided by Faith. Religious Conflict and the Practice of Toleration in Early Modern Europe* (Cambridge, MA, 2007), 358 and Part II, for the various 'Arrangements' Europeans worked out to try to avoid violence.

[29] Stuart B. Schwartz, *All Can Be Saved. Religious Tolerance and Salvation in the Iberian World* (New Haven, 2008), 53.

[30] Natalie Zemon Davis, 'The Sacred and the Body Social in Sixteenth-Century Lyon', *Past and Present*, 90 (1981), 40–70.

Protestantism and Catholicism used the human body as a metaphor for conceiving human alliance, but the Catholic visualized especially the organic connections in the body social—as in the child nourished in the womb of Mother Church—while the Protestants imaged especially the communication network of nerves and ligaments.

In writing 'The Sacred and the Body Social', I hoped in part to reformulate two theories of Max Weber. Rather than his dichotomy of a Protestant transcendent God as against a desacralized world, I suggested a sacred presence in the Protestant world through communication and usages. Rather than his evolutionary model of Protestantism as *the* path toward capitalist acquisition and modernity, I suggested features of Catholic sensibility that could expand and contract with the rhythms of capitalist commercial enterprise. As I had tried to show a common engagement in violent performance by Catholic and Protestant crowds, with certain differences in identifying the sources for and cleansing pollution, so here I tried to show a common engagement in urban and commercial life, with certain differences yielding alternate paths to modernity. The location of the sacred was important in both instances.

The late 1960s and 1970s were also the years of the women's movement, or 'second-wave feminism', as it came to be called, and I was busy teaching courses and trying to conceptualize issues in the history of women and gender. The relation of gender to violence—to the perpetration of violence in warfare, uprisings, protest movements, and personal or family life—was especially perplexing. Some of the early feminist literature tended to idealize women as peacemakers and to see them only as victims of violence. Such a view, devoted to the cause of women though it was, offered little challenge to the nineteenth-century split between the domestic female and the public male. In the words of a republican opponent of the women wishing to bear arms for the French Revolution, 'We must not overthrow the order of nature. Nature has not destined women to kill; their delicate hands were not made to handle steel or to raise deadly pikes'.[31]

I addressed these questions in essays of the 1970s, especially in 'Women on Top' and 'Men, Women and Violence: Some Reflections on Equality'.[32] In the

---

[31] Response of the deputy Dehaussy-Robecourt to the petition of Pauline Léon in March 1792, signed by 315 women, demanding the right of women to bear arms for the Revolution. Paule-Marie Duhet (ed.), *Les femmes et la Révolution, 1789–1794* (Paris, 1971), 115–17.

[32] 'Women on Top', in *Society and Culture*, ch. 5; 'Men, Women, and Violence: Some Reflections on Equality', *Smith Alumnae Quarterly*, April 1977, 12–15, reprinted in Dorothy G. McGuigan (ed.), *The Role of Women in Conflict and Peace* (Ann Arbor, 1977), 19–29.

late medieval and sixteenth-century view of things, both men and women had a capacity for violence: the male humours led to pride, the female humours to anger, and both of these vices were spurs to violence. On the whole, the male temperament was thought more capable of generating violence of an ethical or socially approved kind: the just war or the honourable duel. Women's violence, lit by disobedience and vindictiveness, would more likely lead to more unpleasant disturbance. There were exceptions, to be sure: a biblical Judith, who could rise up and save her people by slaying the drunken general Holofernes; the historical Jeanne d'Arc, leading the French army to righteous battle against the English. Even the poet Christine de Pizan in her *City of Ladies* was of two minds about women and violence: on the one hand, she said that women's weak body 'agreeably excused [them] by default, in so much that they do not do the horrible cruelties and wrongs done to the world by men because of strength'; on the other hand, she described women who had used their courage and strength in great conquests.[33] Her last poem was dedicated to Jeanne d'Arc.

Within this frame, women turned to violence when they wished to, but used loopholes or symbols or festive practices drawn from the cultural system to legitimate or facilitate their actions. Some young women ran off to join European armies dressed as men as one might do at carnival. Mademoiselle de Montpensier leading troops openly against the king during the Fronde was an unusual figure. (It was these practices of inversion that the women soldiers of the French Revolution were trying in vain to replace). The significant participation of women in street protests, including religious riots, drew its legitimation from the belief that women as mothers or as oppressed poor or as simple Christian believers in a hierarchical society could sometimes reverse the order of things, rise up to tell the truth and right wrongs. On the other hand, the allegedly weak brains and poor emotional control of women could provide excuses for uprisings after the fact: women were less 'responsible' than men and could not be held as accountable as men by the authorities.[34]

---

[33] Christine de Pizan, *The Book of the City of Ladies*, trans. Earl Jeffrey Richards (New York, 1998), part I, ch. 14, p. 37.

[34] Among many fine studies of women and violence published since the 1970s, those concerning the early period include Darlene Gay Levy, Harriet B. Applewhite, and Mary Durham Johnson (eds), *Women in Revolutionary Paris, 1789–1795. Selected Documents Translated with Notes and Commentary* (Chicago, 1980); Rudolf Dekker and Lotte van de Pol, *The Tradition of Female Transvestism in Early Modern Europe* (Houndmills, 1989); Arlette Farge, *La vie fragile: violence, pouvoirs et solidarités à Paris au XVIIIe siècle* (Paris, 1986); Cécile Dauphin and Arlette Farge (eds), *De la violence et des femmes* (Paris, 1997);

VII

The 1980s were for me a period of interest in storytelling, that is, in finding out how people told stories about themselves and the events around them and in using such literary evidence as a path to wider understanding of social values and cultural sensibilities. If I started with an analysis of the rhetoric of Judge Jean de Coras's account of Arnaud du Tilh's 'prodigious' imposture of Martin Guerre, I soon embarked on the stories people told of murder, that is, of a capital criminal crime for which they hoped to win a royal pardon.[35]

In each case a homicide had to be narrated in the words of the perpetrator, genuine and colloquial enough so that he or she could repeat them convincingly one day before a judge. The story had to be plausible enough to be attested to before the judge by neighbours or acquaintances of the person seeking pardon. But it also had to be shaped to the legal requirements for a pardon, otherwise this would never be signed by the king's chancellor. The violence of murder was not exactly tamed in the telling, but it could not be described as planned or premeditated, but only as done on the spur of the moment in self-defence, and/or hot anger, or by accident. An honourable duel between two gentlemen had to be recast for the king's official ears as a surge of sudden anger. Village lads who had killed in defence of their honour and repute had to modify their stories in appropriate ways. A long-battered wife could not aim to kill a violent husband; he had to fall on her knife as she was cleaning a chicken for his dinner.

Pardon tales differ from accounts of religious riots published by Catholics and Protestants in their authorship and in their self-presentation. A pardon tale is a collaborative venture between a royal notary and a person, whether an unlettered villager or a country gentleman; descriptions of religious uprisings incorporate popular voices—say, in the last letters of Protestant martyrs smuggled out from prison and reproduced in Jean Crespin's *Livre des Martyrs*, or in the cries, slogans, and quotations incorporated into the pamphlet literature—but authorial control was in the hands of educated and experienced writers. Further, the rules for a pardon plea obliged supplicants to conceal or downplay certain facts about themselves, such as their concern for reputation and esteem or their righteous indignation at abuse, whereas descriptions of religious riots and massacres allowed authors to fully develop their own religious values.

Dominique Godineau, 'De la guerrièrre à la citoyenne. Porter les armes pendant l'Ancien Régime et la Révolution française', *Clio. Histoire, femmes et sociétés*, 20 (2004), 2–17.

[35] Natalie Zemon Davis, *Fiction in the Archives: Pardon Tales and their Tellers in Sixteenth-Century France* (Stanford, CA, 1987).

Nonetheless, the genres resemble each other when it comes to issues of festivity and religion. As religious riots clustered around holy days, liturgical events, and even Mardi Gras, so a significant number of individual homicides are set on days of holiness or festivity, which the pardon tales make intrinsic to the violent action. A young baker knifes a young toolmaker in the town of Senlis on Corpus Christi day 1530: the baker had been playing the crucified Jesus in the theatrical performance to mark the day's sanctity. The two men exchanged insults about the state of each other's genitals, and the baker found the toolmaker's 'dishonest words' not only insulting to him but 'to our Lord Jesus Christ and the holiness of the day'. In 1567 in Novaro, a Protestant officer for the Queen of Navarre killed a turbulent Catholic school teacher, who was also a leader of popular Catholic festivity. Though the killing took place close to Easter and was, the officer claimed, in line of duty, he began his story weeks before at Mardi Gras when his victim, known as Captain Shovelpurse (Pellebourse), led a transvestite carnival through the streets of the town.[36]

VIII

Exploring the representation of violence has been developed in important ways in recent years by such works as Shahid Amin's *Event, Metaphor, Memory: Chauri Chaura, 1922–1992* (1995) and Philip Benedict's *Graphic History: The Wars, Massacres and Troubles of Tortorel and Perrissin* (2007). In the former, Amin compared many accounts of an anti-police riot that took place in the small North Indian market town of Chauri Chaura in 1922.[37] Police had fired into a crowd of Gandhian volunteers who were urging boycott of British products and had killed three persons. Whereupon the volunteers had attacked the police, finally pushing them into the police station, setting it afire, and burning twenty-three men to death. Nineteen men were executed as leaders of the riot; 110 more were condemned to life imprisonment. Amin explored many tellings and retellings of these events: the trial records, especially that of a young farmer who testified against his fellow rioters; the initial condemnation and exclusion of the rioters by Gandhi for their violence and their later reincorporation into the nationalist narrative; and especially the memories of old people who had lived through the events, relatives of condemned rioters or slain policemen. Here violence has another life after the historical happening: it lives in contested and changing accounts and memories, which leave their mark on identity and on the possibilities for hostility or reconciliation in the future.

---

[36] Ibid., 30–1, 33–4.
[37] Shahid Amin, *Event, Metaphor, Memory: Chauri Chaura, 1922–1992* (Berkeley and Los Angeles, 1995).

Philip Benedict's multi-layered study of the historical print series by Jean Perrissin, Jacques Tortorel, and two other artists also reveals new dimensions to the place of violence in the thought and imagination of sixteenth-century people.[38] The *Forty Tableaux or divers memorable histories concerning the wars, massacres, and troubles that have occurred in France in these last years* was published in Geneva in 1569–70 and was, as Benedict shows us, an innovative venture in depicting recent historical information and news in graphic form; a Protestant vision of events, but with some balance to it; and a commercial enterprise reaching an international readership, even beyond the Reformed fold (it appeared in French, German, Italian, and Latin, and Benedict traces a wide ownership and reuse of the *Tableaux*). Violent actions of various kinds constitute the most important news: the Estates General and Colloquy of Poissy of 1561 and the Peace Treaty of 1563 were outnumbered by scenes of battle, siege, execution, and popular massacre.

The popular massacres—Cahors, Vassy, Sens, and Tours—are all perpetrated by Catholics against Protestants, but three scenes of Protestant town seizures portray vindictive and excessive bloodshed: Valence, Montbrison and, most dramatically, the Michelade of Nîmes. (Protestant iconoclasm is not depicted, however; it was left to Catholic artists to portray it with vehemence in their depiction of Protestant 'crimes' and 'cruelties').[39] Benedict gives us the textual sources used by Perrissin and Tortorel for their *Tableaux* and suggests the visual traditions from which they drew: for the popular massacre scenes, paintings of the Massacre of the Innocents and Antoine Charon's *Massacre of the Triumvirs* are among the influences.[40] The early generations of readers of the *Forty Tableaux* must have often witnessed scenes like those portrayed by the Protestant artists. We may wonder whether the prints left an impression on their memories and imagination, as television and film do today on our own expectation of what violence looks like.

---

[38] Philip Benedict, *Graphic History: The 'Wars, Massacres and Troubles' of Tortorel and Perrissin*, Travaux d'Humanisme et Renaissance, 20 (Geneva, 2007).

[39] Pictures of Protestant iconoclasm are found in the manuscript *De tristibus galliae* (1567), Bibliothèque municipale de Lyon, Fonds ancien, MS 156 (reproduced in Davis, 'Sacred and the Body Social', 56, fig. 3); and in Richard Verstegen, *Theatrum crudelitatum haereticorum nostri temporis* (Antwerp: A. Hubert, 1588), "Horribilia scelerata ab Huguenotis in Gallijs perpetrata" (reproduced in Davis, 'The Rites of Violence', in *Society and Culture*, 187, fig. 17). The classic treatment of this subject is by David Freedberg, *Iconoclasm and Painting in the Revolt of the Netherlands* (New York, 1988).

[40] Benedict, *Graphic History*, 116–18, 160.

IX

My own path in the late twentieth and early twenty-first century took me to a different site from which to write about religious violence. In my scholarship, I had been looking at processes of social and cultural exchange, of cultural crossings and mixtures, along with my long-term interest in the polarities of domination and resistance and cultural contrasts and choices. During the mid-1990s, the surge of identity politics worldwide, with its pressure for sharp boundaries and exclusive loyalties, increased my sense of urgency in exploring porous borderlands and cultural entanglements. Then came the Gulf War, the mass murders of 9/11, and the ensuing upsurge of hatred, fear, and war.

Such were the intellectual and political contexts for my writing a book about the man Europeans called Leo Africanus, known to himself as Hasan ibn Ahmed ibn Muhammad al-Wazzan al-Gharnati al-Fasi. Diplomat for the sultan of Fez and observant traveller, al-Wazzan was kidnapped by Christian pirates and delivered to Pope Leo X in 1518. For several years, he remained in Italy, living outwardly as a Christian, and writing books for Christian Europeans about the lands, peoples, and learning that he had known since boyhood: Africa, the theology and law of Islam, Arabic poetry, and more. In 1527 he returned to North Africa and to Islam, leaving several manuscripts in Italian and Latin behind him, one of which, *The Description of Africa*, was to become a learned best-seller.

Al-Wazzan's worlds were infused with violence, much of it connected with religion. From North Africa, he heard with approval of the Sunni Sultan Selim's conquest of the Shia Safavid ruler of Persia, and then witnessed himself the sack of Cairo by Selim's Ottoman troops. In Morocco, he fought at his sultan's side against the Portuguese assaults on the Abode of Islam. On both sides of the Mediterranean, he heard eschatological preaching which called for attacks against the infidels and which identified world conquerors—Charles V or Selim or his successor Suleiman—who must lead the holy war and usher in the Golden Age.

Trickster Travels: A Sixteenth-Century Muslim Between Worlds, as I called the study, described two processes which may be pertinent to the dialogue in this present book.[41] First were the cultural strategies that al-Wazzan drew upon or developed in Italy to survive as a Christian and a Muslim simultaneously—not just as an 'outward' Christian and 'inward' Muslim, but more interestingly as a man with a sustained commitment to Islam but entangled with and influenced by certain features of Christian learning (*not* belief in the

---

[41] Natalie Zemon Davis, *Trickster Travels: A Sixteenth-Century Muslim Between Worlds* (New York, 2006; London, 2007).

divinity of Jesus, but certain approaches to sacred texts). These strategies included finding equivalences between the religions through the experience of translation and scholarly collaboration, and practices of distancing and maintaining ambiguity so as to keep some areas of belief safely apart. (Some of these individual strategies are similar to the 'practices of tolerance' described by Benjamin Kaplan and the adage 'all can be saved' unearthed by Stuart Schwartz).

Al-Wazzan's other accomplishment was one of writing: the creation of texts—especially the great Africa book—which were astonishingly free from the religious polemic and partisanship characteristic of almost all writing of his day. In a sense his circumstances demanded this tone: he was writing his manuscripts in a Christian land and yet, as he said toward the end of the Africa book, he planned to return one day 'safe and sound' to North Africa. He had to write with enough discretion and balance so as not to offend powerful Christian masters and yet to be excusable one day to powerful Muslims who might learn of the manuscript.

But the tone of the Africa book also projects a model state of mind: battles between Christians and Muslims, with a heavy toll in death and enslavement, described without taking sides; references to the Prophet, Muslim holy men, and Islamic learning that are descriptive, sometimes favourable, sometimes not, but free of the invective of the ordinary Christian account and of the litany of praise always found in Arabic rhetoric. To be sure, al-Wazzan condemns the Shia 'heresy' and ridicules certain popular practices among Muslims, but for contemporary European readers this gave greater authority to his picture of the true spirit of Islam.

Al-Wazzan's Africa book did not prevent any religious wars, especially in its published versions, to which European translators and editors added some Christian polemic; but the manuscript still stands as a testimony to the creation of and legitimation for communication across a religious divide, an alternative to bloody confrontation.

As I conclude this reminiscence and reflection on New Year's Day 2010, news comes in from many lands of violence on holy days and at holy sites, and eschatological visions are afloat, sanctioning land seizure and slaughter. But the internet hums, too, with practices of peace and rituals of rebuilding. The essays by my colleagues in this volume will give us new understanding of the mixed and complicated story of the past and the possibilities for the future.

Rites of Repair: Restoring Community in the French Religious Wars*

Barbara B. Diefendorf

In 1564, France was enjoying an uneasy peace after the first of what would prove to be eight civil and religious wars. Catherine de Medici, the queen mother and effective ruler of the kingdom, decided to profit from the peace to show her fourteen-year-old son, King Charles IX, to his kingdom and that kingdom to Charles. For the next two years, the court was on the road, travelling in a wide loop around France. In every major town, the king participated in a formal entry ceremony that presented the sovereign to his people, and the people to their lord, ritually joining the social body to its head (to borrow a metaphor often employed at the time). The welcome each city offered its king was a fine display of urban pride, carefully scripted as an act of submission through welcoming speeches, decorative programs using the king's colours and emblems, and such ritual gifts as the keys to the city.

Ritually displaying the restoration of royal authority, the royal entries at the same time enacted the reconciliation of parties recently opposed in bloody civil war. In Lyons, for example, the young-adult sons of the city's most distinguished families, the '*enfants de la ville*', paraded two by two, Protestant and Catholic side by side. Dressed identically in white satin doublets with capes of black velour, members of the two faiths offered the king and court a show of unity. Only one small sign marked out their different allegiances: the Catholics had affixed jewelled crosses to their caps. A small sign, but a telling one, of the deep divisions that still seethed beneath the apparent harmony of the day, for the cross had become a contested symbol in France's religious wars.

---

* Earlier versions of this chapter were presented at University College Dublin and the Université de Paris-Sorbonne (Paris IV). I am grateful to Tadhg O hAnnrachain and Denis Crouzet for the invitations to present this work in these venues and to them and their colleagues and students for the stimulating discussions that followed. I would also like to thank Jeffry Diefendorf who, as usual, served as my first and keenest reader.

Anyone watching the Lyons entry would have recognized this emblem as a sign of partisan loyalties—a reminder of the white paper crosses that Catholics had fastened to their hats to identify themselves in religious riots; a reminder equally of the many crosses that Protestants had torn down as symbols of Catholic idolatry. And anyone familiar with Lyons's troubled history during the first religious war would suspect that this show of unity was a forced one. Archival sources confirm this to be true. Two weeks before the king's arrival, Marshal de la Vieilleville, charged by the king with overseeing enforcement of the edict of pacification in Lyons, sent an urgent plea to Catherine de Medici, telling her that the Catholic *enfants* refused to march with their Protestant counterparts and urging her to intervene, so as to assure public order, by threatening to punish as 'rebels' and 'disturbers of the peace' those who refused to march peacefully together.[1]

The unity on display for the king's entry was not only forced; it was already being subverted from within. With a population of 60,000 to 65,000 people, Lyons was one of the largest French cities seized and held by Protestants when civil war broke out in March 1562.[2] Retaken by Catholic forces, the city remained teeming with hatreds when a negotiated peace was announced in March 1563. The Protestants had followed up their victory with a swift but thorough campaign to purify the city of Catholic idolatry, and Catholics could not forgive what they saw as the wanton destruction of altars, relics, and churches. Once masters again themselves, they enacted a bloody revenge against their enemies and worked to make sure that such a betrayal could not recur. Building on the secret sympathies of royal officers charged with maintaining the peace, they undermined the bi-partisan municipal government mandated by the king, organized a clandestine militia, and prepared to strike first when war broke out again, as it did in 1567. Lyons's brief experience of Protestant domination was not to happen again.

Lyons's history in the Wars of Religion is both typical and unique. Protestants took over approximately one in three of France's sixty largest

---

[1] Bibliothèque nationale de France, Paris, MS français 15880, fo. 160r. Letter of 30 May 1564 from François de Scépeaux, maréchal de la Vieilleville to Catherine de Medici. On Vieilleville's appointment to oversee pacification efforts in Lyons, see Claude de Rubys, *Histoire veritable de la ville de Lyon* (Lyons, 1604), 399–402. The king's entry took place on 13 June 1564.

[2] Philip Benedict, 'French Cities from the Sixteenth Century to the Revolution', in Philip Benedict (ed.), *Cities and Social Change in Early Modern France* (London, 1989), 24, gives Lyons's population as 58,000 in 1550; Natalie Zemon Davis, 'The Sacred and the Body Social in Sixteenth-Century Lyon', *Past and Present*, 90 (1981), 43, puts it at 65,000 in 1555.

cities by the spring of 1562, even though they represented a militant minority and not the majority in most of these towns.[3] Even many areas still under Catholic domination experienced religious riots, iconoclastic attacks, and the destruction of churches. In general, the Protestants' most enduring successes lay in a broad arc across the South, but each city's experience was different. The story that I have very briefly narrated for Lyons thus cannot stand in for all of France's cities, but it does neatly encapsulate three key elements of the argument that I wish to make as I examine the dynamics that prompted nearly forty years of religious war in France. These elements are, in very summary form: 1) the provocative role of Protestant religious violence; 2) the way the Catholic response served to heighten religious differences; 3) the need for secular authorities ultimately to resolve these differences by separating the civil and religious spheres. A common theme linking all three elements is the way in which sacred and secular rituals were manipulated to maintain—or to undermine—community.

Like other chapters in this volume, 'Rites of Repair' is intended as a response to Natalie Zemon Davis's seminal article on 'The Rites of Violence', first published in *Past and Present* in 1973, and to subsequent studies of the French Wars of Religion, which have been profoundly influenced by Davis's work. Identifying the violent acts perpetrated in the course of religious riots as the products of a vast repertory of gestures rooted in judicial and ecclesiastical practices, Davis revealed an underlying logic to the actions of participants in these riots and showed how their behaviour, however destructive, was nevertheless intended in some way to purge the pollution of heresy and restore sacred and civic communities disrupted by religious discord. As such, she concluded, the violence was justified and even legitimated in the minds of its perpetrators.

In the years since the article's initial publication, these insights have been criticized but also extended and elaborated in various ways. My approach in this essay takes its departure from questions Suzanne Desan raises in a 1989 article about Davis's emphasis on the restoration of community as an underlying motive for religious violence. 'Rather than asserting that existing perceptions of the body social defined violence', Desan concludes, 'one could say that violence over religious beliefs destroyed the existing community and tore

---

[3] For the one in three figure, see Philip Benedict, 'The Dynamics of Protestant Militancy', in Philip Benedict, Guido Marnef, Henk van Nierop, and Marc Venard (eds), *Reformation, Revolt and Civil War in France and the Netherlands, 1555–1585* (Amsterdam, 1999), 48. According to Davis, Protestants never made up more than one third of Lyons's population, and this is almost certainly a larger minority than most cities would have had, 'The Sacred and the Body Social', 47.

it apart in a bloody power struggle as each group fought to draw new communal boundaries'.[4]

Desan's analysis of Davis's argument is largely a theoretical one, rooted in a critique of the kind of cultural anthropology that Natalie Davis was reading when she wrote 'The Rites of Violence'. And yet her comments have been largely vindicated by recent historical research. If a single, common conclusion can be drawn from the growing literature on French religious violence, it is that the religious rioting that spread through the kingdom in the late 1550s and early 1560s played an important—even a crucial—role in tipping the country over into civil war. That same violence became one of the most important barriers to peace, not just in the case of the first religious war but in subsequent wars as well. Becoming endemic, the violence also repeatedly threatened the religious co-existence mandated by the Edict of Nantes and became an excuse for renewing the persecution of French Protestants in anticipation of the Edict's revocation in 1685. But the violence did not just prompt and perpetuate the religious quarrels; it also provoked just the kind of fundamental rupture of the social body—the metaphorical representation of an idealized unitary community—that Desan postulated in her article.

My intention in taking up the problem of community in the religious wars is not to criticize Natalie Davis's foundational article but rather to expand upon themes merely sketched out lightly there. It is important to remember that, when Natalie Davis wrote 'The Rites of Violence', historians still tended to attribute a far larger place to politics and even to economics than to religion as causal factors in the Wars of Religion.[5] Religious rioting was largely dismissed as the work of uncouth mobs and fanatics. Historical writing on the religious wars was often still confessional in inspiration, and the popular violence was embarrassing to both sides. Catholic historians did not like to admit that Catholic preachers were calling for the extermination of heretics, nor did Protestants like to admit that members of Reformed congregations and even ministers were sacking and pillaging Catholic churches. Protestants also preferred for political reasons to depict Catholic leaders and even the king, rather than the people, as their enemy.[6] Natalie Davis's article helped set

---

[4] Suzanne Desan, 'Crowds, Community, and Ritual in the Work of E. P. Thompson and Natalie Davis', in Lynn Hunt (ed.), *The New Cultural History* (Berkeley and Los Angeles, CA, 1989), 63–4, 65.

[5] On the way our understanding of the wars has changed, see Mack P. Holt, 'Putting Religion Back into the Wars of Religion', *French Historical Studies*, 18 (1993), 524–51.

[6] Janine [Garrisson] Estèbe, *Tocsin pour un massacre: La saison des Saint-Barthélemy* (Paris, 1968), 43. Estèbe mentions only the Catholics' calls to massacre and the Protestants' political preferences, thereby displaying her own biases.

historians on a different path by showing how the acts carried out in religious riots were rooted in participants' understanding of their relation to the sacred, their anxieties about profanation of the holy, and their perception of threats to their faith. By analyzing the underlying logic and meaning of crowd violence, Davis cast a new light onto the fundamentally religious character of the Wars of Religion.

A number of historians, myself included, have followed Davis's lead in rethinking the role of religious violence in the wars. To cite but one example, Denis Crouzet's first book, *Les Guerriers de Dieu*, and recently published *Dieu dans ses royaumes* deal exhaustively with the underlying mindset, or *imaginaire* that moved sixteenth-century French people to attack the symbols and persons of their enemies.[7] My own argument may occasionally venture into the realms of the *imaginaire*, for it is impossible to separate the violence from its motives. Taking up the problem of community nevertheless shifts the focus to the ways in which people acted out both attempts to restore community and hostility toward those who did not share their views. Moreover, unlike Davis, who defined her topic as 'religious riot' and tried to separate this violence from that which occurred during war, I will blur the boundaries of war and peace in order to show how intimately the pre-war violence was connected to the slide into war and how the violence did not stop with peace. Where Davis's comparative analysis of the social meanings of religious violence could dispense with the element of change over time, my argument is necessarily linked to the dynamics of cause and effect.

My thesis is quite simply this: Despite their religious differences, Protestants and Catholics held to an ideal of community in which the sacred and the civic were joined. Members of both faiths nevertheless believed that the social body had been dangerously corrupted and could only be restored by purging it of the errors that defiled it. But here they parted ways. For Protestants, the goal was to create a newly purified and godly society; for Catholics, it was to excise the pollution of heresy and restore the sacred to its proper place in the city. These aims were mutually exclusive, and the 'rituals of repair' that each side employed to restore their imagined community excluded the other. Religious rituals of repair were thus double-edged; whatever their avowed intention, they served more to heighten differences than to promote unity. Ultimately, the task of repair had to be left to secular authorities, who worked far harder at this than they have often been given credit for, but against very difficult odds.

---

[7] Denis Crouzet, *Les Guerriers de Dieu: La violence au temps des troubles de religion, vers 1525–vers 1610*, 2 vols (Seyssel, 1990); and Denis Crouzet, *Dieu dans ses royaumes: Une histoire des guerres de Religion* (Seyssel, 2008).

Although I will limit my evidence largely to the period surrounding the first War of Religion, the underlying dynamic is a broader one. Popular religious violence reached a peak around the outbreak of the first religious war, but it continued to recur throughout the wars and even, although with a lesser intensity, under the seventeenth-century regime of the Edict of Nantes. The violence continued because hatred has a long memory, but also, and perhaps more fundamentally, because the ideological roots of these mutual animosities had not changed. It is necessary, then, to begin at the root of these antagonisms.

The revolutionary character of French Protestantism

One of the areas most enriched by recent attempts to 'put religion back into the Wars of Religion' is our understanding of the 'destabilizing and even revolutionary implications' of France's Protestant movement.[8] Until recently, historians tended to depict the demands of Reformed church leaders as limited and defensive. French Protestants merely wanted recognition, they told us; they wanted freedom of conscience and the right to worship as their conscience demanded.[9] To generations who took for granted twentieth-century principles of religious liberty, the argument sounded reasonable, but it was in fact deceptive on two scores. It ignored pre-Reformation realities in treating religion as a private matter of personal choice and, as such, as a matter of personal belief and not belonging. It also misrepresented the Protestants' true aims. Recognition was a last-ditch demand French Protestants made when pushed to the wall. In the more hopeful moments that preceded the first War of Religion, they demonstrated by act and word that their true desire was to revolutionize society by eliminating false worship and idolatry and by renewing morals. Let me take up each of these points in turn.

When Natalie Davis wrote 'The Rites of Violence', she and others of her generation were moving away from a social history rooted in materialist paradigms and inventing new cultural approaches that drew from sociology and anthropology. Among other benefits, this paradigm shift has given early modernists a new understanding of the place of religion in society, and more particularly, a new appreciation for the pre-Reformation equation between communion and community. In an influential essay on 'The Mass as a Social Institution', John Bossy explained how the sacrament of the Eucharist served as a ritual of unity 'whereby the Christian participates in communion,

---

[8] Holt, 'Putting Religion Back'; Benedict, 'The Dynamics of Protestant Militancy', 36.
[9] E.g., N. M. Sutherland, *The Huguenot Struggle for Recognition* (New Haven, CT, 1980).

common union, the wholeness of Christ and of his church'.[10] The notion of the Christian community as 'one bread and one body' was explicit in many sixteenth-century explanations of the Mass, and was acted out in the Eucharist but also in the distribution of holy bread after Sunday Mass.[11]

Borrowing from scripture, the metaphor of the body also expressed the relationship between Christ, the 'head,' and his 'body' the church.[12] Although Christian notions of sin necessarily made salvation at least in part an individual matter, the church's role in mediating Christ's saving grace had a collective dimension in the parish Mass and in a variety of rituals through which divine protection was solicited on behalf of the community. The doctrine of the Real Presence reinforced the sacramental authority of the clergy but also the underlying unity of the social and the sacred. God was not experienced as a distant deity. His presence could be grasped sensually in the sights and sounds of the Mass, which climaxed with the priest's elevation of the consecrated Host. Embodied in the Host, God could be taken out of the church and carried through the streets in elaborate processions that consecrated urban space and ritually unified the social body to Christ, its head. Moreover, God's protection could be solicited directly though ritual and prayer, but also through the mediation of patron saints, whose sacrality spilled over into the relics and images through which they were venerated but could also be approached.

The Protestant Reformation firmly rejected these traditional ways of experiencing divinity. As Natalie Davis points out in another classic article, 'That the sacred could be enclosed in a thing—in a host, in a bone, in a building, in a piece of land—was a notion smacking of idolatry'.[13] Protestants' belief that we are justified by faith alone and their conviction that God tells us to seek him through his Word alone caused them to reject the traditional church's reliance on ritual and ceremony, which they identified as soul-endangering distractions from truth.[14] Protestants did not, however,

---

[10] John Bossy, 'The Mass as a Social Institution, 1200–1700', *Past and Present*, 100 (1983), 34.

[11] Barbara B. Diefendorf, *Beneath the Cross: Catholics and Huguenots in Sixteenth-Century Paris* (Oxford and New York, 1991), 32.

[12] Ephesians, 1:22–3: '[God] hath put all things under his feet, and gave him to be the head over all things to the church, which is his body, the fulness of him that filleth all in all'; Colossians, 1:18: 'And he is the head of the body, the church'.

[13] Davis, 'The Sacred and the Body Social', 58.

[14] Christian Grosse, 'Places of Sanctification: The Liturgical Sacrality of Genevan Reformed Churches, 1535–1566', in Will Coster and Andrew Spicer (eds), *Sacred Space in Early Modern Europe* (Cambridge, 2005), 64.

simply reject divine immanence in favour of transcendence. Rather they sought to redefine how the holy should be present in the world.[15] They found this new definition in scriptural assurances that Christian believers are themselves 'the real temples of the Lord'. Church buildings have no innate sacrality; it is the 'meeting of Christians for the purpose of worship' that 'invests the place with a divine presence, which is both spiritual and social'.[16]

This belief that God was present in the congregation gathered for worship nevertheless represents a clear break from traditions that defined the Christian community in more encompassing terms. Convinced that the broader community was mired in superstition and false practice, members of Reformed churches separated themselves into closed communities of the faithful. The creation of consistories to enforce church discipline and promote higher standards of morality furthered this tendency toward separation, as did the doctrine of predestination, which encouraged believers to identify themselves as chosen ones. Referring to themselves unselfconsciously as 'God's children', '*les enfants de Dieu*', Reformed church members envisioned themselves as part of an extended family from which the non-Reformed were pre-emptively excluded.[17]

But if French Protestants' withdrawal from the broader community was in part due to their desire to create a more godly society, it was also the result of an involuntary expulsion. The condemnation of Protestant teachings forced converts into the shadows, at least until the late 1550s, when the movement grew strong enough in certain areas to emerge publicly, and secrecy only aroused popular suspicion. Borrowing tropes first employed in the early church's campaigns against heresy, Catholic preachers aggravated these suspicions by accusing Protestants of using their clandestine services to engage in lechery.[18] Another favourite trope was the metaphor of gangrene or cancer.

---

[15] Davis, 'Sacred and the Body Social', 59.

[16] Grosse, 'Places of Sanctification', 64.

[17] The expression '*les enfants de Dieu*', occurs, for example, in *La juste et saincte defense de la ville de Lyon* (Lyon, 1563), reproduced in L. Cimber [pseud. of Louis Lafaist] and Félix Danjou (eds), *Archives curieuses de l'histoire de la France depuis Louis XI jusqu'à Louis XIII*, 30 vols (Paris and Beauvais, 1834–41), IV, 198, 209, 212; Jean Faurin, *Journal de Faurin sur les guerres de Castres*, ed. Charles Pradel (repr. edn, Marseille, 1981), 11.

[18] G. Wylie Sypher, ' "Faisant ce qu'il leur vient à plaisir": The Image of Protestantism in French Catholic Polemic on the Eve of the Religious Wars', *Sixteenth Century Journal*, 11 (1980), 59–84; Luc Racaut, *Hatred in Print: Catholic Propaganda and Protestant Identity during the French Wars of Religion* (Aldershot, 2002), 33–5, 52–4, 58–63.

Preachers said Protestants were gangrenous members who needed to be severed from the social body in order to restore it to health.[19]

Protestants were also ritually expelled from the social body in the ceremonies that accompanied the execution of condemned heretics. Approximately 450 convicted heretics were executed in France between 1523 and 1560, a smaller number by comparison with population than were executed in Tudor England or the Habsburg Netherlands, but quite enough to remind Protestants of their outsider status.[20] As David Nicholls has shown, the rituals for the execution of heretics were meant to reaffirm community solidarity against individuals who disturbed the social order. Combining religious and secular elements, the elaborately staged ceremonies began with the victims performing an act of public penitence and climaxed with their execution by burning. 'Heresy had to be driven out of society like disease from the body', says Nicholls, 'and the social body completely cleansed of all impurities'.[21]

This fundamental schism in the Christian community helps explain why, when French Protestants began to act out their hatred of Catholic errors, their actions were so provocative and reprisals were so severe. There was often a pedagogical impulse behind these gestures—what one historian refers to as a '*théologie pratique*' acted out in 'rituals of humiliation and defiling'.[22] The iconoclast who knocked the head off a statue of the Virgin on a street corner wanted to show that the image was an inert bit of carved stone. The blasphemer who seized the consecrated Host during Mass and stomped it under foot wanted to show that it was only bread, a 'god of paste'. Such acts, however, met with astonished incomprehension. From the Catholics' perspective, vandalizing a statue of the Virgin Mary risked the withdrawal of her sacred presence as protector and mediator for the community. Desecrating the Host risked the wrath of God himself.[23] Both gestures were taken as assaults on the entire economy of the sacred and, more particularly, on the very points at which the sacred and the social body were joined. And, indeed, they were intended this way, which is precisely why these acts were so inflammatory.

---

[19] Diefendorf, *Beneath the Cross*, 47, 150.

[20] E. William Monter, *Judging the French Reformation: Heresy Trials by Sixteenth-Century Parlements* (Cambridge, MA, 1999), 54.

[21] David Nicholls, 'The Theatre of Martyrdom in the French Reformation', *Past and Present*, 121 (1988), 50.

[22] Olivier Christin, *Une révolution symbolique: L'iconoclasme huguenot et la reconstruction catholique* (Paris, 1991), 142.

[23] See, e.g., Claude Haton, *Mémoires contenant le récit des événements accomplis de 1553 à 1582*, ed. Félix Bourquelot, 2 vols (Paris, 1857), 375, describing a sacrilege committed in the Sainte Chapelle in 1563.

Incidents of sacrilege and iconoclasm began early in the Protestant Reformation but occurred in a sporadic fashion until the late 1550s, when they became more frequent and spectacular.[24] The upturn correlates with the organization of Reformed churches, the multiplication of Protestant conversions, and a new confidence on the part of these converts. One chronicler, for example, describes a six- or seven-week visit to his city by John Knox in February 1559 as extremely fruitful; 'the ranks of the faithful grew in such a fashion that they dared to preach in broad daylight, where they had previously dared to hold services only at night'.[25] Public worship, however, brought new dangers, and church members began wearing arms to services as early as 1557. As this militancy became more widespread and organized, it became another provocation.[26] Despite heightened tensions on both sides, the Protestant gospel continued to spread. By the end of 1562, more than eight hundred Reformed churches had been founded, with a collective membership of between 1.5 and 2 million people – still only about 10 per cent of France's population, but an astounding rise in a very short time.[27]

As Protestant communities grew, they wanted not just to meet publicly and in daylight but to have places of worship of their own. As a result they began to seize churches in towns where their numbers were greatest. Protestants justified taking churches by their growing numbers, but of course Catholics did not see the situation in the same way, especially when the Protestant takeovers were followed up by the whitewashing of walls and removal of statues, side altars, and crucifixes, so as to adapt the buildings to their new purpose. As far as Catholics were concerned, there was little or no difference between the transformation of churches into Reformed temples and their outright sacking and pillaging.

From the Protestant perspective too, there was an ideological continuity between these acts. Churches needed to be purified of idolatry in order to be suitable places for the right worship of God, but the community needed to be

---

[24] On the wave of Protestant iconoclasm and the motives behind it, see especially Christin, *Une révolution symbolique*; Crouzet, *Les Guerriers de Dieu*, ch. 7, 8.

[25] Guillaume Daval and Jean Daval, *Histoire de la Réformation à Dieppe, 1557–1567*, 2 vols (Rouen, 1878–9), 10–11.

[26] Benedict, 'The Dynamics of Protestant Militancy', 42. In this article, Philip Benedict summarizes previous contributions to our recognition of this revolutionary radicalism but also breaks new ground with the questions he raises about what these beliefs meant in action. My understanding of Protestant militancy owes a lot to his insights.

[27] On the difficulty of estimating the number of Reformed churches, see Philip Benedict and Nicolas Fornerod, 'Les 2 150 'églises' réformées de France de 1561–1562', *Revue historique*, 311 (2009), 529–60.

purified too in order to contain the godly new society the Protestants wanted to create. As Philip Benedict observes, 'wherever the ranks of the movement began to swell toward a position of local dominance, aspirations commonly surfaced for the immediate elimination of the idols from the temple, the ridding of the land of useless religious, and the abolition of the "stinking" mass'.[28] The case of Castres illustrates well the kind of intimidation that Catholics experienced in areas where Protestantism was strongest. Between September 1561 and January 1562, Protestants in Castres seized and 'purified' twelve churches in the city and its immediate surroundings. On 1 January, city officials forbade the saying of Mass. The takeover appears to have been accomplished with little overt violence, but only because local Catholics feared to stand up to the Protestant crowds. A Franciscan preaching Advent sermons was accused of sedition and driven from town with a noose around his neck. A Trinitarian priest caught clandestinely celebrating Mass after the ban was subjected to a roughly mocking charivari. Paraded about town backwards on an ass still wearing his liturgical vestments, he was then seated in the town square for questioning. Asked if he wanted to die for the Mass, he lost courage and said no. His captors took his vestments, missal, and the Host he had prepared for Mass and burned them on the spot. A Protestant chronicler narrates these events unapologetically; he blames the 'papists' for nearly provoking a riot and records the takeover of churches in the following terse phrase: 'all the images and altars in Castres's churches were overthrown'.[29] Protestants in other cities used similar language to describe the seizure of Catholic places of worship. They also employed similar rituals to discredit Catholic priests and dissuade them from celebrating Mass through both mockery and threats.[30]

Significantly, Protestant accounts present these acts not as 'rites of violence' but rather as 'rites of repair' intended to restore worship to evangelical purity and to rid the community of pollution.[31] A Protestant account of the

---

[28] Benedict, 'The Dynamics of Protestant Militancy', 45.

[29] *Journal de Faurin*, 9–12.

[30] See, e.g., Claude de Sainctes, *Discours sur le saccagement des églises catholiques par les heretiques anciens et nouveaux Calvinistes, en l'an 1562* (Paris, 1562), reproduced in Cimber and Danjou (eds), *Archives curieuses de l'histoire de la France*, IV, 384; Haton, *Mémoires*, I, 250–7, on an incident in Orléans; Christin, *Une révolution symbolique*, 141, regarding 'processions burlesques' of broken images through Montpellier; Davis, 'The Rites of Violence', 180–1, on incidents in Montauban, Lyons, and other cities.

[31] This is explicit, for example, in Jean Faurin's justification of the destruction of a Jacobin church and episcopal château outside of Castres on account of the 'infinite number of acts of debauchery' that took place there. *Journal de Faurin*, 25.

capture of Lyons, for example, explains that the first table of the Decalogue commands kings and princes to destroy idols and to 'expel and exterminate idolaters and cleanse public space of such pollution'.[32] It is not surprising, then, that in Lyons, as in many other towns taken by the Protestants at the outset of the first religious war, cleansing churches of 'idols' was, after providing for the town's defence, a top priority for the new regime. As Olivier Christin concludes, 'the abolition of idols thus represents a way of burning one's bridges with the older order of things, a deliberate engagement in the irreparable'.[33]

Recent research has also borne out Natalie Davis's observation that Protestant iconoclasm was not, as it has often been seen, simply the product of angry mobs or wanton crowds. Elites were not just present but actually directed the sacking of the cathedral of Le Mans in 1562 and the pillaging of the abbey of Saint-Florent outside Saumur in 1563.[34] Records also exist that show workers being paid to undertake acts of destruction ordered by local towns and consistories. Much of the iconoclasm was thus less the result of spontaneous rioting than of campaigns organized with the overt or clandestine aid of local and Reformed church officials.[35]

This is not to say that all Reformed church leaders or members agreed that it was right to seize the initiative and cleanse Catholic churches in this way, but the objections they offered were grounded in political caution and not in ideological opposition to the iconoclasm itself. In many towns taken by the Huguenots, officials tried to control the removal of ritual objects from churches by ordering inventories be made and precious materials safely stored. Once war broke out, however, such safeguards proved impossible to maintain. Huguenot leaders saw the seized properties as a way to help pay the costs of war, and the didactic impulse of earlier acts of iconoclasm gave way to looting for gain. Church buildings were demolished to obtain lead for bullets and building materials for the war effort, but looting for personal profit and for the pleasure of destruction inevitably also occurred as order broke down.

If the full impact of this wave of iconoclastic violence has only recently been understood, it is not because these events passed unnoticed. Catholics cried out against the destruction of religious images and churches as soon as they happened, but, as long as the history of the Wars of Religion was still written

---

[32] *La juste et saincte defense de la ville de Lyon*, 206.
[33] Christin *Une révolution symbolique*, 123.
[34] Ibid., 95–6.
[35] Victor Carrière, *Introduction aux études d'histoire ecclésiastique locale*, 3 vols (Paris, 1934–40), III, 386–8.

in confessional terms, Catholic complaints about attacks on religious property were viewed somewhat dismissively as polemic and propaganda. It was only after 'The Rites of Violence' and, more broadly, the turn toward cultural approaches to history in the 1970s that scholars sought to integrate the pillaging of thousands of churches into our understanding of the religious wars. We may never know just how many churches were sacked. Jean de Monluc, bishop of Valence, claimed in 1572 that the Huguenots had destroyed twenty thousand churches and two thousand monasteries.[36] This number may well be exaggerated, but even without a quantitative measure of the damage, the sweeping nature of the violence, which spared few corners of France, and the impact it had on Catholics are now clear.

The Catholic response

At a most fundamental level, witnessing the Protestants' destruction of things they held holy convinced French Catholics that two religions could not coexist side by side. Catholics had always been taught to hate heresy, but the seizure of churches and the spreading wave of iconoclasm made this hatred visceral. No longer an abstract concept, heresy was perceived as a direct threat to the social and sacral community and had to be combated as such. A new Catholic militancy appeared on the eve of the religious wars. Viewed over the long term, this new militancy was part of the spiritual reawakening that resulted in France's Catholic Reformation. In the short term, it contributed to the fierce partisan violence that characterized the religious wars.

The spiritual dimension of this new militancy is evident in the enthusiasm with which Catholics took part in processions, Masses, and other ceremonies intended to repair the pollution of iconoclasm and restore the place of the sacred in society.[37] The use of processions against Protestant heresy dates at least to 1528, when Parisians responded to the vandalism of a statue of the Virgin Mary on a street corner with five days of religious processions in which all of the city's parishes, monasteries, schools, and municipal and royal officials had their turn. King Francis I took part himself in two of these ceremonies.[38] By the time the Wars of Religion began, processions had become a regular response to acts of iconoclasm, either alone or as a preliminary to the

---

[36] Carrière, *Introduction aux études d'histoire ecclésiastique locale*, III, 390.

[37] In the words of Olivier Christin, *Une révolution symbolique*, 178, 'It was necessary both to restore—in every sense of the term, that is to say, to re-establish and to repair—and to exorcise the menace that the sacrileges imposed on the community'.

[38] *Journal d'un bourgeois de Paris sous le règne de François Premier (1515–1536)*, ed. Ludovic Lalanne (Paris, 1844), 346–9.

re-consecration of churches defiled by sacrilege. Many cities also organized them as a form of collective supplication for an end to heresy.[39]

And yet processions were another ritual of repair that could easily turn into a rite of violence. Precisely because Protestants rejected the notion of sacred community that Catholics used religious processions to reinforce, these events became sites where religious differences were publicly acted out, not infrequently with violent results. In December 1560, for example, Protestant youths in Carcassonne broke out a statue of the Virgin from a church and dragged it 'ignominiously through the streets, calling out blasphemies'. They then tried to break apart the statue but, fearing to be caught when dawn arrived, abandoned it in the gutter. Catholics finding it immediately organized a procession to return the statue to its usual place, but some people were too angry to take part in this ritual of repair. 'Animated by an incredible zeal at the sight of this profanation, [they] grabbed arms, abandoned the procession, and ran after all Protestants they even suspected of such an impiety'. Eight people are said to have been killed as a result, and a number of houses were pillaged.[40] Similar events took place in other cities. In Troyes, a procession held to repair the defilement of a statue of the Virgin found with a dead cat hung around her neck was broken up by the sudden rumour that Huguenots were about to attack (when in fact, according to a Protestant chronicler, his co-religionists were hiding at home in fear of the Catholics' anger).[41]

As this chronicler suggests, except in cities where their numbers were very strong, Protestants were often too frightened to interfere directly with Catholic processions. There are recorded incidents of members of the crowd reaching out to grab a passing Host or throw a relic to the ground. There are also incidents of Protestants deliberately cutting through Catholic processions on their way to hear religious services outside the city walls, the only place their worship was permitted. They did this as a deliberate challenge to Catholics' monopoly of sacred space within the city.[42] More often,

---

[39] See, e.g., Jean Lebeuf, *Histoire de la prise d'Auxerre par les huguenots et de la délivrance de la même ville, les années 1567 et 1568* (La Ferté-sous-Jouarre, 2004; repr. of 1723 edn), 85; Andrew Spicer, '(Re)Building the Sacred Landscape: Orléans, 1560–1610', *French History*, 21 (2007), 262–3; Moshe Sluhovsky, *Patroness of Paris: Rituals of Devotion in Early Modern France* (Leiden, 1998), 116–19.

[40] Thomas-Augustin Bouges, *Histoire ecclésiastique et civile de la ville et diocèse de Carcassonne* (Marseille, 1978; repr. of 1741 edn), 311–12.

[41] Nicolas Pithou, *Chronique de Troyes et de la Champagne durant les guerres de Religion (1524–1594)*, ed. Pierre-Eugène Leroy, 2 vols (Reims, 1998–2000), 1, 295–6.

[42] Jérémie Foa, 'An Unequal Apportionment: The Conflict over Space between Protestants and Catholics at the Beginning of the Wars of Religion', *French History*, 20 (2006), 380–1.

however, Protestants showed their disdain for processional traditions and their belief that they constituted idolatry by refusing to hang out the tapestries used to decorate houses along the procession's route or by failing to remove their hats when the Host passed, rather than by actually trying to disrupt the procession. And yet, by the time the Wars of Religion began in the spring of 1562, even such mild gestures of disrespect could cost a man his life, as they did for one spectator at Paris's Corpus Christi Day procession in 1562, when he was heard to disparage the event as idolatrous.[43]

Let us take a moment to put this event into context—not to excuse or accuse, but merely to try to try to understand the volatile atmosphere that pervaded France by May 1562. In the less than three months since war had broken out, Huguenot forces had captured Orléans, Tours, and a string of other towns in the Loire Valley. They had also captured the second and third largest cities in the kingdom, Rouen and Lyons, along with dozens of smaller but still important cities. And every one of these cities had experienced—or was experiencing—the 'cleansing' of churches that Catholics perceived as desecration and wanton destruction. News poured into Paris daily of new outrages—of churches stripped of their most precious relics, altars, and statuary; of priests humiliated, expelled, and sometimes killed. Is it any wonder that, although residing in a fiercely Catholic city with only a very small Protestant minority, Parisians were on edge and fearful of traitors?[44] Or that they, like citizens of many other cities still in Catholic hands, began to attack both the persons and the properties of presumed enemies in retribution for the violence against Catholic properties and persons?

The violence need not have taken place locally. News—or even rumour—of disturbing acts in other towns was often enough to prompt attacks on suspected heretics.[45] When human targets were out of reach, the anger often spilled over onto their properties instead.[46] It is impossible to trace a precise curve of the violence, but clearly violent acts perpetrated on both sides of the religious divide were mutually reinforcing, until the cycle of violence already

---

Haton cites Huguenots in Sens rudely accosting a procession in 1561/2 and says that a number of people were killed in the resulting riot, *Mémoires*, I, 90–4.

[43] Diefendorf, *Beneath the Cross*, 59.

[44] See des Sainctes for the accusation that Protestants were plotting in 1562 to pillage Paris and had 900 of the 'principal houses' marked out, *Discours sur le saccagement des églises catholiques*, 371–3. Haton also demonstrates the conviction that Protestants were plotting to seize Paris, *Mémoires*, I, 240.

[45] Caesar de Nostredamus, *L'histoire et chronique de Provence* (Marseilles, 1971; repr. of 1614 edn), 790–2.

[46] E.g., Lebeuf, *Histoire de la prise d'Auxerre*, 84–5.

building prior to the wars spiralled out of control. The greatest paroxysm appears to have occurred in the summer of 1562, during the first religious war, which was not just fought in the field by armies commanded by great aristocrats but also by more informally organized partisan groups operating on a local level. Militant activists, whose role is still imperfectly understood, helped escalate the cycle of retributory violence I have just been describing into widespread murder and massacre.[47]

They were helped along in this by decrees issued by the Parlements of Toulouse and Paris that appeared to give Catholics free licence to attack their enemies. Declaring Huguenots who took part in the pillaging of Catholic properties guilty of *lèse majesté* and rebellion, and consequently subject to death, the edicts were taken 'as permission to launch a free-for-all attack on anyone suspected of the new religion'. In Paris, we find Huguenots struck down in the street but also incidents of the sort of mock trial that Natalie Davis describes in 'The Rites of Violence', in which 'attackers grilled their prisoners on their religious beliefs and administered whatever punishment—usually death—they considered fitting.[48] In the Midi, we find cases of mass murder. Catholic gangs in Gaillac rounded up Protestants and threw them from high cliffs. In a small town near Toulouse, they set fire to a building where Protestants were gathered for worship and then killed them as they tried to escape.[49] And throughout France, we find the surrender of cities by one side or the other followed by atrocities to opponents captured before they could flee.[50]

As acts of violence multiplied and at the same time spread through local communities in a very personal fashion, the difficulty of making peace

---

[47] A little noticed clause in the Edict of Amboise called on the king's subjects to put an end to 'all associations they might have within or outside of this kingdom, and to no longer collect any fees, enrol any men, or form other congregations or assemblies than those [given] above, and without arms...'. 'Edit et declaration faite par le roi Charles IX de ce nom, sur la pacification des troubles de ce Royaume (19 mars 1563)', in André Stegmann (ed.), *Édits des guerres de Religion* (Paris, 1979), 36. See also Kevin Gould, *Catholic Activism in South-West France, 1540–1570* (Aldershot, 2006), on the creation of militant Catholic associations in towns of south-western France.

[48] Diefendorf, *Beneath the Cross*, 65–6.

[49] *Journal de Faurin*, 14–17.

[50] See Armand Dupin de Saint-André, *Histoire du Protestantisme en Touraine* (Paris, 1885), 82, on the slaughter of Protestants caught in Tours when the town was retaken; Jean Crespin, *Histoire des martyres: persecutez et mis a mort pour la vérité de l'evangile, depuis le temps des apostres jusques a present (1619)*, new edn, 3 vols. (Toulouse, 1885–9) III, 280, on revenge killings; Christin, *Une révolution symbolique*, 202, on the personal and vengeful nature of actions taken in recovered cities.

increased exponentially. The violence that accompanied the religious wars was transformative; it tore the social fabric irreparably. It was one thing for aristocratic leaders to negotiate terms for laying down weapons with the Crown; it was quite another to convince a population scarred by civil war to consent to live peacefully together. By all accounts, the Peace of Amboise issued in March 1563 did little to put a stop to the popular violence. Although the edict ordered the king's subjects to forget the past and to live peacefully together, 'as brothers, friends, and fellow citizens', amnesia could not be so easily legislated.[51] Catholics restored to power in cities retaken from the Protestants used legal proceedings to punish those they held responsible both for seizing the city and for the destruction their churches had endured, but they tolerated and even took part in illegal acts of vengeance as well. City authorities used their legal right to search for hidden arms to harass returning Protestants.[52] They ordered all citizens, regardless of religious affiliation, to hang out tapestries for religious processions and then looked the other way when those who failed in this obligation had their houses pillaged. They confiscated properties belonging to Protestants who had not yet dared to return and auctioned them off to the highest bidders.[53] Venomous preaching and hate-filled sermons also kept things on edge.[54]

I have focused here on the cycle of violence that spun out of control with the first religious war, but similar cycles repeated with each of the subsequent wars. The grand sum of violence was greatest in the first war. The Huguenots never again succeeded in taking as many major cities and so had less opportunity to cleanse churches, and the Catholics had correspondingly less opportunity to exact revenge. The same sorts of incidents nevertheless continued to occur in cities that changed hands and in the undefended countryside through which Huguenot armies passed.[55] The Huguenots failed, for instance, to take Chartres in March 1568. In their retreat, however, they not only burned all the churches outside of the walls and in neighbouring villages, they also destroyed dozens of convents and abbeys in the surrounding countryside for no good military reason.[56]

Such incidents continued because neither side changed its underlying conception of the Christian community and what was needed for it to be holy in the eyes of God. Acts taken by Catholics to repair Huguenot sacrileges only

---

[51] 'Edit et declaration faite par le roi Charles IX', 36.
[52] Pithou, *Chronique de Troyes*, II, 530–1.
[53] Dupin de Saint-André, *Histoire du Protestantisme en Touraine*, 87–8.
[54] Pithou, *Chronique de Troyes*, II, 531–4.
[55] E.g., Lebeuf, *Histoire de la prise d'Auxerre*, 95–130.
[56] Carrière, *Introduction aux études d'histoire ecclésiastique locale*, III, 364–6.

deepened the religious divide. At least ten cities established annual processions to mark the failure of Protestant coups or expulsion of Protestant regimes. Although contested as violations of the edicts of pacification, these processions often continued anyway after a short interval.[57] Serving to reaffirm a city's Catholic identity, they were also occasions for sermons that educated participants about Catholic doctrine, thereby inciting greater devotion but also perpetuating grievances against those who rejected these teachings. Stories of miracles that occurred during the war served the same purposes. Catholics in Lyons used the discovery that the relics of Saint Bonaventure had 'miraculously' survived destruction as evidence of divine favour.[58] Clergy in Auxerre used the Huguenots' failed attempt to break up the reliquary casket of the city's patron, Saint Germain, as a lesson about the holy powers residing in the relics of saints.[59] Citizens of Chartres attributed their escape from the Huguenots' siege to the Virgin's miraculous intervention. Claiming that she was seen standing on the city's ramparts catching cannon balls in her mantle, they erected an image on the spot where the ramparts were nearly breached and celebrated the event with a procession that lasted through the *ancien régime*.[60] Le Puy and Verdun also credited their escape from Huguenot attacks to miracles of the Virgin and honoured this protection with annual processions.

Protestants of course derided these alleged miracles as superstitious nonsense. When Catholic consuls and clergy in Castres dedicated the city to Saint Jacques, whom they credited with ridding the town of plague, indignant Protestants denounced the move as an 'execrable sin against the majesty of God, for [it] took what belonged to God and gave it to Saint Jacques'.[61] Protestants tended to attribute their own close escapes and successes in the wars to divine providence and to the special grace they enjoyed as '*enfants de Dieu*'. They gave thanks with prayers and supplemented petitions for divine

[57] E.g., Jean Burel, *Mémoires de Jean Burel, bourgeois du Puy*, ed. Augustin Chassaing (Le Puy-en-Velay, 1875), 15; Bouges, *Histoire ecclésiastique et civile de la ville et diocèse de Carcassonne*, 313–14; *Briefve narration de la sédition advenue en Tholose, 1562, en may, par les hérétiques* in *Recueil de pièces historiques relatifs aux guerres de Religion* (Paris, 1862), 198–9. Philip Benedict lists ten cities that held processions to celebrate failed Huguenot attacks through much or all of the *ancien régime*, 'Divided Memories? Historical Calendars, Commemorative Processions and the Recollection of the Wars of Religion during the Ancien Régime', *French History*, 22 (2008), 392.

[58] Louis-Antoine-Augustin Pavy, *Les grands cordeliers de Lyon, ou l'église et le couvent de Saint-Bonaventure depuis leur fondation jusqu'à nos jours* (Lyon, 1835), 101–2.

[59] Lebeuf, *Histoire de la prise d'Auxerre*, 211.

[60] Benedict, 'Divided Memories?', 393–4.

[61] *Journal de Faurin*, 29.

assistance with fast days.⁶² The contrasting ways in which members of the two faiths addressed the divinity only added to the distance that separated them and underscored the fundamental incompatibility of their views on the place of the sacred in society. The rituals of repair that each faith used to restore community accented these differences and so could not help to heal the breach. It is necessary to look instead to the rituals of repair employed by secular authorities in their efforts to mend the peace.

The challenge for secular authorities

In histories of the French Wars of Religion it often appears a foregone conclusion that a lasting peace could not be made until a strong king—Henry IV—came to the throne and reconciled parties exhausted by more than three decades of war. This, I would argue, is to look at history through the wrong end of the glass. Taking at face value the mythical greatness of the first Bourbon king and the legendary weakness of the Valois monarchs who preceded him, historians long ignored the serious efforts made to restore and preserve peace during earlier stages of the religious quarrels, just because these efforts ended in failure. As a result, until recently they also ignored the way in which these efforts reconfigured and ultimately extended royal authority by positioning the king as the 'unique guarantor of the common will'.⁶³ The royal tour with which I began this paper was an important element in this process. In the words of one scholar, the tour was an elaborate 'staging of the restoration of royal authority'.⁶⁴ Charles IX was just fourteen when the royal tour began. Although technically of age to rule, Charles was still too young to truly reign, and it is no secret that his mother, Catherine de Medici, was the power behind the throne. This disparity is never evident, however, in descriptions of the royal tour; it was the principle of monarchical authority and not the person of the adolescent king that was on display. Each city represented itself as the 'theatre of one sole power, ornamented with the emblems of its master' and acted out its submission in the ceremonies of the royal entry.⁶⁵ But Charles did not just display his authority in this formal entry. In every city, he set aside time to hear complaints and personally hand down justice. Enacting the traditional role of the '*roi justicier*', he represented himself as standing above factional division, the one impartial judge to whom

---

⁶² E.g., Daval and Daval, *Histoire de la Réformation à Dieppe*, 26, 32, 122.

⁶³ Olivier Christin, 'From Repression to Pacification: French Royal Policy in the Face of Protestantism', in Benedict et al., *Reformation, Revolt and Civil War*, 213.

⁶⁴ Jean Boutier, Alain Dewerpe, and Daniel Nordman, *Un tour de France royal: le voyage de Charles IX, 1564–1566* (Paris, 1984), 285.

⁶⁵ Ibid., 296.

everyone might turn.⁶⁶ He also visited the Parlement in every city he could, presenting himself as the embodiment of the legislative authority the courts were charged to maintain. In similar fashion, he assembled lesser magistrates, members of the legal professions, and members of the nobility in each principal town and lectured them on the obedience due him.⁶⁷

Sixteenth-century France was still a country in which the king's personal presence was an important factor in commanding people's loyalty. The royal tour asserted a real—and not just a symbolic—restoration of monarchical authority. The king's passing visit could nevertheless not resolve all of the remaining issues that needed to be adjudicated for peace to take hold. The Crown assigned this task to commissioners appointed to oversee and enforce the edicts of pacification. Bi-confessional courts were later created to hear legal disputes involving parties of different faiths, but the commissioners constituted the vanguard in the effort to restore peace and dealt on a day-to-day basis with the difficult issues that arose in the bi-confessional state mandated by the edicts of pacification.⁶⁸

About thirty men served in pairs as commissioners for the Edict of Amboise in 1563, and twenty for the Edict of Saint-Germain in 1570. They included both members of the great aristocracy, who could command respect by their proximity to the king, and royal magistrates experienced in the legal issues presented by the peace. Like the king on his royal tour, the commissioners were itinerant and moved from town to town. Jérémie Foa argues persuasively for the seriousness of the commissioners' efforts, their relative success in placing themselves above faction, and the significance of their experience as models for the peace commissioners later employed by Henry IV.⁶⁹ Much of the commissioners' time was spent adjudicating conflicting claims to sacred and civic space. In every town they came to, the issues most needing resolution involved the ruptures of community that had

---

⁶⁶ See Pithou, *Chronique de Troyes*, II, 549–67, for a good description of this ceremony in Troyes. It has been suggested that access to the king's justice was limited, but the symbolism of Charles as '*roi justicier*' is nevertheless important, Boutier, et al., *Un tour de France royal*, 274.

⁶⁷ For examples, see Pithou, *Chronique de Troyes*, II, 568; Haton, *Mémoires*, I, 376–7. See also the discussion in Boutier, et al., *Un tour de France royal*, 242–55.

⁶⁸ Recent reconsiderations of the peace process include Jérémie Foa, 'Making Peace: The Commissions for Enforcing the Pacification Edicts in the Reign of Charles IX (1560–1574)', *French History*, 18 (2004), 256–74; Penny Roberts, 'Royal Authority and Justice during the French Religious Wars', *Past and Present*, 184 (2004), 3–32.

⁶⁹ Jérémie Foa, 'Le tour de la paix: Missions et commissions d'application des édits de pacification sous le règne de Charles IX (1560–1574)', 3 vols, unpublished Ph.D. thesis, Université Lumière-Lyon 2, 2008; and Foa, 'Making Peace', 256–74.

occurred during the war. The commissioners were charged with overseeing the peaceful return of Protestants to their homes in Catholic-controlled cities and of Catholics to their homes in Protestant-dominated towns. They returned churches and monasteries to dispossessed Catholics and appointed places for Protestant worship in conformity with the edicts. They returned offices to those forced out of them and created bi-confessional city governments in an effort to get religious opponents to work together for the common good. The commissioners also dealt with a number of other issues as they tried to resolve disputes that stood in the way of peace, but all of these issues have at their heart the problem of restoring community in the wake of civil and religious war. And while I concur with Foa's conclusions about the importance of the commissioners' efforts, the evidence also persuades me of the enormous difficulties they faced in convincing both sides to forget past quarrels and accept living peacefully side by side.

Catholics returning to Protestant-held cities wanted immediately to re-consecrate sacred space with processions. Monks and priests re-entered Castres, for instance, in a formal procession. Wearing liturgical vestments and bearing crosses, they celebrated Mass in a public square before going on to reclaim the churches from which they had been expelled the previous year.[70] Protestant preaching, meanwhile, was moved to the suburbs by the terms of the edicts—out of the sacred centre and into the liminal spaces outside the walls. In a number of cities, the sites appointed for Protestant services were distant and hard to reach. Protestants appealed repeatedly to commissioners over this issue, but often with little success, as Catholic governors and other officials tended to intervene in support of town councils that claimed that sites in closer proximity to the city might prompt unrest. Implicit—and sometimes explicit—in these arguments was the memory of past violence.[71] Even if the pacification edicts forbade all memory of the harm each side had inflicted on the other, these memories persisted and influenced the terms under which coexistence took place, which is to say that they also influenced the form that community was to take. In the final account, community was not restored; it was permanently changed as a result of France's religious conflicts.

The more Catholics tried to insist on the unity of society and the sacred, the more Protestants were excluded and pushed to the margins. Except in the few towns where they were allowed to hold services, their religious observances

---

[70] *Journal de Faurin*, 26.
[71] Foa, 'Unequal Apportionment', 373; Penny Roberts, 'The Most Crucial Battle of the Wars of Religion? The Conflict over Sites for Reformed Worship in Sixteenth-Century France', *Archiv für Reformationsgeschichte*, 89 (1998), 247–67.

were confined to the domestic sphere. Their conspicuous absence from religious processions gave these occasions an increasingly confessional air. And if sometimes Protestants made their presence known by opening the window of the shop where they worked on a Sunday and singing psalms, or letting the smell of roasting meat penetrate the street on a fast day, these acts only increased the sense of their separation as a defined and restricted minority.[72]

Suzanne Desan was right in postulating that 'violence over religious beliefs destroyed the existing community in a bloody power struggle as each group fought to draw new communal boundaries'.[73] The 'common union' inherited from the Middle Ages had broken down and attempts to restore it through such traditional rites of repair as religious processions served only to heighten religious tensions. A new understanding of community in which politics was separated from religion, and the civic from the sacred, would eventually grow out of the Crown's attempt to place itself above the quarrels as the sole guarantor of the common will. In time, members of both faiths might learn to interact as fellow citizens, living together as neighbours, trading together, and participating together in civic assemblies, while worshiping separately. The first edicts of pacification, the work of the commissioners for the edicts, and the royal tour of Charles IX laid the groundwork for these changes with new assertions of royal authority, but separating religion from politics required more than edicts and decrees. It required a radical change in the way people understood the place of the sacred in society and, by extension, their own relationship to the divinity. Such paradigm shifts are never accomplished quickly or without resistance. If, as Suzanne Desan observed, Natalie Davis left readers wondering whether Protestants and Catholics were 'part of the same community' or 'two opposing communities at war with one another', it is because the very meaning of community was contested in their quarrels.

---

[72] Foa, 'Unequal Apportionment', 381–3. Spicer also notes the 'confessional edge' increasingly evident in Catholic processions, '(Re)Building the Sacred Landscape', 262–3.

[73] Desan, 'Crowds, Community, and Ritual', 65.

Religious Violence in Sixteenth-Century France: Moving Beyond Pollution and Purification

Mack P. Holt

The religious violence resulting from the reformations of the sixteenth century shared much in common with the religious violence of the medieval period that preceded it. It was largely sanctioned by secular and/or ecclesiastical authority. And it tended to break out in places where new religious ideas threatened to subvert established ways of navigating the boundaries between the visible and invisible worlds. Having said that, however, historians usually also argue for both historicity and specificity in trying to analyze religious violence. It is hardly something monolithic, universal, and inevitable as some critics of contemporary religion like Sam Harris and Christopher Hitchens have been eager to suggest.[1] Religious violence has to be understood in the political, social, and cultural contexts that produced it. Indeed, one of the most intriguing questions for scholars of the Reformation generally, and the French Reformation in particular, is why violence among civilians— neighbours killing neighbours—escalated significantly in sixteenth-century France, with levels of popular violence there arguably greater than anywhere else in Europe during the era of the Reformation. How do we explain, for example, the scale of popular violence that erupted in Paris and a dozen provincial cities in France in August 1572, known collectively as the Saint Bartholomew's Day massacres?

One explanation first offered nearly forty years ago is the classic thesis of Natalie Zemon Davis. Influenced by the scholarship of social anthropologists, especially Mary Douglas, Davis proposed that understanding the religious violence of the French Wars of Religion required us to understand it as perceived by its participants. Thus, for Davis this violence was neither random nor spontaneous, but the product of religious beliefs propagated by some (though certainly not all) militant clergy, who claimed that the purity of Christian society was being polluted by the presence of heresy,

---

[1] Sam Harris, *The End of Faith: Religion, Terror, and the Future of Reason* (New York, 2004); Christopher Hitchens, *God is Not Great: How Religion Poisons Everything* (New York, 2007).

and only through the removal of this pollution could Christian society survive. Since neither the church nor the state in France had managed to achieve this, some Christians thought it was up to them to carry out the ecclesiastical and magisterial actions of purification, especially once they convinced themselves that it was the king's will that this purge of French Protestantism be enacted.[2] Davis's intricate analysis of the mock trials carried out over some of the Huguenot corpses, or mock baptisms performed by others, suggests very convincingly that the perpetrators of this violence legitimated their actions by invoking the authority of the magistrate and the priest respectively. Reinforced by the militant sermons of preachers such as Simon Vigor to 'smite the inhabitants of that city [who worship false gods] with the edge of the sword, destroying it utterly and all that is therein', quoting Deuteronomy 13:15, some Parisian Catholics were convinced that both God and king condoned religious violence in order to safeguard Christian society.[3]

'The Rites of Violence' was also significant for emphasizing the importance of religion in the French civil wars. Both the legacy of historians such as Lucien Romier, Jean-Hippolyte Mariéjol, and others who stressed political factors, as well as some of the *Annalistes* who stressed structural factors, resulted in a narrative of the civil wars that tended to see religion as a mask for other more important historical forces.[4] Thus, Davis's article was a pathbreaking and paradigm-changing analysis that transformed the way scholars thought about the religious violence of the period. And that 'The Rites of Violence' explicitly provoked and challenged this older narrative was evident in the immediate response to it by Janine Garrisson-Estèbe published in *Past and Present* shortly after Davis's article first appeared.[5] Estèbe's response reprised the arguments of her earlier book, that the Saint Bartholomew's massacre in Paris was largely the result of economic forces, especially high grain prices. 'There is no doubt', she argued, 'that the Saint Bartholomew's

---

[2] Natalie Zemon Davis, 'The Rites of Violence: Religious Riot in Sixteenth-Century France', *Past and Present*, 59 (1973), 51–91, repr. in Davis's *Society and Culture in Early Modern France* (Stanford, CA, 1975), 152–87. For Davis's inspiration, see Mary Douglas, *Purity and Danger: An Analysis of the Concepts of Pollution and Taboo* (London, 1966).

[3] Davis, 'The Rites of Violence', 51; Barbara B. Diefendorf, *Beneath the Cross: Catholics and Huguenots in Sixteenth-Century Paris* (Oxford, 1991), esp. 145–58.

[4] Lucien Romier, *Les origins politiques des guerres de religion*, 2 vols (Paris, 1922); J.-H. Mariéjol, *La Réforme et la Ligue: L'Edit de Nantes, 1559–1598* (Paris, 1911).

[5] Janine [Garrisson] Estèbe, 'The Rites of Violence: Religious Riot in Sixteenth-Century France: A Comment', *Past and Present*, 67 (1975), 127–30.

[massacre] was a *class crime*, and it is certain that rich Huguenots had been singled out for assault and attack'.[6]

What I aim to do in the rest of this essay is to follow up some additional responses to 'The Rites of Violence' in order to underscore the influence this model has undoubtedly had on scholarship on the Wars of Religion over the last forty years, but also to point to further questions that are still only incompletely understood and warrant further study. For example, as influential and stimulating as Davis's model of purification and pollution has been, it does not explicitly explain why violence broke out in some cities and towns and not in others. Moreover, it does not really address how such social and cultural tensions might be eased once violence broke out so as to de-escalate the violence, as occurred in a number of places in France and elsewhere in Europe. What I argue below, however, is that Natalie Davis's model of pollution and purification does point to some possible answers to these questions. I shall do this by examining two comparative cases alongside Davis's analysis of religious violence in sixteenth-century France: first, late medieval Iberia, where violence among Christians, Muslims, and Jews waxed and waned at various times and in various places in the later Middle Ages; and secondly Dijon, a medium sized city in France, where there was almost no bloodshed and little violence during the Wars of Religion despite a sizeable Huguenot minority living in a largely Catholic community. The conclusion that these cases suggest is that the key to understanding why religious violence occurred in some places but not in others with similar confessional divisions is the legal status of the religious minorities. Relatively peaceful relations among religious communities were possible as long as the minority confession had clearly defined and designated spaces in the community to live and work, and their second-class legal status was well demarcated and did not threaten the hegemony of the majority. In short, religious coexistence could be achieved not by eliminating religious boundaries between confessions, but by clarifying and strengthening them. Religious violence, on the other hand, was always more likely to break out in religiously divided communities where the confessional minority's legal status was either challenged from below by the minority itself or simply eliminated altogether by the majority in an effort to achieve religious uniformity. In both these cases religious minorities could be transformed from unwanted though generally harmless irritants in the community that could usually be tolerated, at least temporarily, to dangerous pollutants that threatened civil order and needed

---

[6] Janine [Garrisson] Estèbe, *Tocsin pour un massacre: La saison des Saint-Barthélemy* (Paris, 1968), 196 (the italics are Estèbe's).

to be eliminated by violence if necessary. But first let's turn to the critics of Davis's model.

I

Denis Crouzet was one of the first to challenge Davis's model of pollution and purification openly in a mammoth monograph published in two hefty volumes in 1990, *Les Guerriers de Dieu*.[7] Less a direct critique of Davis's model than an alternative explanation for religious violence during the sixteenth-century Wars of Religion, Crouzet's book proposed that a widespread eschatological fear of impending doom and a belief that the end of time was near, exacerbated by a wave of astrological prognostication and millenarian prophecy, were ultimately at the foundation of the religious troubles of the period. Thus, for Crouzet the religious violence of sixteenth-century France was more the result of apocalyptic fear and anguish than the natural result of the growth of Calvinism in France. Crouzet does eventually challenge Davis's social explanation for religious violence—though he does it in passing and not until more than 250 pages into his 1,500 page tome.[8] And indeed Crouzet and Davis have since both agreed that there is much that is complementary in their respective approaches despite the obvious differences.[9] What Crouzet has certainly done, however, is to engage with Davis's model and to introduce to the debate the huge corpus of sources printed in the period for further scrutiny.

Another response to 'The Rites of Violence' has been raised by Judith Pollmann in a recent article in *Past and Present*. Pollmann offers a superb analysis of why Dutch Catholics, who were equally as upset and frightened by Calvinists in the Netherlands as their co-religionists in France, for the most part did not employ violence to purify the body social in the Netherlands. She points to the Catholic clergy in the Netherlands as the main reason, as she argues that they tended to see heresy in moral terms rather than as a political and social threat to Catholic existence as some French clergy depicted it. Nevertheless, she frames the article by critiquing 'The Rites of Violence', along with a great deal of other scholarship, principally the work of Barbara Diefendorf, Denis Crouzet, and myself. 'By postulating the inevitability of religious violence', Pollmann argues, 'they signally fail to account

---

[7] Denis Crouzet, *Les Guerriers de Dieu: La violence aux temps des troubles de religion, vers 1525–vers 1610*, 2 vols (Seyssel, 1990).

[8] Ibid., I, 253.

[9] Natalie Zemon Davis, *L'Histoire tout feu tout flame: Entretiens avec Denis Crouzet* (Paris, 2004); and in English translation as *A Passion for History: Conversations with Denis Crouzet*, ed. Michael Wolfe (Kirksville, MO, 2010).

for different patterns that we see outside France'. Instead, she urges us to resist 'the notion that violence was the inevitable outcome of the confrontation between traditional religion and Protestantism, as historians of France have sometimes suggested'.[10] Now, I do not think for a moment that Natalie Davis, nor any of the rest of us for that matter, were arguing that religious violence was inevitable, even in the case of the Saint Bartholomew's massacres in 1572. Moreover, I know that none of us was trying to postulate a universal theory of violence that explained religious violence everywhere in Europe, as Pollmann seems to imply. But she does raise a very important point, which is that the anthropological notions of pollution and purification, while very useful for explaining the motives of religious rioters as well as how they legitimated their actions, are less helpful in explaining why some Catholics chose to participate in violent actions against Protestants while others did not, or why religious violence can break out in one place and not another. For just one obvious example, we know relatively little about what motivated the majority of Catholics in Paris on Saint Bartholomew's night to remain in their homes and not participate in the violence. Indeed, as Pollmann's line of questioning implies, the larger question for historians of sixteenth-century France is not so much to explain the violent actions of the rioters, but to explain why more Catholics did not join them.

Finally, one of Davis's own students has further contributed to this direction of analysis by extending Judith Pollmann's line of questioning. Keith Luria notes in his recent book, *Sacred Boundaries*, that the pollution and purification model of understanding religious violence might be read to suggest that the religious differences between the two confessions may be irreconcilable and that violence between them may seem irreversible. Moreover, even if that is not the case, this model offers few clues about how the violence might be de-escalated, nor does it satisfactorily explain how religious pluralism and co-existence might also occur within the same society.[11] To be fair to both Davis and Luria, a close reading of the book shows that Luria's argument is more critical of how other scholars have made use of 'The Rites of Violence' than of 'The Rites of Violence' itself. But he raises another important question. How do we explain the fact that the visceral emotions that produced such vitriolic rhetoric and collective violence in the sixteenth century eventually gave way, for the most part, to a more peaceful

---

[10] Judith Pollmann, 'Countering the Reformation in France and the Netherlands: Clerical Leadership and Catholic Violence, 1560–1585', *Past and Present* 190 (2006), 83–120, quotations from 87 and 119.

[11] Keith P. Luria, *Sacred Boundaries: Religious Coexistence and Conflict in Early Modern France* (Washington, DC, 2005), especially xiii–xviii.

co-existence between the two confessions in much (if not all) of France in the seventeenth century? Rather than seeing relations between Huguenots and Catholics as an irreconcilable clash of cultures, he urges us to think about these relations as being bounded by the tensions between conflict and coexistence. His book offers convincing evidence that confessional boundaries could indeed become permeable and that both Protestants and Catholics could find ways to live together. And despite the doctrinal differences so emphasized by religious reformers of both confessions, both groups nevertheless shared a common Christian heritage and many social practices. To be sure, co-existence was much easier after 1598, when Huguenots were no longer desecrating Catholic churches and Catholic magistrates were no longer arresting Huguenots as heretics. Moreover, as Barbara Diefendorf demonstrated in the last chapter, even if royal efforts to repair divided communities torn by violence did not succeed during the Wars of Religion, they did lay the groundwork for success in the seventeenth century.[12] Nevertheless, Luria's insights point us in the right direction of how to build on Davis's original ideas in 'The Rites of Violence', especially as we continue to try to understand our own contemporary world in which religious violence still continues to plague us. I am especially struck by his evidence that in certain situations and under certain conditions, it was possible for Catholics and Huguenots in the same community to find ways of living together in peace by permeating or constructing different forms of boundaries between the two confessions. Luria provides some very convincing evidence that in towns such as Niort and elsewhere in Poitou social relations between the confessions were not only peaceful, but there was significant social intermingling including intermarriage.[13] Gregory Hanlon has demonstrated similar patterns in rural Aquitaine in the seventeenth century, as has Robert Sauzet for lower Languedoc and Elisabeth Labrousse for Mauvesin among others.[14] But this was not true everywhere in seventeenth-century France, as Philip Benedict has shown how confessional tensions hardened and even escalated as the two confessions grew farther apart in cities such as Montpellier, a city

---

[12] See Barbara B. Diefendorf, this volume, 30–51.
[13] Luria, *Sacred Boundaries*, 19–46, 155–62.
[14] Gregory Hanlon, *Confession and Community in Seventeenth-Century France: Catholic and Protestant Coexistence in Aquitaine* (Philadelphia, 1993); Robert Sauzet, *Contre-Réforme et Réforme catholique en Bas-Languedoc: Le diocese de Nîmes au XVIIe siècle* (Louvain, 1979); Elisabeth Labrousse, *Une foi, une foi, un roi? Essai sur la revocation de l'Edit de Nantes* (Geneva, 1985). All of this literature and much more is discussed by Philip Benedict, *The Faith and Fortunes of France's Huguenots, 1600–1685* (Aldershot, 2001), 303–7.

almost equally divided between Huguenots and Catholics in the seventeenth century.[15] So, the question remains: why did religious violence break out in some communities with divided religious confessions and not others? And even if we accept that inter-confessional relations in any community could run the entire gamut from peaceful co-existence to violent conflict, what were the specific factors and conditions that tended to shift social relations toward one end of the spectrum or the other?

II

A comparative look at medieval relations between Christians, Muslims, and Jews, primarily though not exclusively on the Iberian peninsula, may be instructive on a number of levels. For a start, medieval Christians considered Muslims and Jews as infidels rather than heretics, and this may help us better contextualize relations between sixteenth-century Protestants and Catholics, either by softening differences we as historians may exaggerate, or by emphasizing similarities we may not see at all. To be sure, the three religious communities of medieval Spain reflect ethnic differences as well as confessional variations, which contrasts significantly with the situation in sixteenth-century France. Nevertheless, the Spanish case helps us break down a number of facile assumptions about the novelty of post-Reformation religious tensions. Second, medieval Iberia presents us with the entire range of relations on the social spectrum, from long periods of relatively peaceful *convivencia* to violent and bloody conflict. The conflict, of course, is well known, and the narrative of the *reconquista* is littered with the polemic of men such as Peter the Venerable, twelfth-century abbot of Cluny, whose anti-Jewish and anti-Muslim writings Dominique Iogna-Prat has expertly analyzed in his book, *Ordonner et excluire*.[16] According to Peter the Venerable, there could be no Christian order unless both Jews and Muslims were excluded from Christian society, though Iogna-Prat is quick to acknowledge that social relations between confessional rivals were not nearly so dependent on such rhetoric, as Christians and Jews had lived peacefully together in Burgundy for 150 years prior to the anti-Jewish rhetoric of Peter the Venerable in the twelfth century.[17] And indeed, we also know from the work of many recent historians of medieval Iberia that social relations were varied and often peaceful. According to Jocelyn Hillgarth, for example, at the same time as the military *reconquista* of the peninsula was fully

---

[15] Benedict, *The Faith and Fortunes*, 317–25.
[16] Dominique Iogna-Prat, *Ordonner et excluire: Cluny et la société chrètienne face à l'hérésie, au judaisme et à l'islam, 1000–1150* (Paris, 1998), especially ch. 10–11.
[17] Ibid., 274.

underway from the tenth century onwards, Jews, Muslims, and Christians mingled and interacted frequently at the courts of the kings of Castile and Aragon, on the island of Majorca, and in taverns all across the peninsula frequented by troubadours, merchants, bankers, and travellers of all types, and Christians even attended Jewish and Muslim weddings and funerals.[18] So, how do we account for both *reconquista* and *convivencia*?

One factor was certainly the power relations between the confessional groups. This could be based on size and number, as well as on the social position the religious minorities enjoyed within the majority confessional community. Mudejars, free Muslims living in Christian Iberia, had been living in Castile and Aragon for two centuries by the mid-thirteenth century and seem to have enjoyed a degree of coexistence and religious freedom prior to the Mudejar revolt of 1264.[19] Jews also lived freely among Christians in medieval Spain. Although hard numbers are not possible, the best estimates suggest that even though there were large Jewish communities in cities such as Toledo, Seville, Burgos, Barcelona, and Valencia, the total Jewish population in Iberia in 1300 was no more than probably 2 or 3 per cent of the population of the Crown of Aragon (out of a total of maybe 1,000,000), and even less than that in the crown of Castile-Léon (out of a total of about 4,000,000). As for the Muslim population, they were far more numerous, especially in the kingdom of Aragon, where they may have made up as much as 35 per cent of the total population, and maybe as much as 50 per cent in the city of Valencia. In the kingdom of Castile-Léon, however, the numbers were significantly lower.[20] What is striking, however, as David Nirenberg has shown, is that even in the kingdom of Aragon where Muslims made up as much as half the population in some areas, relations between Christians and Muslims were generally peaceful until the thirteenth century, when the *reconquista* began to pick up steam under King James I of Aragon.[21] So the size of a minority population alone was not always the critical factor in determining whether religious relations would be peaceful or contentious.

In medieval Iberia what seemed even more important than the size of a minority religious community was its legal status. In different ways, the works of Dominique Iogna-Prat, Hugh Kennedy, Jocelyn Hillgarth, David

---

[18] J. N. Hillgarth, *The Spanish Kingdoms, 1250–1516*, 2 vols (Oxford, 1976–78), I, 155–71.

[19] Hugh Kennedy, *Muslim Spain and Portugal: A Political History of al-Andalus* (London, 1996), 278.

[20] For all these figures and how they were derived, see Hillgarth, *The Spanish Kingdoms*, I, 29–32.

[21] David Nirenberg, *Communities of Violence: Persecution of Minorities in the Middle Ages* (Princeton, NJ, 1996), 23.

Nirenberg, María Rosa Menocal, and Stuart Schwartz collectively suggest that peaceful relations among religious communities were possible as long as the minority group, whatever its size, had clearly defined and designated spaces in the community to live and work, and where their second-class legal status was well defined and did not threaten the majority's hegemony.[22] In Aragon and Catalonia, for example, where numbers of Muslims were significantly higher than elsewhere, Muslims were granted privileges such as the right to practise Islam and even to govern their communities under Islamic law in some areas despite their second-class legal status.[23] Jews were granted even greater privileges, including the right to build synagogues and to worship on Saturdays. As Olivia Remie Constable has suggested, this was probably because Jews had lived for centuries in Christian society without becoming a threat or danger, while Muslims in Iberia had only recently been transformed from infidels and enemies into subjects of a Christian prince. The important point, though, was that their legal status was explicitly defined as being second-class citizens, albeit with certain privileges.[24]

Things had changed dramatically by the end of the fourteenth century, however, as legislation from the Cortés of Castile increasingly challenged the Jews' legal status, rights, and privileges, which also eventually had a knock-on effect on the Mudejars. Clerics and lawyers adopted the anti-Jewish rhetoric of Peter the Venerable of the twelfth century, eventually leading to the pogroms of 1391 and the Inquisition against the Jews in the fifteenth century. By the time of the defeat of Granada in 1492, the legal status of Jews and Muslims had disappeared; they were forced to convert to Christianity or leave Spain altogether. And there was even significant hostility against those who did convert.[25] But as David Nirenberg has suggested, the Holy Week 'rites of violence' against the Jews in Aragon in the fourteenth century 'belong at the center, not the sordid margins of clerical culture in the crown of Aragon'. At the same time, however, before 1492 these annual rites of violence

---

[22] The works of Iogna-Prat, Kennedy, Hillgarth, and Nirenberg are cited in the notes above. Also see Maria Rosa Menocal, *The Ornament of the World: How Muslims, Jews, and Christians Created a Culture of Tolerance in Medieval Spain* (Boston, 2002) and Stuart B. Schwartz, *All Can Be Saved: Religious Tolerance and Salvation in the Iberian Atlantic World* (New Haven, CT, 2009). Perhaps the closest any of these historians comes to making this argument explicitly is in Hugh Kennedy, *Medieval Spain and Portugal*, 273–304. It can be inferred from the work of all of them, however.

[23] Nirenberg, *Communities of Violence*, 23.

[24] Olivia Remie Constable, (ed.), *Medieval Iberia: Readings from Christian, Muslim, and Jewish Sources* (Philadelphia, 1997), 269–71.

[25] See especially Hillgarth, *The Spanish Kingdoms*, II, 126–69.

'used the Jews to re-enact the triumphant place of Christianity in sacred history, while at the same time circumscribing for and assigning to the Jews a place in Christian society'.[26] Thus, even violence could in certain circumstances define and reinforce the very legal status and social space that had the potential to make coexistence possible.

There are obvious difficulties in comparing the changing relations between Christians, Muslims, and Jews in medieval Spain over several centuries with the relations between Catholics and Huguenots in sixteenth-century France over several decades, and I have already alluded to the ethnic dimension of religious tensions in Spain that was completely absent in France. Nevertheless, as the chapters of Barbara Diefendorf and Penny Roberts show elsewhere in this volume, establishing legal boundaries and defined social spaces for religious minorities was critical to determining whether relations between the two confessions could potentially become violent. Roberts's emphasis on peacemaking demonstrates convincingly that the French crown's efforts to establish peace through the royal edicts of pacification that ended each of the civil wars were often the cause of violence breaking out anew. 'Contrary to its intention, the crown's efforts to enforce the peace could enflame existing tensions and exacerbate the very hostilities which it was trying to assuage'.[27] In a very similar vein, Diefendorf argues that the principal reason that so many efforts at repairing the damage caused by religious violence ended in failure during the religious wars were because Protestants and Catholics had divergent and mutually exclusive definitions of community. 'The "rituals of repair" that each side employed to restore their imagined community excluded the other. Religious rituals of repair were thus double-edged; whatever their avowed intention, they served more to heighten differences than to promote unity'.[28] This made it impossible to establish any clear or lasting lines of demarcation between the two confessions living in one community. Above all, both the Spanish and French cases make it clear that religious coexistence could best be achieved not by eliminating confessional boundaries, but by clarifying and reinforcing them. The royal edicts of pacification and other efforts described by Roberts and Diefendorf did not accomplish that in sixteenth-century France, at least on a national level. It could still work on the local level, however.

---

[26] Nirenberg, *Communities of Violence*, 200–30, quotations on 227 and 229.
[27] See Penny Roberts, this volume, p. 77.
[28] See Diefendorf, 'Rituals of Repair'.

III

Now let us turn to a city in France with a significant Huguenot minority where bloodshed and religious violence did not break out after the massacres in Paris on Saint Bartholomew's night, nor at any other time during the Wars of Religion—the city of Dijon in Burgundy. Analysing why bloodshed did not occur in a city seemingly well-positioned for religious violence may help us understand better how and why violence broke out in some places and not in others. A small Protestant community had emerged in Dijon by the early 1550s, though it is difficult to estimate its size.[29] In 1554 one very frightened member of Dijon's city council reported a wildly exaggerated rumour that 'two-thirds of the city were Lutherans'.[30] Nevertheless, by the late 1550s it has been estimated that as many as 500–600 Protestants—largely Calvinists rather than Lutherans—had either converted or settled in the Burgundian capital.[31] The deliberations of the city council throughout this period are replete with reports of 'heretics' who were accused of wanting 'to break, efface and stain the effigy, image and remembrance of the holy and sacred host', or incidents where the 'unfaithful' hurled abuse and insults at Catholic religious processions in the city.[32] The mayor and city council did its utmost to deal with incidents such as these forcefully and publicly, believing that pre-emptive action was the best remedy against an escalation of violence.[33] Things came to a head on All Saints' Day (1 November) 1561, however, when militant Protestants organized a mass demonstration in the centre of the city, which the city fathers wrongly assumed was an attempt by the Huguenots to take the city by force. They had organized themselves on the three previous evenings with meetings of several hundred Huguenots in three different private homes in the city, and the last of these assemblies on 31 October had turned violent when Catholic neighbours began throwing rocks at the Protestants crowding inside.[34] When All Saints' Day finally dawned, a

---

[29] For the origins of the Reformation in Dijon, see Edmond Belle, *La Réforme à Dijon des origins à la fin de la lieutenance générale de Gaspard de Saulx-Tavanes, 1530–1570* (Dijon, 1911), 1–18; Jacques Fromental, *La Réforme en Bourgogne aux XVIe et XVIIe siècles* (Paris, 1968), 9–29; James R. Farr, *Hands of Honor: Artisans and Their World in Dijon, 1550–1650* (Ithaca and London, 1988), 224–36; Mack P. Holt, 'Wine, Community and Reformation in Sixteenth-Century Burgundy', *Past and Present*, 138 (1993), 58–93.

[30] Archives municipales, Dijon [hereafter AM Dijon], B192, fo. 92v (17 July 1554).

[31] This seems the most realistic estimate of Dijon's Huguenot population, which I have calculated from the figures given by Jean Richard, 'Les quêtes de l'église Notre-Dame et la diffusion du protestantisme à Dijon vers 1562', *Annales de Bourgogne*, 32 (1960), 183–9.

[32] AM Dijon, B195, fo. 139v (17 January 1558), B197, fo. 48 (11 August 1559).

[33] See AM Dijon, B198, fo. 138v (15 June 1561), B199, fos. 36v–37 (15–16 July 1561).

[34] AM Dijon, D63 (liasse), 29 and 30 October 1561, B199, fo. 80, 31 October 1561.

group of maybe two hundred Huguenots gathered on the Rue des Forges, a street inhabited by prosperous artisans. Alarmed by the rumour that the Protestants had stolen a silver image of the Virgin Mary from the parish church of Notre Dame nearby, a group of Catholic *vignerons* (wine-growers) sounded the tocsin in their own neighbourhood as a call to arms 'to run against those [Protestants] of the Rue des Forges'. The resulting clash was relatively anti-climactic, however, as there was only one casualty, a Catholic dyer. Thus, it is unlikely that the Huguenots were as heavily armed as the Catholic *vignerons* had originally believed. The Protestant demonstration dispersed quickly and order was restored.[35]

The more relevant point here is the reaction of the members of the city council and the judges in the Parlement of Dijon. The Parlement ordered the city council to investigate the incident, round-up and arrest as many of the Protestants who took part as possible, and they also made it illegal for anyone in the city to harbour Protestant ministers or preachers in their homes or hold any Protestant services in the city.[36] The city council readily agreed to undertake this repression of the Huguenot movement in Dijon and the very next day ordered the banishment of all Protestants from the city.[37] Before this policy could be implemented, however, the Queen Mother and regent for the young Charles IX, Catherine de Medici, issued the Edict of St. Germain, otherwise known as the Edict of January 1562. This edict recognized the Huguenots for the first time under the law. It was a very bitter pill for most French Catholics to swallow, and the reaction in Burgundy underscores how the doctrinal differences between the two confessions were perceived in social as well as doctrinal terms by the laity. Although the edict did recognize the right of Protestants to exist, it was a very limited existence. They could neither meet nor assemble in any town or city in France, publicly or privately, and they could only assemble for worship outside all urban jurisdictions. Furthermore, all Huguenots were still required to observe and obey all restrictions on Catholic feast days and other holidays. All these limitations were placed upon the Protestants out of a desire to maintain public order.[38] And when the Huguenots in Dijon began to contravene these restrictions, the complaints of the mayor and city council were explicitly couched in terms of maintaining public order. In a long list of grievances addressed to Claude

---

[35] AM Dijon, B199, fo. 81 (1 November 1561). This incident is recounted in Belle, *Réforme à Dijon*, 44–6; Farr, *Hands of Honor*, 196; Holt, 'Wine, Community and Reformation', 63–4.

[36] AM Dijon, D63 (liasse), 1 November 1561.

[37] AM Dijon, B199, fo. 81v (2 November 1561).

[38] N. M. Sutherland, *The Huguenot Struggle for Recognition* (New Haven, CT, 1980), 354–5.

de Lorraine, Duke of Aumale, royal governor in Burgundy, the mayor and city council pleaded for the arrest and detention of all those Huguenots who had violated the terms of the edict. There were numerous references to those of the 'so-called reformed religion' and how their behaviour was contrary 'to the honour of God, the service of His Majesty, the defence and protection of this city, [and] the peace and tranquillity of his good, loyal, and faithful subjects'. The twelve specific complaints covered the entire realm of the regulation of the body social: the Huguenots' refusal to observe Catholic feast days, on which 'the so-called reformers work and labour publicly and openly in their shops'; the selling of 'censured and scandalous' books; tavern-keepers and hoteliers who served meat during Lent and other prohibited periods; the celebration of Protestant weddings and baptisms in the seasons prohibited by the Catholic church 'to the great scandal of everyone'; the continued propagation of 'secret pedagogies ... to seduce the poor and tender youth, who are incapable of resisting their odious words'; the 'scandalous singing of the Psalms in public in a loud voice'; and even the Huguenot's opposition to the last mayoral election, in which a militant Catholic defeated a Protestant candidate for mayor in June 1561. This last complaint, the magistrates argued, was contrary to 'all order of the policing of the city and contrary to the inhabitants' right to elect their own magistrates and officers, which had always been a sign of the most famous, ancient, and flourishing republics'.[39]

The centrepiece of this list of grievances to the royal governor, however, was clearly the Huguenot attacks against the Catholic Eucharist. 'They parade openly in front of the Palais [de Justice] and generally everywhere in all public places selling libels, defamations, effigies and other figures of unworthiness and derision of the holy sacrament of the mass'. Moreover, many Protestants had openly blasphemed the sacrament, 'daring impudently to call the holy sacrament *Jean Le Blanc* [John White, or John the Blank]'.[40] Although this was the most explicitly theological of all the magistrates' complaints, it too was understood primarily because of its social implications. Calling the Host *Jean Le Blanc* on account of the colour of the white wafer used in the Eucharist was an explicit profanation of the sacred. Like the Protestant taunts in Paris of 'God of paste' that Natalie Davis has so convincingly described,[41] this epithet cut to the heart of the Catholic doctrine of transubstantiation; *le blanc* was a reference not only to the colour but the inefficacy of the Host. It was also an attack on the specific enfolding together of the body social, body politic, and

---

[39] AM Dijon, D63 (liasse), letter of city council to duke of Aumale [undated but clearly spring 1562].
[40] Ibid.
[41] Davis, 'The Rites of Violence', in *Society and Culture in Early Modern France*, 157.

body of Christ that Catholics believed the Eucharist represented. The magistrates informed the governor that they had already imprisoned those Huguenots who had blasphemed against the holy sacrament by calling it *Jean Le Blanc*, and they urged him 'to seize the initiative and uphold the king's will so that exemplary punishment can be done to eliminate and quell such audacious and seditious speech'.[42] In short, the very definition of community in Dijon as defined by the Catholic city officials was perceived to be under attack by the Huguenots, a point made by Barbara Diefendorf in her essay in this volume.[43]

The repression of the Huguenots in Dijon continued in the spring and summer of 1562, even as the First Civil War broke out farther north. And with the advent of war, the court's policy of recognition of limited Huguenot rights of the Edict of January soon gave way to suppression as well. 'Do everything that you can', Catherine de Medici wrote to Gaspard de Saulx, sieur de Tavanes, lieutenant-general of Burgundy, in June 1562, 'to cleanse the entire region of Burgundy of this vermin of preachers and ministers who have introduced the plague [of heresy] there, as you have already begun to do'.[44] The Queen Mother even used the language of pollution and purification in her missive. And about the same time the mayor of Dijon, Bénigne Martin, complained vehemently to the duke of Aumale, the royal governor of Burgundy, about 'the unlawful meetings [*conventicules*] and assemblies of people who oppose our faith and Christian religion, which is against the edicts of the king'. He went on to urge the governor to inform the king that 'these same black sheep [*dévoiéz*] continue daily in their assemblies in several houses, preaching there in their woeful and accustomed fashion in the middle of the day with their doors open'.[45] Scores of Huguenots in Dijon were frequently arrested in 1561–2 for publicly singing the Psalms in French, which the city's Catholics found especially insulting.[46] Again, the beginning of the First Civil War in the Spring of 1562 meant that the Edict of January never got

---

[42] AM Dijon, D63 (liasse), letter of city council to duke of Aumale [undated but clearly spring 1562].

[43] See Diefendorf, 'Rituals of Repair'.

[44] Joseph Garnier (ed.), *Correspondance de la mairie de Dijon extraite des archives de cette ville*, 3 vols (Dijon, 1868–70), II, 22–3, Catherine de Medici to Tavanes, 4 June 1562: 'vous faciez tout ce que vous pourrez pour achever de nettoyer tout le pays de Bourgongne de ceste vermine de prédicans et de ministres qui y ont mis la peste, ainsi que vous avez bien commancé'. A copy of this letter is also in the city council deliberations of Dijon: AM Dijon, B199, fo. 277.

[45] Garnier (ed.), *Correspondance de la mairie de Dijon*, II, 24.

[46] Archives départementales de la Côte d'Or, B II 60/44, 13 November 1561, 4 September 1561 for just two of many examples.

registered in Dijon's Parlement, and both the mayor Martin and the lieutenant-general, Tavanes, could work in earnest 'to clean' the city and province of the 'vermin' as instructed by the Queen Mother. This would result in a pattern that would be repeated with the outbreak of each successive civil war: arrests of Protestants, heavy fines or seizure of their property, expulsion from the city, and/or pressure to convert to Roman Catholicism.[47] In other words, the Burgundians strove to make sure that Protestants were not just recognized as second-class citizens, but that they also understood that their definition of community was incompatible with Dijon's Catholics.

When the edict of pacification ending the First Civil War was signed at Amboise in March 1563, in theory the limited legal rights of the Huguenots of the Edict of January were restored. Once again the Parlement of Dijon refused to register the edict, and a special commission was dispatched to the court to protest against the edict. At the head of this delegation was Jean Bégat, former *échevin* on Dijon's city council and now a presiding judge in the Parlement of Dijon. Bégat presented a remonstrance to the young King Charles IX in May 1563 outlining the Burgundians' complaints:

> Sire, since you are Christian and carry the title of Most Christian among all Christian kings . . . [and] you believe what the Roman Church believes and know that all contrary doctrine is error . . . how can it be that you would suffer among your subjects a law so contrary and foreign that allows not only the public profession, but also the free and public exercise [of heresy], to the scandal and ruin of your own religion? . . . Religion, Sire, as Plato said, is the only sure bond of charity and peace, forging a similarity of morals and wills in one common measure.[48]

The Parlement of Dijon continued in its refusal to register the edict, and it was only registered when the king appeared in person in Dijon in May 1564 and forced its registration with a *lit de justice*.[49] Thus, as Barbara Diefendorf has outlined, King Charles IX used the royal tour of the provinces in 1564 to re-establish royal authority.

---

[47] Holt, 'Wine, Community and Reformation', 69.

[48] The remonstrance is printed in *Mémoires de Condé, ou recueil pour servir a l'histoire de France*, 6 vols (The Hague, 1743), IV, 356–412, quotations on 361 and 405. For more on this episode, see my 'Burgundians into Frenchmen: Catholic Identity in Sixteenth-Century Burgundy', in Michael Wolfe (ed.), *Changing Identities in Early Modern France* (Durham, NC, 1997), 345–70.

[49] For details see my 'The King in Parlement: The Problem of the *Lit de justice* in Sixteenth-Century France', *The Historical Journal*, 31 (1988), 507–23.

Thus, the pattern of a legal edict limiting Huguenots to second-class status and prohibiting them from worshipping inside the city or making any public practice of their religion would be breached by both Catholics and Huguenots alike. Huguenots invariably refused to accept these restrictions and publicly insulted their Catholic neighbours or sang the Psalms loudly and publicly in French in their boutiques and homes, which amounted to the same thing. At the same time, Dijon's city fathers refused to enforce the edicts, attempting to remove all Huguenots from the city altogether. In short, they instituted a policy of suppression of the 'so-called reformed religion', requiring all Huguenots either to go to Mass with their Catholic neighbours or forfeit their property and right to live within the city walls. Huguenots who were willing to live peacefully under the restrictions of the peace edicts might be allowed to stay, but their houses were searched for arms and munitions and all their servants who were not Catholics were forced to leave the city. Moreover, they could not leave their houses at night, and they were required to keep their boutiques closed on all Catholic feast days and during all services in the parish churches.[50] The mayor and city council were still insisting after the Edict of St. Germain of 1570 that the Huguenots in Dijon, who were 'disturbers of the public peace', were required to refrain from 'singing Psalms, holding assemblies in the city and in the suburbs, or doing anything else contrary to the said edict'.[51]

The programme of suppression certainly worked, however, as there was no Saint Bartholomew's massacre in Dijon as occurred in so many other French cities with significant Protestant minorities in 1572. Indeed, the evidence suggests that most of Dijon's Huguenots either fled the city altogether for places of refuge where they could practise their religion publicly—Geneva, for example—or they succumbed to the pressure to abjure their faith and convert to Catholicism. And those who did abjure were forced to sign certificates of abjuration recording their conversion for the municipality. There is a good deal of formulaic sameness to these certificates, and they obviously reflect the perceptions of the city magistrates who collected them more than the views of those Huguenots who signed them. Nevertheless, they reveal a great deal. First of all, they tell us virtually nothing about religious conversion and abjuration in any meaningful way, because signing one was the only way any Protestant who was imprisoned or whose property had been seized could liberate himself or his goods. This was not mandated by any of the edicts of

---

[50] See AM Dijon, B204, fos. 71 (23 September 1567), 94 (10 October 1567), B205 fos. 29v (2 July 1568), 58v (7 September 1568), 106v (14 January 1569), 129 (15 March 1569), 132v–33v (24 March 1569), 139v (5 April 1569).

[51] AM Dijon, B207, fos. 147–52v (13 February 1571), quotations on fo. 151v.

pacification during the civil wars (and it was explicitly contrary to some of them), but it was the will of the local magistrates: the mayor and *échevins* on Dijon's city council. Moreover, the chronology of these abjurations makes it very clear that whenever large numbers of Huguenots were imprisoned, large numbers of abjurations immediately followed. Of the surviving sample of certificates of abjuration—a total of 287 individuals—76 of them (26 per cent) were dated September 1568 immediately after the outbreak of the Third Civil War ended the Peace of Longjumeau; 147 (51 per cent) are dated between 2 September and 31 October 1572 following the Saint Bartholomew's massacres in Paris and the imprisonment of all Huguenots in Dijon; and 34 (12 per cent) are dated in July and August 1585 following the Treaty of Nemours, when Henry II capitulated to the Catholic League. This accounts for 257 of the 287 person sample: 89 per cent.[52] Thus, there is little question that these abjurations followed immediately after intensive efforts on the part of Catholic magistrates to incarcerate Burgundian Protestants.

The certificates themselves are interesting in their own right, however, for what they do tell us about Catholic perceptions of the Huguenots in their community and what abjuration and reuniting with the Catholic community actually meant. The certificates were drawn up by parish clergy selected by the city magistrates, but they had to be deposited in the town hall with the mayor and council before any prisoner or his property could be released. So although there is a clerical signature on each document, it appears that the contents of the certificates reflect the sensibilities of the magistrates much more than those of the clergy. One of the most striking features about these certificates, for example, is that explicit references to doctrines, beliefs, and Catholic theology generally are almost wholly absent. In only two certificates from the entire sample of 287 could I find any specific reference to doctrine. But what did the other 285 statements of abjuration say, then, if they did not refer to doctrines or sacraments?

The one phrase that occurred over and over again in virtually all the certificates is that each Huguenot promised to '*vivre catholicquement*'. And what did living Catholicly mean for the magistrates of Dijon? It largely meant to live in peace with one's neighbours and in obedience to the king, that is, not to

[52] This includes 175 names on 40 different certificates, all with dates 17–30 September 1568 or 2 September–31 October 1572 [AM Dijon, D65 (liasse)], and 102 names (not 93 as indicated on the wrapper) on certificates dated between 1560 and 1587 (AM Dijon, D66 (liasse)]. For a more detailed analysis of this evidence, see my essay, 'Confessionalization Beyond the Germanies: The Case of France', in John M. Headley, Hans J. Hillerbrand, and Anthony Papalas (eds), *Confessionalization in Europe, 1555–1700* (Aldershot, 2004), 257–73.

commit 'scandalous acts'. It also meant 'to live and die' in the Catholic church, and above all to do one's Easter duties by confessing one's sins and attending Mass. Typical was the metal-polisher Thibault de Rochefort, who denied all those who had testified that he was a Huguenot. 'On the contrary', he attested, 'he had always conducted himself modestly and Catholicly in the obedience of the Roman Catholic Church. And since the beginning of these recent troubles he has always been ready and in arms under the charge of his captain [of the parish] to do service to the king and to the commonwealth whenever they were endangered'. It was only 'heinous enemies and liars' and those of 'sinister opinions' who claim he was now a Protestant, and 'he would prefer to die than to be thought of as such'. He concluded his statement, as so many others had also done, by promising 'to live Catholicly as he had done all his life' and by swearing that 'he was perpetually committed to make humble and faithful service to His Majesty the king and to the commonwealth, and that he would always be ready to risk the last drop of his blood in order to serve the city of Dijon'.[53]

All these examples should not lead us to conclude, however, that all Huguenots either abjured, or that they became Nicodemites, conforming outwardly in their public behaviour simply to gain their release from prison, though doubtless many did do exactly that. These 287 cases of public abjuration did not represent the entire Protestant community in Dijon. While the number of Huguenots in Dijon in 1562 has been estimated to be maybe as many as 500–600 persons (out of a population of about 15,000), many fled the city at the first sign of suppression by the magistrates. Significant numbers went directly to Geneva, in fact, which was far closer than either Lyon or Paris, French cities with sizeable Huguenot congregations. There were also some who remained resolute to their faith and refused to abjure. These were always a minority, as most either fled or abjured and then fled. But some, such as the cobbler Nicolas Hurtault, remained incarcerated for long periods rather than recant their Calvinist faith. Hurtault had been arrested along with his wife in October 1563 when their neighbours complained that they had been 'singing the Psalms of David very loudly in French in their shop'. Once again, it is a rupture in social relations that was at the heart of the issue. Rather than abjure as so many of his co-religionists did and promise 'to live Catholicly', Hurtault stood firm in his faith, at least for a time. Five years later in 1568 he joined dozens of others who abjured in order to be released from prison.[54]

Thus, when news of the Paris massacres reached Burgundy on 31 August 1572, Léonar Chabot, Count of Charny and lieutenant-general of the

---

[53] AM Dijon, D65 (liasse), 11 October 1572.

[54] AM Dijon, D65 (liasse), 2 October 1563 and September 1568.

province, ordered all Huguenots in Dijon to present themselves to the city magistrates at city hall the following day. The Protestants were then herded into the keep of the château for their own safekeeping, though Chabot clearly believed 'that those of the so-called reformed religion were disturbers of the public peace'.[55] David El Kenz has recently demonstrated that it is a myth that Chabot and Pierre Jeannin, a judge in the Parlement of Dijon, disobeyed the orders of the king in order to save the Huguenots' lives—a myth generated largely from Jeannin's memoirs written decades later.[56] There was one Huguenot casualty nevertheless, a sieur de Traves, who was murdered while in prison and his body thrown into a ditch. His crime was that he was a client of the Admiral de Coligny, the focal point of the Paris massacres that began on the night of 24 August. The other 150 Huguenots imprisoned for nearly a month were all released 'after having promised and sworn to live Catholicly'.[57] Thus, the numbers of Protestants in Dijon were gradually reduced between 1562 and 1572, with many abjuring and converting to Catholicism, while others left the city never to return. By 1585 the zealous city fathers could find only 69 suspected Huguenots left in the city, and it seems likely that not all of those were actually practising Protestants.[58]

What the example of Dijon suggests is that despite a very anti-Protestant culture of hostility toward the Huguenots, extending even to illegal imprisonment and seizure of their property, religious violence was not a foregone conclusion after the news of the massacres in the capital reached the city. What had motivated the city fathers from the beginning of the religious struggle was maintaining the unity of the Catholic community in practice and behaviour, as well as maintaining the social and political order. Obviously there were doctrinal implications to these goals, but preventing a breach in the community and maintaining order appear to have been higher on their list of priorities than doctrinal purity. In the end, they managed to achieve both without the violence of a Saint Bartholomew's massacre, because their policy of attrition through abjuration had been working so well since 1562. The irony here is that the political policy in Dijon to ignore, or simply not to enforce, the various peace edicts of 1562, 1563, 1567, and 1570, all of which guaranteed the Huguenots some rights and legal protection under the law, ultimately led to the success in Dijon of reuniting the community around the Catholic majority. It was the crown's policy of limited toleration in the

[55] AM Dijon, B208, fos. 15v–17 (31 August–1 September 1572).
[56] David El Kenz, 'La Saint-Barthélemy à Dijon: Un non-événement?', *Annales de Bourgogne*, 74 (2002), 139–57.
[57] AM Dijon, B208, fo. 23 (22 September 1572).
[58] AM Dijon, B223, fos. 82v–83 (29 October 1585).

series of peace edicts, all designed to prevent violence and civil war, that ultimately ensured their continuation, as Penny Roberts argues in this volume.[59] In the end it was Dijon, and towns like it all over France, that proved more successful than Paris and the dozen other sites of massacres in 1572 in avoiding violence and bloodshed on Saint Bartholomew's Day. But why was that the case?

What I have tried to demonstrate here is that religious violence was neither inevitable nor irreversible once it began in sixteenth-century France. Natalie Davis's pollution model suggests that in communities where Protestants appeared dangerous and threatening—that is, where they practised their religion openly and publicly in contravention of the edicts of pacification—violence could indeed break out. Where local magistrates suppressed the Huguenots and forced them through legal or extra-legal means to abjure their faith and rejoin their Catholic neighbours in the Roman religion, violence was much less likely. In the one case, as in Dijon in 1561, the Huguenots were perceived as vermin to be cleansed and were thought to be very dangerous. Just a decade later, however, they were thought of more as irritants and 'disturbers of the public peace'. With their numbers decreasing significantly after each successive civil war, the Protestant movement in Paris had ceased to be a threat, and those few Huguenots remaining kept out of public view and were forced to accept their second-class status. While individual Huguenots and Catholics could decide not to let religious boundaries completely rule out good neighbourliness, economic activities between the two confessions, or at the extreme, even intermarriage, for most French men and women during the Wars of Religion, these boundaries remained pretty formidable and certainly contributed to the violence among civilians during the civil wars. That is not to say, however, that religious violence was either inevitable or irreversible. For one thing, the legal status of Huguenots was redefined by the Edict of Nantes. From 1562 to 1598, the legal status of French Protestants vacillated between certain legal rights granted by each successive edict of pacification and the attempts to take away those rights in each successive civil war. From the generous terms of the Edicts of Beaulieu in 1576 and Poitiers in 1577 to the outright banning of Protestant practices and beliefs in 1585, crown policy toward the Huguenots vacillated wildly and was never stable or predictable. The situation changed dramatically with the Edict of Nantes, however.[60]

---

[59] See Roberts, 'Peace, Ritual and Sexual Violence'.

[60] See Luria, *Sacred Boundaries*, 316–17; Barbara Diefendorf, 'The Failure of Peace before Nantes,' in Richard L. Goodbar, (ed.), *The Edict of Nantes: Five Essays and a New Translation* (Bloomington, MN, 1998), esp. 8–9.

Although the terms of the published edict seem very similar to the earlier edicts of pacification, the political and religious context was very different after 1598. Henry IV promised not to persecute his former co-religionists if they promised to remain loyal to him and the French monarchy. In short, after 1598 Huguenots were no longer sacking Catholic churches and Catholic magistrates were no longer arresting Huguenots for heresy. Moreover, the edict also granted a clear and precise second-class legal status to the Huguenots, limiting their practice to certain towns but restoring freedom of conscience. Although the French state at every level was to remain Catholic, and even the edict's preamble implied that eventually the monarchy hoped that God would reunite France under one religion, the fact was that the edict provided the means for a peaceful coexistence between the two confessions, not by eliminating the boundaries between the two, but by clarifying and recognizing them. Thus, just as in medieval Iberia, when the state established clearly recognized and stable legal boundaries between the two confessions, peaceful coexistence was at least possible in ways that were less possible during the religious wars. And though Henry IV's son and grandson were not as willing as he was to maintain and safeguard that peaceful coexistence, it is nevertheless true that between 1598 and 1685 in many parts of France the 'rites of violence' were a distant and not very pleasant memory.

Natalie Davis concluded her classic analysis of religious violence in sixteenth-century France by insisting that the 'rites of violence' did not imply any 'rights of violence'. She wanted to make clear that her attempt to understand the motivations and inspirations of the rioters' actions did not in any way justify those actions.[61] In the same vein, I wish to stress here that my analysis of the policies that allowed for a relatively peaceful confessional coexistence in pre-modern Europe—whether in late medieval Spain or in sixteenth-century France—does not imply or suggest that these are justifiable policies for religious coexistence in our contemporary world today. Even to raise such a possibility is both disturbing and depressing. Legally defining religious minorities as second-class citizens and physically and socially proscribing the social spaces in which they could practise their religion only worked in the pre-modern world, however, because nearly everyone in that world—especially urban magistrates—still tended to believe that, at least in theory, religious uniformity was always a better means to maintain community and social order than trying to forge a community divided by rival confessions. Religious coexistence was never perceived by most Europeans in the pre-modern world as a permanent solution to a multi-confessional

---

[61] Davis, 'The Rites of Violence', 91.

community. Nevertheless, as Benjamin Kaplan has recently shown, many bi-confessional or multi-confessional communities could manage to work out ways to live together peacefully, though in nearly all cases it was through legal means that established religious minorities as second-class citizens, who either had to physically exit their towns or communities in order to worship in some other location, or who could worship only in private, either at home or at *schuilkerken*, the so-called 'clandestine churches' hidden in plain sight in the middle of cities and towns. And in unusual cases, different confessions even shared physical worship spaces, though generally not at the same time.[62] These were all policies of accommodation, however, 'fictions of privacy' to use Kaplan's arresting term, not policies designed to protect religious pluralism.

To be sure, the peaceful coexistence of different religions might over time lead to conditions that allowed for a complete change in the central values of a community from religious uniformity to religious pluralism. But that change was a more modern and recent transformation, by no means completed by the Enlightenment at the end of the eighteenth century.[63] Viewed from the beginning of the twenty-first century, however, the world is very different. Even today there are still some extreme fundamentalists—whether Christians, Jews, Muslims, or those of other religions—who continue to yearn for religious uniformity and see modernity and religious pluralism as the enemies of faith. For the overwhelming majority of us, however, the only treatment of religious minorities that can be justified is one that harbours no more 'fictions of privacy' and that supports a community in which members of all faiths have unfettered freedom of worship as well as freedom of conscience. As I have tried to show in this chapter, the values of virtually all Catholics and Huguenots in sixteenth-century France did not allow them to embrace such a community. Nevertheless, the 'rites of violence' that some of them resorted to in the name of their respective confessions were neither inevitable nor irreversible. They were clearly shaped by historical contingencies that varied over time and space, just as they do in our own world today.

---

[62] Benjamin J. Kaplan, *Divided by Faith: Religious Conflict and the Practice of Toleration in Early Modern Europe* (Cambridge, MA, 2007); Benjamin J. Kaplan, 'Fictions of Privacy: House Chapels and Spatial Accommodation of Religious Dissent in Early Modern Europe', *American Historical Review*, 107 (202), 1031–64. For sharing religious spaces also see Jesse Spohnholz, 'Multiconfessional Celebration of the Eucharist in Sixteenth-Century Wessel', *Sixteenth Century Journal*, 39 (2008), 705–29.

[63] See Darrin M. McMahon, *Enemies of the Enlightenment: The French Counter-Enlightenment and the Making of Modernity* (Oxford and New York, 2001).

To give Natalie Davis the last word, 'if we try to increase safety and trust within a community, guarantee that the violence it generates will take less destructive and less cruel forms, then we must think less about pacifying "deviants" and more about changing the central values'.[64]

[64] Davis, 'The Rites of Violence', 91.

Peace, Ritual, and Sexual Violence during the Religious Wars

Penny Roberts

Natalie Davis's 'Rites of Violence' thesis remains the essential starting point for any discussion of confessional division during the French religious wars, as well as proving instructive for how many other historical conflicts might better be understood. The insights it provides to why participants acted as they did has immeasurably increased our understanding of the ritualized nature of such violence. In particular, Davis explored the exceptional brutality meted out by Catholics to their Protestant victims in anthropological and cultural terms. She interpreted it as the removal, purging, and destruction of the pollution in their midst, because the people believed that the authorities were failing in their duty to do so (and the same motivation, she argued, led Protestants to target priests and to participate in iconoclasm). By encouraging us to 'think with' those who carried out these acts, however, the Davis thesis shifted the focus of the debate away from the depiction of the violence itself. This essay will, therefore, offer a reassessment of just what we can know about that violence from the ways in which it was both experienced and represented. First, by considering how widespread and intense it actually was, and how effective were the attempts to appease it; and then, what was both included and left out of contemporary descriptions of such events, and what this can tell us about the attitudes and responses of both faiths. Particularly telling in this regard is the apparent suppression of the discussion or portrayal of sexual assault. An examination of language and cultural context will prove crucial here, as well as comparison with the experience and representation of violence in other arenas of war.

Peace and violence

No doubt, as in all conflicts, the experience of violence for many communities and many individuals in sixteenth-century France varied enormously. It is arguable that too much attention has been paid to the extreme acts of religious violence during the wars, when it is hard to quantify just how endemic and continual (or 'normal') they really were. For the Huguenots in particular, verbal and physical abuse, as well as intimidation and harassment of various sorts, formed a daily hazard. Such incidents were unavoidably tinged with the threat of violence which might eventually result in an assault or even murder. Yet they were far more characteristic of confessional relations than the full-blown massacres on which so much historical attention has been focused to date. Furthermore, recent studies have shown how prolonged periods of coexistence, often deliberately constructed, prevailed in some contexts.[1] This was true not just of France, but throughout Reformation Europe.[2] Like royal peace edicts, such agreements constrained and contained confessional violence locally (or at least tried to do so). Apart from the containment of violence, however, there is a yet more interesting story to be told if we consider the relationship between peace and violence which, at first sight, might seem contradictory but, in some ways, was interdependent.

All conflict presupposes an opposite state of peace which, however, may remain elusive if disputes are not fully resolved. Studies of attempts at conflict resolution, drawing on examples from medieval times to the present day, reinforce this intractability.[3] Although 'war and peace are radically different contexts that induce and constrain violence in very different ways', the presence of or potential for violence during peacetime results from the same antagonisms which propagate war.[4] The apparent juxtaposition between violence and peace conceals the extent to which the two are symbiotically related in practice, particularly at a time of civil strife. Cumulatively, responses to provocative actions by the other faith in sixteenth-century France contributed to the environment in which more sustained violence was possible. When divisions are as entrenched as they were during the religious wars by confessional difference, mired in acrimony and resentment, then efforts at peacemaking may actually exacerbate existing tensions and the chances of a resort to violence.

---

[1] Olivier Christin, 'La coexistence confessionnelle, 1563–1567', *Bulletin de la Société de l'Histoire du Protestantisme Français*, 141 (1995), 483–504; Jérémie Foa, 'Making Peace: the Commissions for Enforcing the Pacification Edicts in the Reign of Charles IX (1560–1574)', *French History*, 18 (2004), 256–74; Penny Roberts, 'Royal Authority and Justice during the French Religious Wars', *Past and Present*, 184 (2004), 3–32.

[2] Benjamin J. Kaplan, *Divided by Faith: Religious Conflict and the Practice of Toleration in Early Modern Europe* (Cambridge, MA and London, 2007).

[3] Diane Wolfthal (ed.), *Peace and Negotiation: Strategies for Coexistence in the Middle Ages and the Renaissance* (Turnhout, 2000); Barbara F. Walter, *Committing to Peace: The Successful Settlement of Civil Wars* (Princeton, NJ, and Oxford, 2002); Yaacov Bar-Siman-Tov (ed.), *From Conflict Resolution to Reconciliation* (Oxford, 2004); Robert L. Rothstein (ed.), *After the Peace: Resistance and Reconciliation* (Boulder, CO, and London, 1999).

[4] Stathis N. Kalyvas, *The Logic of Violence in Civil War* (Cambridge, 2006), 22.

The contradictory role of peacemaking, in particular the implementation of the royal edicts of pacification, as a cause of conflict is striking. It is evident that there were plenty of violent incidents during periods of supposed peace during the religious wars, which in fact outnumbered the years of official strife.[5] But wartime provided some immunity for these actions, whereas in peacetime, arguably, violence had to be justified in other ways; most often as self-defence or to prevent sedition, laying blame squarely at the feet of opponents. Nevertheless, peacetime conditions presented peculiar opportunities for provocation principally through the rights and concessions granted by the crown in its edicts, especially over sites of Reformed worship and burial, such that official sanction actually exacerbated hostilities. Thus, the relationship between peace and violence during the religious wars is closer than we might expect. The crown's attempts to establish peace came about in order to stem confessional violence, including under Henry III strenuous efforts to encourage unity and reform, yet resulted in the intensification of that violence.[6] Contrary to its intention, the crown's efforts to enforce the peace could enflame existing tensions and exacerbate the very hostilities which it was trying to assuage. Peace became a provocation, a cause and a pretext for the violence it was supposed to prevent. At the very least, it created the conditions in which the potential for and the threat of violence was ever present. This was an outcome that even the crown was forced to acknowledge. It was no easy task to reconcile parties so recently divided, to assuage enmities and grudges perpetuated by acts of violence, and to persuade bitter opponents to live alongside one another in peace.[7] The contemporary view of religious toleration was that it was a temporary solution, not a pattern for future coexistence. The longer the wars lasted, the greater were the causes for cynicism and dissatisfaction among a disgruntled populace of either faith. Peace did not seem to be working when conflict so soon returned and grievances were not satisfactorily addressed. As the sociologist John Brewer has recently commented, 'rarely is there a complete cessation of all forms of violence, and the ending of violence in most post-violence societies is only relative'.[8]

---

[5] The edicts or peace agreements in question, and their duration, are: Amboise (1563–7); Longjumeau (1568); Saint-Germain (1570–2); Beaulieu (1576); Bergerac (supplemented by those of Nérac and Fleix, 1577–85); Mantes (restoring Bergerac, 1591–). Full texts of the edicts can be located at http://elec.enc.sorbonne.fr/editsdepacification/ [accessed 16 September 2011].

[6] Mark Greengrass, *Governing Passions: Peace and Reform in the French Kingdom, 1576–1585* (Oxford, 2007).

[7] See Barbara B. Diefendorf, this volume, 30–51, and Mack P. Holt, this volume, 52–74.

[8] John D. Brewer, *Peace Processes: A Sociological Approach* (Cambridge, 2010), 32.

Peace generated anxiety and resentment in a situation where disputes and antagonisms remained unresolved and laid the groundwork for volatile encounters which, ultimately, could and did lead to violence. The impassioned debates regarding the royal policy of toleration were partly shaped by whether it lessened or heightened such tensions; indeed the breakdown of order was the primary concern of local and regional authorities. In view of such uncertainties, it is unsurprising that contemporary opinion was divided over the relationship between peace and violence. In particular, Catholics were concerned about the detrimental impact on peace and order if freedom of worship was granted to local Huguenots. Drawing on their own experience of interconfessional tensions, municipal and regional bodies argued that the presence of Reformed services exacerbated rather than reduced the possibility of violence. When the Edict of January 1562 arrived in the town, the municipal authorities in Dijon opposed its publication allowing 'services in the towns and suburbs of this province and duchy' because of the 'misfortunes and inconvenience' which they believed would follow.[9] Likewise, the estates of Languedoc argued in 1570 that, where there was no exercise of the Reformed religion, there was no 'disorder and scandal'.[10] In contrast, the crown (through its edicts of pacification) and the Reformed church (through its petitions to royal authorities) continued to assert the benefits of permitting services. The Huguenots of Lyon, for instance, urged that for the faiths to live peacefully together, toleration was the answer: 'public worship granted by his majesty to those of the Reformed religion has caused ... no scandal, loss nor diminution in the places where it is held, but on the contrary has been the true means to remove' them, because it brought discipline and order.[11]

However, royal attempts to lessen tensions by offering concessions to the Huguenots, most contentiously official locations at which they could worship, often backfired. They were also a headache for local authorities, as the convenience of access to a site had to be weighed against the potential for disorder, demonstrating why the peace was unable to work effectively in many localities. The proximity of a site to a community was of particular concern. Thus, services in the suburbs of Sézanne and Villeneuve-le-Roy were opposed due to recent disturbances in these towns, whilst at La Ferté-Milon, the services were held in a suburb 'cheek by jowl with one of its biggest

---

[9] Archives Municipales (hereafter AM) Dijon, B 199, fos. 181v–2, 184v (February/March 1562).
[10] AM Toulouse, AA 127, fo. 179v (November 1570).
[11] Bibliothèque Municipale de Lyon, MS (Coste) 426.

parishes' provoking 'trouble and sedition'.[12] Equally, Huguenots were well aware of the risks they took when travelling to and from these sites, both as they passed through town gates and whilst out in the surrounding countryside. Reports of attacks, involving both verbal and physical violence, were commonplace, such as the complaints of Huguenots in Dijon of the 'injuries and excesses that they say take place daily . . . both coming and going to services'.[13] In turn, Catholics were alarmed by the open carrying of weapons by those attending services, another common cause of clashes at town gates.[14] Furthermore, episodes of tit-for-tat violence were not uncommon; fire was a favoured weapon as it allowed perpetrators to remain anonymous, as when Catholics were assaulted at Blois following the burning down of a barn used for Reformed services.[15] Such incidents were a manifestation of the uneasy relationship between the faiths in many places; there was a lack of trust and a belief that the other side had their own best interests and not those of the wider community at heart. Their actions were interpreted accordingly, and so practical measures to enforce peace could and did lead to confrontation. They reinforce the peculiar link between peace and violence, but it is the nature of that violence to which attention will be turned next. Its characteristics may go some way to explaining why relations between the faiths were so fraught, and suggest that significant cultural obstacles had to be overcome if coexistence was to be established and accepted.

Ritual violence

The violent episodes which have traditionally been seen to characterize the French religious wars require further investigation. The gruesome depictions attracted the attention of shocked contemporaries as much as they have modern-day historians. Our understanding of these events (as for Davis) is shaped by the testimony of Huguenot sources, in particular, the *Histoire*

---

[12] Bibliothèque nationale de France, Paris, (hereafter BnF) MS français 18156, fo. 40 (Sézanne, Mar. 1564); 16221, fo. 315 (Villeneuve, May 1567); 17832, fo. 87v (La Ferté-Milon, May 1565).

[13] AM Dijon, D 63 (January & March 1564, May 1565); also B 200, fos. 166, 167, 216 (March–June 1564).

[14] For more on this issue, see Penny Roberts, 'One Town, Two Faiths: Unity and Exclusion during the French Religious Wars' in Thomas Max Safley (ed.), *A Companion to Multiconfessionalism in the Early Modern World* (Leiden, 2011), 265–85.

[15] BnF, MS français 15545, fos. 178, 196 (April 1568); 15546, fos. 279–81, 287 (June 1568). On the deliberate destruction of buildings used for Reformed worship, see Andrew Spicer, *Calvinist Churches in Early Modern Europe* (Manchester, 2007), 173–4, 208.

ecclésiastique des églises réformées au royaume de France.¹⁶ It recounts the sense of 'the greatest and most horrible confusion of the world' as Catholics amassed to participate in the killing of their Protestant neighbours; such observations of collective and sudden madness seem to recur in many civil war situations.¹⁷ Yet is there more to what is described than its ritualized aspects? The mutilation of bodies, disembowelment and other acts of apparent butchery, are a common topos. The account of the disfigurement of a cloth-weaver in Chateauneuf, whose eyes were gouged out and nose and ears cut off, is typical.¹⁸ So, too, is the case in Provence in 1559 of a nobleman targeted by a hostile crowd: 'Amongst other barbarous acts, his guts were ripped from his stomach, dragged around the town, then thrown into its ditches, in the most foul-smelling and filthy place'. Finally, 'His heart and liver were removed, stuck on sticks and carried around the town in triumph'.¹⁹ Similarly, in Villeneuve d'Avignon in 1561, a Huguenot prayer meeting was broken up by papal soldiers who, having murdered seven of those attending, paraded the liver of one victim 'on the end of an iron rod' and offered it for sale for the equivalent of five *deniers*.²⁰ Other accounts tell of Huguenot hearts or livers being bitten or eaten, as by the executioner at Carcassonne; showing off his expertise, he 'skinned five of those who had been killed' during a violent confrontation between the faiths, 'eating the liver of one of them'.²¹ In Bar-sur-Seine near Troyes in 1562, enraged Catholic soldiers tore out and took turns to bite the heart of one of their victims, one of them 'barbarically' declaring 'that he knew well that once before dying he would eat the heart of a Huguenot'.²² Strikingly, an account by the Catholic priest of Provins, Claude Haton, ascribes similar actions to the Protestants at Orléans in 1562. Their target, however, was the heart and entrails of the late king, Francis II, which they reputedly fricasseed and threw to the dogs, and some were even reported to have eaten despite the king having died two years

---

[16] G. Baum and E. Cunitz (eds), *Histoire ecclésiastique des églises réformées au royaume de France* (3 vols; orig. edn Paris, 1883–89; repr. 1974) (hereafter *Histoire ecclésiastique*).

[17] *Histoire ecclésiastique*, II, 685. Kalyvas, *Logic of Violence*, 81–2.

[18] *Histoire ecclésiastique*, I, 821–2. Catholic sources, such as Claude Haton, confirm the taking of ears as trophies, e.g. *Mémoires de Claude Haton*, II, 169–70, 505.

[19] *Histoire ecclésiastique*, I, 420.

[20] *Histoire ecclésiastique*, I, 977–8. Cf. discussion and further examples of this 'ghoulish commerce' and of cannibalism in Davis, 'The Rites of Violence', 83 and n. 100.

[21] *Histoire ecclésiastique*, I, 964.

[22] Nicolas Pithou, 'Histoire ecclesiastique de l'eglise reformée de la ville de Troyes', BnF, MS Dupuy 698 [hereafter Pithou], fo. 241v. There is also a modern edition of this source: Nicolas Pithou de Champgobert, *Chronique de Troyes et de la Champagne (1524–1594)*, éd. Pierre-Eugène Leroy, 2 vols (Reims, 1998).

before.[23] Thus the Protestants compounded their barbarity with treason. The common reporting of such actions by both sides reinforces the sense that we are dealing with the expected characteristics of inhumane behaviour as described by prejudiced opponents.

Amid the horror of such acts, there are some striking elements, the full symbolism of which has not hitherto been recognized. Some historical scepticism of the actuality of the sources and the events they describe is appropriate, not just because of the clear polemical intent of the authors, but since the way in which the violence is depicted is reminiscent of the way that marginal groups were perceived in early modern society. The inversion and mockery of religious ritual suggest clear parallels with contemporary accusations against witches and other deviants.[24] In Troyes in 1562, the bodies of a merchant and his wife (whose throats had been cut) were stripped and publicly displayed, before their killers 'quartered the woman's body, which they arranged in the shape of a cross around the corpse of her husband'.[25] Tales of cannibalism (as discussed above) drew similar comparisons. Jean de Léry cites historical examples of the Jews as perpetrators of cannibalism, whilst also being forced to eat human flesh by their Egyptian captors; descriptions of Jewish involvement in the ritual murder of Christian children were commonplace.[26] Similarly, witches were said to dig up, cook, and consume the dead bodies of babies. The ready association of, and repulsion towards, Catholics with the sacrifice, transubstantiation, and subsequent consumption of Christ's body and blood at the Mass may have been on Protestant minds. Cannibalism and inversion were also common, if sometimes macabre, features of popular festive culture, including references to the sale and eating of Christian flesh as part of a rite of renewal.[27] This anthropophagy remained symbolic, however, and was not acted out in the way that was claimed during these episodes of religious violence.

---

[23] *Mémoires de Claude Haton*, I, 335–6.

[24] By contrast, Faurin cites an 'actual' example of cannibalism in 1573 during the siege of Sancerre, where the famine was so bad that a couple allegedly ate their own child which had starved to death and, as a result, they were burned alive: Jean Faurin, *Journal de Faurin sur les guerres de Castres*, ed. Claude Bazin de Bezons (*Pièces fugitives pour servir à l'histoire de France*: Pièce XV; no place or date of publication), 69.

[25] Pithou, fo. 241.

[26] Jean de Léry, *Histoire d'un voyage fait en la terre du Brésil* (Geneva, 1611), 256, 268. He also cites Micah, 3:3: 'Who also eat the flesh of my people, and flay their skins from off them; and they break their bones, and chop them in pieces, as for the pot'.

[27] See, for example, Emmanuel Le Roy Ladurie, *Le Carnaval de Romans. De la Chandeleur au mercredi des Cendres, 1579–1580* (Paris, 1979), 203, 233.

These stories also contain analogies to butchery in the use of the 'vocabulary of the slaughterhouse' and the way in which victims were killed which, as Davis has argued, allowed perpetrators to distance themselves from their actions.[28] Interesting here, is the symbolic role ascribed to executioners: on the one hand they are associated with the most barbaric behaviour, skinning and butchering victims.[29] In contrast, their restraint in other cases is used to denigrate the actions of the perpetrators of violence: such as showing more mercy towards a condemned Huguenot than the crowd baying for his blood, and risking assault themselves as a result.[30] Natalie Davis draws our attention to the participation of butchers (and their wives) in several assaults, and the use of butchers' cleavers to kill Protestants in Meaux.[31] Indeed, the term 'massacre' seems to have derived its meaning at this time from the French word for a butcher's chopping block.[32] Jean de Léry refers to 'the butchery of the French people' and, amongst other such acts, the cutting of victims' throats as if they were sheep.[33] It may be no coincidence, therefore, that sites where animals had previously been slaughtered were sometimes granted as locations for Reformed worship, as at Lyon and Montauban.[34]

Animals, too, play a comparable role in underlining the inhumanity of Catholic foes who are often compared unfavourably with wild beasts

---

[28] Davis, 'The Rites of Violence', 85. Richard Trexler, *Sex and Conquest: Gendered Violence, Political Order, and the European Conquest of the Americas* (Cambridge, 1995), esp. 17–19. He discusses the use of such vocabulary as a common way of dehumanizing the victim, and the perceived right to butcher a sinner like a beast, including castration and anal evisceration, even drawing analogies with the violence of the French religious wars.

[29] In early modern Germany, executioners and knackers (but not butchers) were considered to pursue a dishonourable trade and were consequently ostracized, see Kathy Stuart, *Defiled Trades and Social Outcasts: Honor and Ritual Pollution in Early Modern Germany* (Cambridge, 1999). Their status in France is less clear. On skinning and butchering, cf. biblical quotation in n. 24 above.

[30] The executioner in Troyes refused to participate in the unauthorized execution of Huguenots following the St Bartholomew's day massacre in 1572, see Penny Roberts, *A City in Conflict: Troyes during the French Wars of Religion* (Manchester, 1996), 148; on disputes between executioners and crowds, see also 45–6.

[31] Davis, 'The Rites of Violence', 85–7.

[32] Mark Greengrass, 'Hidden Transcripts: Secret Histories and Personal Testimonies of Religious Violence in the French Wars of Religion', in Mark Levene and Penny Roberts (eds), *The Massacre in History* (New York and Oxford, 1999), 69.

[33] Léry, *Histoire d'un voyage*, 286.

[34] Spicer, *Calvinist Churches*, 176.

(a recurring theme) and 'enraged dogs'.[35] In the case cited earlier from Provence, a dog 'in whom was found more humanity than in these men' was accused of Lutheranism by his outraged owner for refusing to eat a piece of the murdered man's liver.[36] Further symbolic elements may also be at work, in the prominence given to the consumption of such organs as traditional sources of strength: Jean de Léry certainly believed that murderers ate the hearts and livers of their victims in the belief that it would reinforce their own courage.[37] Dogs are often used in other contexts as being prone to, or emblematic of, cannibalism (from *cane*), so are an appropriate metaphor here. Bodies were frequently said to have been left for, or actively given to, animals to eat, including dogs, birds, and pigs, alongside the oft-attested burning or drowning in rivers of victims.[38] There are possibly echoes of biblical, principally Old Testament, stories here, such as the death of Jezebel, as well as in the stripping naked of victims as the ultimate form of disgrace and suggestive of immoral behaviour.[39] For contemporaries, the ready analogy with the activities of the peoples of the newly discovered Americas was evident. Such a juxtaposition allowed for a damning critique of the cruelties enacted by supposedly civilized Europeans. This was as true of the Protestant Léry as of Michel de Montaigne in his famous essay 'On Cannibals':

> I think there is more barbarity in eating a man alive than in eating him dead; more barbarity in lacerating by rack and torture a body still fully able to feel things, in roasting him little by little and having

---

[35] E.g. *Histoire ecclésiastique*, II, pp. 685–6, including comparison to 'tigers & lions' as well as 'enraged dogs' committing 'the most barbarous and inhumane cruelties'. For similar analogies made by Catholics about Protestants, see G. W. Sypher, ' "Faisant ce qu'il leur vient a plaisir": the Image of Protestantism in French Catholic Polemic on the Eve of the Religious Wars', *Sixteenth Century Journal*, 11 (1980), 59–84, esp. 72.

[36] *Histoire ecclésiastique*, I, 420.

[37] Jean de Léry, *Histoire d'un voyage*, 277; and also on this practice, 282–5. It has been suggested to me that there may also be an etymological play on the French terms for *foie* (liver) and *foi* (faith), although there is no suggestion that this connection is being made in the often far from subtle sources I have consulted.

[38] Ibid., on the feeding of human flesh to dogs in particular, including taking some of the examples from the *Histoire ecclésiastique* cited here, 281, 285, 292–3. Also discussed in Davis, 'The Rites of Violence', 83 and n. 100.

[39] For the defenestration and consumption of the corpse of Jezebel by dogs, see 2 Kings, 9: 33–7 (also cited at the beginning of Davis, 'The Rites of Violence', 51, 83). For just one of the examples of nakedness as a punishment, particularly for whoredom, see Ezekiel, 16. For general images of violence, see Habakkuk, 1: 'for spoiling and violence are before me . . . They shall come all for violence', and Lamentations.

him bruised and bitten by pigs and dogs (as we have not only read about but seen in recent memory, not among enemies in antiquity but among our fellow-citizens and neighbours—and, what is worse, in the name of duty and religion) than in roasting him and eating him after his death.[40]

Aside from the more gruesome details of such tales, it was contrary to both humanity and Christian charity for either faith to deny the other's dead proper burial, provoking further confrontation between the faiths.[41]

Natalie Davis herself comments on the need for historians to be alert to the 'problems... [of analysis] present in all kinds of documents' which cannot be seen as a 'straightforward witness'.[42] Clearly, it is impossible for historians to verify one way or the other whether or not such violent incidents took place exactly as described. The formulaic nature of such accounts does suggest, however, that there was a cultural repertoire of actions which are strikingly characteristic of the treatment of various deviant groups in early modern society. This needs to be recognized if we are to grant the symbolism of such accounts the importance it deserves. The perpetrators are routinely shown to be inhuman, amoral, and barbaric; far from the avenging angels, purifiers of the heretical and seditious elements of society, or the divine agents, of Catholic rhetoric (*pace* Crouzet).[43] Thus, Protestant descriptions may be interpreted as suggesting that their actions made Catholics analogous with those marginalized by society, their deviant behaviour delegitimizing their justification before God for such acts. This tarring of opponents with the brush of deviance by association worked both ways. Conversely, Huguenots, like earlier heretics and witches, were accused of sexual impropriety as well as the killing of infants at secret, often nocturnal meetings.[44] These

---

[40] Michel de Montaigne, *The Complete Essays*, ed. and trans. M. A. Screech (London, 1987), 235–6; Léry, *Histoire d'un voyage*, 277–96, where the violence of the French religious wars and that perpetrated by the Spanish in the Americas is unfavourably compared to the customs of cannibalism among native peoples.

[41] Penny Roberts, 'Contesting Sacred Space: Burial Disputes in Sixteenth-Century France', in Bruce Gordon and Peter Marshall (eds), *The Place of the Dead: Death and Remembrance in Late Medieval and Early Modern Europe* (Cambridge, 2000), 131–48.

[42] Natalie Zemon Davis, *A Passion for History. Conversations with Denis Crouzet* (Kirksville, MO, 2010), 34.

[43] Denis Crouzet, *Les Guerriers de Dieu: la violence au temps des troubles de religion (c.1525–c.1610)* 2 vols (Paris, 1990).

[44] For instance, see esp. Sypher, '"Faisant ce qu'il leur vient a plaisir"', 59–84; L. Racaut, 'The Polemical Use of the Albigensian Crusade during the French Wars of Religion', *French History*, 13 (1999), 1–19. *Histoire ecclésiastique*, I, 144, acknowledges this in relation to the

characteristics all have resonance for the final section: the role of gender and especially sexual violence.

Sexual violence

Natalie Davis remarked in the 'Rites of Violence' that, 'while the number of women killed by Protestant crowds seems to have been very small, observers' reports show about one out of ten people killed by Catholic crowds in the provinces in 1572 was a woman'.[45] Although, as we might expect during conflict, women were much less likely to be victims of violence than were men, the targeting of pregnant women was highlighted as particularly heinous by both sides. Whilst scrutinizing contemporary accounts, another unremarked aspect of the female experience of war is striking: that is the near absence of descriptions of sexual violence. Whilst the sexual dimension of the mutilation to which both male and female Huguenot corpses were subject is well-established—in particular, the castration of men, and the disembowelling of pregnant women, perhaps symbolic of the actual destruction of the next generation—and notions of pollution widely accepted, the lack of rape narratives is remarkable.[46] Thus, whilst Huguenots were frequently accused by Catholic opponents of indulging in lascivious acts—'that they gathered together for debauchery, that they put out the lights and took whichever woman they pleased in the confusion'—the missing dimension of actual sexual assault needs further consideration.[47]

Gratuitous acts of brutality against women (and indeed children) lends pathos to many a narrative of violence, and these stories are often the most detailed and their actions the most ritualized. According to these accounts, women were also often forced to bear witness to atrocities against their husbands or other kin, as well as being victims of violence themselves. During the

---

Affair of the rue Saint-Jacques, as accusations 'with which Satan had tried to defame the early Church'.

[45] Davis, 'The Rites of Violence', 78 and n. 87.

[46] For a similar focus on the violence done to pregnant or lactating Protestant women in seventeenth-century Ireland, see Naomi McAreavey, 'Re(-)Membering Women: Protestant Women's Victim Testimonies during the Irish Rising of 1641', *Journal of the Northern Renaissance*, 2.1 (2010). However, Davis, 'Rites of Violence', 60, n. 24, and 78, n. 87, takes issue with Janine Garrisson-Estèbe's interpretation of such acts as seeking the extermination of a 'foreign race'. Although Jean de Léry supports the idea of a deliberate Catholic attempt to wipe out 'the Huguenot race' ('la race de ces Huguenots'): *Histoire d'un voyage*, 279, as Davis states this should not be interpreted in strictly 'racial' terms.

[47] Faurin, *Journal de Faurin*, 6.

religious wars, women were subject to verbal and physical affronts to their status and virtue. Sexual slurs and acts of degradation (such as their oft-cited pelting with mud or ordure) were typical of Catholic attempts to discredit the moral status of the Huguenot minority. The most notorious such episode was the so-called 'Affair of the rue Saint-Jacques' in Paris in September 1557, when women of high status who had been attending a Reformed service were 'called whores, subjected to all sorts of insults, beaten, their clothing torn, their hoods struck from their heads, their hair dishevelled and their faces soiled and covered with filth and mud'.[48] At Dijon in 1564, it was reported that Huguenot women were insulted and threatened, called 'bitches' ('*chiennes*'), and accused of offering their sexual favours freely; one was kicked, and mud and stones were thrown at them.[49] Such slurs and attacks were an effective means to denigrate the Huguenot community as a whole, because the preservation of a woman's sexual honour was crucial to both her and her kin. The deliberate uncovering of hair had particular resonance in this regard, impugning a woman's chastity.[50] Indeed, it was universally recognized that the reputation of honourable women needed to be safeguarded. In Amiens in 1580, after a series of aggressive approaches to Huguenot women by young men of the town, the Catholic authorities even took action to provide regular protection for those returning from their place of worship outside the city walls.[51] By contrast, it is worth noting an unusually detailed and, therefore, fascinating counter-charge of Protestant violence directed against the Catholics of Blois in 1563. Whilst the Huguenots were accused of having shot a pregnant woman and made threats to 'good people' passing by that there were not enough ropes or trees from which 'to hang the papists', no sexual aggression was inferred.[52]

In view of the sexual connotations associated with the frequenting of Huguenot services, it is perhaps surprising to find so little evidence that the modesty of Huguenot women was physically rather than just verbally threatened. In Troyes in 1562, after a massacre, naked female corpses were reportedly put on public view, their legs splayed and their 'shameful parts'

---

[48] *Histoire ecclésiastique*, I, 143.
[49] AM Dijon, D 63 (8 Mar. 1564), 6 fos: referring to 'leur paillardise charité'.
[50] James R. Farr, 'The Pure and Disciplined Body: Hierarchy, Morality and Symbolism in France during the Catholic Reformation', *Journal of Interdisciplinary History*, 21 (1991), esp. 401–3, 409–12.
[51] Olivia Carpi, *Une République imaginaire: Amiens pendant les troubles de religion (1559–1597)* (Paris, 2005), 86.
[52] BnF, MS français 15878, fo. 190; interestingly, two Huguenot women were the only ones identified among those making such threats.

displayed, with declarations made that 'there is where they bestowed their charity (sexual favours)'.[53] Yet, there is no suggestion that they were at any other stage subject to the other forms of sexual assault we might expect. Even more so in a situation of civil war, and the presence of a vulnerable minority, it is notable that there are so few accounts of actual or attempted rape. There are plenty of general allusions as one in a list of the atrocities of war, however: for example, in Loys le Roy's *Des troubles et differens*, including once again comparison to animalistic behaviour. Here, the perpetrators, in the belief that they were doing God's work, 'tear babies from the bellies of their mothers, or kill them in their cradles, rape women and girls, enslave men, ruin the countryside, burn down houses, towns and castles . . . persecuting each other inhumanely with all kinds of cruelty like wild beasts'.[54] Similarly, irenicist bishop and royal commissioner Jean de Monluc describes in his correspondence the royal regiments sent to Auvergne and Loire in 1568, who committed 'so many terrible murders, so many robberies, raped so many women', that the peasantry found 'the lives and chastity of their women in constant danger'.[55] Even in more focused accounts, references to rape are still very general, as in the violence perpetrated against Huguenots in Le Mans, which describes the cutting of throats 'of virtuous and peaceful men', stabbing stomachs of 'chaste and honest women', and in hearts of 'weak and innocent children'.[56] Yet, characteristically, there are very few specifics of actual events; just as with the blanket assertion made against Admiral Coligny by a Parisian priest as part of the justification of his murder in 1572, that he had been 'the cause of the death of a hundred thousand men and the rape of girls, women

---

[53] Pithou, fo. 242.
[54] Loys le Roy, 'Des troubles et differens advenans entre les hommes par la diversité des Religions: ensemble du commencement, progrez, & excellence de la Chrestienné' (Lyon, 1568), 2v–3. According to Richard Trexler, *Sex and Conquest*, 13–14, the rape of men often accompanied their enslavement during war, so this quotation may also need to be read in this context to suggest sexual violence against both men and women.
[55] *Lettres de Catherine de Médicis*, eds H. de La Ferrière and B. de Puchesse (10 vols, Paris, 1880–1943), III, 353.
[56] 'Remonstrance envoyée au Roy, par la Noblesse de la Religion Réformée du Païs & Conté du Maine, sur les assassinats, pilleries, saccagemens des maisons, séditions, violemens de femmes, & autres excès horribles, commis depuis la publication de l'Edit de pacification', *Mémoires de Condé*, V, 286. Cf description in Franck Viltart, '*Exploitiez la guerre par tous les moyens!* Pillages et violences dans les campagnes militaires de Charles le Téméraire (1466–1476)', *Revue du Nord*, 91 (2009), 475, of 'deflowering of virgins . . . spoiling of matrons . . . forcing of women'.

and nuns'.[57] A consistent thread in all such accounts, whether Protestant or Catholic, is that sexual assault was carried out by soldiers rather than civilians, suggesting that such actions were viewed by their perpetrators as part of the spoils of war despite official prohibition. The circumstances of conflict presented both the justification and the opportunity for such acts.

A more systematic account of the common atrocities which accompanied siege warfare, including rape, is provided by the *Journal de Faurin sur les guerres de Castres*.[58] In July 1562, for instance, the Protestant author refers to the confession of Catholic soldiers to 'theft, rape of women and other inhuman acts', for which they were executed.[59] Their successful prosecution and punishment in this regard is notable, as we shall see, and other cases suggest that the fate of soldiers accused of rape was dependent on circumstance not least, probably, ease of identification. The involvement of the secular courts if the incident was deemed to have taken place outside the normal course of war, on the other hand, allowed it to be tried as a criminal offence in the usual way.[60] Subsequent accounts of the sieges that year of Orange, Sisteron, and Montpellier also cite the rape of women and girls by Catholic soldiers, as well as the displacement of women and children then left vulnerable to attack on the roads, or frightened into giving birth before pregnancies reached full term.[61] By the late 1560s, the behaviour of the troops was seen to be no better: entering Protestant towns 'under guise of the peace' in 1568, then taking 'women, girls by force'; or breaking the terms of surrender that 'women leave town unmolested' by leading 'away the girls' and taking 'them by force' in Fiac in August 1569.[62] They also set fire to the town so that the poor women and families that remained had to flee.[63]

---

[57] From the *Journal du cure de Saint-Leu à Paris*, cited in P. Erlanger, *Saint Bartholomew's Night: the Massacre of Saint Bartholomew*, trans. by P. O'Brian (London, 1962), 253.

[58] Faurin, *Journal de Faurin*. Cf Viltart, '*Exploitiez la guerre*', 486–7, including the commonplace of collective or gang rape following a siege.

[59] Faurin, *Journal de Faurin*, 18; cf. Viltart, '*Exploitiez la guerre*', 488–9.

[60] For example, see *Mémoires de Claude Haton*, II, 265–6, in 1569 a Spanish soldier convicted of raping the daughter of his host was hanged; and 502, another similar case in 1572.

[61] Faurin, *Journal de Faurin*, 20–2.

[62] Ibid., 43, 50–1. Also account of rapes at Castres in 1572, 63. Cf Pithou, fo. 242, on the siege of Bar-sur-Seine, that 'several pregnant women, girls and small children . . . were killed, some raped and taken by force, a good number of both men and women put to ransom'.

[63] Cf. Account in J-L.Rigal (ed.), *Mémoires d'un calviniste de Millau* (*Documents sur la Réforme en Rouergue:* Rodez, 1911), 377–8, on the use of fire and the subsequent rape and ransoming of women at Issoire in 1577, in this case despite royal prohibition; 262 and 457, on the rape of women and girls by soldiers in 1573 and, during peacetime, in 1581.

Unsurprisingly, the atrocious actions of Catholic troops are contrasted with the honourable behaviour of Protestant soldiers, who allegedly left unharmed the nuns that they had turned out of their convent.[64] Assaults on nuns, as on priests, were seen as an act of sacrilege by Catholics, but Protestant violence seems to have been directed primarily against male clergy.[65] Yet, although Faurin's journal suggests that rape was an expected and routine aspect of the French religious wars, those violated remain collective and anonymous. Likewise, the quantification of atrocities provided by another Protestant source lists rape among the acts of violence routinely perpetrated. By these estimates, for ninety-three dioceses, an average of 361 rapes per year from 1560–80 were recorded, an average of eighteen per diocese per year. Although the figures are of debatable veracity, the overall impression is of 'a norm of military and civil violence which is akin to a total disintegration of lawful and ordered society'.[66]

The *Histoire ecclésiastique* contains only one brief account of sexual assault, describing the activities of a militant Catholic group, and the analogy here is that its members are morally as well as politically seditious, emphasizing the link between debauchery and disobedience. 'As for the women and girls, most were raped, the others reserved for marriage to those of their band as they saw fit', and their relatives forced to hand over all their possessions as part of the marriage contract.[67] Generally, the women in the accounts we do have are said to be the victims of soldierly brutality or priestly lust, the latter reinforcing Protestant stereotypes and justifying the targets of their violence. They, thus, underline the immorality of particular individuals: a paedophile priest and a militant who handed over his Huguenot sister to be gang-raped, is compared to the father who murdered his own child. Although it is commonly claimed that rape was not formally or legally recognized as a war crime until after the Second World War, it had been officially condemned since at least the laws of war drawn up in the late Middle Ages, and legal measures

---

[64] E.g. Faurin, *Journal de Faurin*, 46. Cf. Anne Curry, 'The Theory and Practice of Female Immunity in the Medieval West', that sexual violence 'was something the opposition did, never the home side'. I am grateful to Professor Curry for letting me consult this essay prior to publication.

[65] See Davis, 'The Rites of Violence', 77.

[66] For a discussion of this source and a breakdown of its statistics, see J. B. Wood, 'The Impact of the Wars of Religion: A View of France in 1581', *Sixteenth Century Journal*, 15 (1984), 131–68: quotation, 141, on rape figures, 140–1, 157–9.

[67] *Histoire ecclésiastique*, I, 986.

taken to curb its occurrence.[68] In a commission to his judges who were in charge of implementing the royal edicts of pacification, King Charles IX specifically omitted it from a general amnesty for actions committed in the heat of battle, including homicide and pillage, by excluding those who 'had raped a woman' or 'killed a small child or infant'.[69] Even so, its perpetrators were to be punished by their commanders, reinforcing the difficulties of securing justice for such acts.[70] Subsequent legislation reiterated this exemption, including clause eighty-six of the Edict of Nantes, for 'execrable cases . . . as kidnapping and rape of women and girls, arson, murders . . .'.[71] Nevertheless, Nicolas Pithou recounts the story of the attempted rape of a Protestant woman (who is not identified although her husband is) by eight named *harquebusiers* from Troyes in 1568. Two were killed on the spot but, despite being arrested and charged, Pithou claims, the rest were later released without punishment and their accusers imprisoned instead.[72]

Judicial records would no doubt tell us more about actual cases of rape brought before the courts, although the problem with the military dealing with it among themselves would remain. However, it is primarily with the symbolism of literary and memorialist accounts that this essay is most concerned. The evidence for sexual violence in these sources is, on the whole, fairly thin, and likewise only in one Protestant rape narrative is the victim named and the 'beastly' ordeal described.[73] This single account is itself fairly brief, so it will be quoted in full:

> Renée Brulé, wife of René Caillou, was beaten all over her body, and afterwards raped in her husband's presence, by seven brutes (castle guards) one after another. Such a villainous and insolent act would shame the beasts; and nonetheless, despite the complaints made about it, it was not possible to have justice for it. Two days later, a widow living in the suburbs was similarly raped at night in

---

[68] Curry, 'Theory and Practice of Female Immunity', cites Honoré Bonet's *Tree of Battles* and the *Black Book of the Admiralty* in this context, texts dating from the fourteenth and fifteenth centuries; cf Viltart, '*Exploitiez la guerre*', 477.

[69] *Mémoires de Condé*, IV, 500.

[70] Curry, 'Theory and Practice of Female Immunity', confirms this difficulty in implementing justice, whether penance imposed by the Church or penalties applied by secular rulers. See also, Viltart, '*Exploitiez la guerre*', 488–9.

[71] Richard L. Goodbar (ed.), *The Edict of Nantes: Five Essays and a New Translation* (Bloomington, 1998), 57.

[72] Pithou, fos. 338v–41.

[73] At least in the sources which so far I have been able to consult; other accounts may contain similar cases.

her own house (although this time the perpetrators were not identified).[74]

Nevertheless, this is a negligible paragraph of nine lines in a twenty-five-page treatise. The account also contains stories of women stripped and murdered, including a heavily pregnant woman, poor widows, and young girls; a woman shot repeatedly in the breasts; and another spattered by the brains of her dead husband; among which the single account of a rape may seem comparatively unimportant. It is significant that the victim was not safe even with her husband present or in her own home. Indeed, the presence of the husband may be crucial here, as a witness to both his wife's and his own dishonour.[75] In a similar account, by the Calvinist of Millau, a husband attempted to prevent 'seeing himself thus dishonoured and his wife too' in witnessing her rape by Catholic soldiers. Preferring 'to die sooner than see such villainy', he killed one soldier but was murdered by the other two, and his wife subsequently raped.[76]

Conversely, the Catholic priest, Claude Haton, took the opportunity to exploit the wanton reputation of Protestant women when recounting the rape of several notable 'huguenottes' by soldiers near Provins in 1567, despite their attempts to disguise themselves as poor peasants. Seven of the women are identified, six through the naming of their 'cuckolded' husbands, implying that these are more like cases of adultery than of rape. Indeed, despite Haton's acknowledgement that the women were used and abused by the soldiers against their will, and had tried to defend their honour, he shows little sympathy for their plight. Rather he emphasizes their 'charitable' actions and shameless behaviour, 'preserving their lives and ransoms through the effort and employment of their bodies'.[77] One of them was paraded through the streets of Provins, her 'feet, legs and head bare . . . wearing only her chemise and . . . a camisole', and then forced to attend Mass and to renounce her faith. The rest, he observed, did not return to town until the soldiers had moved on, 'no more ashamed than prostitutes who come back from being camp followers'.[78] Finally, to reinforce the point that these women should not be

---

[74] *Remonstrance envoyée au Roy, par la Noblesse de la Religion Réformée du Païs & Conté du Maine, sur les assassinats, pilleries, saccagemens de maisons, seditions, violemens de femmes, & autres excès horrible* (1565), in *Mémoires de Condé*, V, 290.

[75] Cf discussion of this phenomenon in Viltart, '*Exploitiez la guerre*', 487, and that contemporaries claimed that men preferred to see their wives and daughters raped in lieu of a ransom than to lose their own lives, a dubious claim.

[76] Rigal (ed.), *Mémoires d'un calviniste de Millau*, 457–8.

[77] *Mémoires de Claude Haton*, II, 170.

[78] Ibid., 171–2.

considered innocent victims, Haton cites the case of one whose husband had previously caught her in a compromising position with their 'heretic preacher', 'kissing and making love to one another charitably, in a secret place'. As a consequence, the husband was mocked and asked 'which he found more offensive, to have been cuckolded by Catholic soldiers or by his spiritual father'. Unsurprisingly, both sides used such accounts to serve the propaganda purposes of their own cause.

It is useful to remember, when considering such cases as those discussed above, Garthine Walker's assertion that, 'The meaning of rape is historically and culturally specific, and how it is understood depends in part upon a framework of storytelling'.[79] She emphasizes the difficulty of the language used to describe rape, and argues that early modern accounts concentrate on the violent rather than sexual aspect of such acts. This may be instructive to us here, in that the reporting of the violence done to, and the helplessness of, the victims is often the most important feature of the reports. Others have emphasized the lack of a sixteenth-century French term for the crime of rape making its designation problematic, and its legal status ambiguous.[80] Most often in our sources, it is referred to as '*violement*' or '*violation*'. Interestingly, the verb '*violer*', to violate, is also frequently used in the descriptions of the damage being done to the kingdom by the civil war and those who were opposed to peace.[81] The source which accompanies that containing the rape narrative discussed above, and also on the same topic, uses this verb repeatedly in relation to the violation of edicts; of laws human and divine; of good advice and of peace; as well as in an account of an actual rape by a local priest of nine young girls who either died or were subject to medical treatment as a result.[82] Likewise, other contemporaries describe towns and buildings being taken 'by force', 'stripped', 'ravaged', and 'despoiled'.[83] So rapists actual, but much more often figurative, do feature in the sources. Such language is present in other, more recent conflicts too.[84]

---

[79] Garthine Walker, 'Rereading Rape and Sexual Violence in Early Modern England', *Gender and History*, 10 (1998), 5.

[80] Stéphanie Gaudillat-Cautela, 'Questions de mot. Le "viol" au XVIe siècle, un crime contre les femmes?', *Clio: Histoire, femmes et sociétés*, 24 (2006), 59–74.

[81] For a discussion of such metaphors in public discourse during the First World War, see Ruth Harris, 'The "Child of the Barbarian": Rape, Race and Nationalism in France during the First World War', *Past and Present*, 141 (1993), esp. 175.

[82] *Remonstrance envoyée au Roy*, in *Mémoires de Condé*, V, 314.

[83] Cf. description in Viltart, '*Exploitiez la guerre*', 475.

[84] James Mark, 'Remembering Rape: Divided Social Memory and the Red Army in Hungary, 1944–1945', *Past and Present*, 188 (2005), 133–61, esp. 141 on the 'rape of

Interestingly, the absence of rape narratives in the depositions of women in seventeenth-century Ireland has also been noted by several commentators including Mary O'Dowd—'the documented evidence for rape is curiously small'—which suggests that it may be historically contingent, although there are some pictorial depictions of it.[85] In France, too, not only written sources but also printed images have shaped our perceptions of the characteristics of confessional violence in France, principally those of the massacres of Huguenots drawn by Jacques Tortorel and Jean Perrissin.[86] They, too, should be reconsidered in view of how they depict violence against women and for any possible suggestions of sexual assault contained therein.

One of the most familiar scenes is that of the massacre of Vassy, in March 1562. The account in the *Histoire ecclésiastique* cites the death of two or three women and the injury of twenty-four others, whilst forty-two were left widowed with children, and the duchess of Guise had urged that the pregnant be spared.[87] In the engraving women are foregrounded and the target of Catholic assassins, meekly and piously accepting their fate, or protecting their children from the wrath of the soldiery (in a way reminiscent of the biblical massacre of the Innocents), or fleeing the scene in terror; all of which is designed to maximize the pathos of the scene. There is no suggestion of sexual violence or degradation, however. In contrast, the massacre at nearby Sens the following month depicts women stripped and humiliated, and their naked bodies displayed, but again there is no evidence of sexual assault.

In contrast, the massacre at Tours, also in 1562, is more suggestive. Again there is much pathos in the merciless killing and drowning of helpless women and children (Figure 1, keys F, H, & K). They are stripped and humiliated, but there is also a more suggestive positioning of swords indicating sexual

---

the nation'. Clearly we lack the oral testimony on which Mark was able to draw, as well as the contested use of rape narratives in respect to national identity and political ideology.

[85] Mary O'Dowd, 'Women and War in Ireland in the 1640s', in Margaret MacCurtain and Mary O'Dowd (eds), *Women in Early Modern Ireland* (Edinburgh, 1991), 101; see also McAreavey, 'Re(-)Membering Women'.

[86] Philip Benedict, Lawrence M. Bryant, and Kristen B. Neuschel, 'Graphic History: What Readers Knew and Were Taught in the *Quarante Tableaux* of Perrissin and Tortorel', *French Historical Studies*, 28 (2005), 175–229; and esp. Philip Benedict, *Graphic History: The 'Wars, Massacres and Troubles' of Tortorel and Perrissin* (Geneva, 2007).

[87] *Histoire ecclésiastique*, I, 809–11. By contrast, the wife of the seneschal of Agenais was unmoved by 'the cries and lamentations' of the poor women and girls of Azay-le-Rideau 'that she could have easily saved by simply opening the principal door of her house', II, 687.

aggression, against women but also possibly men (keys I & L). The *Histoire ecclésiastique* recounts the episode too, but despite a several-page section on the '*Constance de plusieurs femmes*', all described as virtuous and honourable, including vulnerable teenagers, it makes no suggestion of *sexual* violence per se. However, one young woman is said to have declared to the soldiers trying to convert her (through unspecified threats and even the promise of marriage), 'do with me what you will'.[88] Again the pathos of the fate of small children deprived of their mothers is underlined; so too, the stripping of victims, and that even beasts were appalled at the sight of so many dead bodies on the riverbanks. On the sexual element of the massacre, more suggestive however are the Protestant author Agrippa d'Aubigné's references in his epic poem *Les Tragiques*, which is said to have been influenced by Tortorel and Perrissin's print of the massacre, portraying the events in Tours as the ultimate horrors of the civil war:

> Others {snatched this up}, filled with the hell,
> Overriding pity to **despoil** the beauty,
> Stripping it naked before their plain view,
> Taking pleasure in **soiling** its living whiteness
> To darken with death its colour ingenue.[89]

But even here, despite the language of soiling and despoiling, the contrast is one of purity with wickedness rather than a clear indication that sexual violence actually took place.

If we turn again to the *Histoire ecclésiastique*, we find that it frequently mentions the singling out of local women, as at Tours, deprived of male protection due to absence or death, and we would suspect only one end result: sexual assault. Again there is a suggestive account of events in neighbouring Blois and Mer, where Catholic soldiers 'assembled together many of the townswomen, from which they chose those they liked the look of in order to abuse them villainously, from which several since died of shame'.[90] So again, sexual violence is not explicit, but certainly implicit here. It is important to mention, in contrast, the scene in Richard Verstegan's *Theatre des Cruautez*, a graphic depiction of Protestant violence against Catholics published during the ascendancy of the Catholic League. It mentions the rape of a widow by two soldiers, but the picture of the incident and the accompanying text focuses not on her actual but her symbolic rape with a rod as she is

---

[88] *Histoire ecclésiastique*, II, 695–6.
[89] As quoted in Benedict, *Graphic History*, 183 (taken from Agrippa d'Aubigné, *Les Tragiques*, ed. Frank Lestringant (Paris, 1995), 246–7). My use of bold.
[90] *Histoire ecclésiastique*, II, 679–80.

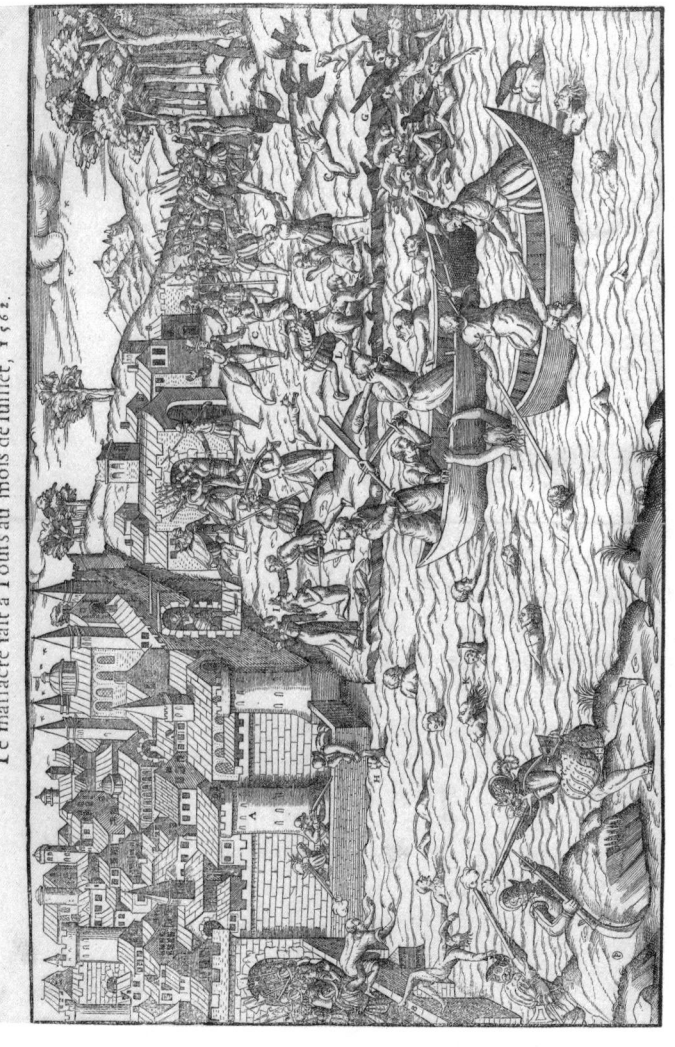

Figure 1. Jean Perrissin and Jacques Tortorel, *The Massacre at Tours, July 1562.* (Bibliothèque Nationale de France, Paris)

subsequently loaded like a cannon with gunpowder and set alight.[91] Here, we are once again dealing with the significance, and vulnerability, of widow status and martyrdom which removes any notion of shame; the woman herself is not identified. According to an earlier account detailing the atrocities of Protestant soldiers at Orléans:

> They had no care, nor regard at all of honestie, shame or chastitie. They stripped an honest mayed stark naked as euer she was borne, in the middes of the streate at Orleans. And when she stood so, openlie among them, ye bawdie ribaudes Sardanapalus souldiours feeled and groped her shamefullye, filthylie, and againste all the lawes of nature, to serche forsooth if she had hidden anie money, aboue the rate of the proclamation, to carie priuilie out of the town about her.[92]

Accompanying a crude woodcut of the scene, in which most of the woman (though clearly naked and being searched) is screened from our view, is a telling verse:

> For shame I both hyde from your eares, and your eyes,
> Howe a mayd was abused in most shamefull wyse.

Once again a veil is drawn over the details of the assault and the identity of the victim.

So what should we make of this reticence in descriptions of sexual violence during the French religious wars? There are several possibilities which suggest themselves as to why so few accounts exist. Whilst the rape of women needs to be carefully extracted from the mass of detail we have of the many atrocities reported to have taken place during the wars, suggestions of assaults on men remain even more elusive. The Calvinist of Millau, having recounted the rape and subsequent death of some women at the hands of Catholic soldiers at Gaillac in 1573, states in a remarkably telling phrase that 'worse still' the soldiers threatened to cut off men's 'shameful parts', by exposing them on a piece of wood sword in hand, unless they were given money. So heinous was 'this inhuman barbarity' seen to be that both Catholics and Protestants,

---

[91] Richard Verstegan, *Theatre des Cruautez des Hereticques de nostre temps* (Antwerp, 1588), 50–1.

[92] Petrus Frarinus, *An oration against the vnlawfull insurrections of the protestantes of our time, vnder pretence to refourme religion Made and pronounced in Latin, in the Schole of Artes at Louaine, the .xiij. of December. Anno. 1565. By Peter Frarin of Andwerp, M. of Arte, and Bacheler of both lawes. And now translated [by John Fowler] into English, with the aduise of the author* (Antwerp, 1566), unpaginated.

'moved, some by pity, others by anger', hunted down the 'perverse' perpetrators.⁹³ This account underlines how rare and shocking such occurrences were in comparison with the incidence of sexual violence against women.

First, we can discount the conclusion that there was just very little rape to report, even though it is generally viewed as a regular weapon of war in order to humiliate and display domination over opponents. Richard Trexler, in particular, outlines the long-established practice in conflicts of the rape of both men and women.⁹⁴ Following Davis's thesis, we could perhaps argue that for the perpetrators sexual congress with their opponents would have been to pollute themselves and to risk perpetuating rather than destroying the next generation of heretics. But this is a quite different concern to that of miscegenation when perpetrated by marginal males. At any rate, sources such as Faurin suggest that rape was in fact an expected and routine part of sixteenth-century French warfare. Rape during wartime is now usually classified as either systematic or opportunistic; both elements might be inferred from the few references we have to its use during the religious wars.

So we might assume that, whilst sexual assault happened, it is rarely mentioned because it was simply too routine to bother with, or perhaps because of early modern prudery. But the sources happily and unrestrainedly describe the disembowelling and mutilation of bodies, and determinedly depict their opponents in the worst possible light. Massive under-reporting of rape is an historical constant of course; between 1540 and 1692, the *parlement* of Paris tried only forty-nine rape cases, which is less than three a decade.⁹⁵ We should remember, however, that we are not dealing with women's own accounts, but chroniclers trying to accuse their opponents of the worst possible atrocities. The rape of virtuous women was a further demonstration of the amoral, inhuman capacity of adversaries, so there was every reason to recount it.

Finally, perhaps since most of the accounts of violence come from Huguenot sources, rapes were not reported in any detail because they did not want to impugn the honour or damage the reputation of their coreligionists by naming the victims. This is the most convincing thesis of those we have. As Ruff puts it, 'rape was a heavy burden of shame for a woman to bear', as indeed it represented the ultimate humiliation for men, explaining at least some of the silence of the sources on sexual violence against them.⁹⁶ There is

---

⁹³ Rigal (ed.), *Mémoires d'un calviniste de Millau*, 262.
⁹⁴ Trexler, *Sex and Conquest*, 13–14, on the rape of women and men as a punishment, an indication of manliness, domination, and shame. On sexual violence against boys during the Burgundian wars see Viltart, '*Exploitiez la guerre*', 487.
⁹⁵ Julius R. Ruff, *Violence in Early Modern Europe, 1500–1800* (Cambridge, 2001), 141.
⁹⁶ Ibid., 143.

no mention of resulting pregnancies in any of the sources looked at, but the possibility may also have required discretion in the interests of both mother and child.[97] The importance of social status is possibly crucial here too, as it is said to have been in Ireland in the 1640s.[98] Yet all women, whether peasant or noble, were vulnerable in the circumstances of war to marauding troops pillaging their property and attacking or killing their menfolk. Although rape was perceived in all circumstances by contemporaries as 'an announcement of enmity', there was most often no opportunity during the religious wars for the usual redress, requiring satisfaction to kin through vengeance, payment or marriage.[99] An exception is the case of the Spanish soldier described by Haton in 1569; despite offering compensation or to marry the girl, the victim and her family refused, and he was hanged.[100] Official suppression might also have been a factor, as in other conflict situations.[101] The crown sought to encourage the faiths to forget and move on from the injuries perpetrated against them during the wars in the interests of peace.[102] Yet, in theory at least, rape was exempt from this prohibition.

Conclusion

The descriptions of the violence perpetrated during the French religious wars remain a rich resource for our understanding of the mores and values of sixteenth-century religious culture and the extremes to which confessional tensions drove those who, in other circumstances, might happily have coexisted alongside one another. This is a vein that should continue to be tapped for the insights it can still reveal, as well as the importance of setting it within its broader cultural and social context. It is not the intention here to detract from the importance of Davis's 'The Rites of Violence' thesis, but historians

[97] Cf. Harris, 'The "Child of the Barbarian"'.
[98] O'Dowd, 'Women and War', 101, on the reluctance to speak and reticence of the deponents, especially if the victim was still alive or of high social standing, as well as the shame of it becoming a matter of public report. Cf. Viltart, '*Exploitiez la guerre*', 488, that Burgundian laws explicitly stated that social status made no difference in the prosecution of rape.
[99] See Stuart Carroll, *Blood and Violence in Early Modern France* (Oxford, 2006), 250–1; Curry, 'Theory and Practice of Female Immunity'.
[100] *Mémoires de Claude Haton*, II, 265–6. Haton considers this unreasonable behaviour by the victim and her family.
[101] E.g. in post-independence India with regard to the rapes which occurred during partition: Brewer, *Peace Processes*, 146.
[102] For more on this issue see Penny Roberts, 'Contested Authority: Peace, Violence and Memory during the French Religious Wars' in R. Pörtner (ed.), *Communities in Conflict: Civil Wars and their Legacies* (Leiden, forthcoming).

have been perhaps too unquestioning about certain aspects of the violence perpetrated during the French religious wars as a result of the reverence in which her analysis is held. It is essential to explore the wider context of confessional tensions: the role of attempts at coexistence and daily experience as well as the occasional dramatic massacre; the nature of the violent acts, and their symbolism beyond that related to religious difference; and the significance of the seeming absence of sexual assault. Although these aspects are not always explicitly described or highlighted in the sources, the clues are there to be found. Furthermore, they can serve to enhance and deepen our understanding of the contemporary experience of the violence perpetrated against both men and women during the religious wars and beyond.

The relationship, and tension, between officially sanctioned acts of violence and justice being taken into the hands of the people, which Davis's thesis did so much to illuminate, is reinforced by such an approach. It identifies both elements of careful observance of the laws of war, and the condemnation of those who failed to honour them, as well as different understandings of the operation of divine law and considerations of common humanity. Equally, it highlights the deliberate defiance of royal directives and legal constraints in the name of the defence of true religion whichever side the actors happened to be on. There is a sense that some felt that different rules applied when it came to the treatment of those who threatened the integrity of their faith, whose beliefs and activities set them apart as deviant and demanded an appropriate response. Thus, the parameters of acceptable behaviour were shifted. Some deployed existing occupations within this changed world of confessional violence, such as executioners and butchers. Others adopted a different role, as judges and officials, than that they normally held. Soldiers, meanwhile, pursued what they saw as the spoils of war. The fate of those they targeted was determined by their gender as much as by their faith. The normal recourse to the rule of law was diverted by myriad other considerations, not least the need to pacify and resolve the causes of tension and conflict. The accounts of religious violence allow us a window into this process which otherwise might have eluded us. Expectations were shaped by the tales of inhumanity and barbarity of the other side, which explains why mutual distrust was so prevalent, peacemaking so protracted, and reconciliation of the faiths so problematic. The rites of violence were thus to shape the challenges of peace.

Massacres during the French Wars of Religion*

Allan A. Tulchin

The Talmud speaks of a pair of inclinations driving human behaviour, the 'good inclination' (*yetzer ha-tov*) and the 'evil inclination' (*yetzer ha-ra*). References to the evil inclination are, however, far more common, to the point where unspecified references to 'the inclination' (*ha-yetzer*) refer exclusively to the evil half of the pair. From the rabbis' point of view, it was easy to understand the inclination to do good. Understanding why people commit evil acts was much more vexing. Scholars living in the aftermath of World War II faced a similar dilemma, and the desire to understand the urge to do evil lies at the heart of most of the scholarly literature on massacres, including Natalie Zemon Davis's 'The Rites of Violence' and other studies of the French Wars of Religion.[1] Davis's article was immensely important and influential, as Stuart Carroll rightly says elsewhere in this volume. I would only add that it is also beautifully written and is stuffed with vividly evocative quotations.

This article will argue, along with Davis, that violence during the Wars of Religion should not be dismissed as merely pathological. However, rather than looking at riots, it will consider massacres, including those committed by organized military forces, a category Davis excluded from consideration—as she emphasizes in her essay about writing 'The Rites of Violence'.[2] My goal was to establish a comparative framework so that I could set my previous research on the Michelade, a massacre in Nîmes in 1567, in context.[3] The

---

* The author would like to thank Anna Leah Berstein Simpson for her research assistance, Bob Kreiser for a helpful reading of the manuscript, and Bill Sewell for bibliographic suggestions.

[1] Natalie Zemon Davis, 'The Rites of Violence', *Past and Present*, 59 (1973), 51–91, at 52. The article was republished as chapter 6 of her *Society and Culture in Early Modern France* (Stanford, 1975), 152–88.

[2] Natalie Zemon Davis, this volume, 8–29.

[3] Allan A. Tulchin, 'The Michelade in Nîmes, 1567', *French Historical Studies*, 29 (2006), 1–35. For other work using a comparative approach, see Philip Benedict,

research for this article began by assembling a list of major massacres (questions of definition are discussed briefly below). As far as I know, no such list has been compiled before.[4] The goal was to examine who committed the massacres, when they occurred, and where. As the list shows, massacres were not equally likely everywhere, nor were they equally spread across the decades from the death of Henry II in 1559 to the Edict of Nantes in 1598. Why? Explaining why massacres were far more likely to occur in some times and places than in others is crucial to understanding why they occurred. Thus my goal here is similar to Mack Holt's, and indeed our conclusions somewhat overlap.[5] I conclude that firstly men in organized military units, not crowds, perpetrated most of the massacres; secondly most violence occurred in the early phases of the wars; and finally, massacres tended to occur in regions where one side was trying to solidify its control, frequently in the context of local coups or seizures of power. These facts suggest that in general, military and political leaders ordered massacres based on rational—usually political—calculations. This does not mean that the decision to commit such violence was made in a calm, deliberative mood. In addition to hatred and fury, the actions of the killers frequently suggest a strong feeling of frustration. The heavily ritualized quality of the violence shows that it was committed in part to send messages to others, but it also shows that those who committed it were in the grip of powerful emotions. Still, as will be seen, people frequently had good reasons for caution or were not under severe threat. Under these circumstances, they were usually able to restrain themselves. People have both

---

'The Saint Bartholomew's Massacres in the Provinces', *Historical Journal*, 21 (1978), 205–25; Judith Pollmann, 'Countering the Reformation in France and the Netherlands: Clerical Leadership and Catholic Violence 1560–1585', *Past and Present*, 190 (2006), 83–120.

[4] The beginnings of a list can be found in G. Baum and E. Cunitz (eds), *Histoire ecclésiastique des églises réformées au royaume de France*, 3 vols (Paris, 1882–9), III, lix. There is also a series of maps showing sieges, battles, and 'other actions' (including massacres) in Fernand Braudel, *The Perspective of the World*, vol. 3 of *Civilization and Capitalism, 15th–18th Centuries* (New York, 1984), 326–7. I have compiled my list from various sources, of which the most useful was Denis Crouzet, *Les Guerriers de Dieu: La violence au temps des troubles de religion, vers 1525–vers 1610*, 2 vols (Paris, 1990). Some of my conclusions are similar to those of David El Kenz, in 'Les massacres au temps des guerres de Religion', *Encyclopédie en ligne des violences de masse*, http://www.massviolence.org/Les-massacres-au-temps-des-guerres-de-Religion [accessed 2 February 2010]. Philippe Dollinger and Philippe Wolff, *Bibliographie d'histoire des villes de France* (Paris, 1967), has also been invaluable.

[5] Mack P. Holt, this volume, 52–74.

violent and altruistic inclinations, and people can think logically even in extreme circumstances.

Beyond these conclusions, it seemed worthwhile to consider what underlying patterns were operative. One potential source of inspiration is the work of social scientists. Since World War II, deaths from wars between states have declined. Sadly, civil conflicts have multiplied. As a result, there is a considerable body of social-scientific theory on the subject, and much of it is clearly relevant to historians.

The Kalyvas model

Among recent social-science studies of civil war, Stathis N. Kalyvas, *The Logic of Violence in Civil War* has been particularly influential, and provides the most helpful suggestions for understanding the massacres of the Wars of Religion.[6] It does not fit the circumstances perfectly, of course. Although Kalyvas cites the literature on the Wars of Religion, including 'The Rites of Violence' and Denis Crouzet's *Les Guerriers de Dieu*, he did not develop his theory with a focus on early modern Europe. Still, Kalyvas's theory is sufficiently useful that it is worthwhile to outline his approach briefly. Kalyvas emphasizes the weaknesses of coarse-grained analysis, and in particular he questions the usefulness of data sets which attempt to categorize civil conflicts across the world. Instead, building his approach from the secondary literature, he applies his model to a very small region of Greece, sixty-one villages in the eastern Peloponnese, during the Greek civil war of the mid-twentieth century. He interviewed over 200 participants, and conducted very substantial archival research. This article discusses a much wider area over a considerably longer time period, and lacks the archival detail, let alone the rich oral material, that Kalyvas was able to obtain. By Kalyvas's standards, therefore, it is a rather broad-brush treatment, and like the work of Judith Pollmann, this article is an overview, with the advantages and disadvantages that a broad scope entails. Indeed the evidence assembled here is insufficient for the kind of sophisticated quantitative testing that Kalyvas undertakes. The conclusions of this article are therefore proffered as provocative suggestions that will need further testing and refinement in future research.

Kalyvas first proposes a distinction between selective and indiscriminate violence. Both, he argues, are usually perpetrated by military men, whether

---

[6] Stathis N. Kalyvas, *The Logic of Violence in Civil War* (Cambridge, 2006). Kalyvas also provides an exhaustive bibliography, including works by historians. I found another major work on this topic, Michael Mann, *The Dark Side of Democracy: Explaining Ethnic Cleansing* (Cambridge, 2005), to be less relevant, and to have a weaker grasp of the historical literature. But its social-science bibliography is also excellent.

soldiers or guerrillas, rather than by civilians. Selective violence, for Kalyvas, is violence directed against known opponents, while indiscriminate violence is collective punishment directed at the community where an incident occurred. As an example, consider the case of Nazi reprisals after attacks on their men. Kalyvas discovered numerous cases where villagers who actively opposed the Nazi occupiers of Greece fled to the mountains after an incident, so that only neutrals or even those prepared to cooperate with the occupation government were left in a village by the time the Nazis imposed collective punishment. Indiscriminate violence was thus sometimes less likely to punish opponents than even purely random punishment. By contrast, Kalyvas defines violence as selective when the perpetrators pick their victims by 'a name list, the visible use of an informer, an arrest following an identity check, or arrests associated with interrogations'.[7]

Selective violence is easy to understand: regimes punish people who oppose them, just as we punish criminals, to deter them and others from committing similar acts in the future. However, even indiscriminate violence can have a deterrent effect, since people may well hesitate to commit acts against a regime when they know that their friends and relatives will suffer for their acts, and communities may be more willing to act against their neighbours, even close relatives, if they know that the community as a whole may suffer. Under certain circumstances, massacres are perfectly logical. It is worth emphasizing, as Kalyvas has done in a recent article, that modern studies have shown that even ethnic identity is constructed, and thus fluid, rather than fixed or innate. For a variety of social, political, and ideological reasons, people shift their allegiances, and therefore various political actors can be tempted to use force to encourage people to shift their allegiances in the desired direction.[8]

Kalyvas limits his theory's 'scope conditions' to circumstances where the regime intends to force people to cooperate, as opposed to cases when a regime chooses a policy of genocide or extermination. Nazi Germany's treatment of Jews and Roma can thus be distinguished from its treatment of Greeks, for example. The Nazis ordered mass killings of Greeks, but they did so to induce compliance. They did not intend to eliminate the Greeks as a group. Kalyvas suggests that an empirical test of whether violence is 'eliminationist' or not is whether opponents have the opportunity to surrender.[9]

---

[7] Kalyvas, *Logic of Violence*, 410.
[8] Stathis N. Kalyvas, 'Ethnic Defection in Civil War' *Comparative Political Studies* 41 (2008), 1043–68. See also the extensive literature cited there.
[9] Kalyvas, *Logic of Violence*, 23–8, esp. 26.

Kalyvas concludes that in fact perpetrators commonly discover that indiscriminate violence is counter-productive. Such violence nonetheless occurs. (Assessing how much violence during civil wars is indiscriminate is, however, sometimes difficult. Frequently evidence is lacking and surviving relatives usually have good reason to insist that the dead 'had nothing to do with it'.) One side may commit indiscriminate violence because it lacks the information necessary to commit selective violence. A related way to look at indiscriminate violence is to see it as a 'quick and dirty' method, since developing sources of information to attack leading opponents using approved, reliable means can be time-consuming and expensive, especially for weak states. Consequently, such methods may be particularly tempting in cases where the central state breaks down and two opposing sides contend in a civil war to replace it. The main danger of indiscriminate violence is that it will alienate potential supporters, who will then turn to the other side. This danger is lessened when the opposing side is weak. In the early stages of a conflict, the incumbent party, over-estimating its dominance, may therefore be tempted to use indiscriminate violence. As the struggle drags on, however, it becomes clear that the insurgents are a force to be reckoned with, and the perceived risks of perpetrating massacre start to outweigh the likely benefits. Thus indiscriminate violence will tend to be perpetrated in the early stages of a conflict.[10]

The same set of issues can have effects which are visible geographically. Kalyvas proposes dividing the territory under contention in a civil war into five zones, depending on the rough degree of control held by each party to the conflict. The regions where the incumbent or the insurgent party has total control he labels 1 and 5 respectively, those where one side has predominant but not absolute control he labels 2 and 4, and those areas where control is approximately equal he labels zone 3. This article will refer to these zones as follows: Zone 1 = Catholic core regions, Zone 2 = Catholics predominant, Zone 3 = neutral, Zone 4 = Protestants predominant, and Zone 5 = Protestant core regions. Kalyvas suggests that indiscriminate violence tends to occur during raids into territory where the perpetrators have few

[10] This paragraph largely summarizes Kalyvas, *Logic of Violence*, ch. 6. A few lines from the conclusion to this chapter (p. 171) seem particularly pertinent: '[The] persistent use of indiscriminate violence points to political actors who are fundamentally weak: this is the case with civil wars in failed states ('symmetric nonconventional wars'), where high levels of indiscriminate violence emerge because no actor has the capacity to set up the sort of administrative infrastructure required by selective violence. In this perspective, the subset of ethnic civil conflicts that display high levels of eliminationist violence could be endogenous to state failure'.

supporters. Since raiders have scant knowledge of the population and no hope or intention of holding the territory for long, they have no incentive to ingratiate themselves with the local population by exercising restraint. Thus Catholics should commit indiscriminate violence during raids in Protestant core regions, while Protestants should commit it during raids in Catholic core regions. Indiscriminate violence may still be irrational, since it serves no useful purpose, but the theory does explain why rational calculations will not restrain the inevitable hatreds and frustrations that build up under wartime conditions.

Kalyvas then goes on to consider the case of selective violence. The theory proposes that in controlled zones selective violence committed by the side in control is unnecessary, since any remaining opponents of the rulers of the area will be too cowed to commit many antagonistic acts. Neutral zones are the eye of the storm. In neutral zones it is extremely difficult for either side to commit selective violence, since potential killers are immediately exposed to retribution from the other side, and thus reluctant to act. Instead, most selective violence will occur in predominant zones. Such violence is particularly likely just after the territory switches from a neutral area into one predominantly controlled by one side. That faction will immediately try to consolidate its control and turn it into a core region by removing its chief opponents.[11] Of course, it is frequently quite difficult to determine the degree of control exercised by each side at a particular time, which is why Kalyvas emphasizes the need for fine-grained, micro-analysis.

What constitutes a massacre?

As noted above, the list (Table 1) consists of 'major' massacres. This restriction is necessary since it is clearly impossible to include every non-combat death in the Wars of Religion. Following Kalyvas, and admitting that any choice is somewhat arbitrary, this article defines 'major' massacres as those events where it appears that at least ten people died, although smaller events are discussed in the text when appropriate.[12] It should be noted that sixteenth-century writers sometimes use the term 'massacre' even when the number of deaths involved was very small. For example, Jean Crespin, in his standard French Protestant martyrology, refers to the 'massacre' of Marsillargues in 1562, in which initially one person was killed, and seven more three days later. (To complicate matters, Baum and Cunitz's edition of

---

[11] Kalyvas, *Logic of Violence*, ch. 7.

[12] Stathis N. Kalyvas, 'Aspects méthodologiques de la recherche sur les massacres: le cas de la Guerre Civile grecque', *Revue Internationale de Politique Comparée*, 8 (2001), 23–42, at 26.

Table 1. Table of massacres during the French Wars of Religion

Year	Month	Place	Perpetrators	Sources
1561	November	Cahors	Catholic	Blaise de Monluc, *Commentaires*, ed. A. de Ruble, 5 vols (Paris, 1864–72), II, 343fn.; Guillaume de La Croix, *Histoire des évêques de Cahors*, trans. L. Ayma, 2 vols (Cahors, 1878–9), I, 3565–6.
1561	November	Grenade	Catholic	G. Baum and E. Cunitz (eds), *Histoire ecclésiastique des églises réformées au royaume de France*, 3 vols (Paris, 1882–9), I, 911.
1561	December	Carcassonne	Catholic	Ibid, I, 963–5.
1562	March	Castelnaudary	Catholic	Claude Devic and Joseph Vaissete, *Histoire Générale de Languedoc*, 15 vols (Toulouse, 1872–92), XI, 378.
1562	March	Limoux	Both	Jacques-Auguste de Thou, *Histoire universelle*, 16 vols (London, 1734), IV, 391.
1562	March	Sens	Catholic	Baum and Cunitz (eds), *Histoire ecclésiastique*, II, 486–7.
1562	March	Vassy	Catholic	Silvia Castro Shannon, 'The Political Activity of François de Lorraine, Duc de Guise (1559–1562). From Military Hero to Catholic Leader', unpublished Ph.D. dissertation, Boston University (1988), 344–82.
1562	April	Caylus	Protestant	Denis Crouzet, *Les Guerriers de Dieu: La violence au temps des troubles de religion, vers 1525–vers 1610*, 2 vols (Paris, 1990), I, 609.
1562	May	Gaillac	Catholic	Devic and Vaissete, *Histoire Générale de Languedoc*, XI, 398.
1562	June	Orange	Catholic	Eugène Arnaud, *Histoire des protestants de Provence du Comtat Venaissin et de la principauté d'Orange*, 2 vols (Paris, 1884), II, 182–92.
1562	July	Morras	Protestant	Ibid, II, 215.
1562	July	Tours	Catholic	Baum and Cunitz (eds), *Histoire ecclésiastique*, II, 681, 694.
1562	August	Amiens	Catholic	Olivia Carpi, *Une République imaginaire: Amiens pendant les troubles de religion (1559–1597)* (Paris, 2005), 80.
1562	August	Bar-Sur-Seine	Catholic	Jacky Provence, 'Bar-Sur-Seine dans la tourmente des guerres de religion', http://pagesperso-orange.fr/patrimoine.barsequanais/301-conf-26-11-98.htm [accessed 25 January 2010].
1562	August	Lauzerte	Protestant	Baum and Cunitz (eds), *Histoire ecclésiastique*, II, 232.

(continued)

Table 1. Continued

Year	Month	Place	Perpetrators	Sources
1562	September	Macon	Protestant	Crouzet, *Les Guerriers de Dieu*, I, 609.
1562	September	Saint Gilles	Protestant	Léon Ménard, *Histoire Civile, Ecclésiastique et Littéraire de la ville de Nîmes*, 7 vols (Paris, 1750–6), IV, 364.
1562	September	Vire	Catholic	Baum and Cunitz (eds), *Histoire ecclésiastique*, II, 844–5.
1562	November	Pithiviers	Protestant	Ibid., II, 234–5.
1562	December	Carcassonne	Catholic	Ibid., I, 963–5.
1563	March	Pamiers	Protestant	Jules de Lahondès, *Annales de Pamiers*, 2 vols (Toulouse, 1882–4), II, 14–15.
1566	June	Pamiers	Protestant	Ibid., II, 22–3.
1567	?	Caraman	Protestant	J. L. Rigal (ed.), *Mémoires d'un calviniste de Millau* (Rodez, 1911), 207–9.
1567	September	Nîmes	Protestant	Allan A. Tulchin, 'The Michelade in Nîmes, 1567', *French Historical Studies*, 29 (2006), 1–35.
1567	October	Tortefontaine (Abbaye de Dommartin)	Protestant	A. Rohault, 'Le livre de Raison d'un Maieur d'Abbeville', ed. A. Ledieu, *Memoires de la societe d'emulation d'Abbeville*, 19 (1897), 133–236, at 206–7, cited in Crouzet, *Guerriers de dieu*, I, 693.
1567	November	Montelimar	Protestant	Alphonse, Baron de Coston, *Histoire de Montélimar*, 3 vols (Montelimar, 1883), II, 282–8.
1568	January	La Rochelle	Protestant	Kevin C. Robbins. *City on the Ocean Sea, La Rochelle, 1530–1650* (Leiden, 1997), 201–4.
1568	April	Auxerre	Catholic	Olivier Chardon, *Histoire de la ville d'Auxerre*, 2 vols (Auxerre, 1834–5), I, 330–3.
1569	December	Saumur	Catholic	De Thou, *Histoire universelle*, V, 550; James Westfall Thompson, *The Wars of Religion in France, 1559–1576* (Chicago, 1909), 372.
1569	August	Orléans	Catholic	D. Lottin, *Recherches historiques sur la ville d'Orléans*, 8 vols (Orléans, 1836–45), I, 476–7.
1567	January	Caraman	Protestant	J. L. Rigal (ed.), *Mémoires d'un calviniste de Millau* (Rodez, 1911), 207–9.
1571	November	Nîmes	Protestant	Ménard, *Histoire de Nîmes*, V, 50–5.
1572	February	Orange	Catholic	Arnaud, *Histoire des protestants de Provence*, II, 212–21.
1572	August	Paris	Catholic	Arlette Jouanna, *La Saint-Barthélemy: Les mystères d'un crime d'état, 24 août 1572* (Paris, 2007).

(continued)

Table 1. Continued

Year	Month	Place	Perpetrators	Sources
1572	August	Angers	Catholic	Philip Benedict, 'The Saint Bartholomew's Massacres in the Provinces', *Historical Journal*, 21 (1978), 205–25. See also Jouanna, *La Saint-Barthélemy*, 190–201.
1572	August	Bourges	Catholic	Ibid.
1572	August	La Charité	Catholic	Ibid.
1572	August	Lyon	Catholic	Ibid.
1572	August	Saumur	Catholic	Ibid.
1572	September	Limoges	Catholic	Benedict, 'The Saint Bartholomew's Massacres in the Provinces'.
1572	September	Orléans	Catholic	Ibid.
1572	September	Meaux	Catholic	Ibid.
1572	September	Rouen	Catholic	Ibid.
1572	September	Troyes	Catholic	Ibid. See also Penny Roberts, *A City in Conflict: Troyes During the French Wars of Religion* (Manchester, 1996), 142–62.
1572	October	Albi	Catholic	E. Jolibois, 'La Saint Barthélemy à Albi', *Revue . . . du Tarn*, 2 (1877), 89–91.
1572	October	Bordeaux	Catholic	Benedict, 'The Saint Bartholomew's Massacres in the Provinces'. See also Jouanna, *La Saint-Barthélemy* 190–201.
1572	October	Gaillac	Catholic	Benedict, 'The Saint Bartholomew's Massacres in the Provinces'.
1572	October	Toulouse	Catholic	Ibid.
1574	July	Aups	Protestant	Gustave Lambert, *Histoire des guerres de religion en Provence*, 2 vols (Toulon, 1870), I, 286.
1575	October	Issoire	Protestant	J. B. Bouillet (ed.), *Annales de la ville d'Issoire* (Clermont-Ferrand, 1848), 101–4.
1579	December	Mende	Protestant	Gustave de Burdin, *Documents historiques sur la province de Gévaudan*, 2 vols (Toulouse, 1847), I, 98–107.
1581	June	Requista	Catholic	Rigal (ed.), *Mémoires d'un calviniste de Millau*, 457.
1595	August	La Chataigneraie	Catholic	Auguste-François Lièvre, *Histoire des protestants et des églises réformées du Poitou*, 3 vols (Paris, 1856–60), I, 245–50.

the *Histoire ecclésiastique* suggests that the 'poor man' killed the first day was from Marsillargues but the killings actually occurred in Sisteron).[13] Of course, some guesswork is involved here: many of the sources do not indicate the number of deaths, while others give wildly exaggerated ones.

This article, like 'The Rites of Violence', is limited to 'religious' massacres, that is, massacres where religion seems to have been the primary motivation. Thus, massacres provoked by private vendettas or other (e.g. economic) grievances are generally excluded. Of course, sometimes motives are mixed: in Carcassonne, for example, the riots of 1561 cannot be called exclusively religious, although religious differences were part of the story. Only massacres where religious motives were clearly minor, such as in the Carnival in Romans, are excluded.[14] In the social-scientific literature and to some extent in popular parlance, 'massacre' also implies that the victims were civilians. By that standard, the killing of sixty Protestant soldiers at Limoux in 1562 after they had surrendered might not count as a massacre. Such events have nonetheless been included because it seems likely that people found it easier to justify breaking faith with enemy forces because of their religious differences. By contrast, events were excluded if the deaths occurred during armed conflict, such as the Catholic soldiers who were butchered during the Protestant takeover of Montélimar in 1587. In this case, most Catholics probably died with weapons in their hands.[15]

Personnel

Most massacres during the Wars of Religion were committed by the military. Some of the men who committed massacres during the Wars of Religion were soldiers, while others were members of civic or other militias. (Stuart Carroll calls the latter paramilitaries, reasonably enough). Consider the example of the Saint Bartholomew's massacre in Paris and its provincial sequels. The civic militia was responsible for the massacre in Paris, and at least three

---

[13] *Histoire ecclésiastique*, I, 983, but see the editorial notation in the index, III, 724. Davis, 'The Rites of Violence', 63, states that the massacre occurred in Marsillargues, but I find Baum and Cunitz's interpretation reasonable, since Marsillargues was heavily Protestant—a Catholic riot there seems implausible, and the text seems to read this way. However, Jean Crespin, *Histoire des martyrs*, 3 vols (Toulouse, 1883–9) III, 213 does not mention Sisteron.

[14] For Carcassonne, see *Histoire ecclésiastique*, I, 963–5. For Romans, see Emmanuel Le Roy Ladurie, *Carnival in Romans* (New York, 1979).

[15] For Limoux, see Jacques-Auguste de Thou, *Histoire universelle*, 16 vols (London, 1734), IV, 391. For Montélimar, see Eugène Arnaud, *Histoire des protestants du Dauphiné*, 3 vols (Paris, 1875–6), I, 441–8.

quarters of the dozen subsequent provincial massacres studied by Philip Benedict were committed under military auspices. Soldiers committed five—in Angers, Bordeaux, La Charité, Saumur, and Troyes. In Gaillac, Captain Mons, the local Catholic military commander, used his troops to imprison the Protestants, then his soldiers escorted the killers into the prison. Civic militias committed three more, in Bourges, Lyon, and Orléans. In Toulouse, a private army under the patronage of the Delpech, an important *parlementaire* family, appears to have been responsible.[16] Likewise, Catholic troops from Troyes massacred an estimated 300 people at Bar-sur-Seine on 24 August 1562, after they retook the château from the Protestants. The high death toll in a small place, if true, substantiates the idea that soldiers were more prone to perpetrate indiscriminate violence.[17]

Massacres in the Wars of Religion thus confirm Kalyvas's conclusion that massacres are usually organized by soldiers or guerrillas. This conclusion is not particularly surprising: the military usually has far more arms at its disposal than civilians do. However, the military has an advantage even more important than weaponry, namely organization. In that sense a massacre is quite unlike a riot: rioters may frequently be violent, but riotous crowds are not efficient at making decisions. Nonetheless, much of the literature on violence during the Wars of Religion conflates riots and massacres, and sixteenth-century conditions provide some justification for analysing the two together. The urban bourgeoisie frequently served in municipal militias, and sixteenth-century soldiers were not trained or disciplined to modern military standards. However, scholars should be wary of believing the lurid reports, which stress the chaotic barbarity even of incidents which were quite ruthlessly organized. To take a modern example, in the Rwanda genocide initial reports suggested that a popular explosion was behind the massacres. Recent research, using autopsy information, has shown that victims of

---

[16] For Paris, see Jouanna, *La Saint-Barthélemy*, 174–5. For Bourges, Bordeaux, Saumur, Angers, La Charité, and Troyes, see Benedict, 'The Saint Bartholomew's Massacres', 216, 221 (fn. 49), 222. For Lyon and Toulouse, see Janine Garrisson-Estèbe, *Toscin pour un massacre* (Paris, 1968), 149, 153. For Orléans, see Lottin, *Recherches historiques sur Orléans*, II, 2. For Gaillac, see Elie-A. Rossignol, *Monographies communales: Etude historique, statistique et monumentale du département du Tarn* (Toulouse, 1864–5), II, 158. The Gaillac case illustrates that some massacres are hard to classify as uniquely civilian or military. The Sens massacre of 1561, as Carroll's contribution to this volume details, provides another example of this: both civilians and the local militia appear to be deeply involved.

[17] Bibliothèque nationale de France, Ms. Français 5995 fo. 229^v, cited in Jacky Provence, 'Bar-Sur-Seine dans la tourmente des guerres de religion', http://pagesperso-orange.fr/patrimoine.barsequanais/301-conf-26-11-98.htm [accessed 25 January 2010].

large-scale massacres were much more likely to be killed with guns, rather than machetes, which suggests that the military and paramilitary forces bore overwhelming responsibility for these events.[18] When massacres are separated out from riots for analysis, the role of the military becomes clear.

Although the military was generally responsible for massacres when victims had to be rounded up, civilian mobs were capable of killing groups of their opponents who had incautiously gathered together. On Sunday, 13 December 1561, for example, a Catholic mob in Cahors surrounded a group of Protestants, who had gathered in a house near a Catholic church for their services. Some members of the crowd then set fire to the building.[19] But the Catholic mob was 'ready-made'—since its members had assembled for Mass—and the Protestant victims right at hand. Little organization was required, and arson is an easy way to kill large numbers of people under the right circumstances. Even if only a few of the Catholics in the mob had intended to murder the Protestants, within minutes the Protestants were doomed.

In some cases, there is evidence that organizers assembled a group to commit a massacre, such as in Castelnaudary, where Protestant reports suggest that canons of the collegiate church of Saint-Michel assembled local toughs, who gathered the mob.[20] Mobs of ordinary citizens were more prone to loot than to murder, as they did in Auxerre in 1561, for example. The few deaths in Auxerre on this occasion contrasts sharply with the far larger massacre that occurred in Auxerre the following year, when Catholic troops seized the town. On this latter occasion, contemporary Protestant reports suggest over a hundred people were killed.[21] Even in the 1562 massacre in Gaillac, where Catholic sources report that a *laboureur*, a yeoman farmer, was in charge, he had help from a detachment of troops sent by Cardinal Strozzi, the bishop of Albi.[22]

---

[18] Philip Verwimp, 'Machetes and Firearms: The Organization of Massacres in Rwanda', *Journal of Peace Research*, 33 (2006), 5–22; Gérard Prunier, *The Rwanda Crisis: History of a Genocide* (New York, 1995). Readers will note that I concur with Penny Roberts' concerns, expressed in her contribution to this volume, about the historicity of some contemporary accounts.

[19] Blaise de Monluc, *Commentaires* ed. A. de Ruble, 5 vols (Paris, 1864–72), II, 343fn.

[20] Claude Devic and Joseph Vaissete, *Histoire Générale de Languedoc*, 15 vols (Toulouse, 1872–92), XI, 378.

[21] For the first incident, see *Histoire ecclésiastique*, I, 852–3. For the second, see Olivier Jacques Chardon, *Histoire de la ville d'Auxerre*, 2 vols (Auxerre, 1834–5), I, 330–3.

[22] For Gaillac, see Devic and Vaissete, *Histoire générale de Languedoc*, XI, 398.

Determining who committed the massacres is usually much easier than determining who ordered them. Those in charge had strong incentives to conceal their responsibility. Some historians have argued that massacres occurred because of the excesses of troops, despite their commanders' wishes. Of course, even today, many military and guerrilla organizations are quite decentralized. In some cases it seems likely that troops committed outrages without having been directed to do so by their commanders. Consider the case of Beaugency, where the Prince of Condé, heading to the relief of Orléans, asked permission to pass through the town. The Catholic governor agreed, but lifted the drawbridge after only half the army had crossed. The remaining troops pillaged the countryside in the immediate vicinity in revenge.[23] Since the troops were reportedly angered because they had been separated from their commander, it seems likely that their acts were committed at their own initiative. However, it is unclear whether any deaths occurred on this occasion. In 1570, by contrast, when Protestant troops went on a similar rampage in Caraman, about thirty kilometres east of Toulouse, the sources indicate that their commanders ordered them to kill priests exclusively, and the sources are also much clearer about the number of deaths.[24]

Since the military committed most of the massacres it is a fair assumption (in the absence of direct evidence to the contrary) that commanders ordered most massacres committed by their men. Other accounts have too often laboured to argue the contrary, for example in analysing the massacre of Vassy in 1562. Vassy is particularly important since it is generally considered to be the event that set off the Wars of Religion. After the massacre, Protestants argued that François, Duke of Guise was a bloodthirsty killer and had planned the massacre. Jacques-Auguste de Thou (1553-1617), the greatest early historian of the period, argued instead that the Duke's men had committed the attack without consulting him:

> While the Duke [of Guise] was stopped, a portion of his men, moved by hate or the desire to pillage, some of them impelled just by curiosity to see a new spectacle, seized the initiative. They began by outraging and verbally mistreating those assembled there [in the barn], calling them several times dogs and rebels against God and the King. The Protestants responded in kind; a hail of stones,

---

[23] For Beaugency, see Lottin, *Recherches historiques sur la ville d'Orléans*, I, 462.

[24] I give the modern spelling for Caraman—the town is called Carmaing in the source. J. L. Rigal (ed.), *Mémoires d'un calviniste de Millau* (Rodez, 1911), 207–9, cited in Crouzet, *Les Guerriers de Dieu*, I, 624.

thrown by the valets of the Duke and some of the Lords who were with him, soon followed the insults. At the same time they dismounted from their horses, and broke the doors of the place, which the Protestants had closed. . . they attacked these poor unfortunates, arms at the ready, and smashed and overturned everything they found.[25]

De Thou, a moderate Catholic, had family connections in the region, and his account has won some acceptance from many modern historians, who also tend to avoid suggesting that Guise ordered the shooting.[26] The massacre was clearly impromptu, since Guise brought only a few men with him. However, Guise himself stated that he was in charge. He explained, in a well-known contemporary letter, that the lordship of the area belonged to his niece Mary, Queen of Scots, and she had entrusted him with its supervision while she was away. Once he was in the neighbourhood, it was impossible for him not to take notice of the Protestants' behaviour, and therefore 'I sent to them two or three of my gentlemen, to indicate the desire that I had to speak to them, following [my men] closely'. They responded by attacking his men, and attempted to make for the door of a nearby building where they had stored a supply of guns. 'However', he wrote, 'their effort could not be otherwise, that I went with my small body of men to control the door. But it could not be otherwise, for which I have great regret, that twenty-five or thirty people died,

---

[25] 'Dans le tems que le Duc étoit arrêté, une partie de ses gens, animés par la haine ou par l'avidité de piller, quelques-uns poussés par la seule curiosité de voir un spectacle nouveau, prirent les devants. Ils commencèrent par outrager & maltraiter de paroles ceux qu'ils trouvèrent assemblés, les traitant plusieurs fois de chiens, & de rebelles à Dieu & au Roi. Les Protestants rendirent injures pour injures ; une grêle de pierres jettées par les valets du Duc & par ceux des Seigneurs qui étoient avec lui, suivit bien-tôt les invectives. En même tems ils descendirent de cheval, ils briserent les portes du lieu que les Protestants avoient fermées, (c'étoit une valle grange;) ils fondirent les armes à la main fur ces malheureux; ils frappèrent & renverserent tout ce qui se rencontra'. De Thou, *Histoire universelle*, IV, 168.

[26] See, e.g., Arlette Jouanna, *Histoire et dictionnaire des guerres de religion* (Paris, 1998), 110, who writes 'les catholiques, furieux, donnent l'assaut'. She follows Silvia Castro Shannon, 'The Political Activity of François de Lorraine, Duc de Guise (1559–1562). From Military Hero to Catholic Leader', unpublished Ph.D. thesis, Boston University (1988), 344–82. Mack P. Holt, *The French Wars of Religion, 1562–1629* (Cambridge, 1995), 48–9, writes 'the first shots were fired by troops of the duke of Guise, as he encountered a group of unarmed Protestants worshipping inside the town of Wassy'. For a different account, which emphasizes that Guise ordered the firing, see Stuart Carroll, *Martyrs and Murderers: The Guise Family and the Making of Europe* (Oxford, 2009), 12–19, esp. 17–18.

and a larger number were wounded'.[27] Guise's own account shows that he was present and ordered his men to prevent the Protestants from leaving the building. He was compelled to order the use of force to protect himself and his men, to prevent the Protestants from getting to their weapons, and to restore order.

In order to conclude with de Thou that Guise's soldiers went off and provoked the incident on their own, one must decide that Guise lied when he said that he ordered his men to go to the barn. Perhaps he felt that to admit that he did not have full control of his troops dishonoured him as a commander. But the simplest explanation is that Guise's account is largely true, except for one detail—namely, the claim that the other side started it by attacking his emissaries. This interpretation is further strengthened by the observation that, although Guise need not have planned the attack long in advance, his decision did have immediate positive consequences for him, since he entered Paris a hero, the idol of the dominant, Catholic party. Vassy also forced the crown to stop temporizing and choose a side—his side. Although Guise probably did not plan to kill the Protestants of Vassy ahead of time, that does not mean that in the moment he could not calculate the political consequences, and decide the result was likely to be in his favour.

Time and place

A simple graph of massacres per year (Figure 1) shows that more massacres were committed in 1562, at the outset of the Wars of Religion, than in any other single year. Catholics committed the majority of these. In some cases, such as at Sens, Protestant sources suggest that Catholic authorities organized massacres to prevent the implementation of the Edict of January, which granted substantial rights of worship to Protestants.[28] A second, smaller peak occurred in 1567, at the beginning of the Second War of Religion. Protestants were exclusively responsible for the 1567 massacres, which were largely linked to the Protestant rising of that year. The third peak in 1572, at the time of Saint Bartholomew's and its provincial sequels, stands out not

---

[27] 'J'envoiay devers eulx deux ou trois de mes gentilzhommes pour leur signiffier le désir que j'avois de parler à eulx, les suivans de bien près', and 'Néantmoins ledict effort ne peut estre si grand que je ne vinsse avec ma petite troupe à estre maistre de leurdicte porte; mais ce ne peut estre (dont j'ay un merveilleux regret) que de l'autre part il n'en soit demeuré vingt-cinq ou trente de tuez, et plus grand nombre de blessez'. 'Correspondence de François de Lorraine, Duc de Guise, avec Christophe Duc de Württemberg', *Bulletin de la Société de l'Histoire du Protestantisme Français* 24 (1875), 209–21, quotations 214–15.

[28] *Histoire ecclésiastique*, II, 486–7.

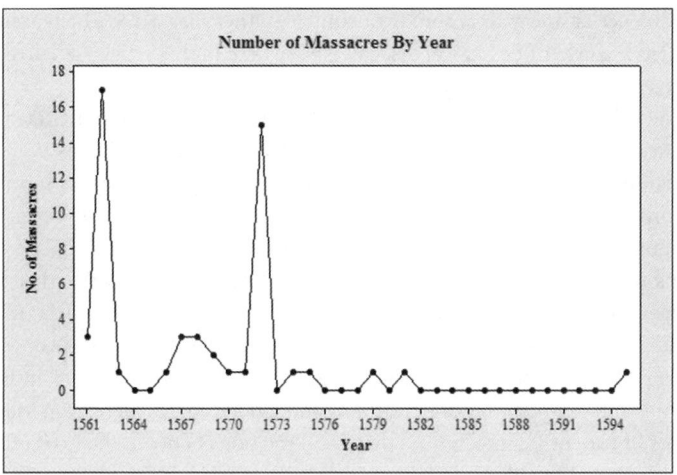

Figure 1.

only because of the number of massacres but also because it constitutes a clear reversal of the previous trend. Denis Crouzet has also noted the decline in violence after 1572, and argues that it represents a growing belief that massacres were ineffective.[29]

When one looks at the timing of specific outbreaks, it becomes immediately evident that many massacres were part and parcel of attempts by one side or the other to seize power. For example, in the massacre at Saint-Gilles (about twenty kilometres south of Nîmes) on 27 September 1562, Catholic forces from Arles had captured Saint-Gilles, a heavily Protestant town, two days earlier. The Protestants of Nîmes could not let a town so near to them remain in enemy hands, and immediately despatched forces to retake Saint-Gilles. They quickly retook the town and destroyed the retreating Catholic forces, who were caught along the banks of the Rhône. A contemporary Catholic account states that the Protestant army pillaged the houses of Saint-Gilles's remaining Catholics, seized all the priests they could find, and the children of the church choir, killed them, and dumped their bodies down a well. Protestants commemorated this event thereafter with psalm-singing.[30] Protestant tactics on this occasion seem to conform to Kalyvas's description

---

[29] Crouzet, *Les Guerriers de Dieu*, II, 145.
[30] Ménard, *Histoire de Nîmes*, IV, 362–4.

of violence as a way to ensure firm control. Other massacres which accompanied seizures of power (all discussed elsewhere in this article) occurred at Auxerre, Limoux, Nîmes, Orange, Tours, and Troyes.

Kalyvas's model predicts that indiscriminate violence is most likely to occur at the beginning of a conflict, and the massacres of the Wars of Religion fit this prediction quite nicely. If the timing of massacres seems to accord with Kalyvas's predictions for indiscriminate violence, however, the geographical distribution of massacres seems more in line with his predictions for selective violence (Figure 2). It is quite striking that neither side perpetrated many massacres in its core regions (Mack Holt's article in this volume makes a similar point). On the Catholic side, Brittany is the obvious example. Although there were significant Protestant communities in both Nantes and Rennes, for example, there were no massacres there. Jean Meyer, in his history of Rennes, argues that good relations between the two confessions reduced the likelihood of a massacre occurring, but it also seems reasonable to posit that one of the reasons for this is that the relatively weak Protestant communities posed no threat. The Catholic majority had no fear that the Protestants would receive outside help, since the main battlefields were far away.[31] Similarly, Béarn and the extreme south-west had no massacres either, again presumably because Protestants felt safe enough in the heartland of the house of Navarre. Protestant Normandy and Catholic Burgundy were also relatively peaceful. Paris, prior to 1572, is another example.

Massacres committed by one side in the core region of the other almost by definition must have the character of raids. However, such massacres were often particularly violent and indiscriminate, which supports the model advanced here. In 1574, for example, Protestant troops under the Baron d'Allemagne, on their way to join the main Protestant forces in Languedoc, seized the town of Aups. They killed 250 people, set fire to the town, and then left. Even by sixteenth-century standards this attack was exceptionally indiscriminate. Likewise, in an unusually late example of a massacre, troops of the Catholic League ventured south in 1595 from Catholic Brittany to La Châtagneraie, a Protestant village north-east of La Rochelle. They caught the Protestants at prayer, and reportedly killed 200 people, including

---

[31] Jean Meyer (ed.), *Histoire de Rennes* (Toulouse, 1972). For Nantes, see Elizabeth C. Tingle, *Authority and Society in Nantes during the French Wars of Religion, 1558–98* (Manchester, 2006).

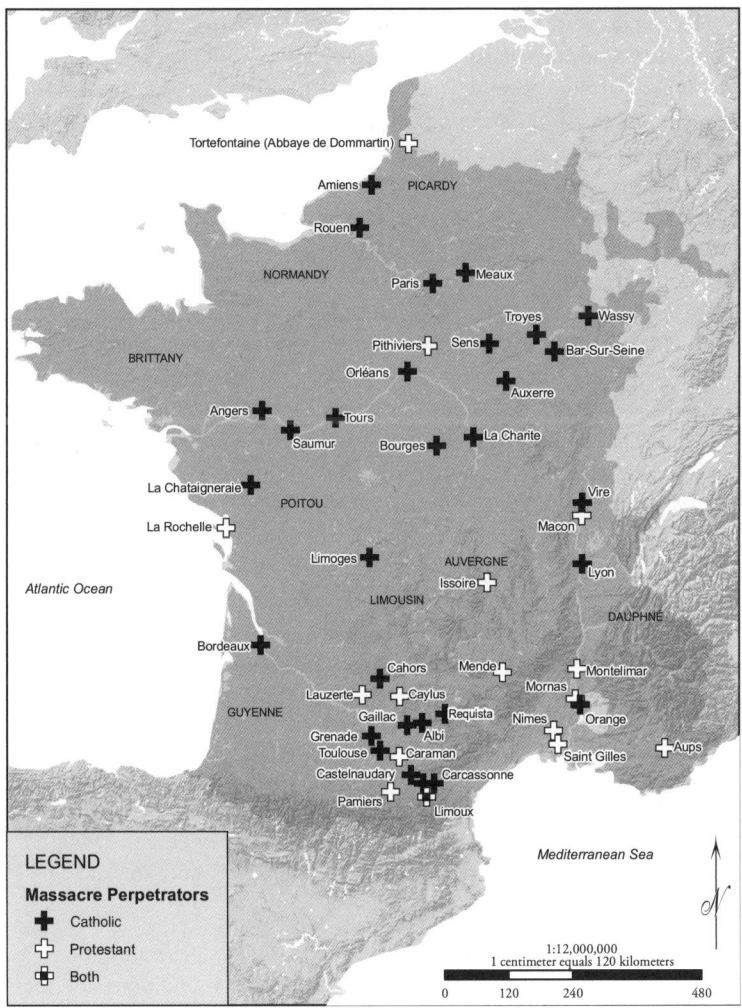

Figure 2. Map of the Massacres

women and children. If this figure is accurate, it is remarkably high for a small village.[32]

---

[32] For Aups, see Gustave Lambert, *Histoire des guerres de religion en Provence*, 2 vols (Toulon, 1870), I, 286. For La Châtaigneraie, see Auguste-François Lièvre, *Histoire des protestants et des églises réformées du Poitou*, 3 vols (Paris, 1856–60), I, 245–50.

The vast majority of massacres, however, occurred in three regions: firstly, in a broad belt south of Paris, committed largely by Catholics; secondly, along the upper Garonne around Toulouse, and thirdly along the Rhône valley. Along the Rhône and Garonne both Catholics and Protestants were responsible. Many of the Catholic massacres south of Paris are easy to explain: this was a border region for Catholics where they were trying to consolidate control in response to Protestant attacks. Most of the time, Protestant forces headed up the Loire towards Paris, and thus the region around Orléans was especially strategic. Likewise, the Rhône and Garonne were heavily Protestant, but both were highly mixed regions, very much seen as up for grabs in the early phases of the wars. So for example, Nîmes, slightly west of the Rhône, was mostly Protestant, while Avignon was largely Catholic, and Valence also Protestant. This mix was a recipe for trouble, and the map shows the results. The largest Protestant massacres were committed in this region. In Lauzerte, for example, it is noteworthy that a Protestant source, the *Histoire ecclésiastique*, reports that Protestant troops killed 567 people, including 194 priests. Protestant forces also committed an enormous massacre in nearby Caylus. The emphasis on priests shows the influence of Protestant theology, but of course priests were also crucial leaders of the Catholic cause.[33]

In previous publications Philip Benedict and I both concluded that massacres tended to occur in regions where one side was predominant, but not in their core regions where they had exclusive control. He wrote:

> In general, several common characteristics can be discerned which unite the twelve cities in which violence flared in 1572. . . . In all, the Huguenots formed a minority of the population, but often a threateningly large minority. In all, they were politically impotent, having been systematically barred from exercising power since the end of earlier civil wars.[34]

In my study of the Michelade, I ventured a similar generalization: 'The Michelade suggests that there are two essential preconditions for mass murder: an overwhelming superiority of force and a fear that the weaker party nonetheless poses an existential threat to the stronger one'.

There is considerable evidence in the sources that closely divided areas tended to be relatively free of violence—contemporaries even commented

---

[33] For Lauzerte, see Baum and Cunitz (eds), *Histoire ecclésiastique*, II, 232. For Caylus, see Crouzet, *Les Guerriers de Dieu*, I, 609.

[34] Benedict, 'The Saint Bartholomew's Massacre', 220–1.

on it. In the small Norman town of Vire, for example, the Protestant *Histoire ecclésiastique* comments:

> The town was composed, like all the others of the region, of people of both religions, not only among the common people, but also among the best and richest families, so the result was that neither dared attack the other [and] the town remained in relative peace.

Eventually, after Protestants attempted to take over Catholic churches, relations between the two religions degenerated, and local Catholics in alliance with troops perpetrated a massacre.[35] Kalyvas argues that the danger of reprisals goes a long way towards explaining the absence of massacres in neutral zones, and such reprisals did in fact occur. For example, in November 1562, the prince of Condé hanged some Catholics in Orléans after the duke of Guise hanged some Protestants in Rouen. The Protestant massacre in Mornas that same year was in explicit response to the Catholic massacre of Orange perpetrated by papal troops, and likewise Protestants staged a massacre in Rabastens in 1562 in response to the Catholic massacre of Gaillac. The battle cry for the Protestant troops in Mornas was 'Kill, kill! Let them pay for Orange!' and afterwards, the dead were dumped into a boat, which was set to float down the Rhône with a message attached to it: 'O you people of Avignon! Let these merchants pass, since they have already paid duty at Mornas'.[36] Note that both the Catholic killings and the Protestant reprisals occurred early in the wars and in the three key zones of contention discussed above—the belt south of Paris, the upper Garonne, and the Rhône. The reprisals were also staged as near as possible to the original incidents. Protestant leaders wanted to send a clear message: although Catholics were the overwhelming majority, they could not commit massacres with impunity. After several incidents like these, it is not surprising that the number of massacres fell precipitously.

Judith Pollmann concludes, on the basis of her comparison of the French and Dutch cases, that the different attitudes of the French and Dutch clergy

---

[35] 'Estant la ville composée, comme toutes les autres de ce pays là, de gens de deux religions, non seulement quant au commun peuple, mais aussi quant aux meilleures & plus riches familles, cela fut cause que les uns n'osans assaillir les autres, la ville demeuroit en quelque paix'. *Histoire ecclésiastique*, II, 844–5.

[36] For Orléans, see Lottin, *Recherches historiques sur la ville d'Orléans*, I, 442–4. For Mornas, see Lambert, *Histoire des guerres de religion en Provence*, I, 159–61. The quotation reads, 'O voi d'Avignone! Lasciate passare questi mercanti, perche an pagato il dazio a Mornas'. For Rabastens, see de Thou, *Histoire universelle*, IV, 387.

explain the relative absence of massacres in the Netherlands.[37] Pollmann's interpretation is certainly possible—the French sources are replete with explicit statements that the clergy urged Catholics to murder Protestants. But the clergy may have been more prone to demand action in France because the Valois were so weak and incapable of forceful repression after 1559 compared to the Habsburgs. It is also possible the Dutch clergy feared tit-for-tat reprisals like those just described above, which were easily imaginable in the crowded plain of the Netherlands.

Even more striking evidence for pressures to restrain violence in areas where neither side had a clear preponderance of control is the phenomenon of 'pactes d'amitié', local peace treaties agreed upon by both religions in particular communities. These have recently been studied by Jérémie Foa. They were heavily concentrated in the Rhône valley, in a way quite consistent with the model proposed here. As Foa puts it, 'These pacts are . . . precisely situated and dated. All were born in effect in disputed zones where religious minorities were sufficiently strong that they could be neither ignored nor muzzled'.[38] It is also noteworthy that Montpellier, which was particularly finely balanced between Protestants and Catholics, escaped a major massacre.[39] In sum, although detailed proof is impossible without further research, the geography of massacres confirms the main predictions of the model proposed here, namely that the most indiscriminate massacres tended to occur in raids into opponents' core territory, secondly that selective violence tended to be committed by parties in predominant but not exclusive control, and finally, areas with a rough balance of control were frequently uneasy islands of calm in the hurricane. In such areas, each side hesitated to attack the other and leaders of both religions in local communities were prone to band together to protect themselves against outside armies, who were generally responsible for the most spectacular violence.

---

[37] Pollmann, 'Countering the Reformation'.
[38] 'Parfaitement datés, ces pactes sont en outre précisément situés. Tous naissent en effet dans des zones disputées où les minorités religieuses sont suffisamment fortes pour n'être ni ignorées ni bâillonnées . . .' Jérémie Foa, 'Les Usages de l'Amitié: Pactes d'amitié et serments d'obéissance au début des guerres de Religion', unpublished paper delivered at the Sixteenth Century Society Conference in Geneva, 29 May 2009. My thanks to Jérémie for giving me a copy of his paper, and permission to cite it here.
[39] Louise Guiraud, *La Réforme à Montpellier*, 2 vols, *Mémoires de la Société Archéologique de Montpellier*, 2nd series, vols 6–7 (1918).

Motives

So far this article has focused on who committed massacres, and when and where they were committed, rather than why, an inherently more difficult question to answer. To some extent the question is also too broad. There were many different perpetrators, and the Catholic and Protestant forces were not monolithic. Nonetheless, an acceptable explanation of motivation should explain the patterns described above. The very clarity of those patterns suggests that an overall logic was at work. Existing theories can also be reconsidered in the light of this new evidence. For example, Crouzet argues that Catholics, faced with the dramatic upsurge of Protestantism in the late 1550s and early 1560s, believed that Antichrist, to be followed by Armageddon and the End of Time, was at hand.[40] The large number of massacres in 1562 is consistent with this analysis, but it does not explain the regional distribution of massacres, nor the heavy involvement of military forces. Instead, the involvement of the military, and the likelihood that many if not all of the massacres were ordered by military commanders, suggests that it is more likely that perpetrators were motivated by the pragmatic considerations that Kalyvas ascribes to perpetrators of selective and indiscriminate violence.

There is another possibility, however, namely that the massacres involved genocidal or what Kalyvas calls 'eliminationist' violence, which he excludes from his theory. Some popular accounts of the Wars of Religion take this view. As Pierre Miquel put it, Catholics and Protestants during the Wars of Religion 'did not have as [their] goal to dominate the adversary, but to destroy it, to reduce it—as the inquisitors did—to ashes'.[41] While according to Kalyvas's theory a desire to control leads to selective and indiscriminate violence, eliminationist violence stems from the very religious, cultural, and ideological factors that many recent historians have identified as the primary causes of the massacres in the Wars of Religion.

It is highly likely that some leaders wanted to eliminate the other side absolutely, while others did not. This article argues that most massacres were not genocidal, but clearly, most is not all. Indeed, genocidal violence need not take the form of a massacre—'ethnic cleansing', to use the modern

---

[40] Crouzet, *Les Guerriers de Dieu*, I, ch. 3–6.
[41] 'La guerre des Religions n'est pas une guerre civile, comme celle des Armagnacs et des bourgignons. Elle est inexorable, elle dresse l'homme contre l'homme. Elle n'a pour but de dominer l'adversaire, mais de le détruire, de le réduire—comme le font les inquisiteurs—en cendres'. Pierre Miquel, *Les guerres de religion* (Paris, 1980), 22. Crouzet, *Les Guerriers de Dieu*, II, 111, suggests that some of the provincial Saint Bartholomew's massacres may also have been intended to exterminate the Protestants, through either death or conversion.

term, can be just as effective. In Amiens, for example, in late May, 1562, the municipal government created a 'roll of people of the new religion', and then proceeded to expel a certain number of 'inveterate or obstinate' Protestants. Similarly, in Carcassonne, in March 1562, while the Protestants were outside the town celebrating their services, Catholic leaders locked the city gates and refused to let them return home. (Catholic relatives of the Protestants pleaded in vain on their behalf.) The effect was to expel them from town.[42] However, it should be underlined that in Amiens, only selected 'inveterate' Protestants were targeted, suggesting that the goal was not really to eliminate the whole body of Protestants—the town's leaders expected that the rest of the group, deprived of their most active members, would recant. Both of these episodes also occurred at the very start of the Wars of Religion, when expectations on both sides were at their height, and according to Kalyvas, when massacres and indiscriminate violence are most likely. In Orange in 1571, it is reported that conspirators 'gathered in the church of Saint-Martin, where they renewed their plot to kill all of the Protestants of Orange, and decided that if any Catholic should speak of saving one of them, he should be the first to be put to death'.[43] Although this description makes it sound like the Catholic party committed itself to practise genocidal violence, in fact some Protestants were ransomed, while others were not killed but instead forced to attend Mass. It is also unclear whether the incident actually occurred, since it comes from Protestant sources who would not normally have had access to the internal deliberations of their opponents, and who had every incentive to invent such stories. Nonetheless, the massacre in Orange was exceptionally bloody. More commonly, however, it was perfectly possible for people to convert, as the many abjurations in the aftermath of the Saint Bartholomew's Massacre show. Victims of true genocide have no such option.

To argue, as this article does, that the pattern of violence during the Wars of Religion was consistent with selective and indiscriminate violence rather than with genocidal violence, we have to consider what patterns we should expect genocidal violence to have. While neither the personnel nor the timing of the massacres excludes the possibility that massacres during the Wars of Religion

---

[42] For Amiens, see Olivia Carpi, *Une République imaginaire: Amiens pendant les troubles de religion (1559–1597)* (Paris, 2005), 80. For Carcassonne, see Devic and Vaissete, *Histoire Générale de Languedoc*, XI, 379.

[43] 'Se réunissent dans l'église de Saint-Martin, où ils renouvellent leur complot de tuer tous les protestants d'Orange, et décident que si quelque catholique parle de sauver l'un d'eux, il sera mis à mort le premier'. Eugène Arnaud, *Histoire des protestants de Provence du Comtat Venaissin et de la principauté d'Orange*, 2 vols (Paris, 1884), II, 215.

were genocidal, this article will argue that the regional distribution of massacres makes this interpretation unlikely.

Consider Kalyvas's five geographical zones and consider how genocidal or what he calls 'eliminationist' violence would have to be distributed across them. If selective violence is concentrated in areas under the predominant control of one side, while indiscriminate violence (especially after the initial outbreak of war) is concentrated in raids on the other party's core territory, how would we expect genocidal violence to be distributed, and does the violence in the Wars of Religion match that paradigm? Surely, the Shoah is the paradigmatic case of genocidal violence. Michael Marrus and Robert Paxton have proposed an explanation of why the percentage of Jews murdered varied so dramatically from one European nation to another. They argue that two key factors determined the result: (1) the Nazi regime's interest in promoting the racial purity of the local non-Jewish population, or of clearing it of Jews to prepare it for German settlement, and (2) Nazi power over the region in question. In short, deaths were highest in those areas at the centre of Nazi interest and control.[44] This explanation can be extended to suggest a more general model for genocidal violence. Genocidal violence can be quite selective, in the sense that members of the target group must be carefully identified, but once members of the group are identified, genocidal violence should be limited only by the limits of the power of the persecuting group, and the location of the targeted community.

Genocidal violence is the mirror image of indiscriminate violence: if indiscriminate violence frequently takes place during raids on the opposing side's home territory, genocidal violence should take place on the core territory of the perpetrators. Thus in the Wars of Religion Catholics should have perpetrated massacres in their core regions, places like Brittany, Picardy, and so forth. They should also have perpetrated massacres in other regions to the extent they were able, so there should have been many massacres in areas where they were predominant, and fewer in areas over which they had little control. Of course, more massacres could have occurred in regions where Catholics were predominant than core regions if the number of Protestants was higher there, but potential victims in core regions should have been particularly prone to persecution. However, as we have seen, Catholic massacres were uncommon in core Catholic regions, even where there were significant Protestant communities. If Catholics wanted to exterminate Protestants, they would surely have done so where it was easy, in places where they held overwhelming control. The survival of Protestant

---

[44] Michael R. Marrus and Robert O. Paxton, *Vichy France and the Jews* (New York, 1981) 356–72.

communities in places like Rennes suggests that Catholics wished to reduce the Protestant political threat, and to reduce the military dangers Protestant minorities posed in threatened towns, rather than to eliminate Protestants wherever they could be found. Extermination was not the predominant motive.

Kalyvas's sharp distinction between selective and indiscriminate violence is not especially helpful for the sixteenth century, and the massacres discussed here have aspects of both selective and indiscriminate violence. They resemble indiscriminate violence in a number of respects. By limiting the discussion to events where more than ten people died, this article effectively excludes much 'pinpoint' violence that was more likely to be selective than large-scale massacres. Although large-scale violence can be quite selective, sixteenth-century troops were undisciplined and poorly paid, so we should not expect surgical strikes. Attempts to use violence against specific targets frequently degenerated.

Some massacres were clearly the result of indiscriminate violence. In Orange, for example, Catholic residents cooperated in 1562 with an army of papal troops from Avignon who were besieging the city. Once inside, the army not only defeated the Protestants but went on a rampage, killing Protestants and Catholics alike.[45] Still, it would also be wrong to call all massacres indiscriminate. Unlike some modern political movements, sixteenth-century Protestants and Catholics were morally obligated to declare their religious allegiance publicly every Sunday, so there were relatively few problems of identification, given a modicum of local knowledge. A particularly good case of selective massacre is that of Tours in 1562. After the city's capture by Catholic forces, their commander, the duke of Montpensier, first killed a butcher whom he found selling meat during Lent. Then 'He . . . sent to fetch the most important men of the Religion, who had been named and suggested to him, and made some prisoners, without telling them why, and ordered others not to leave the house of the archbishop, where he [Montpensier] was lodged'. The Protestant party seized Tours shortly afterwards. Immediately after retaking it Montpensier had local monks write a confession of faith which every inhabitant had to sign before witnesses or be put to death. The actual massacre that followed was a bloody, and inevitably somewhat disorganized affair, but clearly Montpensier was trying his best to strike at hard-core Protestants.[46] One way for Protestant

---

[45] For Orange, see Arnaud, *Histoire des protestants de Provence*, II, 186–8.

[46] 'Il . . . envoya querir les principaux de la religion, qu'on luy avoit nommez & recommandez, desquels il fit constituer quelques uns prisonniers, sans leur dire pourquoy, & entre

armies to perpetrate selective violence despite their lack of local knowledge was to target clergy exclusively—their hair and clothing helped identify them.

Conclusion

Most massacres during the Wars of Religion were committed by troops and civic militias, in regions that were key to the consolidation of control by each side, as part of attempts to seize power or in the immediate aftermath of successful attempts to do so. They occurred especially often at the outset of the wars, when both sides still hoped for a quick victory. These conclusions confirm Stuart Carroll's argument, made elsewhere in this volume, that in sixteenth-century France, violence was 'highly politicized'. It should also be emphasized that although this article documents a fair number of massacres, in the end the relative absence of massacres is more impressive: most of the time, after the initial outbreak of war, in regions that were not in jeopardy of falling to the other side, massacres were rare.

It is hard to read accounts of massacres without being mesmerized. For reasons of propaganda, each side liked to expatiate on the gory violence committed by the other, and each tried to blame the righteous but excessive ardour of its humbler supporters for any excesses. Historians should be aware that such stories, although sometimes true, are tropes. Analysis of this language has its uses—this article has already noted Crouzet's analysis of the decline of religious violence in the aftermath of Saint Bartholomew—but the excessive focus on the analysis of texts has hitherto occluded understanding of who committed the massacres, and of where and when they were committed. Historians should not miss the pattern beneath the embroidery.

If we are riveted by the details of sixteenth-century accounts of massacres, it is no accident. In many instances, both sides committed deliberate and spectacular violence to achieve a clear, rational end, namely to cow the other side into quiescence or conversion. Under these circumstances, historians should always consider it likely that leaders gave the orders that set massacres in motion. This consideration applies in particular to the Saint Bartholomew's massacre. Barbara Diefendorf, in the most influential recent account of the massacre, argues that Henri, Duke of Guise's remark, as he encouraged his men to assist in killing the Protestant leaders, was crucial. After learning of Coligny's death he told them: 'Courage, soldiers, we have begun fortunately, let's go to the others, for the King commands it . . . it is the King's will, his

---

autres leur fit commandement de ne pas bouger de la maison de l'Arcevesque, où il estoit logé'. Baum and Cunitz (eds), *Histoire ecclésiastique*, II, 681, 694.

explicit command'.[47] The bourgeois militia, dominated by Catholic extremists, took these words for orders and went into action. Diefendorf calls Guise's remark 'reckless'. Her term suggests Guise had no notion that his words might have serious consequences, and no role in the events that followed. This conclusion, while not ruled out by the evidence, is hard to confirm. At least two facts point the other way: firstly there is strong evidence that Guise was deeply involved in the initial attack against Admiral Coligny. In addition, the militias seem to have been fully activated, well-coordinated, and above all organized. Every *quartier* seems to have got the news on time, and all participated. Others besides Guise could have done the organizing, but certainly he is a plausible candidate. It is also understandable that Catholic leaders were tempted to try the tactic of massacre in 1572, although it had not served them well in 1562, when they had last used it extensively. The Catholic leadership must have found the unusual concentration of Protestant leaders in Paris extremely tempting.

Although ordinary people in the sixteenth century frequently carried out large-scale massacres, they did not generally plan or direct them. Instead, leaders who had enormous gains and losses at stake, and who therefore had far fewer compunctions than the rest of us, were responsible. In a face-to-face society, with poor policing, most people needed the friendship, or at least the benevolent neutrality, of their neighbours. People also felt considerable pressures to conform, and the many riots of the period are vivid reminders of the dangers that befell those who too heedlessly violated community norms. Nonetheless, among ordinary people, there was a great deal of practical tolerance.[48] Beyond such attitudes, ordinary people also had good, practical reasons not to initiate massacres—they were a nasty, dangerous business. The older scholarship, against which Davis was reacting in 'The Rites of Violence', tended to portray massacres as the product of the crude instincts of the excitable mob. If anything, this article suggests that ordinary people were too docile. More of the blame for sixteenth-century France's bloodiest massacres should be allocated to those who gave the fatal orders.

---

[47] Barbara Diefendorf, *Beneath the Cross: Catholics and Huguenots in Sixteenth-Century Paris* (New York, 1991), 99. Diefendorf quotes the passage cited in the text from Goulart, but I have used the slightly expanded version given by Jouanna in *La Saint-Barthélemy*, 168. Her interpretation follows Diefendorf's, as does Carroll's (see *Martyrs and Murderers*, 215).

[48] Benjamin J. Kaplan, *Divided By Faith: Religious Conflict and the Practice of Toleration in Early Modern Europe* (Cambridge, MA, 2007), and Stuart B. Schwartz, *All Can Be Saved: Religious Tolerance and Salvation in the Iberian Atlantic World* (New Haven, 2008).

The Rights of Violence*

Stuart Carroll

There are very few articles written forty years ago that continue to remain essential reading for undergraduate students. 'The Rites of Violence' is one of those select few. Its place in the historical canon is assured for five reasons. First, it was a major contribution to the assault on social science structuralism. Afterwards, religion or crowd behaviour could no longer be reduced to a set of social and economic variables. Secondly, Davis showed that patterns of ritual could be decoded to uncover the participants' sense of a riot's significance and validity.[1] Ritual endowed violence with legitimacy and meaning: Protestant violence, Davis argued, targeted idols, in accordance with Mosaic Law; Catholics on the other hand drew on the ludic rites of folk culture to purge the community of polluting heretics. Thirdly, Davis restored the role of human agency. Her rioters were not a faceless crowd. Her crowd had a place for women and children too. Fourthly, her interest in anthropology led her to the conclusion that religious violence was a culture clash between opposing conceptions of the sacred. 'The Rites of Violence' marks an important caesura in historical writing. Culture, Davis suggests, is the driving force of historical change.[2] It marked a break with social history and points to the rise of the cultural turn. Finally, the article is indicative of the shifting centre of the historical discipline, as Europe lost its intellectual hegemony to the United States. Davis's expansion of the themes first raised in 'The Rites of Violence' in her subsequent work made her an iconic figure. She was the torchbearer for the New Cultural History, an inspiration to a generation of younger historians.

The first substantive critique appeared a decade later when Mark Greengrass looked in vain for Davis's model in Toulouse. The violence

---

* Thanks to Shane O'Rourke and David Clayton for helping me to think through the conceptual issues.
[1] S. Desan, 'Crowds, Community and Ritual in the Work of E. P. Thompson and Natalie Davis', in L. Hunt (ed.), *The New Cultural History* (Berkeley, CA, 1989), 48.
[2] Ibid., 50.

there between 13 and 17 May 1562 was notable for the high level of bloodshed and the desecration of corpses. But, as Greengrass pointed out, this was not a popular riot. It was a struggle between two paramilitary groups for control of the city in the context of a civil war that erupted over the Protestant right to worship, which had been granted by the monarchy under the Edict of January in 1562.[3] More recently, Allan Tulchin has used another case study—the Protestant massacre of Catholics in Nîmes in 1567—to argue that Davis's organizing categories do not hold water. According to Tulchin, religious violence has little to do with the sacred and everything to do with numbers: where the Protestants were a majority among the elite, as in Nîmes, they were also capable of killing Catholics in large numbers.[4] A more general question has been posed by Judith Pollmann. If religious violence were the result of a culture clash one would expect to see the pattern replicated elsewhere in sixteenth-century Europe. But one does not. In the Netherlands Catholics were on the whole Erasmian and averse to violence.[5]

This paper is not an addition to these critiques. In my opinion, recent re-evaluations enhance and nuance Davis's argument, but they do not demolish it. Her argument remains broadly convincing. 'The Rites of Violence' continues to resonate because it contains important truths about intercommunal violence. Popular religious violence had its own rhythms, structure, and logic that were autonomous of socio-economic forces and not necessarily dependent on the political context. My purpose is rather different. I wish to provoke some reflection on the category of the 'religious' itself. 'The Rites of Violence' had a profound effect on historical writing everywhere, one that was felt most keenly in histories of sixteenth-century Europe. In the intervening years since 'The Rites of Violence' was first published, the revisionists put religion back into the Wars of Religion.[6] This was an important corrective. No longer could we view religious motives as a form of false consciousness which masked class or political ambitions. The Wars of Religion were a struggle for salvation.

---

[3] M. Greengrass, 'The Anatomy of a Religious Riot in Toulouse in May 1562,' *Journal of Ecclesiastical History*, 34 (1983), 373–88.

[4] Allan A. Tulchin, 'The Michelade in Nimes, 1567', *French Historical Studies*, 29 (2006), 1–35. At the 2008 Warwick conference in her honour, Davis contended that Nîmes was a coup d'état. Here (and by extension Toulouse) we are looking at politicized violence that is different from the religious riot.

[5] J. Pollmann, 'Countering the Reformation in France and the Netherlands: Clerical Leadership and Catholic Violence 1560–1585', *Past and Present*, 190 (2006), 83–120.

[6] M. Holt, 'Putting Religion Back into the Wars of Religion', *French Historical Studies*, 18 (1993), 524–51.

The high point of the attempt to marry the new religious history with social and political history was Philip Benedict's deeply researched local study of Rouen, which appeared in 1981.[7] By now, however, Davis was moving in a different direction. In 'The Sacred and the Body Social' she argued that Catholicism and Protestantism were akin to languages or syntaxes, whose discourses and metaphors can be interpreted to reveal how religion shapes a sense of urban community and solidarity.[8] Influenced by the symbolic anthropology of Clifford Geertz she proceeds from the symbols toward an elucidation of their meaning, from the abstract to the concrete. Catholics and Protestants each had a different amalgam of cultural reference, a 'grammar' or a 'syntax' stemming from central notions of their creeds; these 'conceptual structures' and 'collective images', were vehicles for interpreting experience and in the measure that they differed from each other, rendered mutual incomprehension likely. When people 'interact through religion,' two different schemata of reference will lead to misunderstanding and conflict, despite whatever shared cultural patterns may exist.[9]

The Wars of Religion were thus to be understood as a clash of cultures. The nemesis of social history followed soon after. In 1991 Denis Crouzet published *Les Guerriers de Dieu*. For Crouzet the Reformation amounted to a psychological transformation, the Wars of Religion a Manichean struggle between two opposing economies of salvation. Crouzet's debt to Davis was explicit: 'Catholic and Protestant aggression was *primarily* an expression of culture . . . the crisis was *above all* a cultural cleavage'.[10] Factors other than religion are peripheral. It is difficult to do justice to such a rich and stimulating work in such a short space. One of the great benefits of *Les Guerriers de Dieu* has been to refocus our attention on the lexicon of odium and the ingrained mental attitudes that made sectarian violence so difficult to contain. The rhetoric of hate has rarely been more vividly brought to life. One of the key problems raised by *Les Guerriers de Dieu* is methodological: the projection of an entire culture from a collage of texts is predicated on the notion that discourses are holistic and not subject to a plurality of meanings and

---

[7] P. Benedict, *Rouen during the Wars of Religion* (Cambridge, 1981).

[8] *Past and Present*, 90 (1981), 40–70.

[9] For a trenchant critique of this approach: G. Hanlon, *Confession and Community in Seventeenth-Century France: Catholic and Protestant Co-existence in Aquitaine* (Philadelphia, 1993), 10–11.

[10] D. Crouzet, *Les Guerriers de Dieu: la violence au temps des troubles de religion vers 1525 – vers 1610*, 2 vols (Paris, 1991), I, 75: 'les aggressions catholiques et huguenotes furent d'abord des expressions culturelles . . . la crise fut avant tout une dissociation culturelle'. The emphasis is my own.

interpretations. Even if we accept that confessional discourses were coherent and interpreted uniformly, a further leap of faith is required and we must accept that the relation between action and psychological commitment is consistent and presume that religious belief equates to an 'all encompassing causal relation'.[11] Even if we accept that Crouzet's hermeneutic virtuosity makes for a convincing *Zeitgeist* at a general level, it cannot account for the peculiar local chronology of violence. The link between religious mentalities and everyday practice is much more complex: the demonization of the 'other' and eschatological fears were hardly absent in states that did not experience inter-communal religious violence on the French scale.[12] In order to explain the decline of religious passions in the 1570s Crouzet has to invent an equivalent cultural shift. These dramatic mental and cultural shifts in such a short of period of time ask quite a lot of simple folk.

But there is a more fundamental objection to interpreting the civil war and religious violence as the product of a culture clash. Essentialist views of culture tend to simplistic interpretations of the dynamics of temporal change. Is not culture itself shaped by social and political processes? In order to illustrate the problems raised by culture as an interpretative tool, let us take the example of Clifford Geertz, the guru of the New Cultural history, who encouraged cultural historians to distance themselves from social and economic historians.[13] The dominant role he attributed to culture as the prime mover in human affairs left little role for politics. He was therefore unable to account for change and conflict. Critics have accused him of mythologizing Balinese society as traditional and unchanging; his method of 'thick description' is also 'static description'. His work was non-political in another sense. His cultural paradigm did not take account of the interplay of local, national, and international politics. In particular, his analytical framework was unable to come to terms with the dramatic events of 1964-5, when an unprecedented wave of violence swept Indonesia, leaving tens of thousands dead. The massacres scarred Balinese society. In his eloquent decoding of the Balinese psyche through the cockfight, however, the political violence was relegated

---

[11] Hanlon, *Confession and Community*, 10.
[12] On the case of Lutheranism on the eve on the Thirty Years War: M. Meumann, 'The Experience of Violence and the Expectation of the End of the World in Seventeenth-Century Europe' in J. Canning, H. Lehmann, and J. Winter (eds), *Power, Violence and Mass Death in Pre-Modern and Modern Times* (Aldershot, 2004).
[13] For a critique: A. Kuper, *Culture: the Anthropologists Account* (Cambridge, MA, 1999); V. Crapanzano, 'Hermes' Dilemma: the Masking of Subversion in Ethnographic Description,' in J. Clifford and G. Marcus (eds), *Writing Culture: the Poetics and Politics of Ethnography* (Berkeley, CA, 1986).

to a footnote, the symptom of a deep, suppressed lust for violence that he had discerned in the Balinese cock-fight.[14] This is not to deny the importance of religion or culture for the understanding of events. We cannot make sense of religious violence through politics alone. Much of the violence described by Davis and Crouzet had a structuring logic, followed a cultural pattern. On the other hand, we should be wary of cultural determinism, of arguing that identities and social actions are reducible to the cultural.[15]

Politics does not appear in 'The Rites of Violence' and if you did not know the subject you would be hard pressed to realise that there was a civil war going on. This is not a surprise. It was a quite understandable reaction to outdated political history. For the 1970s generation politics was synonymous with personalities and the court, while popular culture was 'valorized', since it was seen as an articulation of resistance to the dominant culture.[16] Davis refers to her rioters as the 'people' in the streets. She is careful to exclude soldiers and officials. And as a follower of Durkheim, Davis placed a strong emphasis on the unifying aesthetic of culture, its role as a mechanism for the maintenance of order. Thus Catholic violence is restorative, purging the community of infection and returning it to a pristine state. This is a plausible and convincing argument. But it is not the whole picture. The danger of leaving the politics out is that an 'emphasis on the cohesiveness of community and the forcefulness of its legitimacy leads to inadequate attention to the issues of transformation, conflict and power'.[17] It is not always easy to distinguish the popular riot from the officially sanctioned massacre. Popular violence was most likely to be bloodier and more effective where it was organized and led. We should add that attempts to distinguish between popular 'religious' violence and elite 'political violence' are fraught with difficulties.[18] The new confraternities of the Holy Sacrament, which were often involved in anti-Protestant violence, were characterized by devotional practices wholly different from the medieval bean feasts they replaced. They shared with their Protestant enemies distaste for the vulgarities of popular culture.

---

[14] 'Deep Play: Notes on the Balinese Cockfight' in *The Intrepretation of Cultures* (London, 1993).

[15] To suggest that violence is largely the product of culture can lead to a simplistic cultural reductionism, such as that propounded in Daniel Goldhagen's controversial (and flawed) explanation of the Nazi genocide.

[16] G. Strauss, 'The Dilemma of Popular History', *Past and Present*, 132 (1991), 130–49.

[17] Desan, 'Crowds, Community and Ritual', 65.

[18] The tenor of Davis's critique of Tulchin: see note 4 above.

The context within which religious violence occurs is crucial to understand its dynamism for another reason. For religion is not to be equated solely with belief and culture. Religion is a protean force. The Reformation, as Ethan Shagan has argued, cannot be reduced to the sum of individual conversions.[19] There is no doubt that communities were in large measure shaped and ordered by religious belief. But nor was it, as Gregory Hanlon has argued, an autonomous category of experience. 'It accommodated well with others in the field of social ordering ... Individuals chose their position to please God, but also with an eye to reducing conflicts with their families, their neighbours, their prince'.[20] For communities are collectives based on aid, conflict, aggression, and sharing. They were constructed, changed over time and can only be grasped as an historical process. Davis explored one facet of community. This led her to downplay others. Individuals were members of churches but they were also members of different sub-groups each with their contradictions and fractured loyalties. We assume the dominance of doctrine over the 'ecumenism of everyday life' at our peril.[21] This grudging accommodation was not expressed in the language of 'tolerance' and 'intolerance', which was an essentially elite religious discourse that implied a relationship between recognized and recognizable religious communities. The common people were likely to use a different terminology; one that rarely appears in the most frequently consulted sources. In early modern England terms such as 'getting on' and 'getting along' deploy the language of neighbourliness and commonality rather than that of religion and difference:

> These two related phrases describe the key social priorities of groups to improve one's social, political and cultural standing on society—and how to achieve this while also 'getting along'—that is to say, maintaining good relationships with the dominant group. It was national political events, real or imagined which upset the relationship. It was during these periods of breakdown that the secular language of neighbourliness struggled to be heard above the language of religious intolerance.[22]

---

[19] E. Shagan, *Popular Politics and the English Reformation* (Cambridge, 2003), introduction.
[20] Hanlon, *Confession and Community*, 279.
[21] The term is Willem Frijhoff's: W. Sheils, ' "Getting on" and "Getting Along" in Parish and Town: English Catholics and their Neighbours', in B. Kaplan, R. Moore, H. van Nierop and J. Pollmann (eds), *Catholic Communities in Protestant States: Britain and the Netherlands, 1580–1720* (Manchester, 2009).
[22] Ibid., 68.

In France, too, peacemaking was a mundane activity and disputants invariably promised henceforth to leave in 'peace' or 'amity' when they reconciled. Olivier Christin has discovered a dozen community peace pacts dating from 1567; modelled on the idea of contract, they deployed the language amity and fraternity and stressed the obligations of civic over sacred order.[23] But the traditional language of neighbourliness also endured. In 1588 the Protestants and Catholics of the Upper Auvergne renounced war and brigandage and 'swore to live in good neighbourliness and not to take up arms even if the war becomes general throughout the kingdom'.[24]

As David Sabean has argued there are as many communities as there are mediated relationships, and he stresses the negative and positive elements of sharing and conflict that comes with the bonds of affinity, blood kinship and neighbourliness.[25] Religion played a fundamental role in all these relationships, but it did not govern them. Communities consisted of hierarchies, factions and clienteles, all of which helped to shape social action. I argue that the uncoupling of the category 'religion' from the micro-political and the everyday social environment has gone too far. This paper seeks to reconnect them. My aim is to place the religious violence into its local political and social context and to question how far it is possible or desirable to distinguish between (elite) 'political violence' and (popular) 'religious violence'. In the early modern period we uncouple the religious from the political with great difficulty. This is even more difficult with a phenomenon as elusive and multi-faceted as violence.

I discuss below three major incidents—two massacres and an assassination—during 1561-2. This was a veritable crucible of violence which did so much to sharpen attitudes, forge memories and draw the boundaries of confessional difference. I suggest that it was in this period in particular that religious violence was highly politicized; that it was, at least in this phase, in the words of Mark Greengrass, more about 'rights' than 'rites'.

Vassy

My interest in these questions was first sparked by research into the most important incident of religious violence in sixteenth-century France. The ways in which an event can utterly transform and reshape history has been brought into sharp focus by 9/11. Vassy was such an event. On 1 March 1562

---

[23] O. Christin, *La Paix de la religion: l'autonomisation de la raison politique au XVIe siècle* (Paris, 1997), 122–30, 311–18.

[24] S. Carroll, *Blood and Violence in Early Modern France* (Oxford, 2006), 224.

[25] D. Sabean, *Power in the Blood: Popular Culture and Village Discourse in Early Modern Germany* (Cambridge, 1984), introduction.

fifty Protestants were massacred in the small Champenois town. Thus began a conflict that shook Europe for thirty-six years. For Protestants and Catholics across sixteenth-century Europe the massacre was not an obscure incident in a far-off town, rather it was a profoundly local event, the first salvo in the greater struggle between good and evil. The printing presses rolled with news of Vassy not only in French, but also in German, Dutch, English, and Latin. In France, news of the massacre spread terror among Protestants: throughout the kingdom congregations held hastily organized musters, drew up rolls of those able to bear arms and hatched plots to seize control of towns. A new word 'massacre' was added to the political lexicon.[26]

Despite Vassy's significance it has been the object of remarkably little scholarly interest. This is perhaps because Vassy does not meet Davis's criteria for a religious riot, though she does refer to it when she talks of Catholic 'rioters' there destroying Huguenot property. These 'rioters' were in fact the retinue of the local magnate, François duke of Guise. Vassy's impact on the combustible religious atmosphere of France is undeniable. But this is not the only reason why we need to pay more attention to Vassy. For the road to Vassy has lots to tell us about something that has been forgotten in the intervening years since 'The Rites of Violence' was first published. Vassy reminds us of another variable: the role of class, or at least, social friction, as a cause of violence. It also reminds us that Calvinism posed a challenge to the social and political order.

My interest in Vassy derived from research on the Guise family and the growing conviction that we had got them wrong.[27] Far from being the leaders of the ultra-Catholic party on the eve of the civil war, they were firmly in the ranks of the Catholic moderates, part of the Erasmian tendency analysed by Pollmann, who made no secret of their opposition to toleration, but who were at the same time opposed to mass burnings and committed to freedom of conscience, requiring only outward conformity. There was a notable exception to this family trend: the most formidable enemy of Vassy's Protestant community was Antoinette de Bourbon, dowager duchess of Guise, who lived at Joinville only a few miles away. While a good case can be made for the evangelical credentials of her sons, Antoinette was pretty much the most straightforward ultra-Catholic you can imagine. Her piety was as famous in her own day as it was conventional. Every day on the way to Mass she

---

[26] M. Greengrass, 'Hidden Transcripts: Secret histories and Personal Testimonies of Religious Violence in the French Wars of Religion', in M. Levene and P. Roberts (eds), *The Massacre in History* (New York and Oxford, 1999).

[27] S. Carroll, *Martyrs and Murderers: the Guise Family and the Making of Europe* (Oxford, 2009).

passed a coffin, which was placed in her bedchamber 'in order that the spectacle would serve as a perpetual reminder of the day of her death'. Hers was a medieval piety, at odds with the new currents of contemplative belief associated with Erasmus and his fellow humanists. Her confessor, the Dominican Pierre Doré, was the butt of clever humanist jokes: Rabelais alludes to his preposterous sermons as Master 'Dungpowder' in *Pantagruel*. Twice, in 1533 and 1557, heretics had burned beneath her eyes in Joinville town square. No wonder that Protestants referred to her as their 'capital enemy'.[28]

So it was with some surprise when I opened a fragment of Antoinette's account book for the period of Lent 1560, which survives in the British Library that I saw that this records not one but two visits to Joinville from her old friend, Françoise d'Amboise.[29] What is remarkable is that she was a Protestant, having converted around 1558. It is possible that she kept this hidden from her host; but this seems unlikely. For in the borderlands of Champagne, it was the Guise and not Françoise who were out of joint. The princely houses of Croÿ, the family into which Françoise had married, of Orléans-Longueville, Luxembourg, La Marck, and Clèves-Nevers, all of them neighbours, friends and kinsmen of the Guise, shared two things in common. First was their close links to the empire and antipathy for the house of Habsburg. Secondly, and perhaps most significantly, by the end of 1561 each clan was headed by a Protestant. It is a story that is little known. Of all the social groups in sixteenth-century France, the princes were the sole group in which Protestantism approached a majority in 1561. They remained firm in their faith during the First Civil War. However, they also remained loyal to the monarchy and opposed to the Edict of January 1562. Some remained neutral; others fought their co-religionists, and can be categorized as Protestant loyalists.

What has this got to do with 'The Rites of Violence'? Well for the house of Guise, I would argue, the world was first and foremost viewed through the prism of hierarchy and social snobbery and this was reflected in their faith. We should not be surprised at this. Indeed, the religious reformations themselves, Catholic and Protestant, were propelled by concerns about order.[30] The Guise attitude to heresy too was entirely conventional. Heresy and sedition are synonymous. Heretics are naturally people of the lower orders. In 1525, the Guise had taken part in the crushing of the German Peasants War. The slaughter of thousands of Alsatian Anabaptists was not only justified; it

---

[28] G. Baum and E. Cunitz (eds), *Histoire ecclésiastique des églises reformées au royame de France*, 3 vols. (Paris, 1883–9, repr. Nieuwkoop, 1974), I, 158.
[29] British Library, London, Additional Mss 21361.
[30] Hanlon, *Confession and Community*, 279.

was something to celebrate. But when the heretics were your fellow princes, your neighbours, and your kinsmen, it was a different matter. The Guise were flexible on matters of faith and indulgent towards those princes who showed conformity. Contrary to received historical opinion, even the Guise were capable of everyday ecumenism. The political ramifications of this stance are not relevant to my purposes in this article. What I briefly wish to show is how social assumptions help to explain what happened at Vassy.

Principally this means we have to rethink the relations between politics and religion in the years before the outbreak of civil war. In 1561 there was a widespread consensus among the Catholic elite that some form of compromise would have to be reached. This explains the Guise interest in Gallican reform along Lutheran lines. Historians have traditionally dismissed this as a ruse to divide the Protestant camp. Missing from the historiography, which has become dominated by technical theological issues, is the social context which made Lutheranism so attractive to the French princes. By the 1550s Lutheranism had become a socially conservative, princely reformation, which crucially, maintained the Mass, the ultimate symbol of union and the guarantor of the traditional body social. The French princes looked with envy at the control over the Church exercised by their German neighbours. Here was a princely reformation that guaranteed social order. This enamel (Figure 1) of the Guise family completed at the time of Vassy is traditionally interpreted as a defence of the real presence. On one level it is. But a further clue to its purpose is the motley crew of heretics it depicts being crushed by Antoinette de Bourbon in her chariot. There are several medieval sectaries, the Anabaptists, as well as Hus, Calvin, and Beza. There is one notable absentee: Martin Luther. This enamel celebrates the Guise triumph over heresy and their rapprochement with the Lutherans.[31]

If the duke of Guise's identity was primarily that of a 'Guerrier de Dieu' we would expect his rhetoric to be consistent with his actions. But this is not so. It would have been easy for the duke to play to the Catholic gallery and justify his actions at Vassy on religious grounds. He did not do so. Such a thing would have been foolish since many of his neighbours and kinsmen were Protestants. But he did not justify himself on legal grounds either: after all by the terms of the Edict of January services inside Vassy were illegal and, as provincial governor, his intervention hardly unwarranted. No: the duke chose to justify himself with regard to social assumptions. During an interview with the English ambassador three weeks later he did not mention religion at all but complained of the 'arrogance' of vassals who dared to

---

[31] J. Harrie, 'The Guises, the Body of Christ, and the Body Politic', *Sixteenth Century Journal*, 37 (2006), 43–58.

Figure 1. *Triumph of the Eucharist and the Catholic Faith* (Copyright the Frick Collection)

challenge his authority. His public justification is even more instructive. He contrasted the seditious plebeian rabble who challenged his authority with his own aristocratic stoicism: he had displayed the 'moderation and patience' of a Pericles and the 'magnanimity' of a Scipio.[32] This was not a post-hoc rationalization of events either. The previous year the duke had told Throckmorton that there would have to be some form of Gallican reformation, but that he feared the Calvinists because they were 'Levellers', who wished only 'to pluck down an old building which consists of good and bad stuff'.[33]

Even those who are convinced by the argument that Guise was motivated more by social prejudice than by religious commitment will rightly warn

---

[32] 'Mémoires-journaux de François de Lorraine duc d'Aumale et de Guise, 1547 à 1563', in J.-F. Michaud and J.-J.-F. Poujoulat (eds), *Mémoires pour servir à l'histoire de France*, 2nd series, 10 vols (Paris, 1836–54), VI, 474.
[33] J. Stevenson (ed.), *Calendar of State Papers Foreign, 1560–1* (London, 1865), 462.

against making general assumptions from an individual case. But on the eve of Vassy in 1562 the duke of Guise was not alone. Only one Catholic prince signed up to the Edict of January. Most of his Catholic peers and several Protestant princes supported the Guise position.[34] The reasons for this were various. But what united this group at the apex of French society was their rejection of the Edict of January as a matter of principle, unable to accept the novelty of a monarchy where two rival religions were officially recognized. How much better the solution was in Germany, where the princes chose the religion of their subjects, or England, where only outward conformity was required. They were unable to disentangle matters of conscience from issues of sovereignty. They accepted freedom of conscience, but they had little interest in supporting public worship in the towns. Their conservatism was reinforced by any sign of rebellion amongst the urban faithful with its worrying overtones of Swiss-style communalism. It could be argued that the aristocracy was different, that they were likely to be motivated by self-interest than by thoughts of salvation. To do so runs the risk of arguing that there is a distinction between an aristocratic and a plebeian mentality; that social status shapes identity as much as belief. This seems unlikely: princes too lived in a community, even if it was rather more rarefied and heterodox than most.

I wish to infer something rather different from my blue-blooded case study. I would argue that in recent years we have become too reticent about locating faith in the nexus of social and political relations; that the recent historiography has overestimated the unity and cohesiveness of communities and of the Catholic community in particular. Before Trent, as Pollmann reminds us, Catholicism was not dogmatic but a spectrum of beliefs. The Catholic community was a creation of the Wars of Religion. Before the wars the Catholic response to heresy was varied: many were prepared to admit that the Protestants had some good ideas and blamed the failings of the Catholic clergy and not Satan for the presence of heretics in their midst. In 1562 all except the militant and super-pious minority or the totally unscrupulous were making difficult choices, trying to compromise between their obligations to God and their obligations to their neighbours. The opinions, analogies, and taxonomies of heresy they had were mediated not just by notions of the divine and the sacred, but by the practical sense of the self and others, the everyday interaction with kin and neighbour. The response to heresy was blunted by indifference and the complex tangle of social

---

[34] For some preliminary observations with a map showing the Guise's Protestant neighbours: S. Carroll, 'Les Guises et le luthéranisme' in A. Boltanski and F. Mercier (eds), *Le Salut par les armes: noblesse et défense de l'orthodoxie XIIIe–XVIIe siècle* (Rennes, 2010).

relations.³⁵ No wonder Protestant numbers grew so rapidly in France. Unlike acts of violence, mundane amicable interactions and everyday accommodations rarely leave a historical trace. How representative of Catholics was the petty gentleman Gilles de Gouberville? Gilles was a good Christian and neighbour, who worked tirelessly to settle disputes and avoid conflict. He heard a Protestant sermon at Pentecost 1562, but was otherwise wary of militants on either side. He reported the following conversation on 3 August, revealing relativist attitudes that are an antidote to the rhetorical absolutes which filled pamphlets and sermons:

> On my return I found *Contrôleur* [Thomas] Noel and Jehan France walking in the fields. We talked until we came to the rue d'Argouges. While we were talking about religion and the great divisions and controversies of opinions there are these days between men, France said: 'If I had my way, a new God would be made who was neither a Papist nor Huguenot so that it could no longer be said that so-and-so is a heretic or Huguenot. To which I said 'Unus est Deus ab eterno et eternus. We cannot make Gods since we are just men.' It seemed to me that Noel was very offended at France's words.³⁶

Noel's shock is a little surprising: he was a Protestant who would soon change sides. This exchange underlines the blurring of religious identities on the eve of the confessional age.

Violence is unpredictable. Its potency lies in its ability to transform the political scene and the social environment; once a fragile consensus is shattered, a chain of events is unleashed. Vassy imperilled the fragile accommodations and the everyday ecumenism that characterized many communities. The stereotypes of hate now became self-fulfilling; the militants had been justified and were emboldened. In the tense weeks that followed Vassy the spaces for accommodation narrowed significantly, as fear and rumour lent credence to the rhetoric of hate. The Protestants were better organized and throughout April congregations held hastily organized secret musters, drew up rolls of those able to bear arms and hatched plots to seize control of towns, in which they were remarkably successful. Violence was bloodiest where Catholics put up resistance, as in Toulouse.

---

[35] Mark Greengrass talks of the 'confused living experience' in his conclusion to L. Racaut and A. Ryrie (eds), *Moderate Voices in the European Reformation* (Ashgate 2005). In the English context Shagan has described the material benefits of accommodation, or what he refers to as collaboration.

[36] M. Foisil (ed.), *Le journal du Sire de Gouberville*, 4 vols (Pont Neuville, 1993–4), III, 806.

Bloodshed was not inevitable, however. In several towns that did not fall to the Protestants the overriding concern of the Catholic authorities, despite the fear of attack or treachery, was not persecution but the preservation of peace in the community. Events at Châlons-sur-Marne and Nantes, for example, look very similar to the situation that prevailed in the Low Countries, where the authorities were primarily concerned about the maintenance of civic order. Elizabeth Tingle has noted in Nantes 'the relatively small amount of bloodshed in the city, compared with other communities'.[37] Peace was probably harder to maintain where both sides were more evenly matched, where a well-armed Protestant minority posed a serious threat, such as in Troyes. But even here the two communities agreed at first that 'everyone will live and converse unanimously and amicably together without reproaching one another regarding one or other of the religions'.[38] In the meantime they continued to arm. On 12 April the Protestants made a vain attempt to seize the city. The arrival of the governor of Champagne, the duke of Nevers, did much to restore order. Nevers's sojourn was controversial, not least because, though a Protestant, he was loyal to the crown. His conduct was denounced by Protestant chroniclers as a dereliction of his duty to God.[39] This presumed that he should place his duty to God above that of the *bien public*. Civic order and authority were under threat throughout 1562 and he cracked down hard on anyone considered to be a rebel. He prosecuted the war vigorously (he was killed at the battle of Dreux). Nevers distrusted the urban congregation, which much to his annoyance had sent troops to the rebel lords, and he was happier in the company of the bishop, Caracciolo, a fellow aristocratic Nicodemite, in whose residence he stayed outside the city walls. The Protestants of Troyes were subject to harassment and intimidation by the Catholic garrison, but on the whole his efforts to maintain order were largely successful. The large-scale bloodshed that occurred elsewhere was avoided.[40]

The bloody episode that occurred in Valognes in 1562 is often cited as a classic example of inter-communal religious violence. The cadavers of the

---

[37] E. Tingle, 'A Mini-Colloquy of Poissy in Brittany: Inter-Confessional Dialogue in Nantes in 1562' in Racaut and Ryrie (eds), *Moderate Voices in the European Reformation*, 55.

[38] 'vivront et converseront tous unanimement et amyablement ensemble sans reprocher l'un à l'aultre pour le fait de l'une ou l'autre des religions': P. Roberts, *A City in Conflict: Troyes during the Wars of Religion* (Manchester, 1996), 102.

[39] Nicolas Pithou, *Chronique de Troyes et de la Champagne (1524–1594)* ed. P.-E. Le Roy and I. Palasi, 2 vols (Reims, 1998–2000), I, 408–502.

[40] According to Pithou's account two Protestants were murdered that summer. But he makes it clear that this was the work of soldiers and not the locals. At Bar-sur-Seine 140 Protestants were massacred, but again this was the work of soldiers, following an assault.

Huguenot victims were ritually displayed in the town, and 'some women had pulled out their eyes with needles'.[41] What is less well known is that the community had previously made a determined effort to avoid bloodshed. Resisting calls from outside to arm the people and expel the Protestants, they summoned an 'assembly of several officers and good bourgeois of each religion, who agreed to keep the people of both religions in peace under the King's Edict'.[42] This sort of cross-confessional co-operation occurred in other places in Normandy, most notably at Caen. It worked for a while in Valognes too. When there was an alarm on the day after Pentecost the bi-confessional militia restored order. But militias were notoriously unreliable and prone to infiltration by militants.[43] The killings which occurred on Sunday 7 June 1562 were not the result of confrontation of 'the people' in the street, but the result of a group of Catholic militiamen firing their arquebuses at a group of Protestant notables. Most of the Protestants escaped with the help of their Catholic neighbours.[44] The context of the violence in Valognes was all important. Pressures from outside were intense: the town was on the front line between Catholic Cherbourg and Protestant St Lô. It is too often forgotten much of the fighting in the civil war took place, not between the main field armies but between hastily raised local levies, in which the lines between professional soldiers and the people became blurred. Around Valognes the traditional conventions of chivalry had already been abandoned: the Protestant captain, the sieur de Hermesis, was killed by elements of the Cherbourg garrison 'using cruelty that was more than barbarous against this young gentleman, cutting off his arms and legs'.[45] Within days of the massacre at Valognes, Protestant troops entered the town to take their revenge, killing a Franciscan monk.

Beza was contemptuous of his co-religionists who tried to 'run with hare and run with the hounds' ('*nager entre deux eaux*'), though it is worthwhile remembering that Catholic-Protestant relations in Caen were to be much

---

[41] Crouzet contrasts this to the more matter-of-fact report of Gouberville: 'les femmes de Valognes venoient encore donner des coups de pierre et de baston sur les ditz corps': *Les Guerriers de Dieu*, I, 49.

[42] *Histoire ecclésiastique*, II, 836–7: 'assemblee daucuns officiers & bons bourgeois de l'une et de l'autre religion s'estans accordés de tenir le people des deux religions en paix sous l'Edict du Roy'.

[43] Benedict, *Rouen during the Wars of Religion*, 42–5.

[44] The women were protected from rape. See also Penny Roberts, this volume, 75–99.

[45] *Histoire ecclésiastique*, II, 843: 'usant de cruaute plus que barbare envers ce jeune gentilhomme, luy fist couper les bras & jambes'.

more harmonious than in towns which experienced a Protestant coup in 1562. Caen is one of a number of examples where the imperative of civic order took priority over religious unity. This supports Davis's contention that we distinguish between the behaviour of elites and the people in the streets. The actions of the elite often reveal a commitment to a humanist and civic agenda and an aversion to internal disorder. The people were committed to a concept of sacred order, which legitimized violence when the magistrates failed to act. But sixteenth-century communities were factional and hierarchical and this sort of 'popular' riot was less in evidence during the crucible of violence in 1562 than at other times. What made France different from other states which experienced the Protestant Reformation was the level of resistance by Catholics in a large number of cites. This can partly be explained by the success of Catholic polemic. But as the next example shows, the people not only required mobilization, they required organization and leadership.

Sens

The events at Sens were perhaps the deadliest of the massacres that occurred in the tense and rumour-filled weeks that followed Vassy. The events are crucial to Crouzet's thesis. According to him, the Catholic violence there was marked by such a fury that it demonstrates 'the internal logic of holy war'.[46] Davis refers to the events there twice, emphasizing the initiative displayed by the peasants who arrived in the town for the feast of St Savinien on Sunday 12 April 1562.[47] She was correct to identify a classic religious riot in which ritual plays a major role in structuring the action. The fighting seems to have begun spontaneously when the Catholic procession and the Protestant congregation collided, the Protestants apparently offering little resistance; children figure prominently in the desecration of corpses, which were ritually cleansed by being dumped in the Yonne. When the article was reprinted in *Society and Culture in Early Modern France*, Davis used this picture (Figure 2) of Sens to illustrate this rite of purification, which apparently mimicked exorcism. This is part of the picture, but it is not the whole of it.

Sens is also important because it was the subject of an unusually detailed and plausible report, clearly based on eye-witness testimony. Although the

---

[46] Crouzet, *Les Guerriers de Dieu*, I, 395.
[47] Her information comes from the Provins priest, Claude Haton. According to him, the pastor called on his flock to 'exterminer ceste vermine papalle'. In contrast, the priest officiating at the pilgrimage of St Savinien orders his flock to be orderly and not cause trouble. Haton's account does not tally with the eye-witness accounts cited below.

Figure 2. Jean Perrissin and Jacques Tortorel, *The Massacre at Sens, Burgundy, April 1562* (Bibliothèque Nationale de France, Paris)

original is lost it survives in a German translation.[48] Even more unusually, we have the report of a Catholic eyewitness, the *procureur de la communauté*, Balthasar Taveau.[49] Most unusually of all these two documents, while their interpretations of the events differ, agree on the crucial details of the chronology.

The city was a largish administrative and ecclesiastical centre of 16,000 inhabitants, which included a Protestant congregation of 600 or so. What the Protestants lacked in numbers they compensated for in quality: Beza was well connected in the city.[50] They had support among the large clerical community: the Cardinal of Châtillon was abbot of Saint-Jean-les-Sens, which seems to have been a centre for evangelization. Just as significant was the support of the dean of the cathedral and vicar-general of the archbishop, who was described as 'not [among] the most scrupulous who were in the Catholic Church'.[51] But the 'avowed leader of the Reformers at Sens' was Jacques de Spifame, who had only recently resigned as bishop of Nevers and abbot of Saint-Paul-les-Sens. His main residence was at the nearby château of Passy, but Spifame was a significant figure in the national leadership and often absent. The Protestants' main strength was among the office-holders. They were well represented in the legal community, and in particular the local *bailliage* court, where they were represented by no less than four *conseillers* and the *procureur du roi*, a commensal of Spifame and his man on the consistory. Their dominance of the organs of *police* is confirmed by the fact that the town provost, his lieutenant and the local *prévôt des maréchaux* were all Protestants.[52]

---

[48] *Historia. Wie iämerlich und erbärmlich die armen Christen der Reformierten Euangelischen Kirchen zu Sens, auss haimlichen practicken des Cardinals von Guise, Ertzbischoffen daselbst, vmbracht, geschmächt, vnd verhergt worden sind* (n. p., 1562).

[49] Taveaux wrote down these reminiscences ten years later. He was, however, one of the leaders of the Catholic party: A. Challe, *Histoire des guerres du calvinisme et de la Ligue dans l'Auxerrois, le Sénonais et les autres contrées qui forme aujourd'hui le département de l'Yonne* 2 vols (Auxerre, 1863–4), I, 339–43.

[50] F. Bitton, *Histoire de la ville de Sens* (Paris, 1943), 52.

[51] L. Bourquin (ed.), *Mémoires de Claude Haton*, 4 vols (Paris, 2001–7), I, 216, 459–60. The archbishop, the Cardinal of Guise, was a courtier and like most pre-Tridentine prelates left the administration of the archdiocese to men like these.

[52] The first Protestant from Sens to be executed was a lawyer, Jean Langlois. The Protestant party can be reconstructed from the German *Historia*, the *Histoire ecclésiastique* and the 'Extrait des Mémoires d'un protestant de Sens sur les massacres et saccagements de cette ville au mois d'avril 1561' printed in Challe, *Histoire des guerres du calvinisme et de la Ligue dans l'Auxerrois*, I, 343. See also F. Chandenier, 'Gilles Richeboys, deuxième imprimeur sénonais', *Bulletin de la société archéologique de Sens*, 30 (1916), 198–289.

Despite the disparity in numbers, the Protestants were a powerful group. As a consequence the city elite were dangerously divided. The first public sign of division occurred during the elections for the 1560 Estates-General, which seem to have been contested: a Protestant and a Catholic were returned for each of the Second and Third Estates of the *bailliage* of Sens.[53] Matters came to a head over elections to the city council on Holy Innocents Day 1561. The Catholics carried the day by mobilizing their supporters and taking advantage of their superior numbers: 'everyone gathered for the election in the largest numbers that anyone had ever seen for such an assembly'.[54] They were led by the *lieutenant criminel* Robert Hémard, whose assiduous heretic hunting in 1557-8, resulted in several arrests, one burning in the city itself and three more who were sent for execution in Paris.[55] Hémard had been mayor since 1561. However, Sens saw no popular riots before the Edict of January. As one might expect in a conflict involving the social elite, violence was the direct result of a dispute about rights. Following the Edict of January, Hémard tried to prevent the building of a Protestant temple in Sens, arguing that it had not been registered by the Paris Parlement, and that any attempt to do so was illegal. When the Parlement finally published the Edict, he changed tack and on 22 February 1562 printed the council's deliberations, encouraging the Lenten preachers to preach against it.[56] The first violence occurred on Easter Sunday, 29 March. According to the *Histoire ecclésiastique*, the official Protestant account, a troop of Protestants on their way home to Courtenay from the Sunday service at Sens had been attacked by Catholic boatmen at Paron, just outside the city walls. They had to be rescued by a troop of Protestant gentlemen. The clash was a serious matter. The Protestants agreed to suspend their services in the meantime and send their pastor away—there would be no Protestant service on Sunday 12 April.[57]

At first sight this looks like a classic case of popular action, undoubtedly stirred by preachers. But there are reasons for believing that the clash at Paron was not spontaneous. There was a logic in operation, channelling Catholic fury into effective action. The Protestants would have been well aware that the

---

[53] Lalourcé and Duval, *Recueil des pièces originales et authentiques concernant la tenue des Etats Généraux*, 9 vols (Paris, 1789), I.

[54] Challe, *Histoire des guerres du calvinisme et de la Ligue dans l'Auxerrois*, I, 55 and 339, gives the names of three Catholic Alderman, in addition to Taveau, the *procureur de la commaunauté*.

[55] *Histoire ecclésiastique*, I, 157; Jean Crespin, *Histoire des Martyrs*, 3 vols (Toulouse, 1885–7), II, 562, 660, 667.

[56] Challe, *Histoire des guerres du calvinisme et de la Ligue dans l'Auxerrois*, I, 50.

[57] A serious qualification of Haton's garbled account of the events.

clash was not happenstance. For the lord of Paron was none other than Robert Hémard, who owned several other fiefs in the vicinity and was the biggest landowner to the immediate west of the city. The lordship of Paron not only gave Hémard appreciable revenues, but as lord he owned numerous houses and collected rent from no less than 62 properties in the city.[58] Every year on 14 September the lord of Paron would place a seat and a table on the bridge over the Yonne and collect his dues from the inhabitants of Sens. Paradoxically, at one time the lord of Paron had been responsible for the spread of heresy in the town not its repression. The previous incumbent, Etienne Bierne, a rich financier, was a Protestant. So horrified was he at the thought of his Catholic elder son, Edme, inheriting his property he went to the unusual step of imposing the condition on his son 'not to receive any priest in his house at Chesnoy'.[59] He was right to be alarmed. When Edme, who was childless, came in turn to dispose of the inheritance in 1556 he favoured his Catholic relatives, which included his brother-in-law, Hémard, at the expense of his Protestant younger brother.[60]

Hémard's growing power and prestige in the city was also underpinned by his connections at court. In addition to his royal and municipal office, he was also *bailli* of the archbishop, the Cardinal of Guise. On the day after his tenants had clashed with the Protestants, he visited his master at Melun. But conspiracy was not confined to the Catholics. The prince of Condé had already issued orders mobilizing the churches in defence of the Edict of January and Tours fell on 30 March. In Sens the Protestants were well organized and had long employed an armed guard for their protection.[61] Preparations in the towns of Champagne were well advanced, but there were fatal delays as orders were awaited from the provincial governor, the duke of Nevers; a Protestant, he had pledged his support to Condé, but now dithered. This was to prove fatal to the Protestant cause in the region. In the next few days the Catholics took the initiative in Sens, seizing the municipal artillery, establishing a militia, which was paid for by the clergy. The city gates were secured.[62] On Friday 10 April the Catholic magistrates held a meeting, at which, the Protestants later claimed, a plot was hatched to exterminate them.

---

[58] For this and following: M. Roy, *Le Chesnoy lez Sens. Histoire d'un fief et de ses seigneurs* (Sens, 1901–5).

[59] Ibid., 142.

[60] Ibid., 144–5.

[61] *Histoire ecclésiastique*, II, 490. According to Taveau the armed guard under Mombaut had been in Sens for a year: Challe, *Histoire des guerres du calvinisme et de la Ligue dans l'Auxerrois*, I, 340–1.

[62] *Histoire ecclésiastique*, II, 488.

Evidence for this came in the evening when a number of arrests were made, in which a printer was wounded. Subsequent events suggest that this is unlikely, and that if there was an extermination plot it was poorly executed and had an extremely odd chronology. The militia was a threat. It consisted of fifty to sixty bourgeois who recruited among elements—boatmen (a group Hémard knew well) and butchers—who often appear in accounts of Catholic violence. But a total strength of 150-300 hardly constituted overwhelming force.[63]

Hémard and his satellites laid a different plan at their meeting.[64] On 5 April the Constable Montmorency had torn down the Huguenot's Parisian house of worship near the Porte Saint-Antoine. This was what the Catholic leadership in Sens had been trying to do for the previous month. Sunday 12th offered an excellent opportunity to tear down the meeting house, because the arrival of pilgrims for St Savinien's Day would offset Protestant superiority among the social elite. It is the Catholic Claude Haton, whose knowledge of the events was second-hand, who stresses the popular and spontaneous nature of the events of 12 April. The blame is placed squarely on 'heretics' on the one side and 'the people' on the other—both groups naturally prone to sedition. He conveniently exonerates the magistracy. The magistrates should have been responsible for maintaining order, especially since only the day before the massacre, the royal council had issued an order that the Edict of January must be upheld. Haton's version of a spontaneous riot is not sustainable.[65]

Our more detailed and coherent eyewitness account, on the other hand, makes a clear distinction between the militia (*söldner*) and the rabble (*pöfel*). That morning the procession was led to the abbey of Saint-Pierre-les-Sens, where one of the leaders of the Catholic faction was a functionary.[66] From here the Catholic militiamen escorted the St Saviniens' Day pilgrims out of the city and, as they stood guard, the common people (*gemainen pöfel*), at the mayor's command systematically razed the temple. The mayor had been

---

[63] The conspiracy began with a meeting of seven magistrates who then signed up fifty or so more supporters. They in turn recruited among the butchers and boatworkers, making a total of 300: Challe, *Histoire des guerres du calvinisme et de la Ligue dans l'Auxerrois*, I, 54–5. The organization is remarkably similar to other Catholic networks like the Paris Sixteen, which also spread along horizontal and vertical ties.
[64] Made explicit by Taveau, who was present: Challe, *Histoire des guerres du calvinisme et de la Ligue dans l'Auxerrois*, I, 341.
[65] The role of the Guise is ambiguous. Hémard seems to have got the final approval of the archbishop, Louis de Guise, before pulling the temple down. But a Guise sanctioned extermination plot is unlikely since on the 11 April they had agreed to uphold exercise of the Edict of January outside of Paris: *Histoire ecclésiastique*, II, 493.
[66] For this and following: *Historia*, 7.

petitioning for months for this opportunity. At this stage religious zeal was directed against the Protestants' house of worship and not on their bodies. The paraphernalia of war gave proceedings an official air. A trumpet was sounded. Drum rolls are elsewhere mentioned in the Protestant accounts. After eating—it was a feast day after all—the second part of the plan was put into action: the arrest of the Protestant leadership. This was done rather incompetently. One man was arrested, most escaped. There were the usual problems with militiamen: some were intent on pillaging the homes of their targets, others drank the wine cellars dry, and others were well disposed to their Protestant neighbours. However, even the official Protestant account agrees that no one was killed in the morning, a fact confirmed by the Catholic Taveau.[67]

The Protestants were momentarily caught of their guard. Their captain was not in the city. Mombaut, a Gascon, had responsibility for the Protestant churches in the Sénonais and, since there was no service in the city that morning, he was presumably attending to his duties in the countryside, where Protestantism was surprisingly well entrenched.[68] Matters turned bloody when it became clear that the Protestants were going to resist. Mombaut returned to the city in the afternoon and gathered a band of Protestants in a fortified house in the parish of Saint-Pierre le Rond, where they were strongest.[69] They were well armed: the lawyer la Fosse had managed to don a helmet and corselet. The subsequent heroics of this mixed band of lawyers and gentlemen, as they made sorties into the streets, fought hand-to-hand with halberds and swords and pushed the Catholics out of the neighbourhood, caused Protestant propaganda to get carried away. Mombaut, we are told, slipped out on one occasion to try to reach an arms cache 'belonging to certain gentlemen of the gendarmerie company of the

---

[67] *Histoire ecclésiastique*, II, 491–2 ; Challe, *Histoire des guerres du calvinisme et de la Ligue dans l'Auxerrois*, I, 341. All the evidence suggests that the people were promised pillage in payment for their demolition work, and that was why certain houses were marked with crosses.

[68] Almost certainly Bertrand de la Vaissière, seigneur de Monbeau: *Histoire de la famille de la Vassière* (Aurillac, 1928). Intriguingly, the château of Monbeau, not far from the banks of the Lot, was at the centre of the triangle formed by the small towns of Fumel, Tournon, and Penne in the Agenais. The role of la Vaissière's tenants in the murder of his close neighbour the baron of Fumel (see below) is well attested. La Vaissière was absent from his homeland, but his implication in events there is further evidence of the intimate nature of religious violence in this period.

[69] Again, the sources are in remarkable agreement. Taveau suggests that there was more than one house: Challe, *Histoire des guerres du calvinisme et de la Ligue dans l'Auxerrois*, 341.

Admiral, at that time in garrison in the said town of Sens'.[70] This aside helps to explain Protestant over-confidence the previous week: the city was garrisoned with a friendly armed unit, belonging to one of the Protestant leaders, Admiral Coligny. But, as in Toulouse, they found themselves outnumbered by the influx of outsiders from the surrounding region. And they were outgunned: the Catholics brought up artillery to batter the fortified house. It was only after Mombaut had been killed and his unit dispersed that the riot began.[71] 'Victory! Victory! Your Captain is dead'. Mombaut's body was desecrated and his corpse dragged through the town. 'Guard your pigs here we have the pigman' shouted the children 'and at each crossroads they burned his body with oven spits. They called the captain and the Huguenots of Sens the pigs because their preaching place was in the pig market. The children, having dragged the captain through the streets, went and threw him in the Yonne with his other pigs'.[72] Over the next two days, the Protestants listed fifty-two houses that had been pillaged and claimed that up to a hundred of their number were killed. The Catholics mentioned eleven deaths. The higher number seems more likely.[73]

Sens shares many characteristics with other acts of violence during the civil wars, most notably the Saint Bartholomew's massacre in Paris, in which the popular religious riot was a consequence of the failure of the Catholic authorities to maintain sufficient control of its militia. The rioting it caused was not respectable. As events spiralled out of their control, the Catholic magistrates were able to re-impose control only with difficulty. Orders issued on the 13 April to cease the violence were ignored. Some of the killing was ritualized. Other victims simply had their throats cut. Some of the killing had little to do with religion at all. Several officials who do not seem to have been Protestants were attacked and killed, including a Catholic magistrate who was murdered as he left Mass 'under the pretext of religion'.[74]

---

[70] *Histoire ecclésiastique*, II, 490.
[71] That Mombaut was the first Protestant victim is stated explicitly by Taveau, *Histoire des guerres du calvinisme et de la Ligue dans l'Auxerrois*, I, 341.
[72] *Mémoires de Claude Haton*, I, 216.
[73] Challe, *Histoire des guerres du calvinisme et de la Ligue dans l'Auxerrois*, I, 62–3, 343. The *Histoire ecclésiastique* claims 100 deaths and 100 houses pillaged. The papal nuncio mentions 80 victims.
[74] *Histoire ecclésiastique*, II, 492–3; Challe, *Histoire des guerres du calvinisme et de la Ligue dans l'Auxerrois*, I, 64. Sense had to be made of this butchery and it came on the evening of 13 April when rumour spread of a miraculous vision witnessed by priests in St Hilaire church. The bells were rung and the 'women in the town held a candlelight procession, each of them saying that this massacre was approved as if from God's own mouth'.

Where was the garrison? We do not know. But the answer as to why the Protestants failed to put up stiffer resistance in Sens may lie beyond the town. Many Protestants travelled for as much as half a day in order to worship at Sens, and had been subjected to intimidation. On the same day that the Catholic magistrates launched their coup in Sens another Protestant meeting house was razed outside the small town of Céant-en-Othe twenty miles to the west. Protestantism was well entrenched among the rural *artisanat* in the wooded uplands of the Othe, but the effort of protecting outlying communities left Protestant forces overstretched. In the summer of 1562 the Othe was the scene of a forgotten but particularly brutal rural civil war. Protestant communities came under attack from a Catholic band, the *pieds-nus*, or shoeless, which also besieged châteaux of the local gentry. Like the urban rioters Davis describes, these peasants were not acting as formal agents in an official capacity. However, they were officered by men from the Sens militia, which highlights the role of what one might call cadres in the organization and spread of violence.

Outsiders to the community played a prominent role in the violence at Sens; they were to be found among the victims and the killers. Some of the bloodiest examples of urban violence occurred when peasants, such as the St Savinien's Day pilgrims, intervened.[75] They were unconstrained by the ties of neighbourliness and kinship which tempered intra-urban conflict. The special treatment to which Captain Mombaut's corpse was subjected was in part because he was an outsider. Like many of the victims in Paris in 1572 he was a Gascon. He was distinguished not only by his dress, but by his southern accent and manner. The interplay between urban and rural violence, a factor hardly touched upon by the historiography, is also feature of our final case study.

Fumel

There is one episode of Protestant violence that stands out above all others during these years, one that neatly encapsulates the relationship between social tensions and religious violence: the murder and mutilation of the baron of Fumel on 23 November 1561. It was a cause célèbre. Davis quotes the official Protestant account that he was killed 'not for religion but for his tyrannies', for 'those of the Reformed Religion made war only on images, which do not bleed, while those of the Roman religion spilled blood with every kind of cruelty'.[76] Let us see how far this was true.

---

[75] A point made by Greengrass about the fighting in Toulouse.
[76] Natalie Zemon Davis, 'The Rites of Violence: Religious Riot in Sixteenth-Century France', *Past and Present*, 59 (1973), 76.

Catholic and Protestant sources differ only on what sparked the incident.[77] According to the investigation conducted at the behest of Fumel's widow, her husband was ambushed at between 3 and 4 pm on 22 November by half-a-dozen armed Protestants, who were lying in wait as he returned from hunting. No motive was given, except that they shouted 'long live the Gospels!' and swore to kill him. The Protestant version is different: Fumel had tried to disperse the faithful on their way to a service, hitting a deacon on the head with his pistol. What happened next is more certain. Fumel was forced to retreat to his castle. That evening the Protestants summoned help from the neighbouring churches. The following morning sharp-shooters mortally wounded the baron. The Protestant host, now numbering some 1500 to 2000 people, stormed the château, whereupon their victim was set upon by the mob and his corpse horribly mutilated.

Was Fumel's murder a religious riot or a peasant *Jacquerie*? There is evidence for both. Fumel was a cruel lord. The peasants pillaged his château and the house of the baronial receiver; they burned his archive. But the language of the rioters was religious. They called him a 'wicked persecutor' and left the scene of the crime singing psalms. Historians remain divided. For Henry Heller this is a clear example of 'class war'. To Janine Garrisson-Estèbe it was a peasant *Jacquerie*, 'popular, bloody, and spontaneous'.[78] However, I would agree with Denis Crouzet, who argues that Fumel's murder was indeed a religious riot.[79] He places the murder in the context of wider events in the Agenais, where, to all intents and purpose civil war was already under way. For Crouzet, the chronology of mounting religious tensions is crucial to understanding the events at Fumel. It was only one of a number of such attacks on Catholic seigneurs during 1561. These men were trying to stop the Reformation by force. The synod of Haute-Guyenne responded by

---

[77] M. de Mas-Latrie 'Arret de Montluc après la révolte des Protestants de Fumel contre leur seigneur, en 1561', *Mémoires de la societe royale des antiquaries de France*, 2 sér. VII (1844), 319–48; *Histoire ecclésiastique*, I, 885–98; A. de Ruble, *Lettres et commentaires de Blaise de Monluc*, II, 329–69, IV, 122–7; 'Documents pour servir à l'histoire des guerres de religion dans l'Agenais', *Revue de l'Agenais*, 9 (1882), 41–57. See also A. Durengues 'Le Protestantisme en Agenais, *Revue des Questions Historiques*, 112 (1930), 331–72.

[78] J. Garrisson-Estèbe, *Les Protestants du Midi*, 166–7. S. Brunet, *De l'Espagnol dedans le ventre. Les catholiques du Sud-Ouest de la France face à la Réforme, (v. 1540–1589* (Paris, 2007), refers to the events of 1561 as a 'peasants' war' (p. 82). This seems unlikely: links to the 1548 *gabelle* rebellion are even more tendentious, as the focus of resistance then was further to the north. The expert on peasant uprisings in the region, Y.-M. Bercé, also rejects the *Jacquerie* label: 'Retour sur le drame de Fumel, novembre 1561 – avril 1562, *Revue de l'Agenais*, 132 (2006), 543–58.

[79] Crouzet, *Les Guerriers de Dieu*, I, 515–23.

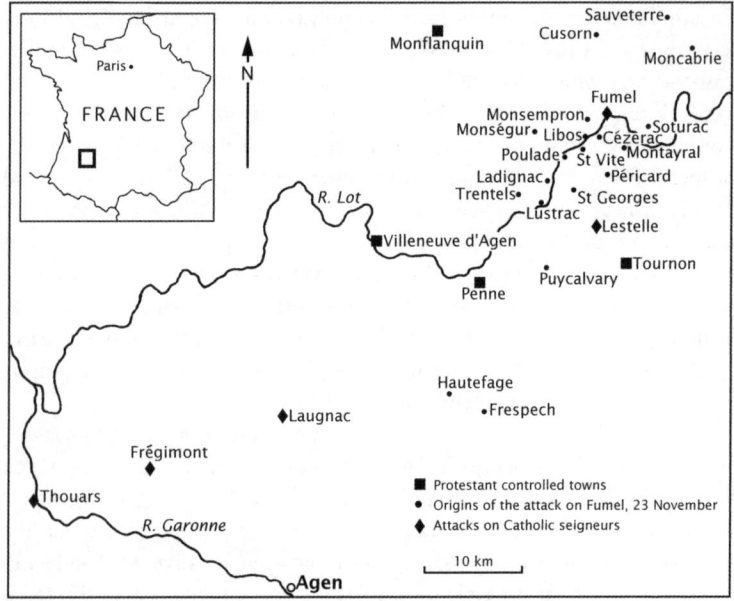

Figure 3. Map of towns and villages near Fumel

organizing militarily. A summer of escalating violence culminated in the week before Fumel's murder with a Catholic riot in Cahors, which left over twenty Protestants dead, and a week after Fumel's death when the Protestants took over Agen and abolished the Mass.

The towns and villages that were contiguous with the barony of Fumel (Figure 3) were at the heart of the Protestant offensive. The small town of Monflanquin was completely cleansed of popery by the end of 1560.[80] In the New Year the inhabitants of the towns of Penne and Villeneuve, just downstream on the banks of the Lot, chased the Franciscans out of town and destroyed the abbey of Saint-Eysses. When two local lords tried to stop iconoclasm at the neighbouring village of Tournon in the summer of 1561 they were confronted by a crowd of two to three thousand locals, who arrested them and then set about cleansing the church as planned.[81] It was the

---

[80] J.-P. Tamizey de la Roque, *Documents inédits pour servir à l'histoire de l'Agenais* (Paris, 1874), 82; 'Les temples protestants de Monflanquin aux XVIe et XVIIe siècles', *Revue de l'Agenais*, 40 (1913), 235; Durengues, 'Le Protestantisme en Agenais', 346–7.

[81] Durengues, 'Le Protestantisme en Agenais', 350–1.

inhabitants of places like these who answered the summons to Fumel on the evening of 23 November.

So Fumel's murder was not a *Jacquerie*. It was well organized and followed a pattern. Where Crouzet and I diverge is over what is inferred by the category of religious violence. For this religious riot had political overtones; social conflict also played a role. First of all, the assailants who attacked Fumel were not peasants. They were villagers. Of the 209 named suspects, there were forty-four artisans and fourteen notables.[82] Crucially, there was not a single nobleman involved. Fumel had several high status Protestant neighbours but they seem to have remained aloof from the violence.[83] The leadership came from the small towns. As well as men of the law and former priests, the leadership consisted of the leading citizens of Fumel, including its consuls. Although there was much fanfare about the severity of the repression, as so often during the Ancien Régime, the law was always more terrifying in appearance than reality. The ringleaders were never caught and never executed.

Secondly, had the rural notability—more literate, more wealthy, more numerous and more confident than it had ever been before—killed a member of the petty gentry then it would hardly be worth a mention. But Fumel was a man of significance.[84] He was a former ambassador to the Sultan, captain in the royal guard and styled himself 'haut et puissant messire'. And as Crouzet first pointed out, Fumel was not the only Catholic nobleman to be attacked. Already in the summer of 1560 a force of four thousand Protestants, ostensibly supporting the house of Bourbon in its dispute with the Guise, was in the field, releasing a minister from captivity, 'following some bloody fights'.[85] Between July 1561 and February 1562 there were numerous attacks on Catholic lords. In August, Protestants attacked the châteaux of Frégimont and Thouars. These belonged to an even bigger fish than Fumel: François I de Montpezat. The Montpezat had a fearsome reputation in the region. This was why Henry III would later choose François's son to captain the Gascon royal

---

[82] Bercé, 'Retour sur le drame de Fumel', 551.
[83] The Caumont-La Force were the major Protestant presence in the region: Garrisson-Estèbe, *Les Protestants du Midi*. Their stronghold at Castelmoron was, however, over 50 km upstream on the Lot. Jeanne de Biron's château at Gavaudun, across the Lémance river, was a much closer centre of Protestant evangelization: *Revue de l'Agenais*, 26 (1899), 112.
[84] For this and following : H.-G. O'Gilvy, *Nobiliaire de Guienne et de Gascogne. Revue des familles d'ancienne chevalerie ou anoblies de ces provinces, antérieures à 1789*, 4 vols (Bordeaux, 1856–83), I, 1–18.
[85] J.-R. Marboutin, 'Le Château de Savignac', *Revue de l'Agenais*, 31 (1904), 520.

guard, the *Quarante Cinq*. His security responsibilities extended to murder and assassination.[86] Murder was a routine weapon of Montpezat rule in the Agenais. When a Catholic priest publicly criticized their conduct, François's uncle, who was popularly known as the 'Maltese dragon', had him murdered at the altar. François himself was the instigator of attacks on the Protestant churches at Libos, Tournon, and La Plume. The Protestants responded by trashing the seigneurial church at Laugnac.

Confessional violence did not take place in a vacuum. Family politics shaped religious identity in the Agenais. François de Montpezat's elder brother Antoine, 'a character who was not only violent and unbalanced but also jealous and a stirrer' was a Protestant. Having been disinherited by his father, he was fighting against his younger siblings for his rightful portion. Troops loyal to him had already attacked the châteaux of Laugnac and Frégimont in January 1558. The evidence suggests that Antoine was already leader of the Protestants' armed wing in the region. His insurgent activities expanded over the next two years and he emerged as a significant Protestant captain in 1562.[87] Fumel would have been unable to remain aloof from this bloody feud and the violence it unleashed: Antoine de Montpezat was his brother-in-law. The dangers of opposing Antoine were made explicit when, around this time, he had another brother-in-law, Jean-Georges de Rochechouart, murdered—an act that clarified the Montpezat succession and enabled the brothers to make peace in 1564.[88]

Peasant revolt will not help us explain the nature of Protestant-Catholic violence in the Agenais. Nor I think will 'The Rites of Violence'. More

---

[86] Ibid.; J. Hazon de St Firmin, *Un Assassin du Duc Henri de Guise. François II de Montpezat, Baron de Laugnac, capitaine des Quarante-Cinq. 1566–1590* (Paris, 1912); A. de Bellecombe, *Histoire du château, de la ville, et des seigneurs et barons de Montpezat et de l'abbaye de Pérignac* (Auch, 1898).

[87] Laugnac and Frégimont had been seized by Antoine's brother-in-law Jean-Georges de Rochechoaurt seigneur de Plieux: Archives Nationales, Paris, JJ 263b fo. 153, April 1565 and fo. 235. Antoine, known usually as either the seigneur of Savignac or Thouars, appears in the Protestant army in Guyenne in 1562 with the nickname 'Captain Rossillon': *Histoire ecclésiastique*, III, 77. Antoine's lieutenants in 1558 also seem to have joined the Protestant cause: des Cours was a relative, probably brother, of the leader of the Protestant soldiers in 1560: Marboutin 'Le Château de Savignac', 520. Pierre de Labay sieur de Lescalle was a gendarme in the company of the king of Navarre from 1558 until 1571: J.-J. Monlezun, *Histoire de la Gascogne depuis les temps les plus reculés jusqu'à nos jours*, 6 vols (Auch, 1846–50, repr. Nîmes, 2002), VI, 161–2.

[88] L. Massip, 'La ville et les seigneurs de Cancon en Agenais', *Revue de l'Agenais*, 30 (1890), 257, 372. Montpezat and Fumel had married respectively the sisters Françoise (1526) and Gabrielle (1536) de Verdun.

pertinent for Protestants were their rights. The Protestant struggle for recognition had brought them into conflict with the traditional political elite. As the traditional elite fractured, the lead in the Agenais was taken by small towns, often bastides like Monflanquin and Fumel, which had a fierce history of independence, in which Protestants were well organized to take control in municipal elections and institute a top-down Reformation, which left the consuls firmly in control of the local consistory. They were well used to using the law against the local nobility and this is how they first proceeded when faced with the Catholic backlash. The two Catholic noblemen arrested at Tournon for harassing the faithful were also accused of murder and abduction. A similar operation was planned at Fumel. Indeed, the Protestant leadership had obtained a warrant in August. This time, however, the operation was botched. But even after the murder, they attempted to provide a fig-leaf of legality by launching a counter-suit against Fumel's widow. These are the actions of men confident in the law. No wonder the ringleaders escaped execution.

And the language they used in defence of their rights was that of the *bien public*, the commonwealth. They called Fumel a 'wicked persecutor', a biblical term, but they also called him a 'tyrant', a word that was rare in the Geneva Bible, but which was a commonplace of medieval political culture. When persecution was stepped up in 1559 and 1560, during the Guise-dominated regime of Francis II, religious and political tyranny became synonymous. The flood of pamphlets attacking the Guise had a broad appeal, as Quentin Skinner has pointed out: 'Once we see how little of their ideology was distinctively Calvinist, we are bound to ask whether they may have been concerned . . . with appealing to the uncommitted, seeking to reassure those thinking of joining the cause, and above all attempting to neutralise as far as possible the hostile Catholic majority'.[89] Republican language was also used to justify the Reformation in the Agenais. The consuls of Mézin ran the priests and monks out of town otherwise they would 'turn the world upside down and disturb the Republique'.[90] And the crowd at Fumel were doing the same: fighting for the commonwealth not just against an enemy of the faith, but against a lord who was notorious for his wickedness. In Calvinist psychology the two were related.

It would be wrong to see the hunger for some form of Reformation in rigidly confessional terms. Many of the insurgents who attacked Fumel were tenants of his neighbour, Antoine de Poton de Raffin; a courtier and seneschal

---

[89] Q. Skinner, *Visions of Politics*, 3 vols (Cambridge, 2002), II, 263.
[90] Tamizey de la Roque, *Documents inédits pour servir à l'histoire de l'Agenais*, 85.

of the Agenais, he was the most powerful man in the region. Though Raffin was a Catholic, he took an entirely different view to the breakdown of order in 1561. A month prior to the assassination on 11 October, he oversaw the reorganization of the Agen municipality, establishing a bi-confessional city council, in which half of the twenty-four councillors were Protestants.[91] What clinches the non-confessional and political aspects of the Fumel case is what did not happen on 23 November. In a region which was witnessing one of the most intense iconoclastic campaigns of the Reformation there are no reports of the despoliation of sacred sites. Fumel church was left untouched; the Cluniac priory of Monsempron was left alone. No wonder, as the *Histoire ecclésiastique* points out, Catholics too were happy to join in the attack on the baron.

Davis was correct in identifying one significant pattern in religious violence. Catholics were the champions of killing. But she overstates Protestant restraint. Until very recently the historiography of the French Reformation supported this view of the Protestants as essentially victims, since it concentrated largely on their struggle for recognition. But the paradoxical nature of French Calvinism is revealed in the *Histoire ecclésiastique*'s official account of Fumel's murder. The murder was condemned as 'inexcusable', and the faithful were reminded that vengeance belongs to God alone. But it also believed that Fumel was getting his just desserts for the barbarous tyrannies that he had brought back from Constantinople. One of the ringleaders was avenging his father, who had been condemned to the galleys by Fumel's legal chicanery. The other was the son of a man whom the baron had tied to his horse and dragged back and forth across the Lot. Fumel was struck down by two persons chosen 'by a singular providence'. This construal of divine vengeance was commonly used by Protestants to justify their acts of violence. The Fumel incident also reminds us of the liberating effect of the popular Reformation, one that cannot be confined to a narrow confessional history. It was a religious riot, but one that articulated social grievances; it was an attack both on a persecutor and on a tyrant; it was part of a wider struggle for rights in which a rural notability challenged powerful Catholic aristocrats.

Moreover, Fumel's murder was not an isolated occurrence. For the Protestants called upon a novel form of violence with which to achieve their wider religious objectives: political assassination. This began in 1557 with an unsuccessful attempt on the life of King Henry II. But the first shots in France's civil war were fired in Scotland. The overthrow of the Guise regime there in 1559 inspired their French co-religionists with similar patriotic ideals

[91] J. Beaune, 'Deux sénéchaux d'Agenais (aux XVIe siècle)', *Revue de l'Agenais*, 33 (1906), 63.

to resist the 'foreign' tyranny at home and call the Guise to account at the hitherto moribund Estates-General. Protestants posed, with some success, as the scourge of unpopular officials. The insurgents' targets were selective: the Guise, their servants and unpopular officials. The assassination of tax collectors we can assume was popular among Catholics and Protestants alike. Once civil war began, this violence acquired the trappings of the due legal process. The sack of Bayeux by Protestant troops under Coligny on 4 March 1563 was followed by the summary execution of taxmen and priests. Among the victims was the *contrôleur du domaine*, Thomas Noel, whom we encountered six months before in irenic conversation with his friend Gilles de Gouberville. The *Histoire ecclésiastique* found Noel's apostasy reprehensible, but that was not the reason for his death. He, 'one of the most cunning men in the region', and his colleagues were getting their just desserts because of their rapacity, which had 'marvelleously exhausted the whole region, in such a way that the majority [of people] had abandoned their houses'.[92] The number of victims was relatively small and, in contrast to the popular character of much Catholic violence, these 'lynchings' were *populist*. But in a hierarchical society, the quality of the victims was more important than numbers in impact. As a contemporary saying had it you cannot compare 'salmon with frogs'. Assassinations spread terror among Catholics which explains why the murder of the duke of Guise on 1 February 1563 had such a disproportionate effect.

After thirty years of revisionism, recent research is once again rediscovering the political and social radicalism of the Calvinist Reformation.[93] Religion was pervasive in sixteenth-century society and contemporaries saw the problems that confronted them—political, social, or economic—and their solutions in moral terms. The idea of a Godly Reformation that returned the world to its pristine state gave fresh meaning to all manner of resentments. While the dominant voices of French Protestantism were replete with discourses about the need for passive obedience to the powers that be, the actions of their followers was often in stark contrast. In the 1560s the tombs, effigies, and monuments of the kings of France were the object of systematic iconoclastic destruction: at Cléry, the most important shrine devoted to the Valois, the effigy of Louis XII, kneeling in prayer, was treated to the charade of a mock execution before being smashed. If kings were not sacred it followed that they

---

[92] *Histoire ecclésiastique*, II, 857.
[93] For a starting point: 'P. Benedict, 'The Dynamics of Protestant Militancy: France, 1555–1563' in P. Benedict et al. (eds), *Reformation, Revolt and Civil War in France and the Netherlands, 1555–1585* (Amsterdam, 1999).

were mere mortals subject to God's retribution like us.[94] John Foxe's Latin martyrology, which was translated into French in 1561, reinforced this point in its preface by explaining that God uses the most insignificant individuals to exemplify his glory. Kings may come and go; political empires will decay. The only enduring empire is that of the 'captain-general of God's elect'. These ideas spread rapidly: summoned to surrender in the name of the king in February 1562 Jehan du Verdier, king's advocate in the seneschal court of Armagnac, replied 'What king? We are the kings, he that you speak of is a little turdy kinglet; we'll whip his breech and set him to a trade, to teach him to get his living as others do'. No wonder that several French Protestant princes took umbrage and threw in their lot with the Guise.

From 1559 Protestants developed the idea of a commonwealth in which sovereignty was shared between the monarch and the people represented by the Estates-General. This Republican (in the traditional sense) ideology was immensely attractive, even to those who found their religious beliefs abhorrent. The diary of the priest Claude Haton, has been plundered by religious historians for its insights into popular belief and culture. But they missed something. Haton also recorded the anti-monarchical, anti-seigneurial, constitutionalist language of his parishioners. Haton was radicalized by the fight against the Reformation. He uses a Republican language to denounce monarchical tyranny. The monarchy had been desacralized, preparing the way for the experiment with elective monarchy. His parishioners were able to imagine the king's death 'desiring his death and the extermination of his entire lineage'.[95] His sharpest invective was reserved for the local gentry, invariably referred to as 'genspillehommes' or 'genstueshommes'. Haton learned to trust in the poor. Unlike Montaigne, he preferred the common opinion, 'the voice of the people, there is the voice of God'. This was the language of social antagonism. It was not a new language. Nor can it be located in Haton's relationship to the means of production. It was directly inspired by his reading of the Gospels.

Conclusion

As well as the British School of Marxists and social anthropology, 'The Rites of Violence' was also inspired by the first stirrings of the public debate in the west on the origins and nature of the Holocaust. It was a prescient article too, given the revival of ethnic and religious violence in the wake of the end of the Cold

---

[94] For this and following: M. Greengrass, 'Regicide, Martyrs and Monarchical Authority in France in the Wars of Religion' in R. von Friedeburg (ed.), *Murder and Monarchy; Regicide in European History, 1300–1800* (Basingstoke, 2005).

[95] *Mémoires de Claude Haton*, IV, 112, 215, 318, 359, 445.

War. The lessons derived from more recent research on the popular motivation for participation in the Final Solution in Eastern Europe are however ambiguous. Ideological factors have been downplayed. The expropriation of Jewish property is now recognized as a major contributory factor. Violence offered all sorts of opportunities for the unscrupulous. At the end of *Neighbors*, his study of the murder of the Jews of Jedwabne by their Polish neighbours in 1941, Jan Gross remains perplexed: 'the Holocaust . . . was a heterogeneous phenomenon . . . we must see it as a mosaic composed of discrete episodes, improvised by local decision-makers, and hinging on unforced behaviour, rooted in God-knows-what motivations, of all those who were near the murder scene at the time'.[96]

I do not wish to conclude from this that we should retreat down the cul-de-sac of stagnant empiricism. It would be wrong to conclude that there was no structure to religious violence. We owe Davis a great debt for showing us that was not the case. 'The Rites of Violence' shows us that there is another path that leads to more fruitful pastures. To my mind, better points of comparison are to be found in other states which are characterized by economic under-development and a weak state. Post-colonial sub-Saharan Africa, for example, has been particularly prone to ethnic and religious violence and civil war. From the origins of the Biafran war to the recent riots in Kenya and Nigeria the rites of violence identified by Davis, in which victims and corpses are subject to ritual degradation and mutilation is depressingly familiar. The genocide in Rwanda, in which between 500,000 and 800,000, perhaps one-eighth of the population, were killed in three months, has stimulated some of the best work.

Rwanda was utterly unlike the Holocaust in that the Hutu militias did without technical expertise or firearms. Most of them were unemployed or underemployed adolescent males imbued with the assurance that that they were acting out the will of their country's leaders with the support of the majority of their compatriots. The killing was meticulously organized and by the time it had started, the militias numbered around 30,000—one militia member for every ten families—and had nationwide coverage with representatives in every neighbourhood. Early research argued that cultural factors were paramount in mobilizing the Interahamwe, 'those who stand (fight, kill) together', and Impuzamugambi, 'those who have the same (or a single) goal', militias to carry out their pogroms. Popular resentment of the Tutsis was animated by radio propaganda. Discourses of hate are never produced in a vacuum and the Rwandan genocide followed culturally specific forms.

---

[96] J. Gross, *The Destruction of the Jewish Community in Jedwabne, Poland* (Princeton, 2001), 81.

The violence in Rwanda was rooted in specific cultural dispositions, since 'we are, each of us, functions of how we imagine ourselves and of how others imagine us'.[97] Myths and stereotypes were internalized. 'In the discourse of Hutu extremism, Huthu autochthony is opposed to the foreignness of the Tutsi'.[98] The killing was structured by a mythic logic, which, in much the same way as Davis's riots, gave rise to rituals and techniques of cruelty.

More recent research has exposed this interpretation as simplistic. It might be added that culture served as an alibi for the international community: Rwandans were simply killing each other as they were wont to do, for primordial tribal reasons, since time immemorial.[99] Fieldwork based on killers' testimonies has found that 'pre-existing hatreds tended to be personal and individual, not collectively aimed at an entire ethnic group'.[100] The mounting evidence is that situational factors, especially fear and uncertainty, were far more important in explaining the dynamics of violence than culture and identity. It was civil war, the consequence of a Tutsi insurgency since 1989, which provided the Hutu oligarchy with its best weapon yet against pluralism. Before the civil war, communities had been highly integrated and there is little evidence that mass killing was the result of 'deep, pre-existing antipathy and prejudice'.[101] The Rwandan genocide was a political crisis fed by poverty, social division, and war. Responsibility for the genocide went all the way to the top: it was openly discussed in cabinet meetings and it was organized by top-ranking government officials and members of the army. The genocide was a struggle for Hutu power. On the local level planners included mayors and members of the police. Patron–client networks were the skein of the conspiracy. The nation was urged to unite against a common enemy—all Tutsis were potential accomplices of the insurgents. The genocide was the culmination of assassinations and mini-rehearsals, but civil war was the most consequential factor, legitimizing mass killing and justifying extreme measures. War not only legitimates killing as an acceptable practice, it creates a culture of violence.

The scale of the bloodletting in sixteenth-century France was more limited. The reasons for this are not just technological. By and large French communities were not irrevocably divided, as the current historiography would have us believe, between two hostile confessional groups intent on violence.

---

[97] P. Gourevitch, *We Wish to Inform You that Tomorrow We Will be Killed with Our Families: Stories from Rwanda* (London, 2000), 71.
[98] C. Taylor, *Sacrifice as Terror: the Rwandan Genocide of 1994* (Oxford, 1999), 30.
[99] Gourevitch, *We Wish to Inform You*, 154.
[100] L. A. Fujii, *Killing Neighbors: Webs of Violence in Rwanda* (Cornell, 2009), 183.
[101] S. Straus, *The Order of Genocide: Race, Power and War in Rwanda* (Cornell, 2006), 199.

Politics played a significant role in the two major 'seasons' of inter-communal violence which occurred in 1561-2 and 1572. I do not wish to infer from this that we reduce the ritual cruelty Davis uncovered to surrogates for political action. Rather, I suggest that, instead of using rites as a simple model or template for religious violence, it is more fruitful to understand them as one of a set of variables, as part of a larger dynamic. In Rwanda, cultural factors may partly explain the very large numbers of deaths.[102] This works less well for France where popular religious riots on their own rarely produced large numbers of victims. In both cases organization and leadership were factors that led to a higher body count. The existence of bi-confessional communities throughout Europe suggests that violence was neither inevitable nor the product of a dialectical *Kulturkampf*. The formation of distinct and mutually hostile confessional communities was a consequence rather than a cause of violence. Recent research has underlined the intimate and banal causes of inter-communal violence, 'for the many people who are not naturally bloodthirsty, civil war offers irresistible opportunities to harm everyday enemies'. This is pertinent to the sixteenth-century French case, because as Stathis Kalyvas goes on to explain, 'civil war privatizes violence'.[103] Local and personal grievances were often transformed into lethal violence; only after it occurred was the violence endowed with religious meaning. Civil war also made possible a new type of politics that was based on religious identity, in which the elites legitimized and often encouraged popular violence.

The lessons of recent ethnic conflict for the historian of sixteenth-century Europe are clear. In reviewing the evidence from Africa, Mahmood Mamdani states that: 'Ethnic cleansing is rarely spontaneous: it requires elite conspiracies and methodical popular organisation'.[104] The privileging of macro-level causal explanations and ill-defined categories, such as 'ideology', 'belief' or 'culture', will not help us explain how violence escalated or was contained. As analytical categories they are static concepts that of themselves cannot explain violence's peculiar dynamics. The political context matters because particular circumstances, which generate fear and insecurity, can cause people to commit harm that they might not otherwise have been prepared to commit. My contention is that it would be more rewarding to study sixteenth-century religious violence in the context of micro-politics, understanding the conspiratorial role played by local groups, such as urban factions

---

[102] Scott Straus, however, plays down cultural factors altogether and highlights the role of geography and the state.

[103] S. N. Kalyvas, *The Logic of Violence in Civil War* (Cambridge, 2006), 389.

[104] 'The Invention of the Indigène', *London Review of Books*, 33 no.2 (20 January 2011), 31.

and paramilitary cadres, and viewing the events through the prism of everyday social relations. The response to Protestantism and civil war was mediated by these relationships and the nature, chronology, and level of violence thus differed according to the local context. My contention is supported by the growing body of work on genocide which highlights the key role played by social ties and group dynamics in leading ordinary people to join in the violence.[105]

---

[105] The seminal work is C. Browning, *Ordinary Men: Police Battalion 101 and the Final Solution in Poland* (New York, 1992). See also Fujii, *Killing Neighbors*, 187.

Prophets in Arms? Ministers in War, Ministers on War: France 1562–74

Philip Benedict

Late in France's First Civil War (1562–3), just after the duke of Guise had been struck down by a Huguenot assassin, the minister of the Reformed church of Valence, Loys Normand, sent a letter to the churches located in the vicinity of Valence and Montélimar.[1] He urged them to send troops to the Protestant military commander of the province, the count of Crussol, who was mustering forces to come to the aid of besieged Grenoble. In what is almost certainly a reference to Guise's killing (although this is never made absolutely explicit in the document), Normand first announced that even though the faithful had shown themselves ungrateful for the benefits and victories that God had given them, the Almighty had

> struck down and killed the tyrant who had sought by all means to encourage foreign nations, kings and potentates to exterminate His poor churches... and to banish from the Kingdom the fruits of his worthy Gospel, in order to maintain popish superstition and idolatry, overcome (?) the faithful children of God, massacre and sack their women and children, and loot and pillage their goods and houses. But this good God punishes them just as He formerly did Sennacherib.[2]

---

[1] Archives Départementales de la Drôme, Valence, E 3338/11, Loys Normand to 'messieurs et freres des églises de Valentinois et circonvoisins comme Estelle, Livron, Loriol, Monthellimart et son ressort', Valence, 1 March 1563, partial copy made by a deacon of the church of Montélimar. The duke of Guise was shot on 18 February 1563 and died on 24 February. Grenoble came under siege on 1 March and was relieved by Crussol on 4 March.

[2] The story of the Israelites' dealings with the mighty Assyrian king Sennacherib is recounted in 2 Kings 18–19. During the reign of King Hezekiah, Sennacherib overran and conquered Judah, but the Lord promised to preserve the surviving remnant of the Israelites. An angel of the Lord struck down thousands in the Assyrian camp by night, and Sennacherib withdrew. He was subsequently killed by his sons. In March 1563, the Protestants controlled most of Dauphiné, but nationally they had lost control of the great

After suggesting to the churches that they hold services to give thanks for their deliverance, Normand went on to urge those who received the letter to send all their forces to Crussol's side at Romans, 'where milord the count has gone to deliver, by this blow and with the aid of our benevolent God, all of the churches of this province from oppression'. Acting by virtue of an unspecified charge given him by Crussol, he also told them to make a register of all 'seditious and rebellious' individuals who refused to cooperate, and to deal with them promptly. The copy of this letter that comes down to us was made by a deacon of the church of Montélimar and sent on to the church of Dieulefit. The minister or elders at Dieulefit must have in turn communicated it to the then-Protestant civic authorities since the letter was subsequently kept in the municipal archives amid a series of other orders concerning the mustering and payment of troops. Whether Normand was a member of the political council attached to Crussol or simply chaplain to his troops, we find here a minister disseminating both military and political instructions via the churches of the region during the First Civil War. He likened the war to the freedom struggles of the ancient Israelites and construed it as being fought to prevent the extermination of Christ's Gospel and the protection of his children, their houses, and families.

Since Natalie Zemon Davis first argued so persuasively in 'The Rites of Violence' that to understand the 'preconditions for guilt-free massacre' historians needed to pay more attention to the core values of those who spilled so much blood in the streets of France between 1560 and 1598, students of the French civil wars have, in Mack Holt's memorable phrase, 'put religion back into the Wars of Religion'.[3] A long series of local studies have repeatedly suggested that the rise of religious divisions sparked violence in the localities even before leading grandees raised the banner of revolt at the centre, thereby undermining the previously dominant interpretation of the civil wars as stemming chiefly from the rivalries between the aristocratic houses of

---

majority of cities they had taken early in the war. The analogy between their situation and that of the Israelites conquered by the Assyrians was thus apt, and the allusion to Sennacherib an expression of faith and hope.

[3] Natalie Davis, 'The Rites of Violence: Religious Riot in Sixteenth-Century France', *Past and Present* 59 (1973), 51–91, also published in Alfred Soman (ed.), *The Massacre of Saint Bartholomew: Reappraisals and Documents* (The Hague, 1974), and in Davis, *Society and Culture in Early Modern France* (Stanford, CA, 1975); Mack P. Holt, 'Putting Religion Back into the Wars of Religion', *French Historical Studies*, 18 (1993), 524–51.

Guise, Montmorency, and Bourbon.[4] Detailed examinations of networks of aristocratic clientage have likewise sapped this older view by showing that clientage ties only weakly explain party affiliation during the initial decades of the religious wars.[5] Denis Crouzet's massive, stimulating thesis of 1990, *Les Guerriers de Dieu,* followed the trail blazed by Davis to offer an explicitly culturalist account of 'la violence au temps des troubles de religion' that recast the entire story of the French Wars of Religion as a dialectic of religious and intellectual change that found expression in crowd action.[6] Crouzet has in turn inspired a raft of younger French scholars to undertake innovative cultural studies of later sixteenth-century politics. That religious convictions shaped the politics of the later sixteenth century is now the prevailing orthodoxy in both French and Anglophone historical writing about the French religious wars.

But just how did religious belief beget violence and civil war? Here, the consensus evaporates and some of the limits of the past generation's innovative work become clear. If most specialists agree with the general proposition

[4] Philip Benedict, *Rouen during the Wars of Religion* (Cambridge, 1981) was the first monograph to study the wars from the vantage point of a single community and to emphasize the inadequacy of Romier's emphasis on aristocratic factionalism. Among the many local and regional studies that have followed, those that have most enriched our understanding of the dialectic between religious change and political conflict at the local level include: Barbara B. Diefendorf, *Beneath the Cross: Catholics and Huguenots in Sixteenth-Century Paris* (Oxford, 1991); Marc Venard, *Réforme protestante, Réforme catholique dans la province d'Avignon* (Paris, 1993); Penny Roberts, *A City in Conflict: Troyes during the French Wars of Religion* (Manchester, 1996); Mack P. Holt, 'Wine, Community and Reformation in Sixteenth-Century Burgundy', *Past and Present,* 138 (1993), 58–93; Michel Cassan, *Le temps des guerres de religion. Le cas du Limousin (vers 1530–vers 1630)* (Paris, 1996); Philip Connor, *Huguenot Heartland: Montauban and Southern French Calvinism during the Wars of Religion* (Aldershot, 2002); Thierry Amalou, *Une concorde urbaine. Senlis au temps des réformes (vers 1520–vers 1580)* (Limoges, 2007); and idem, *Le Lys et la Mitre. Loyalisme monarchique et pouvoir épiscopal pendant les guerres de Religion (1580–1610)* (Paris, 2007).

[5] Revisionist studies revealing the extent and limits of aristocratic clientage during the civil wars include Kristen Neuschel, *Word of Honor: Interpreting Noble Culture in Sixteenth-Century France* (Ithaca, 1989); Stuart Carroll, *Noble Power during the French Wars of Religion: The Guise Affinity and the Catholic Cause in Normandy* (Cambridge, 1998); Mark W. Konnert, *Local Politics in the French Wars of Religion: The Towns of Champagne, the Duc de Guise, and the Catholic League, 1560–1595* (Aldershot, 2006); Ariane Boltanski, *Les ducs de Nevers et l'Etat royal. Genèse d'un compromis (c.1550–c.1600)* (Geneva, 2006).

[6] Denis Crouzet, *Les Guerriers de Dieu. La violence au temps des troubles de reigion, vers 1525–vers 1610* (Seyssel, 1990).

that religion drove the Wars of Religion, they offer different opinions about which religious convictions were most important in stimulating and legitimating the religious violence. 'The Rites of Violence' highlighted the importance of beliefs about pollution: if Catholic crowd violence was directed chiefly against people—the heretics in their midst—while Protestant crowd violence was aimed principally at things—images, the consecrated host, or other objects of false worship—this was because both sought to purge the community of forms of defilement that threatened to bring God's wrath upon it.[7] Crouzet located the initial cause of religious violence in the growing mood of eschatological anxiety within Catholicism that both led France's Catholics to respond violently to the presence of heretics within their midst and made the Calvinist message of predestinarian solafideism appealing since it liberated believers from anxiety about how they would be received at the last judgment. My 1999 essay on 'The Dynamics of Protestant Militancy: France, 1555–1563' identified the rise of Protestantism as the chief destabilizer of the religious status quo and argued that Reformed militancy arose from a three-fold dynamic.[8] First, Calvin's powerful critique of false worship and Nicodemism convinced believers that they were doing their duty to obey God, not man, in seceding from the established church and in setting up Reformed assemblies, even though such assemblies were forbidden by law. Once established, such assemblies then could justify arming themselves for protection against attack by bands of angry Catholics in the name of self-defence. Second, the biting polemical attacks on false forms of Catholic worship and on the greedy priests who benefited from them that were central to the propaganda of the years 1555–62 generated violent anger among some new converts, who took to direct action to drive out the Mass and the priests. Third, once the Edict of January 1562 granted the Reformed freedom of worship within the kingdom, the Protestants felt themselves justified in taking up arms to protect the rights they had just obtained in the name of defending the law and the king's will, of self-protection, and of obedience to divine commandment.

Studies during the past thirty years have focused primarily on understanding episodes of crowd violence, with the prevalent approach being to explore the messages conveyed by widely circulating pamphlets, printed sermons, or prevalent rituals to show how these illuminate the forms and targets of collective action. Far less explored have been the roles that the churches and their

---

[7] Davis, 'The Rites of Violence'.

[8] Philip Benedict, 'The Dynamics of Protestant Militancy: France, 1555–1563' in Philip Benedict, Guido Marnef, Henk van Nierop and Marc Venard (eds), *Reformation, Revolt and Civil War in France and the Netherlands, 1555–1585* (Amsterdam, 1999), 23–50.

clergy played in organizing, abetting, justifying, and even fighting the structured military combat of the eight civil wars that historians usually enumerate during these years. This is where some of the details conveyed by Loys Normand's letter are likely to come as a surprise even to specialists, notably the fact that a minister should have sent instructions to other churches about political and military measures that needed to be taken, and that these instructions should have ultimately been communicated to the municipal authorities of a small town. The rhetoric of Normand's letter is also of the highest interest, notably its allusion to the Assyrian king Sennacherib, the enemy of Judah.

This article seeks to explore these less well understood aspects of the interaction between religion and politics during the French Wars of Religion by focusing on two questions concerning the Protestant party during these conflicts. First, just how directly were ministers involved in the military mobilization and political decision-making of the period? Ulrich Zwingli's death at the battle of Kappel is a vivid reminder that Protestantism's redefinition of the status of the clergy called into question the principle that priests should not bear arms—a principle in any event imperfectly enshrined in late medieval and sixteenth-century Catholicism, as the participation in war of more than one bishop makes clear.[9] Davis's 'The Rites of Violence' noted that the minister Jacques Ruffi bore arms in the Huguenot takeover of Lyon. He was not the only minister to fight in the civil wars. Even if only a minority of French Reformed ministers did so, many more were in a position to influence policies concerning war and peace as chaplains and advisers to great noblemen, as members of Protestant political assemblies, and as leading voices within the consistories and synods that coordinated the political strategy of the Reformed churches and that were called upon for counsel in cities under siege. This leads directly to the second question that will be explored here: When ministers were asked to express their opinions in such contexts, what policies did they argue for, and on what grounds? Here I will seek to refine the concept of 'prophetic politics' that I have elaborated elsewhere and to

---

[9] On the participation of bishops in the French Wars of Religion, see Frederic J. Baumgartner, *Change and Continuity in the French Episcopate: The Bishops and the Wars of Religion 1547–1610* (Durham, NC, 1986), 149–54. Lesser clergymen also bore arms on occasion. During the Second Civil War, Charles IX appealed to those clerics who wished to go to war and to carry arms to do so, and Pope Pius V provided those who did so a bull of absolution. Ibid., 151. The priest-historian Claude Haton was a member of the civic militia of Provins. *Mémoires de Claude Haton*, ed. L. Bourquin et al., 4 vols (Paris, 2001–9), I, xiii.

determine how prevalent this manner of thinking about political action was among Huguenot ministers and laymen.

An ample literature of extremely high quality already exists about the views of Calvin, Beza, the 'monarchomachs' and, to a lesser extent, Pierre Viret and Peter Martyr Vermigli concerning the right of resistance to unjust authority.[10] The goal here is not to go over this well-trodden ground once more, although the conclusions of this research are pertinent and will be drawn upon when appropriate. For all their importance as the opinion leaders of French Protestantism, Calvin, Beza, Viret, and Vermigli were just four of the hundreds of French-speaking ministers who built the initial French Reformed churches and directed them through the storms of the Wars of Religion. Recovering the actions and ideas of some of the other, more obscure ministers in situations close to the actual smoke and fire of battle seems a more urgent research priority. A key source that I have used for this purpose is the compilation of local histories of churches from throughout the kingdom covering the years 1555–63, the *Histoire ecclésiastique des églises réformées au royaume de France*—a source that Davis also drew upon heavily in 'The Rites of Violence'.[11]

---

[10] Key titles include Quentin Skinner, *Foundations of Modern Political Thought*, 2 vols (Cambridge, 1978), II, 189–348; Harro Höpfl, *The Christian Polity of John Calvin* (Cambridge, 1982); W. Nijenhuis, 'The Limits of Civil Disobedience in Calvin's Latest Known Sermons: The Development of His Ideas on the Right of Civil Resistance' in *Ecclesia Reformata: Studies in the Reformation*, 2 vols (Leiden, 1972–94), II, 73–100; Max Engammare, 'Calvin monarchomaque? Du soupçon à l'argument', *Archiv für Reformationsgeschichte*, 89 (1998), 207–26; Robert M. Kingdon, 'The First Expression of Theodore Beza's Political Ideas', *Archiv für Reformationsgeschichte*, 55 (1955), 88–99; Theodore Beza, *Du droit des magistrats* ed. Robert M. Kingdon (Geneva, 1971); Ralph Giesey, 'Why and When Hotman wrote the *Francogallia*', *Bibliothèque d'Humanisme et Renaissance*, 29 (1967), 583–611; *Vindiciae, Contra Tyrannos* ed. George Garnett (Cambridge, 1994); Robert D. Linder, *The Political Ideas of Pierre Viret* (Geneva, 1964); Robert M. Kingdon, *The Political Thought of Peter Martyr Vermigli: Selected Texts and Commentary* (Geneva, 1980).

[11] *Histoire ecclésiastique des églises réformées au royaume de France*, eds G. Baum and E. Cunitz, 3 vols (Paris, 1883–9) (henceforward *Histoire ecclésiastique*). This work was based on memoranda about the early history of the different churches drafted at the request of the national synod of 1563 and sent to Geneva, where these memoranda were drawn together by Theodore Beza and supplemented with substantial additional material from his own papers or copied from other printed Huguenot histories. Although Beza occasionally altered details of the relations to ensure a coherent presentation of certain particularly contested questions, he generally preserved the character and outlook of the memoranda. The local histories in the volume can be seen on close reading to represent a

Ministers in political decision-making and war

Both theory and practice conspired to make it extremely hard for the Protestant party to define the precise extent and limits of ministerial participation in political decision-making and war during the French civil wars. To begin with, Calvin's views on the relationship between church and state were complex, if not contradictory. On the one hand, he distinguished between the two realms of ecclesiastical and civil power. The former exercised authority over matters of the spirit, the latter over outward behaviour. On the other hand, he asserted that these two forms of authority were 'conjoined'. Magistrates had a duty to uphold both tables of the Law and to defend true religion and its ministers. Ministers were obliged to proclaim what Christian ethics taught about questions of public authority.[12]

One way of resolving the tension between these two principles was sketched out by Theodore Beza in his letters. In 1575 he wrote to Lord Glamis of Scotland that bishops should not sit in Parliament 'for the bishop has nothing to do in ordering mere civil affairs'.[13] Eight years previously, he had explained to Coligny that 'since all actions, either public or private, must be made in good conscience, there are no such actions that the pastors should not examine to ensure that proper account is rendered to God'. Saul and Jehoshaphat had come to grief because they failed to solicit and follow the advice of priests or prophets. The prophet Jeremiah had rightly criticized the political decisions taken by the kings of Judah. While ministers should not be allowed into the councils of princes, an appropriate group of them—and not just one, 'for in the Church of God there is no king but Jesus Christ'—should be consulted whenever princes embarked on actions that 'touch in some manner the domain of ecclesiastics'.[14]

If these principles suggest clearly enough that ministers should not fill political offices or sit in assemblies that made political decisions but should be consulted collectively for their opinions on many such matters, the manner in which the Reformed churches developed in France made it difficult to separate ministers, consistories, and church synods so neatly from political and military decision-making. Once the churches established their network of national and provincial synods in 1559–1560, these synods

---

range of perceptions about the events of the time. The work is best considered a collective, multi-authored history.

[12] *Calvin: Institutes of the Christian Religion* ed. John T. McNeill, 2 vols (Philadelphia, 1960), III.xix.15, IV.xx; Höpfl, *Christian Polity*, 122–4.

[13] *Correspondance de Théodore de Bèze*, Henri Meylan et al. (eds) (32 vols to date, Geneva, 1960 –) (henceforward *Correspondance Bèze*), XVI, 173.

[14] Ibid., VIII, 270–4.

collaborated with local churches and their consistories in organizing petitions for freedom of worship and in putting in place military units to protect the cause or the king in case of attack. The call to arms that spread within the Huguenot party in the wake of the massacre of Vassy and the prince of Condé's seizure of Orléans was disseminated both by noblemen in the suite of the prince of Condé and by the network of Reformed churches, consistories, and ministers. Each church was asked to contribute men and money to the cause. Subsequent Huguenot mobilizations likewise depended in varying degrees upon both aristocratic and ecclesiastical networks. Even before the outbreak of open civil war and the Protestant seizure of many cities that accompanied it, the cause had had to grapple with the question of whether consistories and ministers should be given a role in making political decisions in the dozens of towns across the Midi where Protestantism had grown strong enough by 1561 to take over Catholic churches, gain control of the municipality, purge churches of their 'idols', and put an end to the Mass.

In light of Calvin's distinction between the ecclesiastical and the civil realms, many churches were clearly troubled when ministers and consistories were drawn into making decisions about how to pay for troops or when to use force. The provincial synod of Dauphiné and the Lyonnais held in November 1561 decided that henceforward synods would 'only treat matters pertaining to religion alone'; financial affairs would be put in the hands of competent deputies.[15] Between March 1561 and March 1562 the churches of Castres and Nîmes established political councils separate from their consistories to 'see to the exterior governance (*police*) and necessities of the church'. Ministers did not sit in these councils, but the councils were instructed to 'confer and communicate' with the consistories.[16] The decisions taken during the First Civil War by the Protestant-controlled Estates of Languedoc and Dauphiné to organize the military, fiscal, and political affairs of the substantial portions of those provinces under Huguenot control likewise established distinct

---

[15] 'Articles arrestez au Synode tenu à Lyon le xxv novembre 1561', Bibliothèque Municipale de Grenoble, MS R 7054, 177, published in Eugène Arnaud (ed.), *Documents protestants inédits du XVIe siècle* (Paris, 1872), 33. Nicolas Fornerod and I are currently preparing a new edition of this and other early acts of the provincial synods of the French Reformed churches.

[16] Bibliothèque nationale de France, Paris, MS français 8666, fo. 70; Philippe Chareyre, 'L'installation de la discipline calviniste d'après le premier registre du Consistoire de Nîmes 1561–1563' in D. Bollinger et al. (eds), *Jean Calvin. Les visages multiples d'une réforme et de sa réception* (Lyon, 2009), 138; Jacques Gaches, *Mémoires sur les guerres de religion à Castres et dans le Languedoc: 1555–1612* (Paris, 1879), 10–11.

military and political councils in which ministers were not represented.[17] Yet pastors were present and played an important role at the meeting of the provincial estates of Dauphiné that established the new structures of authority for the province in December 1562.[18] They likewise participated in the meeting of the Estates of the Protestant-controlled Vivarais in the same month.[19] The role of Loys Normand in spreading the word for troops to assemble in Romans in March 1563 suggests that even after the provincial estates designated a system of military command that excluded the churches and their ministers, pastors remained involved in the dissemination of military instructions. A decade later, as the Reformed churches struggled to re-establish and reorganize themselves after the shock of the Saint Bartholomew's massacre, ministers were again represented in the assemblies that coordinated this effort. They made up a third of the delegates at the political assembly of Montauban in August 1573 and five per cent of those at the political assembly of Millau in December 1573.[20]

Beza's own biography also illustrates how difficult it was to separate ministers from 'mere civil affairs'. In the summer of 1560 he travelled from Geneva to Nérac to meet with Antoine de Navarre. Although he preached regularly while in Nérac, the chief purpose of his trip was to convince Antoine to champion the Reformed cause by aggressively asserting his right to lead a regency government and then promoting Reformed rights of worship. It appears that Beza and Calvin were jointly engaged in raising money for troops that they were willing to place at Antoine's service if he were prepared to grasp the nettle.[21] When the First Civil War broke out, Beza was once again in France. He quickly joined those around the prince of Condé, was among those advising him during the critical days prior to his seizure of Orléans, probably ghost-authored his subsequent manifestos justifying his actions, wrote independently to the Reformed churches of the kingdom urging them to send men and money for the Protestant cause, and served as one

---

[17] Jean Loutchitzki (ed.), 'Collection des procès-verbaux des assemblées politiques des réformés de France pendant le XVIe siècle', *Bulletin de la Société de l'Histoire du Protestantisme Français*, 22 (1873), 514–15; Abbé Brisard, *Histoire du Baron des Adrets* (Valence, 1890), 155.

[18] Brisard, *Baron des Adrets*, 66, 145.

[19] Auguste Le Sourd, *Essai sur les Etats du Vivarais depuis leurs origines*, 2 vols (n.p., 1926; reprinted Valence, 2002), I, 243–4.

[20] Janine Garrisson-Estèbe, *Protestants du Midi 1559–1598* (Toulouse, 1980), 183, 185.

[21] Alain Dufour, 'L'affaire de Maligny (Lyon, 4–5 septembre 1560) vue à travers la correspondance de Calvin et de Bèze', *Cahiers d'Histoire*, 8 (1963), 269–80; idem, *Théodore de Bèze*, Histoire littéraire de la France publiée par l'Académie des Inscriptions et Belles-Lettres, vol. 42 (Paris, 2002) 359.

of the cause's treasurers and fund-raisers.[22] He was also present at the battle of Dreux—unarmed, he stressed in reply to Claude de Sainctes' accusation that his flight from the field endangered his fellow minister François Perrussel, also present.[23] After his subsequent return to Geneva, he followed events in France closely, wrote to a succession of Huguenot noblemen, and recurrently played an active role rallying assistance for the oft-endangered Reformed churches. In early 1573, for instance, he was involved in the planning of a military expedition involving refugee Huguenot noblemen that set out from Geneva to revive the dormant churches of Dauphiné and that vainly attempted to seize Grenoble. The following year he helped to organize an expedition against Mâcon and Chalons-sur-Saône.[24] He and his fellow members of the Geneva Company of Pastors were also frequently asked by the magistrates of that city for advice about its political affairs.

That Beza stressed that he was unarmed at Dreux shows that the example of Zwingli and the several dozen other ministers who fought and died at Kappel did not inspire subsequent generations of Reformed theologians to consistently reject the distinction between clergy and laymen concerning participation in war. As might be expected in light of his general clericalism, Calvin opposed ministers bearing arms. When he learned of the role that Jacques Ruffi had played in the Protestant takeover of Lyon, he wrote a sharp letter of reprimand to the corps of ministers of the city: 'We would be traitors to God, to you, and to all Christendom if we did not tell you that it is not fitting for a minister to be a soldier or a captain. It is even worse for him to leave the pulpit to bear arms. Worst of all is it to confront the governor of a city with a pistol in hand and to threaten him with boasts of one's forces, for here are the words that have been reported to us by credible witnesses: 'Monsieur, you must do this because we've got control [*nous avons la force en main*]".[25] Peter Martyr Vermigli likewise argued that it was not lawful for ministers of the church to fight, since they must avoid all things that hinder their function. He nonetheless made an exception for situations when a city was suddenly attacked by an enemy. In this instance, 'the minister of the church may rightly take arms

---

[22] Dufour, *Bèze*, 375–7; Scott M. Manetsch, *Theodore Beza and the Quest for Peace in France, 1572–1598* (Leiden, 2000), 24–5.

[23] Theodore Beza, 'Ad F. Claudii de Xaintes responsionem altera Th. Bezae apologia' in *Tractationum Theologicarum*, 2 vols (Geneva, 1582), II, fo. 362; *Responsio F. Claudii de Sainctes parisien theologi ad Apologiam Theordori Bezae, editam contra Examen Doctrinae Calvinianae et Bezanae de Coena Domini* (Paris, 1567), fo. 155.

[24] *Correspondance Bèze*, XIV, appendix 4; Manetsch, *Beza*, 76–7.

[25] *Iohannis Calvini opera quæ supersunt omnia*, ed. G. Baum, E. Cunitz, and E. Reuss, (Brunswick, 1863–1900), (henceforward *Calvini Opera*), XIX, no. 3785, cols. 409–10.

and repell violence, and doe that which becommeth a good citizen'. Once regular soldiers have arrived to defend the city, he should lay down his arms and return to his original office.[26]

The treatise on the ministry of Jean de L'Espine, the prominent Augustinian who threw off the cowl just prior to the colloquy of Poissy and became one of the most important Huguenot authors of devotional treatises during the final three decades of his long life, shows that other Reformed ministers were prepared to defend more extensive ministerial participation in war. It was not permitted for ministers or prophets to take up arms to establish or spread the word of God, L'Espine argued, for God's truth had no need of human force to win souls. Spreading doctrine at the point of the sword was a practice of Muslims and Papists. However, ministers, like other Christians, could take up arms to combat efforts by the enemies of religion to overturn the church's discipline and freedom to proclaim true doctrine. In support of this position, he adduced a number of Old Testament examples: the high priest Phinehas, who killed Zimri for consorting with a Midianite woman in the Israelite camp [Numbers 25:1–18]; the prophet Elijah, who slew the false prophets of Baal [1 Kings 18:40]; the high priest Jehoiada, who secretly raised the young king Joash during the regency of Queen Athaliah, then sparked the uprising of the Levites that placed him on the throne [2 Chronicles 23]; and the priest Mattathias, who killed a royal commissioner who forced the Jews to make sacrifices and touched off the revolt of the Maccabees [1 Maccabees. 2: 23–69]. L'Espine also cited a number of instances from previous centuries when Catholic bishops took part in battles. 'Did not our fathers see the Cardinal of Sion riding among the Swiss battalions and acting as a captain at Marignano?' The Papists are thus in no position to criticize us if 'ministers, to uphold their freedom of conscience, the discipline and government of their Churches, the privileges that the King has given them, and finally their homes, hearths, and lives, take up arms to oppose the evil designs of their opponents who seek nothing other than to exterminate them and scatter the flock of Jesus Christ'.[27] L'Espine's vision of what was at stake in the civil wars, it will be noted, was identical to Loys Normand's. That L'Espine devoted an entire chapter of his work to the question of whether or not it was permissible for a pastor to take up arms to defend his religion suggests that this was a question with which many were grappling at the time.

---

[26] *The Common Places of the most famous and renowmed Divine Doctor Peter Martyr* (London, 1583), part 4, 287, col. 1.

[27] Jean de l'Espine, 'Du Ministere de l'Eglise' in *Seconde partie des Opuscules theologiques* (Geneva, 1598), fos. 348–50, esp. 350.

Ample evidence exists that ministers did fight in the civil wars. One pastor, Martin Taschard, had already assumed an important military role before the First Civil War broke out. An erstwhile *avocat au siège présidial* who left Montauban for Geneva in 1553, Taschard had been ordained as a minister in Geneva in 1557 and dispatched to the Waldensian valleys of Piedmont. There in 1560–61 he led an armed squadron of 100 harquebusiers that seized and 'purified' churches in the Val Pragelato and Val Germanesca, then played an essential role in the successful armed defence that the churches of these valleys mounted against the duke of Savoy's effort to outlaw their assemblies. When the peace of Cavour granted the Reformed rights of worship, Taschard was specifically exempted from this permission and banished because of his military involvement.[28] He returned to Montauban to become pastor there, in a city that already had emerged as one of the centres of Huguenot militancy and would soon be centrally involved in the military campaigns of the First Civil War. During the fighting around the city in the summer of 1562, the *Histoire ecclésiastique* tells us, 'even the ministers joined the bands of their churches'.[29]

One might be tempted to attribute the military involvement of the ministers around Montauban to Taschard's example or influence, but this was not the only place where ministers fought in this or later civil wars. In the Gevaudan the minister Anthoine Copier captained the troops that took Mende in July 1562. After the city fell, he 'with several others . . . began to run everything, especially the public purse'.[30] In the Loire valley Pierre Denise 'did the work of a soldier more than of a minister' throughout the First Civil War, while (at least according to the Catholic chronicler Jean Louvet) the minister Henri Salvert was one of the Huguenot captains during the brief

---

[28] The literature on the Reformation and resistance in the Waldensian valleys is extensive. For information about Taschard's role see Giovanni Jalla, *Storia della Riforma in Piemonte fino alla morte di Emanuele Filiberto 1517–1580* (Florence, 1914), 175, 179, 185ff; idem, 'Le Refuge dans les Vallées Vaudoises. Les relations entre la France protestante et le Piémont pendant le règne d'Emmanuel-Philibert (1559–1580)', *Bulletin de la Société de l'Histoire du Protestantisme Français*, 85 (1936), 8, 14; Giorgio Tourn, 'Pastori e cappellani nelle guerre valdesi', *Bollettino della Società di Studi Valdesi*, 176 (1995), 16–18; Euan Cameron, *Waldenses: Rejections of Holy Church in Medieval Europe* (Oxford, 2000), 274–9. The importance of the war and peace in these valleys for subsequent events in France has recently been underscored by Cornel Zwierlein, 'La Pace di Cavour nel contesto europeo' in P. Gajewski and S. Peyronel Rambaldi (eds), *Con o senza le armi. Controversistica religiosa e resistenza armata nell'età moderna* (Turin, 2008), 67–98.

[29] *Histoire ecclésiastique*, III, 101.

[30] *Histoire ecclésiastique*, III, 226.

Protestant occupation of Angers.[31] At the outset of the long siege of La Rochelle in 1572–3, the numerous ministers who had taken refuge decided that 'those among them who were the most disposed to do so should do such faction of war as their health permitted'.[32] Not every minister with the strength to fight was prepared to do so. In Montauban in 1562 one pastor urged to assume a position as captain of a regiment of troops, Jean Constans, refused on the grounds that this was contrary to his vocation.[33] The decision of the pastors in La Rochelle in 1572–3 suggests that the consensus viewpoint in their ranks was that they could fight if they had the strength to do so and believed this to be part of their calling.

We will never know what percentage of Protestant ministers in France actually bore arms. Those who did not do so were expected to contribute to the war effort in other ways. The most important of these lay in providing spiritual support to Protestant armies when they went on campaign, a clerical function that medieval treatises had already insisted upon, and that Reformed ministers continued to consider essential. Before Condé's army left Orléans for the campaign that culminated in the battle of Dreux, the prince attached ministers to each regiment of his troops at the behest of the numerous pastors who had taken refuge in the city, both so that the clergymen could lead prayers and offer exhortations, and 'to restrain the men so that they do not go beyond due measure'.[34] Reports of battles during the civil wars occasionally note the presence of ministers with the troops. At Moncontour, according to an eyewitness, a minister at the side of the captain Saint Cyr took part in the

---

[31] Public Record Office, London, State Papers 70, vol. 73, no. 469(III), fo. 33; Jean Louvet, 'Journal', *Revue de l'Anjou*, (1854) no. 2, 261.

[32] 'Et fut arreté entre les dits ministres que ceux d'entre eux qui estoyent les plus dispos feroyent telle faction [sic? 'action'?] de guerre que leur santé le permettroit'. [Simon Goulart], *Memoires de l'estat de France sous Charles Neufiesme* (3 vols, 'Meidelbourg: Henrich Wolf' [Geneva], 1576), II, 329–30.

[33] *Histoire ecclésiastique*, III, 87.

[34] Lancelot Voisin de La Popelinière, *Histoire de France*, 2 vols (La Rochelle, 1581), I, fo. 338. The attachment of ministers to the army in this manner was already specified in the April 1562 *Traicté d'association faicte par monseigneur le Prince de Condé avec les Princes, Chevaliers de l'ordre, Seigneurs, Capitaines, Gentilshommes et autres de tous estats qui sont entrez ou entreront cy apres en ladict Association*: 'Pour estre conduicts soubs l'obeissance de la parole de Dieu, nous entendons avoir en noz compagnies de bons et fideles Ministres de la gloire de Dieu, qui nous enseigneront sa volonté, et ausquels nous presterons audience telle qu'il appartient'. *Mémoires de Condé*, 5 vols (London, 1743), III, 260. *The Common Places of . . . Peter Martyr*, part 4, 287, col. 1, also insisted upon it.

discussion that led him to launch an attack.[35] When a Protestant raiding party surprised and took Nîmes in 1569, the presence of mind of the minister Deiron, who accompanied it on its nocturnal mission, proved essential to its success. Just as Deiron began to exhort the men prior to the raid, a strange light illuminated the sky and spread consternation among the troops. Deiron recalled the pillar of fire that God used to guide the Israelites toward the Red Sea and restored calm with assurances that this was a comparable sign of God's support for their undertaking.[36]

Ministers also assumed a wide variety of tasks in Protestant-controlled cities under siege. They regularly were assigned to the different guard stations set up throughout the city to keep watch over its defences 'to say prayers there and to remain there day and night to exercise vigilance that no offense was given to God and no betrayal committed'.[37] In Orléans in 1563, after saying prayers each morning at the guard stations at 6 a.m., the ministers joined the rest of the population in working on the city's fortifications. In La Rochelle in 1572–73, ministers were expected to lead morning and evening prayers at each watch station, to preach on Sundays when conditions permitted it, to help repair the city's fortifications as these came under attack, and to 'do such faction of war as their health permitted'. They also accompanied the patrols that went through the city at night checking on the state of the fortifications, since they were thought to be particularly trustworthy watchmen. Before or during sieges, as we shall shortly see in more detail, the urban authorities also regularly solicited their opinion or that of the church consistory about important military or political decisions that had to be taken. Sometimes they asked them to join them for key deliberations. Occasionally ministers accompanied the local military commander to negotiating sessions with the enemy.[38]

Prophetic politics?

Whether responding to a city's council's request for advice or participating themselves in the deliberations of a political assembly, Huguenot ministers

---

[35] Agrippa d'Aubigné, *Histoire universelle* ed. André Thierry, 11 vols (Geneva, 1981–2001), III, 136.

[36] Léon Menard, *Histoire civile, ecclésiastique et littéraire de la ville de Nismes*, 7 vols (Paris, 1750–58), V, 51.

[37] *Histoire ecclésiastique*, III, 114, an account of the 1562-3 siege of Montauban. For examples of ministers distributed among watch stations in besieged Grenoble (1562), Orléans (1563), and La Rochelle (1572-3) see ibid., III, 345; La Popelinière, *Histoire de France* (Orléans, 1563), II, 335; *Memoires de l'estat de France sous Charles Neufiesme*, II, 329–30.

[38] See below, 185–92.

did not speak with one voice on the pressing questions of war and peace that faced the cause. On the whole, however, they seem to have advocated resistance without surrender more often than noble Protestants, frequently seeing parallels between the events of their time and the histories and prophecies of the Old Testament, and arguing that God would not abandon his chosen people so long as they retained trust in Him, even when the situation looked dire.

The initial decision to take up arms in 1562 was a particularly critical moment of decision for the members of the Reformed churches. For the first time every local church and all of their noble members found themselves confronted by the question of how to respond to a call for mobilization. Although this was presented as being in defence of the king, it involved disobeying the expressed will of the crown and accepting the argument that the king and queen mother had been taken captive by the Catholic Triumvirate and that the statements issued in the crown's name were thus illegitimate. In the wake of the massacre of Vassy, a first call to be on guard in the event of violence and to prepare to come to the aid of other churches that might be attacked was distributed through the network of churches. After the prince of Condé and the grandees who had rallied around him seized Orléans on 2 April, manifestos issued in his name were in fact likely to have been authored by Beza. These justified the seizure of the town on the grounds that the massacre of Vassy was merely the first act of a larger plan by the Catholic Triumvirs to deprive the Protestants of rights of worship that had been granted to them in response to the demands of the Estates-General by the Edict of January. They also argued that not only was it legitimate to take up arms to defend these legal rights; it was necessary to do so to defend the authority of the king and queen mother, who had been illegally sequestered by the Triumvirs and forced to act against their will. The treaty of association sworn by Condé and all those who rallied to his banner engaged those who signed on to lay down their lives if necessary to defend and liberate the king and to preserve the liberty of conscience granted by the Edict of January. They were also to comport themselves in an exemplary fashion according to God's laws. At the same time that the leaders of the Protestant party in Orléans sought to engage as many of the faithful as possible in this sworn national association, the leaders of each individual congregation also had to decide whether or not to take pre-emptive action locally to forestall rumoured initiatives on the part of their Catholic enemies to deprive them of their rights of assembly or even slay them all.[39]

---

[39] Pierre-Hyacinthe Morice, *Mémoires pour servir de preuves à l'histoire écclésiastique et civile de Bretagne*, 3 vols (Paris, 1742–6), III, 1302–3; *Correspondance Bèze*, IV, 71–2, 254–60;

Protestant assemblies that would appear to have been primarily ecclesiastical in character since the sources identify them as 'colloquies' and 'synods' were held in several parts of the country to debate what to do. Alas, no minutes of these meetings have been preserved, so only their decisions can be determined, not the nature of the arguments advanced amid the debates. According to the *Histoire ecclésiastique*, the churches around Toulouse held a colloquy in that city in April 1562 after an envoy sent by Condé reported that the Edict of January had been overturned. The Prince had taken the churches under his protection, and several good towns had already joined his sworn association.[40] The assembly decided against joining the association or taking any other immediate action, much to the dismay of the delegate from Montauban, which was preparing to resist a punitive action threatened against it by the royal lieutenants in the region, and whose delegate could only extract a promise that the assembly would send men to aid the city if it was 'tyrannically assailed' and if its resistance was found legitimate. Over the next month tension continued to mount in Toulouse. A local Protestant nobleman who had met with Condé organized a plan to seize the city's gates. Catholic judges received letters asserting that the Edict of January no longer had to be respected and began to discuss how Protestant worship might be banned. After the Reformed were forbidden to celebrate the Lord's Supper at Pentecost for fear that this might spark trouble, the church's leaders met to decide how to react. The sources agree that a minister who had already spoken from the pulpit about the need to act, Jean Barrelles or Cormier, was the critical figure in rallying the fraction of the church that felt that no more delay could be tolerated to attempt a pre-emptive strike to take over the city. The undertaking failed after four days of bloody street fighting.[41] After its failure, Barrelles fled to Nîmes and Lyon along with a

---

Mémoires de Condé, III, 221–55, 258–69. For the tense situation in certain cities that sought to preserve religious coexistence in the weeks and months following Vassy see in particular Greengrass, 'The Anatomy of a Religious Riot in Toulouse in May 1562', *Journal of Ecclesiastical History*, 34 (1983), 374–6; Roberts, *A City in Conflict*, 100–9. Many comparable situations are reported in the *Histoire ecclésiastique*.

[40] *Histoire ecclésiastique*, III, 74.

[41] *Histoire ecclésiastique*, III, 12–13; La Popelinière, *Histoire de France*, I, 312–14; Claude Devic and Jean Vaissete, *Histoire générale de Languedoc*, 16 vols (Toulouse, 1872–1905), XI, 383, XII, 14, 18; Greengrass, 'Anatomy of a Religious Riot', 376. Barrelles, a former Franciscan, studied in Geneva 1559–61. The author of the relevant pages of the *Histoire ecclésiastique* deems him 'bravehearted and zealous' but also 'impetuous' and 'not led by the spirit of God'—this last judgment presumably an inference from the failure of the Protestant coup to take Toulouse.

group of church members who managed to survive. In exile he pressed his refugee flock to contribute money for a military expedition to retake Toulouse. They pledged to do so, then quickly lost courage after learning of the fall of Mâcon and scattered to Geneva without providing the money, whereupon Barrelles sent a list with their names to Calvin and urged him to remonstrate with them about their breach of promise.[42]

In Saintonge and Aunis, debate about the proper course of action seems to have been particularly intense. In August or September 1562, up to sixty ministers from throughout the province attended a 'synod' convoked at Saintes. After 'all doubts and objections were amply debated according to divine and human law', it was decided that the action undertaken by Condé was both necessary and legitimate. Following the assembly the minister Charles Leopard was dispatched to visit the nobleman François de Belleville to urge him to fight the good fight.[43] The decision of this assembly, however, did not lead the Protestant governor of La Rochelle, Guy Chabot de Jarnac, to deviate from the policy of neutrality that he pursued for that city throughout the First Civil War—a policy that was opposed by the minister Ambroise Faget, who was excluded from the city for his more militant stand.[44]

These cases reveal the range of ministerial responses to the question of whether to respond to Condé's appeal and aggressively seize the initiative in the spring and summer of 1562, or to stay calm and resist the call to arms. Some followed the path of caution. This was true not only of the majority of those present at the colloquy of Toulouse. The *Histoire ecclésiastique* credits the minister Brunel with holding the Protestants of Limoges back from violence.[45] If Ambroise Faget was expelled and subsequently barred from re-entering La Rochelle because of his opposition to Jarnac's course of neutrality, that still left other ministers in office who can be presumed to have gone along with the policy of neutrality. The 1563 national synod of Lyon dealt with the case of a Limousin minister who initially consented and contributed to the taking up of arms but then, after the war went badly for the Huguenots in the region, withdrew from serving his church and obtained permission to live unmolested in his house by falsely denying his initial

---

[42] *Calvini Opera*, XIX, no. 3846, Pierre Viret to Pierre d'Airebaudouze, Lyon, 2 September 1562.

[43] *Histoire ecclésiastique*, II, 981.

[44] Ibid., 980.

[45] Ibid., 990. Cf. Michel Cassan, 'Les choix politiques et confessionnels de la ville natale de Jean Dorat durant la seconde moitié du XVIe siècle et les débuts du XVIIe siècle' in C. de Buzon and J.-E. Girot (eds), *Jean Dorat poète humaniste de la Renaissance* (Geneva, 2007), 49.

engagement in the association.⁴⁶ Other ministers, such as Barrelles and the majority of those present at the synod of Saintes, supported Condé's association and pushed for pre-emptive action to defend the cause. As we shall see shortly, once the wars were underway, a clear majority of ministers advocated resistance *jusqu'au bout*. It should be underscored that a fraction of the many noblemen who had joined the Reformed Church prior to April 1562, probably an even larger fraction than of the cause's pastors, had hesitations similar to those of the colloquy of Toulouse and either remained neutral in the war, fought with the crown rather than joining Condé's association, or initially rallied to Condé's standard but then, once the tide turned against the Protestant cause, withdrew from his army and retired to their estates or joined the royal troops.⁴⁷

The documents surrounding the initial decisions taken in 1562 to take up arms or to attempt to preserve the religious peace do not spell out the arguments advanced in the Protestant assemblies where these issues were debated. However, two exceptional sources, Theodore Beza's rich correspondence and certain of the most detailed Protestant narratives of events within Huguenot cities under siege in the civil wars, do allow us to hear the voices of different ministers once the wars were underway as they intervened directly in debates about how to prosecute wars and whether or not to accept proposed peace offers. Such sources are extremely precious if we are to grasp the nature of the convictions that motivated Protestant fighting, so they deserve the closest attention.

To understand better how religion could spark or intensify violence in early modern Europe, historians must move beyond arguing that the various

---

⁴⁶ Jean Aymon, *Tous les synodes nationaux des Églises réformées de France*, 2 vols (The Hague, 1710), I, 43.

⁴⁷ Among the high nobility Jarnac, who had been a member of the Reformed church since 1560 and had ordered the images removed from the churches of his seigneurial town, was just one of those who could not be drawn into fighting for the Protestant cause. Others who had joined the Reformed church but refrained from fighting for it included François II de Cleves, duke of Nevers, governor of Champagne, Leonor d'Orléans, duke of Longueville, and Henri-Robert de La Marck, duke of Bouillon, governor of Normandy. For the numerous defections that began to thin the ranks of the Protestant armies as the war advanced, see *Mémoires de Condé*, II, 50; David Potter, 'The French Protestant Nobility in 1562: The "Associacion de monseigneur le Prince de Condé"', *French History*, 15 (2001), 313–15; Neuschel, *Word of Honor*, 40–2; and especially Denise Turrel, 'Un sobriquet des guerres de Religion: les guilbedouins, déserteurs saintongeais de la cause protestante' in J. Mondot and P. Loupès (eds), *Provinciales. Hommage à Anne-Marie Cocula*, 2 vols (Bordeaux, 2009), II, 963–75, the best study to date of this phenomenon.

participants in the conflicts conventionally labelled wars of religion sincerely believed in their religious convictions, and explore exactly what elements of a given religion's doctrines and practices encouraged its adherents to resort to violence in specific situations.[48] To the list of specific religious convictions that have already been shown by previous studies to have encouraged violence in the context of Catholic-Protestant confrontations in early modern Europe, we might wish to add an outlook that I labelled 'prophetic politics'. By this I mean the conviction that the Old Testament books of the Bible offer a history of God's treatment of His chosen people that provides enduring principles of proper political conduct. Since the Old Testament contains numerous examples of small but righteous groups winning victory against all rational expectation, a logical corollary of prophetic politics could have been to incite those who believed themselves to be God's chosen people to undertake or continue wars that they might not otherwise undertake, secure that God was on their side and would bring them victory.

The concept of prophetic politics was first suggested to me by the dedicatory epistle that Theodore Beza addressed to Gaspard de Coligny in 1565 to accompany Calvin's commentaries on the first twenty chapters of Ezekiel.[49] Here, Beza explained to the Protestant champion that amid the combats to which he had been called to defend the true church of Christ, 'a diligent comparison of the prophetic and historical writings will strengthen you like nothing else, for this is the sole foolproof method of guarding against making erroneous conjectures about what is to come on the basis of observations of past events, as people commonly do'. By studying these books of the Bible, he could 'stand among the counsels of God himself and behold the true causes of change'. By comparing what actually happened in history with the predictions of the prophets, he could act 'in God's manner and on God's advice'. Since the same God determined the outcome of biblical events as those of all times, the maxims that can be drawn from Scripture are perpetual and unchanging, 'indeed more certain and infallible than all the principles of the mathematicians'. To be sure, understanding the prophetic books was not always easy, for the prophets often spoke obscurely, so it was important to rely

---

[48] Philip Benedict, 'Religion and Politics in the European Struggle for Stability, 1500–1700' in Philip Benedict and Myron P. Gutmann (eds), *Early Modern Europe: From Crisis to Stability* (Newark, Del., 2005), 120–38, also published in slightly different form as 'Religion and Politics in Europe, 1500–1700' in Kaspar von Greyerz et al. (eds), *Religion und Gewalt: Konflikte, Rituale, Deutungen (1500–1800)* (Göttingen, 2006), 155–74.

[49] *Correspondance Bèze*, VI, 15–21; *Calvin's Old Testament Commentaries*, vol. 18, *Ezekiel I* trans. D. Foxgrover and D. Martin (Grand Rapids, 1994), 3–8.

on the counsel of an experienced, reliable student of Scripture who understood their distinctive idiom. Calvin was one such man. Had not his commentaries on Daniel, written when the colloquy of Poissy had sparked hope that a calm harbour lay just ahead for the Reformed churches of France, warned that the churches soon would have yet harder battles to fight, and had not the First Civil War indeed soon followed? Beza's goal in stressing these points, he demurred, was not to put ministers on the thrones of kings or in the seats of magistrates, but to show how important it was for princes to study the prophetic and historic books of the Bible and to rely on expert guides to help them.

Just what did Beza mean when he said that the historical and prophetic books of the Old Testament offered a science of politics more certain than all the principles of mathematics? How directly did he think that political decision-makers could apply examples of effective action suggested in the Bible to contemporary situations deemed analogous? The letters and memoranda that Beza and his fellow Geneva ministers wrote to great noblemen or to the Genevan government when they solicited ministerial advice reveal that they did not systematically reason from Old Testament example when offering immediate political advice—or that if they did so they did not cite their sources when speaking to lay authorities. Take for instance the *avis* concerning the legitimacy of a war with Savoy addressed by the Company of Pastors to the authorities of Geneva in 1582 in response to their request for an opinion as to whether or not it was appropriate to undertake a war in response to the continued Savoyard harassment of the city's commerce and provisioning.[50] The memorandum began by defining when wars are just and unjust according to principles derived from medieval just war theory. Despite the horrors of war, wars are legitimate so long as they are defensive in character, based on right, and only undertaken after all attempts to negotiate other forms of resolution of the injustices done to the aggrieved party have been exhausted. In this instance, the pastors judged, the repeated intrusions, violence, and pillaging of lands that they believed belonged to Geneva, 'notably the damage done to temples and buildings belonging to the public together with the obstruction of the holy ministry', made any war undertaken properly defensive and just, should peaceful efforts to convince the enemy to cease such violence and withdraw from the contested localities prove unavailing. Such efforts should include recourse to impartial arbiters. It was not part of the ministers' charge, they judged, to tell the magistrates just how they should

---

[50] *Registres de la Compagnie des Pasteurs de Genève, tome IV 1575–1582*, eds Olivier Labarthe and Bernard Lescaze (Geneva, 1974), 434–8. Beza's is the first signature on this document.

undertake the fight if it came to war. They nonetheless felt obliged to warn them to be on guard against two *extremitez* that could offend God. The first would be to 'make merry [vous esgayer]' or to trust too much in your own power should God offer you ample means to conduct the war successfully 'instead of continually abasing yourself before the Lord and placing all your confidence in Him'. The second would be to lose courage if you found yourselves outnumbered by the enemy, 'considering that the power of the lord is not subject to human strength' and that God's extraordinary favour had clearly sustained 'this republic' and the 'Seigneurs des Ligues' on many past occasions. Above all, however, it was imperative that the magistrates attend to the flaws in the administration of justice within the republic, support the holy ministry in the reformation of vice, and act against the 'traffic in loans, fornication, gambling, idleness, gluttony and other such forms of dissolution ... by which the indignation of God has been so inflamed against us that he has visited upon us the scourges of famine, plague and war'. It was also important that a good code of military justice be drawn up and enforced should war ensue. At no point is direct Old Testament example invoked to provide a guide to action. The general principles of ethics regarding war derive from just war theory. At the same time, there is a strong sense that God's protection has blessed the republic but that to retain these blessings strict ethical behaviour had to be upheld within the army and in society at large.

A very similar outlook characterized most letters of advice Beza wrote to prominent French noblemen about political matters. Sometime around 1575, for instance, he wrote to Henry of Navarre about how he should govern his territories in south-western France after escaping from his captivity at court and returning to the Reformed faith. The letter includes conventional pieties—the king should keep God's word always before him, be of upright conscience, keep his promises, avoid flatterers, and uphold justice. It also includes more specific points of advice directed to the present situation—the king should cooperate with the prince of Condé, the house of Montmorency and the Reformed churches, he should set up an inner council of wise men composed if possible of equal numbers of Protestants and Catholics, he should stay on good terms with duke Casimir of the Palatinate. He should not listen to those who would try to convince him that free and regular meetings of representative bodies weakened the authority or dignity of rulers, but instead maintain well ordered assemblies as the true means to make rulers serene in their conscience, loved by their subjects, feared by their enemies, and blessed by God. Every meeting of the inner council should open with a prayer. Lastly, he should take particular care to ensure that his ears were never polluted with blasphemies and dirty words.

Again, there is no direct use of Old Testament examples.[51] At the same time, however, some of the themes here recur insistently in his letters to great noblemen and suggest that he inferred some broader rules of political conduct from Old Testament example. Repeatedly in his letters to noblemen he stressed the need to make the psalms 'your discipline and rule of conduct', reprehended them for their vices, and urged with particular intensity that blasphemy and other vices not be allowed to proliferate in their armies or at their courts. Rather than drawing direct lessons from specific incidents of Old Testament history, Beza appears to have been guided in his letters of advice to rulers by a looser sense that God favoured those who cleaved tightly to His word and punished those who did not. Even when one was outnumbered, one must not lose hope, for God had recurrently defended the small number of His chosen people from great danger. At the same time, excessive trust in one's purely human force or any lapse from upright behaviour was likely to stimulate God's wrath and bring political reverses.[52]

The view that exemplary morality needed to be maintained among the troops if God was to grant his people victory seems to have been widely shared among the French Reformed ministers. When Condé's men were about to leave Orléans in 1562 for the campaign that culminated in the battle of Dreux, the ministers in the city approached him and urged him to

---

[51] *Correspondance Bèze*, XXX, 365–8.

[52] Despite the relative paucity of arguments by direct analogy with specific Old Testament examples in Beza's letters of advice to rulers in advance of events, he clearly viewed events in hindsight by analogy with Old Testament situations in his private letters. As the first conflicts between Henry III and the princes associated with the Catholic League began in France after the 1585 measure outlawing Protestantism, Beza thought immediately of the Midianites killing one another in their confusion when at war with Gideon's little band. Ibid., XXVII, 199. When Henry of Navarre, in whom Beza had placed so much hope and from whom he received a pension, converted to Catholicism in 1593 and a Polish minister wrote to him to say that 'your David—so you called him in your last letter to me—has degenerated most miserably into a Saul', Beza kept the faith by refiguring Henry IV as Samson, who turned his back on the true religion but ultimately laid down his life to defeat the Philistines and restore peace to Israel. Manetsch, *Beza and the Quest for Peace*, 260–1. When writing to his fellow ministers, Beza was also more likely to cite biblical texts in support of political advice than when writing to noblemen or magistrates. For instance, a 1587 letter to Abraham Musculus that once more reiterates the need for the strictest discipline within armies to avoid setbacks includes a series of Old Testament citations to justify the point, including: references to Phineas slaying the Israelite soldier who married a Midianite woman and thus saving Israel from great punishment (Numbers 25:6–7), and Moses' stern warnings to the Israelites in the desert to obey the Lord's commandments (Deuteronomy 7–9). *Correspondance Bèze*, XXVIII, 77.

purge his units of all thieves and fornicators 'in order to turn aside God's wrath'.[53] In 1574–8, when warfare had become a permanent feature of life in religiously divided regions, the minister and consistory of the small Rouergue town of Pont-de-Camarès waged a persistent campaign to bring the garrison of nearby Mounès under their sway and to put a stop to the soldiers' depredation of the surrounding countryside. After the elder named to lead morning and evening prayers for the garrison had words with and injured a soldier who refused to heed him, the prayer services ceased and the garrison was cut off *en bloc* from the church.[54] The arguments that armies must choose pious men as both soldiers and captains, put their whole trust in God, and maintain good laws even while on campaign all recur as well in the one treatise on war published by a Huguenot minister during the Wars of Religion, the 1588 *Discourse on Warre* of Bertrand de Loque (né François de Saillans). 'It is a maxime... that if God be in the middest of our host, to conduct and preserve it, the effect shall alwaies be good and happy', Loque wrote in this treatise dedicated to Henry of Navarre. 'Victory dependeth not of the multitude of fighting men, but of the grace and favour of God'.[55] Prior to writing this treatise, Saillans had served as a minister in the households of both the moderate duke of Bouillon and the militant viscount Turenne, after first gaining notoriety in the armed seizure of Valence's Franciscan convent during the Easter season of 1560.[56]

In addition to this widely shared view that moral discipline was essential to military success, certain ministers, especially those in cities under siege, drew more direct lessons from Old Testament examples and found signs amid the dramas in which they were involved that recalled God's dealings with His chosen people. Evidence of this stronger version of prophetic politics may be found in the *Histoire ecclésiastique*'s long relation of the 1562–3 siege of Montauban, an account that also reveals particularly clearly the role ministers

---

[53] *Histoire ecclésiastique*, II, 233–4; La Popelinière, *Histoire de France*, I, 338.
[54] Frank Delteil, 'Institutions et vie de l'Eglise réformée de Pont de Camarès' in Michel Peronnet (ed.), *Les églises et leurs institutions au XVIème siècle* (Montpellier, [1978]), 100.
[55] Bertrand de Loque, *Discourses of Warre and Single Combat* (London, 1591), 21, 27. James Turner Johnson, *Ideology, Reason, and the Limitation of War: Religious and Secular Concepts, 1200-1740* (Princeton, NJ, 1975), 107–9, provides an excellent short synopsis of this tract.
[56] François Joubert and Salomon de Mérez, *Mémoires de divers événements en Dauphiné notamment pendant les guerres de religion* ed. E. Maignier (Grenoble, 1886), 24; J. Brun-Durand, *Dictionnaire biographique de la Drôme*, 2 vols (Grenoble, 1900–01), II, 102–4, 328–9; Eugène and Emile Haag, *La France protestante*, 10 vols (Paris, 1846–59), VII, 120–1.

could play in sustaining resistance in a town under siege.[57] During the First Civil War Montauban emerged as one of France's leading Protestant strongholds by successfully resisting three royalist and Catholic sieges, the third and longest of which lasted from October 1562 until March 1563. Soon after this final siege began, the enemy commander asked to open negotiations with the city and its military commander, the captain Laboria. The ministers in the city opposed all negotiations 'alleging that through such means the hearts [of the defenders] would be weakened and their faith in God sapped'.[58] They nonetheless accompanied Laboria and the other military men and political officials to the various parleys with envoys from the attacking forces. These envoys were usually chosen from among former fighters for the Huguenot cause, the better to convince the defenders that their resistance was unjust. At the first parley on 17 October, Laboria replied to the demand to capitulate with what the author of this account later judged to be 'virtuous' firmness. The Montalbanais, Laboria said, would 'defend the city for the king by whose edict and consent they had been granted the exercise of their religion ... since they were assured that God would defend them in so just an enterprise'. Signs of trouble to come were already manifest, however, for prior to the meeting Laboria angrily told the ministers, when they offered advice contradictory to his, that they were acting as if they wanted to make themselves cardinals.[59]

Over the subsequent weeks Laboria's faith in the wisdom of resistance gradually eroded, as did that of one of the eight ministers in the city, Pierre Du Croissant. The other ministers worked to sustain the resistance and oppose any concessions to the enemy. They also continued to take part in negotiating sessions and, when Laboria sought to gather support for peace terms among the population by speaking in various public and private forums, opposed him directly with counter-arguments. In rallying support for the cause and offering advice about policy, the ministers often drew inspiration from Old Testament examples and observed signs that God was with them. The minister Martin Taschard assured the defenders that so long as they had faith in God, He would give the men the hearts of lions and the women the hearts of men, which proved true, the history reports, since some

---

[57] *Histoire ecclésiastique*, III, 111–54. It seems probable that this account was written by the minister Jean Constans or by somebody very close to him, since the account quotes directly and at length words spoken by him in a small gathering at which he was the only person present who would subsequently remain loyal to the Protestant cause.

[58] Ibid., III, 116. Is this an echo of Deuteronomy 20 with its emphasis on fearlessness and stoutheartedness within an army?

[59] Ibid., III, 116.

women armed themselves and joined the men on the ramparts.[60] To reassure the Montalbanais that they would not starve during the siege, Taschard cited the words of 2 Kings 19:29: 'This year you will eat what is ripe, and the second year what grows without being sown; and the third year sow and reap'. A field near one of the towers of the city subsequently gave a rich crop of wheat even though it was not sown, while a field belonging to Taschard in a nearby community also produced a harvest of millet even though it had not been sown for six years.[61] As October advanced, the ministers as a group formally opposed further negotiations with the attackers 'with several lively remonstrations and the express witness of Scripture, notably the story of Nehemiah and other similar passages'.[62] Their opposition failed to prevent a new parley from taking place on 28 October, but once again a minister, Jean Constans, accompanied Laboria to the meeting. When one of the enemy captains warned them of dire consequences for the city if it did not submit, Constans replied that God would respond to whatever they attempted. The captain, clever former Protestant that he was, reminded Constans and Laboria that they should not count on miracles, since their own faith insisted that the age of miracles was long since over. Just at that moment, a rainbow appeared in the sky, and Constans told him 'Turn around, monsieur, and you will see the arc that God has placed in the clouds so that no flood will drown us'. The captain had also learned his Bible well enough to know that God had sent a rainbow to Noah as a sign of his protection after the flood, and was silenced.[63] Here the Old Testament provided both a means for interpreting natural phenomena as signs of God's providential concern for his children and direct examples that could be used in urging a specific course of political action.

As Laboria continued to try to win people over to the cause of a negotiated peace, the consistory grew so alarmed at his lobbying that it sent two ministers to the city council to urge it to take measures against him, threatening that if the council did not act it would appeal for a general assembly of the citizens. The consuls replied by sending a delegation back to the consistory to communicate several demands. One was that the seneschal's lieutenant be admitted to their assembly ex officio. 'It was immediately replied to them that the power of the magistrates and ecclesiastical jurisdiction were two different things according to Jesus Christ and the perpetual practice of the Christian

---

[60] Ibid., III, 119.
[61] Ibid., III, 134.
[62] Ibid., III, 120. Nehemiah oversaw the rebuilding of the walls of Jerusalem despite plots by the ungodly and subsequently became an exemplary governor of Judah.
[63] Ibid., III, 120.

church ... The examples of kings Saul and Ozias, who sought to usurp the power of sacrifice, were not forgotten'.[64] Another demand was that the consistory explained, with 'reasons founded on the word of God', why it was not licit to negotiate with enemies and make truces with them. The consistory's reply deserves to be quoted at length:

> The response ... was that indeed it is not forbidden to speak with or to make arrangements with infidels, or more broadly with one's enemies, given that Jesus Christ orders us to love even our enemies, and that the apostle wants us to have peace with all men; but what he adds, namely that this should be done insofar as is possible, shows that one must carefully consider the circumstances lest one offend God or one's neighbour or lest one bring about one's own downfall in the name of charity and peace, given that David said that he hates the enemies of God, that Jesus said that one cannot serve two masters, and that Paul said there can be no accommodation between light and darkness. As for the current situation, the words and deeds of those with whom it is a question of negotiating show more clearly than day not just that they are detestable and execrable people who seek nothing other than the lives and goods of those they assail, but also that they have expressly taken up arms to exterminate the religion from top to bottom ... Furthermore, the religion of the enemy explicitly states that it is not necessary to keep faith with heretics, so that if there are any conscientious people among them, they would think themselves damned if they kept a pact with us. Furthermore, even if Terride [the Catholic commander] and his captains were moved by some humanity to offer and keep equitable conditions, they could not do it as they do not exercise sovereign authority, which is instead exercised by those who have taken advantage of the king's youth, and notably the Parlement [of Toulouse].[65]

For this general question of the ethics of war and peace, the ministers replied not with reference to the Old Testament but by citing many of the key passages from the New Testament recurrently mobilized by Christians over the

---

[64] Ibid., III, 131. It should be noted that the presence of royal officials at consistory meetings had been expressly ordered by the Edict of January ('L'édit de Nantes et ses antécédents (1562–1598)' éditions en ligne de l'Ecole des Chartes, http://elec.enc.sorbonne.fr/edits depacification/edit1/, article 8 [accessed 16 September 2011]).

[65] *Histoire ecclésiastique*, III, 131–2.

centuries to counter Christ's command to turn the other cheek. Their reply also shows that as early as 1562 an enduring theme of Protestant anti-Catholicism had already taken shape: Catholics could not be trusted in political affairs since it was an article of faith for them that one must not keep agreements made with heretics.

Evidently, the consistory's reply convinced the consuls of the legitimacy of resistance, for they persisted in this course and brought together Laboria and the ministers to broker a reconciliation, sealed with an embrace. Shortly thereafter, however, Laboria slipped out of town. The city continued to refuse peace overtures, to endure bombardments, and to repulse attacks for five more months. The peace of Amboise finally brought an end to the siege and guaranteed the continuation of Protestant worship.[66]

Another instance where we can recover some of the content of ministerial arguments is during the long and critically important royal siege of La Rochelle in the aftermath of the Saint Bartholomew's massacre.[67] After the Protestant citadel refused to open its gates to the royal governor Armand de Gontaut-Biron, a loose blockade began in November that proved incapable of preventing supplies and reinforcements from entering the city. Charles IX turned to the former Protestant governor of the city François de La Noue and asked him to undertake a mission to convince it to recognize Biron and open its gates in return for freedom of conscience and the preservation of its privileges. La Noue journeyed to La Rochelle and, after meeting with a group of ministers to obtain their counsel and to convince them of his good faith, was allowed to enter the town and meet with the urban authorities. They convinced him to assume a share of its military command, which he accepted after explaining his motives to Biron. The besieging royal forces soon received substantial reinforcement, and the king's brother, the duke of Anjou, arrived to take charge of the attacking army in February. One of his first actions was to offer new terms to the city. A majority of the city council made an initial determination in favour of rejecting these, and then placed the question

---

[66] Ibid., III, 133–54.

[67] The two fundamental contemporary accounts of events within the besieged city are *Memoires de l'estat de France sous Charles Neufiesme*, II, 306, 329–32, 417, 431–4; and Bibliothèque nationale de France, Paris, MS 19869. Key modern accounts include Arlette Jouanna et al., *Histoire et dictionnaire des guerres de religion* (Paris, 1998), 207–12; Henri Hauser, *François de La Noue, (1531–1591)* (Paris, 1892), 34–60; James Supple, 'The Role of François de La Noue in the Siege of La Rochelle and the Protestant Alliance with the Mécontents', *Bibliothèque d'Humanisme et Renaissance*, 43 (1981), 107–22; James B. Wood, *The King's Army: Warfare, Soldiers, and Society during the Wars of Religion in France, 1562–1576* (Cambridge, 1996), ch. 10.

before a general assembly of those within the town. At this meeting a refugee minister speaking on behalf of his peers spoke strongly against entering into a separate peace. It was imperative to 'preserve the unity and association that must exist among all of the faithful'. Furthermore, the articles proposed in the king's name could not be trusted, since the king had already forbidden the exercise of the Reformed religion throughout the kingdom, even though he had claimed in his letters written after the Saint Bartholomew's massacre that he wished to see the previous edict of pacification that permitted Reformed worship upheld. One of La Rochelle's ministers, speaking in the name of the consistory, echoed his call for unity and resistance. After a lay refugee from Saint Jean d'Angély reminded those present of how the resolve of that city had been undermined by too frequent negotiations when it had been under siege in 1569, the assembly decided not only to reject the terms, but also to avoid face-to-face negotiations in the future, and to demand that any peace proposals be communicated to it in writing.[68]

At La Noue's urging this last decision was quickly reversed and a new parley undertaken. Before it met, the council put a series of questions to the ministers, who chose to reply only to the question they considered the most important: was it permissible for the city to make a separate peace? Five pastors were delegated to speak before the council. Their response had four points. First, the vigour of all individual members of the church depended upon their union with their leader Jesus Christ in the communion of the saints, which obliged them to pursue the well-being of their brothers and sisters as fervently as their own. In support of this they adduced the examples of the Reubenites, the Gadites, and the half-tribe of Manasseh who heeded Joshua's command to join in the conquest of the Promised Land even though they were safely established on the other side of the Jordan (Joshua 1:12–18), as well as that of Uriah, the upright warrior who refrained from sleeping with his wife Bathsheba when David brought him home from the front, heeding the injunction for sexual abstinence for those engaged in holy war (2 Samuel 11:8–11). Second, La Rochelle had made a pact with the brethren of Nîmes and Montauban to communicate and cooperate with one another. They were obliged to keep their promise, as Joshua had done with the treacherous Gibeonites, for after Saul had violated the same promise, God had punished Israel with a grievous famine (Joshua 9:3; 2 Samuel 21:1–2). Third, even if the city were to fall into dire necessity, it should keep its hope in God's aid and recall the examples of Judith, who properly rebuked those of Bethulia who limited the time within which God might aid them by deciding to surrender within five days (Judith), and of the inhabitants of Samaria, who, prepared to

---

[68] *Memoires de l'estat de France sous Charles Neufiesme*, II, 306.

eat their own children rather than surrender under siege, were delivered by the Lord in their moment of greatest distress (2 Kings 6:24–7:20). In any event—and this was the ministers' fourth point—such extreme dedication was not even necessary in this instance because by God's grace La Rochelle had sufficient provisions to last for three more months.[69] When one of the ministers in the city, André de Mazières, a pastor in the region since 1557, learned at the conclusion of the meeting that La Noue inclined toward a negotiated settlement, he grew so agitated that he tagged alongside the iron-armed captain as he returned to his lodgings, reprimanded him as a 'perfidious traitor and a deserter of his party', and slapped him across the face. Although La Noue responded with equanimity to this affront, he chose to leave the city several weeks later and to withdraw from the conflict because he could not accept the policy of resistance. The majority of the city council and local population remained firm in their resistance, even when several months later three hundred of those inside the walls, including some leading citizens, signed a petition arguing that the time had come to negotiate a peace.[70] La Rochelle held out successfully for four months after the March negotiations. The attacking army—its ranks more than halved by disease, casualties, disillusionment, and defection—packed up and withdrew. By the peace that followed, rights of Protestant worship were restored to La Rochelle, Nîmes, and Montauban.

As these two examples vividly illustrate, the more belligerent ministers of Montauban and La Rochelle under siege appear to have held to a stronger version of prophetic politics than Theodore Beza. Acting as guardians of both the morality and the loyalty of the city's defenders, offering counsel about peace negotiations and even, in the case of Montauban, taking part in them alongside the city's military commanders, these ministers saw those within the besieged cities as the equivalents of the different tribes of Israel and urged staunch resistance since they could be confident that God would defend his chosen people. Old Testament history was cited both to guide military policy and to illuminate the proper relationship between magistrates and ministers, priests, and king. The Montauban ministers Jean Taschard and Jean Constans also interpreted in the light of Old Testament history a variety of natural phenomena as quasi-miraculous signs of God's providential concern for his children, evidence that he would indeed protect them against all dangers. At the same time, the language of prophetic politics was not the only way in which the siege was perceived and questions of political strategy debated.

---

[69] Ibid., II, 332.
[70] Ibid., II, 431–4; Kevin C. Robbins, *City on the Ocean Sea: La Rochelle, 1530–1650: Urban Society, Religion, and Politics on the French Atlantic Frontier* (Leiden, 1997), 208–14.

When Montauban's city council asked the consistory to justify from Scripture the more general principles behind the policy it was supporting, the consistory replied chiefly with New Testament citations. It also accused the enemy of brutality and claimed that the very principles of its faith rendered it untrustworthy in any negotiation.

While groups of ministers recurrently urged the rejection of peace initiatives that did not grant the full conditions sought by a sworn Protestant association, they did not always do so in the language of prophetic politics. In March 1563, after the prince of Condé had negotiated initial terms for what would become the Edict of Amboise and submitted them to the 72 ministers who had taken refuge in Orléans, the ministers drafted a written protest against the agreement and urged that the party fight on till the full rights of worship accorded in the Edict of January were restored and the crown agreed to punish the perpetrators of the massacres of Vassy and Sens. In this case, their protest simply enumerated the terms concerning religion that the ministers believed had to be part of any peace before asserting: first, that they had been sent to specific places to preach the word of God and had a sacred obligation to return to those places even if the terms of a peace forbade it; and second, that the Protestants had taken up arms to ensure that the Edict of January was maintained and should not abandon this cause. Behind the advocacy of such a line of conduct may have lain the conviction that God would protect His children no matter how weak they might appear by the light of carnal reason—the war had gone badly for the Huguenot cause and Orléans was under siege at the time—but here one finds no deployment of Old Testament example to this effect.[71] The same is true of the response of the ministers who had taken refuge in La Rochelle during the Third Civil War to a request of the Queen of Navarre and her council that they make their opinion known on the articles concerning religion under discussion in the peace negotiations of 1570.[72] The language of prophetic politics was just one of several ways in which Huguenot ministers reflected on politics, one that perhaps was particularly likely to come to the fore in moments of extreme crisis, in cities under siege or in the wake of the Saint Bartholomew's massacre and the numerous defections that followed it. As Arlette Jouanna has pointed out,

---

[71] *Histoire ecclésiastique*, II, 368–70.

[72] 'Responce des ministres du sainct Evangile, qui sont retirez de toutes parts de ce Royaume en la ville de la Rochelle à cause des guerres A la Royne de Navarre, et a son conseil sur la demande à eux faicte par sa Majesté, sur cest article du pourparlé de Paix, concernant l'exercice de la Religion' in *Histoire de nostre temps, contenant un recueil des choses memorables passee et publiees pour le faict de la Religion et estat de la France, depuis l'Edict de pacification du 23 jour de Mars 1568 jusques au jour present* ([La Rochelle, 1570), 736–8.

reliance on Old Testament example was particularly extensive at this latter moment. A proposal about how to organize resistance that circulated within the Huguenot crescent late in 1572 bore the title *Daniel's Decree* in some versions because it was attributed to the prophet. François Hotman asked Heinrich Bullinger whether the example of the city of Libna's rebellion against the tyrannical king Joram (2 Kings 8:16–22) might not legitimize La Rochelle's return to its former independence, while a versified translation of the canticle of Deborah likened the city to the prophetess fighting the Canaanites.[73]

One final instance where ministers opposed the terms of a peace proposal merits attention, not for what it reveals about their political language, but for the insights it provides into the political dynamics of the Huguenot cause. At the December 1562 meeting in Montélimar of the provincial estates of the parts of Dauphiné controlled by the Protestants, a central question before the deputies was whether or not to accept peace terms negotiated between the Protestant regional chieftain, the baron des Adrets, and the royal and Catholic governor of the province, the duke of Nemours. The truce they had tentatively agreed upon had four components. First, all of Dauphiné would recognize the authority of the duke of Nemours. Second, des Adrets would serve as his lieutenant when he was absent from the province. Third, all inhabitants would enjoy freedom of conscience and worship, but only in the privacy of their homes. Fourth all ministers would leave the province—because, added Jacques-Auguste de Thou by way of explanation, they 'were regarded as the real instigators of the troubles'.[74] Unsurprisingly, the ministers present in the assembly were among the most vehement opponents of this proposal, which was defeated.[75] Among their ranks, it might be noted, was Jacques Ruffi, representing the allied province of the Lyonnais.[76] Evidently Calvin's denunciation of his bearing arms during the Protestant takeover of Lyon had not diminished his stature amid Lyon's Huguenot leadership. The baron des Adrets can thus be placed alongside the captain Laboria in Montauban in 1562, the prince of Condé in April 1563, and François de La Noue in 1573 in the category of Protestant military commanders prepared to accept a peace that the cause's ministers rejected. Contrary to what one would be led to expect by the argument of Lucien Romier and others that an essentially

---

[73] Jouanna et al., *Histoire et dictionnaire*, 205–8; Donald R. Kelley, *François Hotman: A Revolutionary's Ordeal* (Princeton, NJ, 1973), 42.
[74] Jacques-Auguste de Thou, *Histoire universelle*, 11 vols, (The Hague, 1740), III, 352; cf. *Histoire ecclésiastique*, III, 356.
[75] De Thou, *Histoire universelle*, III, 351–3; *Histoire ecclésiastique*, III, 354–63.
[76] Brisard, *Baron des Adrets*, 149.

peaceful Protestant movement was only drawn into violence when noblemen became important within it, the ministers as a group seem more often to have advocated fighting on when the situation grew difficult than the cause's aristocratic military commanders and were perceived by at least some contemporary observers as the true authors of the troubles.

This is not to say that battle-hardened noblemen were always insensible to the counsels of ministers citing Old Testament examples or urging that victory went to the upright and not to the strong. To be sure, after the ministers at Orléans protested against making peace in 1563, the prince of Condé kept them at a safe distance from the negotiations and quickly finalized an accord. François de La Noue's *Political and Military Discourses* reveal him to have been a man whose judgments about questions of strategy rested upon experience, close observation and considerations of prudence, not biblical prophecy. Such considerations, alongside ones of honour and the loyalty he owed to the crown, seem to have entered into his decision to leave La Rochelle after the city refused the negotiated settlement that he urged it to accept.[77] Yet even Henry of Navarre, no paragon of Christian virtue in every aspect of his conduct, was sufficiently susceptible to the argument that God was unlikely to reward an unrepentant sinner with victory that, after being admonished by Philippe Duplessis Mornay for never having made public reparation for the notorious scandal of his affair with the daughter of a magistrate of La Rochelle, he agreed to admit his fault publicly before the church of Pons just prior to the battle of Coutras.[78] At the core of Agrippa d'Aubigné's vision of history and politics, the leading student of this topic has observed, lay the conviction that 'when the true church places its confidence in God alone, all the powers of the world can avail nothing against it, but when it counts on its own physical strength, or when it forgets the lesson given by the little shepherd David and reinforces itself with men who are not part of it, then God weakens and curses it'.[79] The ideal that the Huguenot ministers sought to impose of an upright Christian army fighting with a firm faith that God would preserve it so long as it cleaved to His cause and commandments had at least some purchase among the aristocracy, even if pastors were its most insistent champions.

---

[77] La Noue, *Discours politiques et militaires* (Basel, 1597); Johnson, *Ideology, Reason, and the Limitation of War*, 106–7; Supple, 'Role of La Noue in the Siege of La Rochelle', 110–12, 118–22.

[78] Hugues Daussy, *Les Huguenots et le roi. Le combat politique de Philippe Duplessis-Mornay (1572–1600)* (Geneva, 2002), 402.

[79] André Thierry, *Agrippa d'Aubigné, auteur de l'histoire universelle* (Lille, 1987), 81.

In the line of the past generation's work that has put religion back into the Wars of Religion, this essay has sought to explore what Protestant ministers, famous and less famous, said and did during the structured military conflicts of the period. A range of attitudes and actions has been revealed. While Calvin and Beza distinguished between the temporal and the spiritual spheres, they also insisted that temporal rulers should consult with the collectivity of God's ministers before taking any political decision with implications for the spiritual realm. Since both municipal authorities and military commanders regularly did so when the Huguenots found themselves in situations of wartime political authority, this gave ministers the opportunity to express their views about what actions should be taken. Beyond these situations of advisory influence, ministers were occasionally represented within Huguenot political assemblies and played a role in mobilizing troops for the cause and communicating political instructions among the churches. Regularly joined to army units or guard posts as chaplains and moral watchdogs, some of them also bore arms in the conflicts, a course of action that Jean de L'Espine defended but Calvin condemned.

No single line of conduct or mode of thinking about politics governed their actions or arguments when they were faced with critical decisions about what course of political or military action to follow. A fraction hesitated to respond aggressively to the initial call to arms in 1562, withdrew from a conflict after initially encouraging mobilization, or advocated accepting peace in situations where proffered conditions divided a community between war and peace parties. Inside besieged Montauban in 1562–3, one minister in eight favoured a negotiated settlement. More often, however, ministers emerged as partisans of uncompromising struggle, more prone to advocate fighting on when the situation grew difficult than aristocratic military commanders. At the same time they seem consistently to have sought to ensure strict morality and a firm faith in the ultimate victory of the cause within the Protestant armies, viewing these as essential to securing divine favour. The civil wars, in their eyes, were nothing short of struggles to defend the true faith and its adherents against extermination. The fact of having entered into a sworn association before God intensified the obligation to persevere in its defence.

At the same time, it does not appear that a consistent outlook that can be dubbed that of prophetic politics systematically governed all ministerial interventions in public debates. The general principles enunciated in Beza's prefatory letter to Coligny appear logically to announce a strong theory of prophetic politics according to which the historical and prophetic books of the Bible offer concrete examples of successful policies to be imitated in analogous situations. However, in those memoranda where Beza actually gave advice to political leaders he did not draw precise policy proposals from the Old Testament, contenting himself with the looser lesson that God did not abandon His children so long as they cleaved tightly to His commandments, and thus that rulers and armies that respected a good moral order were more likely to win success in battle than those who did not. In certain of the sermons or memoranda written by other, less celebrated Huguenot pastors in cities under siege, however, Old Testament analogies were more explicitly and precisely used to justify a course of struggle against difficult odds. Other memoranda did not invoke Old Testament example at all. Whether or not the ideal type 'prophetic politics' finally proves to be coherent enough to endure as a tool for understanding early modern political motivation, it does seem clear that certain ministers, and even certain noblemen, were impelled to fight on during the Wars of Religion because of their intense identification with the ancient Israelites and their conviction that God would preserve them and ultimately allow them to triumph over their enemies as numerous Biblical examples showed that He had done for the Hebrews, no matter how seriously they were outnumbered. It also appears that this manner of thinking was particularly likely to come to the fore in circumstances of crisis. Most significantly, in French Protestantism's most desperate hour, in the wake of the Saint Bartholomew's massacre when Protestant worship survived in only a few towns, it seems to have been critical in rallying the resistance that preserved the cause. As we continue to seek to understand better the place of religion within the Wars of Religion, exploring more fully the prevalence, force, and consistency of this outlook would seem to be a high priority.

Rites of Torture in Reformation Geneva*

Sara Beam

Natalie Zemon Davis's groundbreaking work on religious riots established that French commoners saw the rituals of justice as a means of cleansing their communities of sinners. Religious rioters often enacted mock trials against perceived heretics analogous to those undertaken by law courts: the systematic searching out, interrogation, and sometimes torture and execution of religious deviants. Davis's coining of the term 'rite of violence' revealed how the religiously motivated actions of the French crowd had a ritual logic that justified them in the eyes of the participants. We now know that the riots discussed by Davis exploded in France in the 1550s just as royal judges at the *parlements* threw up their hands at the possibility of suppressing heresy through the courts.[1] French crowds appropriated the role of the judge for themselves because they felt that the courts were tempting the wrath of God by evading the active persecution of heresy. But what about communities where justice was vigilant, where heretics and other deviants were righteously pursued by the authorities? In Reformation Geneva, city residents were faced with a situation opposite to that confronting French urban dwellers: rather than lamenting the hesitation of authorities to curb religious deviance, as early as the 1540s Genevans were more likely to riot in protest *against* the rigidity of the authorities' imposition of religious conformity than to ask for more.[2] In Calvin's city, the government directed legislation and its criminal court toward creating a godly state. French men and women took violent

---

* This research was undertaken with the generous financial support of the Social Sciences and Humanities Council of Canada. I would especially like to thank Erin Kelly, Gary Kuchar, Larry MacDonald, Andrea McKenzie, Laura Stokes, and Jill Walshaw for their comments on an earlier draft of this article.

[1] E. William Monter, *Judging the French Reformation: Heresy Trials by Sixteenth-Century Parlements* (Cambridge, MA, 1999).

[2] William G. Naphy, *Calvin and the Consolidation of the Genevan Reformation* (Manchester, 1994), 146–53; Karen Spierling, *Infant Baptism in Reformation Geneva: The Shaping of a Community, 1536–64* (Aldershot, 2005).

action because they felt the royal administration was not taking responsibility for purging heresy; in contrast, the Genevan church and government worked together to impose religious conformity through liturgy, civic ritual, and rites of violence such as torture.

Until now, most studies of justice in Geneva have not emphasized the link between the violence of judicial practice and Reformed religion.[3] Here I seek to explore that relationship, specifically with regard to the practice of torture. The term 'rite of violence' is useful in this context because it reveals the ways in which public rituals that were more judicial than religious in content were deployed in the Reformation period in an attempt to create purified confessional communities.[4] Analogous to the actions of French crowds, the practice of torture in Geneva allowed city officials to differentiate the godly citizen from the deviant and to justify the elimination of these condemned individuals. The effort to build a Reformed community in Geneva obviously had many facets, including Calvin's rousing sermons, the new liturgy of Sunday services, catechism classes, psalm singing and full lay participation in communion.[5] Nevertheless, torture and its corollary punishments, banishment and execution, were also important means by which city authorities created

[3] Christian Broye, *Sorcellerie et superstitions à Genève (XVIe–XVIIIe siècle)* (Geneva, 1990); Robert M. Kingdon, *Adultery and Divorce in Calvin's Geneva* (Cambridge, MA, 1995); E. William Monter, *Enforcing Morality in Early Modern Europe* (London, 1987); William G. Naphy, *Plagues, Poisons, and Potions: Plague-Spreading Conspiracies in the Western Alps, c.1530–1640* (Manchester, 2002); Michel Porret, *Le Crime et ses circonstances: de l'esprit de l'arbitraire au siècle des Lumières selon les réquisitoires des procureurs généraux de Genève* (Geneva, 1995); Bernard Lescaze, 'Crimes et criminels à Genève en 1572', in *Pour une histoire qualitative: études offertes à Sven Stelling-Michaud* (Geneva, 1975), 45–71; Sonia Vernhes Rappaz, 'La noyade judiciaire dans la République de Genève (1558–1619)', *Crime, Histoire and Société*, 13 (2009), 5–23. See in contrast, Erich Hans Kaden, *Le Jurisconsulte Germain Colladon, ami de Jean Calvin et de Théodore de Bèze* (Geneva, 1974).

[4] Edward Muir, *Ritual in Early Modern Europe* (Cambridge, 1997); Susan Karant-Nunn, *The Reformation of Ritual: An Interpretation of Early Modern Germany* (London, 1997).

[5] Christian Grosse, *Les Rituels de la Cène: le culte eucharistique réformé à Genève (XVIe–XVIIe siècles)* (Geneva, 2008); Robert Kingdon, 'Worship in Geneva before and after the Reformation', in Karin Maag and John D. Witvliet (eds), *Worship in Medieval and Early Modern Europe: Change and Continuity in Religious Practice* (Notre Dame, IN, 2004); Karen Spierling, 'The Complexity of Community in Reformation Geneva', in Michael J. Halvorson and Karen E. Spierling (eds), *Defining Community in Early Modern Europe* (Aldershot, 2008), 81–101. These efforts to build a Reformed community were informed by a conception of Protestant martyrdom at the hand of Catholics. See Charles H. Parker, 'French Calvinists as the Children of Israel', *Sixteenth Century Journal*, 24 (1993), 227–48.

the Reformed city whose godly aspect visitors like John Knox were so quick to praise.

Torture in Geneva was defined as the short-term application of pain designed to elicit a truthful confession during a criminal trial. The first references to torture being applied in Geneva appear in the fourteenth century, and the procedure was officially condoned in city statutes as early as 1387.[6] Legislation passed in 1568 established that torture should only be employed with the approval of the criminal court during trials in which 'the criminal, shown to be guilty by sufficient witnesses or physical evidence of that which he is accused, does not want to confess'.[7] As in the rest of continental Europe, the Genevan practice of torture rested on Roman law foundations that required a confession from the accused in order to obtain a full proof of the crime.

Although torture was first and foremost a judicial procedure, it also functioned as a rite of violence in Reformation Geneva. The prevalence of God and the devil in legal opinions and in interrogation sessions, the symbiotic relationship between the Consistory and the criminal court at the *Petit Conseil* in the prosecution of moral crimes, and the persistence with which Genevan interrogators sought out the spiritual degradation of the criminal's soul testify to its role as a purifying ritual imposed by the criminal court to clarify who did and who did not belong to the Reformed community of the faithful.

In addition to establishing the ways in which rites of torture helped to create a godly community in Reformation Geneva, this chapter has a second aim: to investigate how Genevan criminal procedure, which was strongly influenced by French law, in part because so many judicial experts living in Geneva during the Reformation were French refugees, compared with judicial practice at local courts of first instance within France during the same period. Whereas the records of French appeal courts represent the practice of torture as a strictly legal procedure, indirect evidence suggests that local courts of first instance used it in an effort to cleanse their communities of heresy and deviance. This case study of torture in Geneva, a city located on the borders of France, raises interesting questions about the assumptions of religious neutrality that French historiography usually attributes to the royal courts during the Wars of Religion.

---

[6] Edward Peters, *Torture* (New York, 1985); John H. Langbein, *Torture and the Law of Proof: Europe and England in the Ancien Régime* (Chicago, 1977); Olivier F. Dubois and Martine Ostorero, 'La Torture en Suisse occidentale', in Bernard Durand (ed.), *La Torture judiciaire: approches historiques et juridiques*, 2 vols (Lille, 2002), II, 541.

[7] Ibid., II, 547–8; Émile Rivoire and Victor van Berchem, *Les Sources du droit du canton de Genève* (Geneva, 1930–3), III, 250.

Torture was a linchpin of criminal justice during the sixteenth century, in France no less than in Geneva, but its investigation within France is frustrated by incomplete records. Important research has been done at the Paris *parlement*, the highest appeals court for the Ile-de-France region encompassing several million inhabitants, that demonstrates how enthusiasm for torture began to wane at that court as early as the mid-sixteenth century. The Paris records reveal that neither God nor the devil make much appearance during the torture sessions. This is not to imply that Parisian judges never thought of God in the torture chamber, but it does suggest that at the *parlement* torture was justified by a search for crime not for sin.[8] Tantalizing fragmentary records from other French courts demonstrate that the Paris *parlement* experience should not be taken as normative and suggest that torture remained an important means of obtaining confessions through to at least 1600.[9] In contrast, the Genevan archives are full of thousands of detailed criminal trials, records that enable a close examination of the logic of judicial practice. In addition, clear reliance on divine law justified the application of torture in Geneva. God is everywhere in the Genevan records: in the torture interrogations, in the case summaries, in the legal opinions developed by lawyers, and in the final sentences. The point here is less to draw absolute distinctions between Catholics and Protestants, since we know from the German evidence that religion could certainly play an important role in the Catholic torture chamber, but rather to explore the explicit references to godly justice in the Genevan records and to consider to what extent such considerations could have shaped judicial practice in French courts of first instance as well.[10]

---

[8] Alfred Soman, 'La justice criminelle aux XVIe –XVIIe siècles: le Parlement de Paris et les sièges subalternes', in *Sorcellerie et justice criminelle: le Parlement de Paris (16e–18e siècles)* (Hampshire, 1992), 38–49; Bernard Schnapper, 'La justice criminelle rendue par le Parlement de Paris sous le règne de François Ier', *Revue Historique de Droit Français et Étranger*, 52 (1974), 252–84.

[9] Gérard D. Guyon, 'Recherches sur la méthode jurisprudentielle criminelle du Parlement de Bordeaux au XVIe siècle', in Jack Poumarede and Jack Thomas (eds), *Les Parlements de province: pouvoirs, justice et société du XVe au XVIIIe siècle* (Toulouse, 1996); Bernard Schnapper, 'La répression pénale au XVIe siècle: l'exemple du Parlement de Bordeaux (1510–1565)', *Recueil de mémoires et travaux, publié par la Société d'histoire du droit et des institutions des anciens pays de droit écrit*, 8 (1971), 1–54; Annie Charnay, *Paroles de voleurs: gens de sac et de corde en pays toulousain au début du XVIe siècle* (Paris, 1998); Veronique Pinson-Ramin, 'La torture judiciaire en Bretagne au XVIIe siècle', *Revue Historique du Droit Français et Etranger* 72 (1994), 549–68.

[10] Wolfgang Behringer, *Witchcraft Persecutions in Bavaria* (Cambridge, 1997); Lyndal Roper, *Witch Craze: Terror and Fantasy in Baroque Germany* (New Haven, CT, 2004).

Aware that torture did not always yield the truth but anxious to ensure that it do so, early modern European jurists hemmed the procedure in with strict rules about when and how it could be applied.[11] Torture was generally employed only in difficult cases in which two neutral eye witnesses could not be found or when defendants were accused of particularly serious crimes. Accused criminals were rarely tortured during their first interrogation and usually first had the opportunity to reflect on their fate for several days while detained in prison. In Geneva, torture did occur behind closed doors, but it was not a secret or an illegitimate procedure. Defendants were tortured in a public building under the auspices of elected city councillors, and in the presence of a scribe as well as of the *lieutenant criminel*. Torture sessions were scripted events, beginning with the same gestures and invocations and following a set series of movements in time and space. During interrogations with torture, the words spoken were carefully recorded, an exchange that was captured in Geneva in a question/answer format with the replies of the accused usually recorded in the third person. Judicial records are of course complex texts mediated by considerations of genre and the desires of judges to represent themselves as fair and responsible. Such texts can never provide transparent access to the experiences of the torture chamber, but they do reveal the ways in which the court sought to represent its procedures and the range of possible outcomes that could be imagined and sanctioned.[12] As a result, these documents are most useful for exploring the world-view of the judges who controlled not only the questions asked during an interrogation but also the records produced from such sessions.

In Geneva, truth, conscience and sin were concepts constantly evoked by the interrogators during torture sessions and were coupled with the physical pain to produce a transformation in the defendant. Torture was a rite that sought to test the innocence or discover the guilt of the accused; no matter what s/he confessed, the defendant's relationship with the judges, with society, and with God was irrevocably altered by the experience.[13] In Geneva, defendants who stubbornly refused to confess to a serious crime were confronted first with a panel of judges and then with the torture equipment in a measured encounter designed to intimidate and to elicit a baring of the soul.

---

[11] Peters, *Torture*; John H. Langbein, *Prosecuting Crime in the Renaissance: England, Germany, France* (Cambridge, MA, 1974).

[12] Natalie Zemon Davis, *Fiction in the Archives: Pardon Tales and their Tellers in Sixteenth-Century France* (Stanford, CA, 1987); Michel de Certeau, *La Possession de Loudun* (Paris, 1980); Edward Muir and Guido Ruggiero (eds), *History from Crime* (Baltimore, 1994).

[13] Muir, *Ritual in Early Modern Europe*; Victor Turner, *The Ritual Process: Structure and Anti-Structure* (New York, 1969).

Individuals were tortured at the *Evêché* near St Peter's Cathedral, the former residence of the Catholic bishop that had been transformed into the Reformed city's civic prison.[14] In preparation for a torture session, the judges of the Genevan criminal court, who were delegates chosen from the elected executive council of the city, the *Petit Conseil*, gathered in an interrogation room in the prison.[15] At the outset of the encounter, the judges asked the prisoner 'to come to the truth' or 'exhorted [him] to tell the truth'.[16] On 10 June 1549, Genevan resident Jacques Bard, accused of having traded in false coins, was brought before the judges and was asked to swear to 'tell the truth that everything he had confessed was real'.[17] Jacques admitted that he had used false coins and he blamed his actions on the devil, a claim that the judges took very seriously. Despite his protests that his confessions were 'true', the lieutenant in charge of criminal matters deemed his replies to be inconsistent and decided that torture should be applied 'so that the truth is forced from his mouth'.[18] Taken into a small triangular courtyard in the prison complex, Jacques was shown and attached to the torture instrument before having a change of heart and vowing to tell all. He was thus untied and brought back into the room where the judges were assembled. After a few more questions, the lieutenant, still unsatisfied with Jacques' responses, ordered him to be put into restraining irons overnight. The following day, Jacques still refused to reveal the provenance of the false coins to the judges. As a result, the lieutenant authorized 'one pull of the *corde*', a centuries-old procedure by which defendants were raised on a pulley with their hands tied behind their backs. This operation caused great pain and often dislocated the shoulders of the accused.[19] Jacques endured the *corde* for fifteen minutes before revealing that he, together with his brother Jean, had clandestinely manufactured the false coins and had deliberately subverted the

---

[14] Walter Zurbuchen, *Prisons de Genève* (Geneva, 1977), 52. For an understanding of the confessionalization of civic space, see Judi Loach, 'The Consecration of the Civic Realm', in Andrew Spicer and Sarah Hamilton (eds), *Defining the Holy: Sacred Space in Medieval and Early Modern Europe*, (Aldershot, 2005), 277–300. The interrogations in which torture was threatened and undertaken were called 'Répétitions devant les messieurs' and in some cases the attending judges' names were listed. See Archives de l'État de Genève (hereafter AEG), Procès criminels série 1 (hereafter PC1), 1394 interrogation 14 March 1567; AEG, PC1 1238, interrogation 13 November 1564.

[15] Rivoire and Berchem, *Sources*, II, 492; III, 250.

[16] AEG, PC1 1421, interrogation 15 November 1567; AEG, PC1 1267, interrogation 27 February 1565; AEG, PC1 1173, interrogation 21 January 1564.

[17] AEG, PC1 456, interrogation 10 June 1549.

[18] Ibid.

[19] Ibid., interrogation 11 June 1549.

authority of the Genevan government. Jacques elaborated more fully on the range of his accomplices and the techniques used in creating the false coins during three more interrogations without torture in the weeks that followed.[20] These final interrogations were as valuable as those conducted under torture for they allowed the court to claim that his confession had been 'repeated several times'.[21] A few days after his last interrogation, Jacques was deemed to have sinned 'without fear of God and of justice', sentenced to have his head cut off and be left to rot on the gibbet.[22] The torture session was the turning point in this trial because it transformed him from a sinner and a casual criminal who had made a bad decision to buy something with a false coin into a systematic law-breaker who had deliberately subverted the laws of the city.

Torture could be fine-tuned to the case at hand: the length of time the accused hung from the *corde*, whether from one arm or both, and whether or not s/he was dropped sharply to the floor to increase the pain, all varied.[23] But the steps taken by the executioner before torture was applied and the kinds of questions asked by the judges were consistent. Torture was highly regulated, structured by set criteria for determining its need, set truth-testing questions, and a limited number of permissible techniques. Its formulaic nature conducted at the request of elected public officials invested the procedure with claims to legal certainty. As we will see, the ways in which Genevan judges also invested the procedure with the status of a spiritual ordeal and employed it to find those who had abandoned God reveal that torture was also a rite of violence.

---

[20] Ibid., interrogations 12, 19, and 27 June 1549.

[21] Ibid., final sentence 13 July 1549.

[22] Ibid., case summary 13 July 1549.

[23] Although the *corde* and the *estrapade* overwhelmingly predominated, various torture methods were occasionally practised in Reformation Geneva, including sleep deprivation, confinement in a very small cubicle called the *cachot*, attachment with irons to restrict movement in prison, heating the feet, and the *beurrière*, a human churn using pressure and the weight of the body to cause pain. In the cases of restraining irons, the *cachot* and sleep deprivation, though these practices did not take place during the interrogation session itself, sixteenth-century references to these techniques as torture and special means to encourage confession justify their inclusion in this list. See AEG, PC1 2876, PC1 960; Broye, *Sorcellerie et superstitions*, 54; André-Luc Poncet, *Les Châtelains et l'administration de la justice: dans les mandements genevois sous l'Ancien Régime (1536–1792)* (Geneva, 1973), 236, n. 128; Sonia Vernhes Rappaz, 'La noyade judiciaire à Genève (1558–1619)', mémoire de licence, University of Geneva (2007), I, 88; Zurbuchen, *Prisons*, 52.

Whereas torture was a well-established legal procedure in Geneva before the Reformation, its use seems to have peaked during the middle decades of the sixteenth century. The prevalence of its practice in the mid-sixteenth century has until now gone largely unnoticed in part because of the way that criminal cases are organized in the archives. Nineteenth-century archivists produced detailed summaries of over two thousand court cases prosecuted in Geneva before 1600, but these case summaries do not consistently include references to torture when it was applied. Unlike in France, few of these cases have been redacted, transcribed, and published.[24] As a result, the striking reliance of the *Petit Conseil* on torture during the sixteenth century can only be determined through a careful reading of entire case files. With the notable exception of studies focused on witchcraft and plague-spreading trials, the full extent of torture as a legal procedure in Reformation Geneva has thus been left unexplored.[25]

Genevan judges tortured defendants accused of a wide variety of crimes that were considered serious enough to warrant the death penalty. Despite laws that clearly defined crimes for which a capital sentence was necessary, Genevan judges did not always choose to enforce the law to its fullest extent and, as a result, the criteria for determining whether torture was warranted in a given case shifted over time.[26] At the height of Genevan judges' willingness to use torture, which preliminary research suggests was in the 1560s, judges in Geneva tortured both men and women for a variety of capital crimes including homicide, infanticide, sedition, witchcraft, counterfeiting, theft, arson, adultery, sodomy, rape, and prostitution. Between 1560 and 1563, an analysis of trials for the above-mentioned crimes reveals that torture was used to obtain confessions from at least 34 per cent of defendants accused of these crimes, a number that suggests that the practice was routine when defendants refused to confess.[27] Analogously, over 84 per cent of individuals who were

[24] For exceptions, see Raymond Christinger and J. E. Genequand, 'Un procès genevois de sorcellerie inédit', *Genava* 17 (1969), 113–38; Michel Porret et al., *L'Ombre du diable* (Chêne-Bourg, 2009); Sophie Simon, *'Si je le veux, il mourra!' Maléfices et sorcellerie dans la campagne genevoise (1497–1530)* (Lausanne, 2007).

[25] Broye, *Sorcellerie et superstitions*; E. William Monter, 'Witchcraft in Geneva', *Journal of Modern History*, 43 (1971), 179–204; Naphy, *Plagues, Poisons, and Potions*.

[26] Poncet, *Châtelains*, 373–97.

[27] This figure is based on an analysis of 138 individuals tried for homicide, murder, assassination, infanticide, treason, conspiracy, burglary, theft, adultery, prostitution/procuring, heresy, bigamy, rape, abortion, sodomy, arson, counterfeiting, and witchcraft brought before the Genevan *Petit Conseil* between 1560 and 1563 that are still extant. The actual number of cases of serious crimes tried by the *Petit Conseil* during this period may have been double that number. In contrast, a century later, in a sample drawn from

executed in Geneva during the same time period had been tortured.[28] Hanging someone by the *corde* was the standard procedure, but this was often intensified by dropping the individual sharply to the ground, a technique known as the *estrapade*. Suspects could also be tortured repeatedly. In 1563, Etienne Fallas, accused of assassination, was subjected to the *estrapade* twice on 17 September, to the *corde* twice on 28 September and the *corde* at least once more on 14 October.[29] The aim of these torture sessions was clear: the judges sought a confession of guilt that was consistent with the physical evidence and witness testimony they had already gathered. Yet they did not stop there. Even after establishing the basic facts of a crime, Genevan judges often continued to question the defendants on whether they had abandoned God. The judges' persistence regarding the spiritual state of the accused is notable and is one element that suggests the procedure was regarded as a means of godly justice.

Of course, torture in Geneva should not be understood in solely religious terms. Geneva during the Reformation was a fledgling city state in an unstable relationship with its neighbours. A community of some 10,000 residents, Geneva had only established its independence from the house of Savoy in the 1520s. Its transformation from rule by a prince-bishop to fully formed state took over a decade as the city appropriated ecclesiastical revenues and adapted existing governmental institutions to self-rule. Over the next thirty years, political authority remained unstable as competing elites sought to dominate the city. Soon after the return of John Calvin in 1541, Geneva faced an onslaught of French exiles fleeing religious intolerance, a wave of immigration that almost doubled the population of the city and exacerbated political divisions. Only towards the mid-century did the political system stabilize as the city's indirectly elected *Petit Conseil* increasingly wrested judicial and executive authority from the larger, more democratic councils.

---

the years 1650–3 involving seventy-one trials for the same crimes, only nine per cent of the accused were tortured. These numbers are necessarily tentative because of the large number of missing cases, particularly for the sixteenth century. Nevertheless, comprehensive lists of all completed trials for the years 1552, 1562, and 1572 confirm the overall patterns found in the extant cases. See Bernard Lescaze, 'Crimes et criminels', 45–71; E. William Monter, 'Crime and Punishment in Calvin's Geneva, 1562', *Archiv für Reformationsgeschichte*, 64 (1973), 281–6. Torture was not employed in Geneva, even for capital crimes, if a confession could be obtained through interrogation alone. See AEG, PC1 903, 1167.

[28] According to the 1560–3 full trial records, twenty-seven individuals were tortured among the thirty-two criminals executed.

[29] AEG, PC1 1139, interrogations 17, 28 September and 14 October 1563.

During the second half of the century, a relatively narrow oligarchy of native Genevan and French immigrants emerged as the unchallenged leaders of the city.[30] When understanding the practice of torture in Geneva, it is important to remember that this was a new and relatively fragile state surrounded by larger and more powerful neighbours.

Historians have clearly established that some of the most violent uses of torture, during the witch hunts of the late sixteenth and early seventeenth centuries, occurred in the small, hinterland states of western Europe: in what was to become Switzerland, along the contested eastern border of France, and in the states in the south-west of the Holy Roman Empire. In some of these polities, torture was applied with great intensity, and it was not uncommon for the defendants accused of serious crimes to be subjected to multiple torture sessions that unsurprisingly produced damning confessions. Small states with uncertain political futures and judicial courts whose decisions were not subject to a rigorous appeals procedure were often more violent in their imposition of justice than law courts in the well-established monarchies.[31] Thus a rise in the use of torture in Geneva during the sixteenth century is not surprising. As a relatively small oligarchy came to dominate city governance through the *Petit Conseil*, it would be expected that the practice of torture might be a means to assert authority in the newly minted city state. Thus torture in Geneva need not have been a rite of violence; secular legal precedence and the vulnerable political situation of the city were sufficient to explain the intensification of the practice during the sixteenth century.

Yet to stress political causes is to ignore the many ways in which Reformed faith and the need to actively regulate its bounds shaped Genevan judicial practice. Torture functioned as a rite of violence by shaping the questions and answers in the torture chamber. Genevan judges used torture to explore the sinful nature of the criminal's soul not only during trials for clear cases of deviant belief such as heresy but also during trials for public order crimes like murder and theft. Torture rites created narratives of sin that justified the

---

[30] Naphy, *Calvin and the Consolidation*; E. William Monter, *Studies in Genevan Government (1536–1605)* (Geneva, 1964); Liliane Mottu-Weber, Anne-Marie Piuz and Bernard Lescaze, *Vivre à Genève autour de 1600*, II: *Ordre et désordres*, (Geneva, 2006).

[31] H. C. Erik Midelfort, *Witch Hunting in Southwestern Germany 1562–1684: The Social and Intellectual Foundations* (Stanford, 1972); Robin Briggs, *Witches and Neighbours: The Social and Cultural Context of European Witchcraft* (London, 1996); Robert Muchembled, *Le Temps des supplices: de l'obéissance sous les rois absolus (XVe–XVIII siècle)* (Paris, 1992); Laura Stokes, *Demons of Urban Reform: Early European Witch Trials and Criminal Justice, 1430–1530* (New York, 2011); E. William Monter, *Patterns of Witchcraft in the Jura* (Berkeley, CA, 1971).

purging of polluting criminals from the community and sought to cement bonds of confessional unity among city residents. The frequency of the use of torture during the middle decades of the sixteenth century can in part be explained by the urgency of its task. It was only in 1555 that Calvin was able to oust his political enemies from the city and to secure a *Petit Conseil* that consistently supported his programme of religious reform. During the decades that followed, the Reformed Church intensified its efforts to force sometimes reluctant city residents to conform to God's law: to attend church services regularly, to refrain from corrupting activities such as dancing and gambling, and to avoid myriad sexual sins. The *Petit Conseil* and the Reformed consistory together sought to educate Genevans in the ways of right living, and torture, alongside the visible punishments of banishment and execution, were important means of doing so.

Because judges sitting in the Genevan criminal court were not men trained in the law but amateurs who served as judges as part of their overall political duties, they frequently turned for expert advice to university-trained lawyers, who, during the middle of the sixteenth century, were all French and men of deep Reformed faith. One of the lawyers consulted was none other than John Calvin. Calvin never held political office in the city, though it is generally agreed that he exercised wide political influence during the decade preceding his death in 1564. As such, he was consulted on a number of criminal cases during the early 1550s, in one of which five male youths were accused of the capital crime of sodomy.[32] Given the serious nature of the crime, Calvin and three other jurists deemed that harsh punishment must be imposed on these young sinners because 'there would be a danger that our Lord make manifest with more horrible punishments that which man had wished to conceal and that his anger envelop others' if they did otherwise.[33] Calvin feared not only for the souls of the defendants, but also for the spiritual corruption of the judges. In this case, given the tender age of the accused, the jurists recommended punishment by their parents for the youngest two boys; the older three were sentenced to temporary incarceration under a bread and water regime, and to a public flogging in front of a burning pyre as a reminder that mercy had saved them from a fiery fate. This legal opinion reflects not only a horror of sodomy but also a faith that God was attentive to the judges' actions. God's wrath was to be feared should the jurists shirk their duty; public

---

[32] John Witte and Robert M. Kingdon, *Sex, Marriage, and Family in John Calvin's Geneva* (Grand Rapids, MI, 2005), 71–2; Verhnes Rappaz, 'Noyade judiciaire à Genève', I, 108.

[33] Ibid., II, 77–9.

punishment of infamous criminals was a means of showing obedience to divine law.[34]

Most legal opinions recommending torture and execution were not signed by Calvin, but rather by his close associates, most frequently during the height of the Reformation by another university-trained lawyer named Germain Colladon. Committed to the Reformed faith, Colladon left France in 1550 for Geneva where he established residency and became an important advisor on legal matters. Colladon drafted the city's new criminal and civil statutes in 1568, and offered well-respected legal opinions in hundreds of criminal cases during the second half of the sixteenth century.[35] Oftentimes, Colladon was consulted repeatedly during the same case: he developed the questions posed to the accused, weighed in on the need for torture, and recommended a final sentence. Colladon, steeped in Roman law and contemporary French procedure, justified his decisions in favour of torture on several grounds, including 'divine law'.[36] References to scripture and to God's law pepper his legal opinions and vindicate his recommendations of violent torture and harsh physical punishments. Often Colladon chose to recommend torture because the crime that the defendant was accused of having committed threatened 'in a scandalous manner a church reformed according to the Word of God' or involved a 'defamation of God'.[37] Colladon clearly shared Calvin's view that the law was an arm of godly justice that should be used to correct, punish, and provide an example of Christian living to the community at large. Although the judges of the *Petit Conseil* did not always follow Colladon's advice, they usually tortured accused criminals when he recommended doing so.[38] Thus, by turning to Colladon for legal advice, the judges sought and found confirmation that torture was a justified way of fighting God's battles in the temporal realm.

God was believed not only to be watching from above but also to be present in the torture chamber in a way that was analogous to the earlier tradition of the judicial ordeal. Ordeals of fire and water, designed to test the guilt or

---

[34] Marianne Carbonnier, 'Le droit de punir et le sens de la peine chez Calvin', *Revue d'Histoire et de Philosophie Religieuses*, 54 (1974), 187–201.

[35] Kaden, *Colladon*, 96–9.

[36] Ibid., 81–2; AEG, PC1 911, *avis de droit*. For the strong influence of Roman law on Colladon in particular and on Genevan jurists more generally, see Langbein, *Prosecuting Crime*; Vernhes Rappaz, 'Noyade judiciaire dans la République', 16–17.

[37] AEG, PC1 911, *avis de droit*; AEG, PC1 1173, 2nd *avis de droit* of Colladon; AEG PC1 928, *avis de droit*; Kaden, *Colladon*, 82–3.

[38] The *Petit Conseil* sometimes chose to impose a milder sentence that the one Colladon recommended. Ibid., 80 n. 266; AEG, PC1 1089.

innocence of the accused before God, had of course been outlawed by the Catholic church as early as 1215, but the practices persisted well into the early modern period.[39] The 'swimming' of witches to see whether they would float—a sign of the witch's pact with the devil and hence her guilt—was an enduring if exceptional judicial procedure in the eastern borderlands of France and in south-west Germany throughout the sixteenth century.[40] Educated jurists repudiated the ordeal, in part because there was no precedent for it in Roman law, but notions that God and the devil were present in the torture chamber were never completely eliminated. Belief in the devil and in his powers on this earth was prevalent in the sixteenth century even among doctors, theologians, and judges. Both Catholics and Protestants agreed that the devil was less powerful than God and most thought that he required human intermediaries to effect evil on earth. But many also believed the devil was a tangible force, not a metaphor for acting in bad conscience, but an agent of evil who could haunt individuals and corrupt their souls. It was commonly held that the devil could aid the accused in the torture chamber and protect him/her from confessing the truth by means of an amulet, a salve or merely the strength of the pact that bound them together. Although the devil could protect individuals from pain, the pain of torture was also considered to be a penitential ritual, a possible means of cleansing the soul of the devil's influence.[41] Once free of the devil, the suspect could finally admit the

---

[39] Robert Bartlett, *Trial by Fire and Water: The Medieval Judicial Ordeal* (Oxford, 1987); Jacques Chiffoleau, 'Sur la Pratique et la conjucture de l'aveu judiciaire en France du XIIIe au XVe siècle', in *L'Aveu, Antiquité et Moyen Age: actes de la table ronde* (Rome, 1986), 341–80; Edward Peters, 'Destruction of the Flesh—Salvation of the Spirit: The Paradoxes of Torture in Medieval Christian Society', in Alberto Ferreiro (ed.), *The Devil, Heresy, and Witchcraft in the Middle Ages* (Leiden, 1998), 131–48; Lisa Silverman, *Tortured Subjects: Pain, Truth and the Body in Early Modern France* (Chicago, 2001); Andrea McKenzie, 'This Death Some Strong and Stout Hearted Man Doth Choose: The Practice of Peine Forte et Dure in Seventeenth- and Eighteenth-Century England', *Law and History Review*, 23 (2005), 299–304.

[40] For the swimming of witches, see Arlette Lebigre, *La Justice du Roi: la vie judiciaire dans l'ancienne France* (Paris, 1988), 197; Richard van Dülmen, *Theatre of Horror: Crime and Punishment in Early Modern Germany* (Cambridge, 1990), 14–17. There is no evidence of witches being tested by an ordeal of water in Geneva. See Broye, *Sorcellerie et superstitions*; Isabelle Jeger, 'Répression de la sorcellerie dans la région Genevoise avant la Réforme', *Schweizerische Zeitschrift für Geschichte*, 52 (2002), 127–32; Monter, 'Witchcraft in Geneva'.

[41] Stuart Clark, *Thinking with Demons: The Idea of Witchcraft in Early Modern Europe* (Oxford, 1997), 590–3; Dülmen *Theatre of Horror*, 15–23; Dubois and Ostorero, 'Torture en Suisse', 562–3.

truth and confess his sins not only before the judges but also before God. Thus the authority of torture was enhanced by its association in the minds of many Christians with the tangible power of God and the devil on the soul of the accused. Unadulterated truth produced by a purified soul was a possible outcome of a torture session.

These beliefs were certainly in play during torture sessions in Reformation Geneva. Once defendants were attached to the torture instrument and before they were lifted on the pulley, the interrogator often threatened them with God's judgment, asked questions about the state of their conscience, or accused them of being in league with the devil.[42] These questions served several purposes, including assessing the possibility that the devil might help defendants resist the pain of torture and encouraging them to confess their sins before God in the hopes of achieving forgiveness and redemption.

In turn, accused criminals evoked God's presence for their own purposes. Threatened with torture but before they were attached to the pulley, defendants sometimes fell to their knees in a position of prayer and abnegation to beg mercy of the judges and to swear before God that they were telling the truth.[43] Once attached to the *corde* and in pain, the tortured frequently called out 'my God have pity on me' or swore his/her innocence before God. Unlike the rest of the utterances transcribed during the interrogation, scribes sometimes recorded direct pleas to God under torture in the first rather than the third person, a choice that heightened the immediacy of the plea and suggested that the moments when the accused was subjected to the pain of torture were outside of the normal realm of experience.[44] The time when the defendant was attached to the *corde* was a liminal experience that had the potential to transform the accused into a righteous innocent, a shameless sinner, or humble penitent. Some defendants took advantage of the authority afforded by the torture rite to invoke God's all-knowing nature in their favour. When Petramande, wife of Jean-François Morel, was threatened in 1567 with torture on suspicion of adultery, she boldly claimed that she would never confess, not even if they tore her into a 'thousand pieces'. When lifted by the *corde*, she reasserted her innocence and claimed that the judges were 'wrong to torment her' since 'she would never commit such an act, as God

---

[42] AEG, PC1 1028, interrogation of Guillauma Epaula 6 April 1562; AEG, PC1 900, interrogation 15 November 1567; Broye, *Sorcellerie et superstitions*, 69.

[43] AEG, PC1 1090, interrogation 8 January 1563; AEG, PC1 1028, interrogation of Henriette Chesalier 8 April 1562.

[44] AEG, PC1 1238, interrogation 13 November 1564. See also AEG, PC1 1824, interrogation 11 March 1601.

knows'.[45] In this case, the judges found Petramande's appeals to God convincing: soon after, the judges gently lowered and detached Petramande from the pulley and, five days later, freed her from prison. Although questions about the devil and God can be found at other moments in the trial, invocations and pleas directed to God while under torture were recorded with a great attention to detail that reveal the extent to which they were granted weight in the evaluation of the accused's testimony.

Of course, this is not to say that God's presence made the outcome of the torture session certain. Although Colladon and other legal experts consulted by the *Petit Conseil* often recommended torture as a means of obtaining truth, their legal opinions also expressed some scepticism about the reliability of confessions produced under duress, especially when the testimony varied day to day.[46] Nevertheless, these same well-educated lawyers also recommended searching some accused because they suspected their resistance to torture was enhanced by the presence of an amulet provided by the devil.[47] Torture as a rite of violence was ambiguous and fraught with difficulties of interpretation, but the idea that God and the devil were battling for the soul of the accused was very much present in the minds of Genevan authorities. Torture was a legal procedure first and foremost, but it was also a liminal ritual during which the veil that separated the spiritual from the temporal realm could be lifted.

These considerations were particularly apparent in trials against suspected witches, a phenomenon that peaked in Geneva during the 1560s and 1570s.[48] Strongly informed by demonological theory that predicated the power of the witch on his/her relationship with the devil, judges questioned defendants about their relationship to God, their presence at the Sabbath, and when they had first made a pact to serve the devil. In 1567, Eustache de Bourgel, a well-established Genevan *bourgeois*, was tortured with the *estrapade* and the *corde* on at least three occasions before he admitted to having met the devil some eighteen years earlier and having been in league with him ever since. But the interrogations continued after he confessed to these heretical sins, for the judges sought not only confirmation of Bourgel's spiritual pollution but also proof of his physical crimes against his fellow city residents. Only after he admitted to having poisoned some soup that he fed to a young

---

[45] AEG, PC1 1394, interrogation 12 March 1567. See also AEG, PC1 1139, interrogation 14 October 1563.

[46] AEG, PC1 1028, Colladon's *avis de droit*; AEG, PC1 1139, *avis de droit*; Kaden, *Colladon*, 85–91.

[47] Poncet, *Châtelains*, 376.

[48] Broye, *Sorcellerie et superstitions*; Monter, 'Witchcraft in Geneva'.

girl who subsequently died were the judges satisfied and ceased their questioning.[49] Similarly, Guillauma Epaula, wife of a fisherman, was subjected to a session with the *corde* to pressure her to confess not only that she had abandoned God for the devil but also that she had spread poisoned grease on objects in order to sicken her neighbours.[50] Both their state of spiritual alienation from God and the *maleficia* they had performed were crucial to successful witchcraft prosecutions in Geneva.[51] In these respects, accused witches were not so very different from other sorts of accused criminals who were brought before the *Petit Conseil*.

Although there was a more concerted focus from the outset of a witchcraft trial on questions of faith and spiritual deviance, these matters also arose in the trials of those accused of more mundane crimes. For any Christian, a crime was also a sin and the sign of a corrupted soul, but in Geneva the search for spiritual pollution was particularly probing. Contradicting Michel Foucault's claims about the nature of early modern justice, Genevan judges were rarely content with a simple confession of the crime.[52] Instead, during the Reformation the Genevan criminal court sought to uncover the entire moral universe of the accused in the expectation that the committing of a heinous crime was predicated on a life of sin.[53]

Even during trials for straightforward murder or theft, the moral and spiritual aspects of the case often transformed interrogations under torture from procedures of criminal investigation into rites of spiritual purification. In 1567, Jean Delachenal was arrested in Nyon and transferred to Geneva to be tried for murder and brigandage. His initial confessions were wildly inconsistent and so torture was applied. Having been subjected to restraining irons in prison and then to the *estrapade* during an interrogation, he confessed to having participated in the murder of not one, but two, men over the course of the last seven years.[54] During the interrogations, the judges asked as many questions about the numerous sins he had committed in his adult life as they did about the homicides for which he had been brought in. Frequent thefts, repeated instances of extramarital sex, blaspheming against God and even physically abusing his family members were confessions that very much

---

[49] AEG, PC1 1421, interrogation of Eustache Bourgel 14, 15, 17 November 1567.

[50] AEG, PC1 1028, interrogation of Guillauma Epaula 8 April 1562; AEG, Jur. Pen. A3, fo. 19v, 7 April 1562.

[51] Monter, 'Witchcraft in Geneva', 192.

[52] Michel Foucault, *Surveiller et punir: naissance de la prison* (Paris, 1975).

[53] This is similar to the English experience. Andrea McKenzie, *Tyburn's Martyrs: Execution in England, 1675–1775* (London, 2007).

[54] AEG, PC1 900, interrogation 1 April 1560.

interested the judges. Even though Delachenal had confessed enough to warrant the death penalty and bring an end to his torments, the judges persisted. They began asking Delachenal about the devil, much as they did when faced with an accused witch: did he believe in God? Did he believe in the devil? Did he believe in the possibility of hell? At first, Delachenal claimed that he believed in God, but denied everything else, an unsatisfactory response; eventually he admitted to believing in the existence of the devil and of hell, but he consistently denied having met the devil or having been in league with him.[55] He did acknowledge, however, that his wife had acted as his good conscience, frequently reprimanding him for his bad behaviour and judging him harshly for the murders he had committed. He also expressed great regret for his sins and admitted that his own feelings of remorse were so great that sometimes he could not eat.[56] After eight interrogations of this nature, during two of which he was tortured, the judges were finally satisfied that they had discovered the full extent of his sins and crimes, and, as a result, sentenced him to death. In the final sentence, his descent from sin into crime was described in the following manner:

> that since your youth, having forgotten all fear of God, you abandoned yourself to enormous crimes and sins such as blasphemy, illicit sexual relations, adultery, theft, lies, robbery, murders and brigandage, and having beaten and hit your own mother.[57]

The rhetorical ordering of Delachenal's crimes is telling. Although it is clear that he was not executed because he attacked his mother, the narrative constructed by the interrogations and the torture sessions depicted a man who had long since lost God and any sense of morality. The murders he had committed were merely the last in a long line of sins that demonstrated his unworthiness and the Genevan judges' righteousness in executing him. Delachenal's case, though unusual in its focus on family interactions, was far from exceptional in its exposure of the accused as a morally depraved individual through the purging experience of torture.[58] As in witchcraft trials, both the physical crimes committed and the evidence of a spiritual stain on the soul were the subject of the torture interrogation; these aspects were assessed together when the final sentence of banishment or execution was issued.

---

[55] Ibid., interrogation 1, 2 April 1560.
[56] Ibid., interrogation 2 April 1560.
[57] Ibid., case summary.
[58] See, e.g., AEG, PC1 903, PC1 1010.

The importance of torture as a rite of violence can also be seen in the means by which certain defendants reached the torture chamber and the kinds of crimes that the Genevan government thought serious enough to warrant capital sentences. The Genevan criminal court very rarely tortured individuals for relatively minor crimes such as petty theft or even extramarital sex. But the wide range of moral crimes that the judges did consider worthy of testing with pain is striking, even for the sixteenth century. The frequency with which moral and sexual deviants were tortured must in part be attributed to the Consistory and its close relationship, particularly after 1555, with the *Petit Conseil*.[59]

The first line of defence against the religiously and morally deviant in Geneva was the Consistory, the body of pastors and elders (chosen from among the members of the city's three governing councils) that regulated the Christian comportment of city residents. First established by Calvin in 1541, the Consistory made great efforts to identify city residents who were not attending church, espousing heretical beliefs, or speaking out against God, as well as those defying moral regulations. Unlike the *Petit Conseil*, the Consistory did not have the authority to torture, banish, or execute the social and religious deviants it uncovered. Most individuals found guilty by the Consistory were either instructed and/or fined; only the most determined and recalcitrant recidivists were denied access to communion, the Consistory's harshest penalty. In cases of particularly determined sinners who had clearly broken the law, the Consistory also had another option: to refer cases to the *Petit Conseil* for consideration.[60]

Referring cases of social deviance, including sexual misconduct, to secular criminal courts was not uncommon during the sixteenth century. Historians have demonstrated that a marked rise in the efforts of government officials to regulate the moral and sexual conduct of their subjects/citizens occurred during the late medieval period. Whereas this responsibility had been the purview of church courts prior to 1450, part of the process of state building in much of western Europe involved the assumption of these responsibilities by temporal officials and the association of good citizenship with conforming to

---

[59] Nevertheless, even after 1555, the *Petit Conseil* and the Consistory did not always work in concert. See Naphy, *Calvin and Consolidation*; Bernard Lescaze, "Funus Consistori, O Miserere!' l'Égalité de traitement devant le consistoire de Genève autour de 1600', in Danièle Tosato-Rigo and Nicole Staremberg Goy (eds), *Sous L'Oeil du consistoire: sources consistoriales et histoire du contrôle social sous l'Ancien Régime* (Lausanne, 2004), 40–55.

[60] Ibid.; Grosse, *Les Rituels de la Cène*, 353–422; Scott M. Manetsch, 'Pastoral Care East of Eden: The Consistory of Geneva 1568–82', *Church History*, 75 (2006), 274–313.

a prescribed set of social norms.[61] That the Genevan criminal court enforced social discipline is thus not at all unusual. Nevertheless, Geneva did stand out for the range of moral crimes it chose to test by torture and to punish with banishment and execution. This tendency to punish sexual infractions relatively harshly coincided with the coming of Calvin's Reformation: before the 1540s, such cases were exceptional and rarely resulted in death sentences.[62]

Adultery was the most notable sexual crime prosecuted by the *Petit Conseil*, but both men and women suspected of a wide swathe of sexual transgressions including incest, prostitution, sodomy, extramarital sex, abortion, bigamy, and rape were also tried and tortured by the criminal court.[63] Between 1560 and 1563, 22 per cent of those tortured in Geneva were accused of these sexual crimes, a rate far higher than in most French or German jurisdictions.[64] The numbers of individuals the *Petit Conseil* punished severely for sexual crimes is also striking. In 1562, nine of thirty-one banishments and five of thirteen executions were issued against individuals found guilty of sexual crimes.[65] This harsh treatment of sexual deviants relied on referrals from the Consistory: between 1546 and 1557 almost half of those accused of sexual irregularities were referred to the *Petit Conseil* with the knowledge that for infractions like adultery torture, if not execution, was likely to result.[66] Close

---

[61] Philip Benedict, *Christ's Churches Purely Reformed: A Social History of Calvinism* (New Haven, CT, 2002); R. Po-Chia Hsia, *Social Discipline in the Reformation: Central Europe 1550–1750* (New York, 1989); Alan Hunt, *Governance of the Consuming Passions: A History of Sumptuary Law* (New York, 1996); Raymond A. Mentzer, *Sin and the Calvinists: Morals Control and the Consistory in the Reformed Tradition* (Kirksville, MO, 1994); Lyndal Roper, *The Holy Household: Women and Morals in Reformation Augsburg* (Oxford, 1989); Guido Ruggiero, *The Boundaries of Eros: Sex, Crime, and Sexuality in Renaissance Venice* (Oxford, 1985); Frank Rexroth, *Deviance and Power in Late Medieval London*, trans. Pamela E. Selwyn (Cambridge, 2007).

[62] Few Genevan women were banished for adultery before 1540. See AEG, PC1 161, PC1 346; Naphy, *Calvin and the Consolidation*, 181.

[63] Kingdon, *Adultery and Divorce*; William Naphy, 'Sodomy in Early Modern Geneva', in Tom Betteridge (ed.), *Sodomy in Early Modern Europe* (Manchester, 2002), 94–111; Liliane Mottu-Weber, ' "Paillardises", "anticipation" et mariage réparation à Genève au XVIII siècle', *Schweizerische Zeitschrift für Geschichte*, 52 (2002), 430–47; Michel Porret, 'Le crime des filles "séduites et abandonees" ', in Johann Heinrich Pestalozzi (ed.), *Sur La Législation et l'infanticide: vérités, recherches et visions* (Bern, 2003), 163–87; Cornelia Seeger, *Nullité de mariage, divorce et séparation de corps à Genève au temps de Calvin* (Lausanne, 1989).

[64] Soman, 'Justice criminelle', 43; Dülmen, *Theatre of Horror*, 47.

[65] Monter, 'Crime and Punishment', 281–6.

[66] Witte and Kingdon, *Sex, Marriage, and Family*, 62–79.

surveillance of residents' personal behaviour by the Reformed church contributed to a society in which the testing of sexual crime under torture was more frequent in Geneva than in many other European communities.

The language of torture sessions and of final sentences makes it clear that sexual deviants were being condemned on religious grounds. In 1561, when Guillaume Branlard was accused of sodomizing another man, he was asked during his first interrogation 'if he did not know that it is a crime detested by God and by man and for which God judged and condemned many people', a statement with which he quietly agreed.[67] Similarly, when Pierre Gardet was accused of having committed adultery with a woman while her husband slept with them in the very same bed, the act was deemed to be 'so horrifying' that he was interrogated repeatedly, tortured, and, when he finally confessed, sentenced to death.[68] The very methods used to execute individuals convicted of these sexual crimes also made their spiritual pollution explicit. Whereas most criminals who were executed in Geneva were hanged, sexual deviants were dispatched in ways that highlighted that their behaviour defied 'nature'.[69] Sodomites were often burned at the stake, a punishment usually reserved for heretical witches. Those convicted of rape and incest, as well as female adulterers and women guilty of infanticide, were usually drowned, a punishment that was deemed by Colladon to be a more merciful adaptation of burning. Both these punishments evoked the ordeals of fire and water and mirror the retributive violence of sixteenth-century French rioters eager to cleanse their communities of dangerous heretics.[70] Torture was often the means by which these accused criminals exposed their sins to the judges; their public punishment displayed their alienation from God before the wider community.

The prevalence of torture in the prosecution of sexual deviance is somewhat in tension with recent studies on the Consistory. Extensive research undertaken in the difficult Consistorial records over the last two decades has produced a wealth of new studies that examine the dynamics of spiritual correction in Geneva. When considering the amendment of religious behaviour, the disciplining of women, the education of parents and the policy of excommunication, historians have stressed that the Consistory sought to

[67] AEG, PC1 971, interrogation 17 August 1561.
[68] AEG, PC1 1267, final sentence against Pierre Gardet. Gardet was interrogated eight times and tortured at least once with the *corde* on 27 February 1565.
[69] Verhnes Rappaz, 'Noyade dans la République', 15.
[70] Natalie Zemon Davis, 'The Rites of Violence: Religious Riot in Sixteenth-Century France', *Past and Present*, 59 (1973), 51–91; Denis Crouzet, *Les Guerriers de Dieu: la violence au temps des troubles de religion vers 1525–vers 1610* (Seyssel, 1990).

correct, protect, and educate its flock with an eye to the spiritual reintegration of the sinner. As a result, they have argued that living in Geneva was less religiously repressive than Calvin's decisive writings about social mores and obedience to God's law might suggest, and have stressed the degree to which members of the Consistory acted as spiritual counsellors to their flock.[71] This literature is compelling, but needs to be framed in a wider context that acknowledges the degree to which both spiritual and temporal authorities interacted and often cooperated in Geneva at the height of the Reformation. The fact that so many individuals accused of sexual infractions were referred to the criminal court and that so many legal opinions recommending torture were written by Calvin's close associates reveals how the Consistory's pastoral role was in part made possible by the threat of the iron fist of the *Petit Conseil*. A full picture of the disciplinary regime of Reformed religion in Geneva must take into account the degree to which torture was a rite often employed against those who deviated from the rigid sexual and moral regime imposed by the Reformed church.

Torture was applied in Geneva during the Reformation both to determine whether a crime had been committed and to expose the hidden sinners living amongst the faithful. An awareness that God was watching and the possibility that the devil shaped the outcome of the torture session informed the judges' actions. Torture was often employed as a rite of violence that justified the elimination of the individual from the community. Sins against God predominated in the torture chamber as questioners probed deeply until the spiritual core of the criminal's soul was revealed. Through their use of torture and execution, Genevan judges sought to identify individuals whose punishment could instruct the urban community about the bounds of the sacred. Although historians have long seen the Servetus case as a symbol of the possibility of retributive violence against the heretic in Reformation Geneva, his experience before the *Petit Conseil* is generally seen to be exceptional.

---

[71] Robert M. Kingdon, 'The Geneva Consistory in the Time of Calvin', in Andrew Pettegree, Alastair Duke, and Gillian Lewis (eds), *Calvinism in Europe, 1540–1620* (Cambridge, 1996), 21–34; Christian Grosse, 'Rationalité graphique et discipline ecclésiastique: les registres du consistoire de Genève à l'épreuve (XVIe–XVIIIe siècles)', *Bulletin de la Société de l'Histoire du Protestantisme Français*, 153 (2007), 543–59; Manetsch, 'Pastoral Care'; Jeffrey R. Watt, 'Calvinism, Childhood, and Education: The Evidence from the Genevan Consistory', *Sixteenth Century Journal*, 33 (2002), 439–56; Karen E. Spierling, 'Making Use of God's Remedies: Negotiating the Material Care of Children in Reformation Geneva', *Sixteenth Century Journal*, 36 (2005), 785–807; Jeffrey Watt, 'Women and the Consistory in Calvin's Geneva', *Sixteenth Century Journal*, 24 (1993), 429–39.

Examining the torture sessions of more mundane cases—crimes ranging from adultery, to coining, to murder—reveals that the search for the ungodly was a regular aspect of torture in Calvin's city.

When comparing torture in Geneva to its practice in French law courts, at first the differences are striking. Historians of France usually represent torture as a secular judicial procedure during the Reformation.[72] Very few records of torture sessions remain for the sixteenth century, with the exception of a series at the *Parlement* of Paris beginning in the 1580s. These interrogations are brief and the individual is usually only tortured once (though s/he had usually been subjected to torture, perhaps multiple times, at a lower court before arriving at the *parlement*). During the torture session, the questions are focused on the facts of the crime; the devil rarely makes an appearance in these accounts except in witchcraft cases. Very rarely does anyone confess to anything.[73] But the historian does well to keep in mind that the *Parlement* of Paris was a politically and religiously moderate court caught between radical Catholics and the vacillating policies of the monarchy during a period of religious strife and intermittent civil war. The *parlement* magistrates thus had every reason to represent their procedures as being above religious considerations.[74] In contrast, courts of first instance and even provincial *parlements* were less hesitant to torture. Both appeals to the *parlements* and the efforts of their magistrates to correct abusive torture practices at the local level suggest that convictions for moral crimes such as adultery, extramarital sex, blasphemy, and witchcraft were frequently made on the basis of confessions obtained through torture during the sixteenth century.[75] Although the *parlements* sometimes reversed or modified the harsh sentences issued by the lower courts, many cases never reached a more lenient appeals court. By regarding

---

[72] Soman, 'Justice criminelle'; Lebrigre, *Justice du Roi*; Benoit Garnot, *Justice et société en France aux XVIe, XVIIe et XVIIIe siècles* (Paris, 2000); Antoine Astaing, *Droits et garanties de l'accusé dans le procès criminel d'Ancien Régime (XVIe–XVIIIe siècle)* (Aix-en-Provence, 1999). One notable exception is Silverman, *Tortured Subjects*.

[73] Archives Nationales de France, x2b 1330.

[74] Barbara B. Diefendorf, *Beneath the Cross: Catholics and Huguenots in Sixteenth-Century Paris* (New York, 1991); Sylvie Daubresse, *Le Parlement de Paris ou la voix de la raison (1559–1589)* (Geneva, 2005); Nancy L. Roelker, *One King, One Faith: The Parlement of Paris and the Religious Reformations of the Sixteenth Century* (Berkeley, CA, 1996).

[75] Laurence Montazel, 'Les parlements de France et la torture judiciaire du XVe au XVIIIe siècle', in *La Torture judiciaire*, II, 622–7; Alfred Soman, 'Les procès de sorcellerie au Parlement de Paris (1565–1640)', *Annales: Economies, Sociétés, Civilisations*, 32 (1977), 800–12.

the experience of the *parlement* as typical, French historians describing judicial procedure after 1562 have perhaps dismissed the impact of religion on the practice of judicial torture at other royal courts rather too quickly. That torture could function in Geneva as a rite of violence is clear; whether it was also sometimes deployed in this way by French courts of first instance during the Wars of Religion is a hypothesis worth considering.

From Christ-like King to Antichristian Tyrant: A First Crisis of the Monarchical Image at the Time of Francis I

Denis Crouzet
Translated by Philippa Woodcock

In her groundbreaking article on the 'Rites of Violence', Natalie Zemon Davis was interested principally in the gestures which allowed the perpetrators of violence, both Catholics and Calvinists, to be able to forget that their victims were human beings. 'The rites of violence allowed this dehumanization to occur' activating a repertoire of gestures, cries, and symbols which formed part of a logic of dehumanization. This was not unconscious violence, but a quest for legitimization which rested on semiological foundations. 'An arsenal of punitive and purifying traditions', which should, thus, be perceived as a 'basis' for violence, a past which provided the very code for aggressive practices; this is what can be called the Davis 'model' or paradigm.[1]

From massacres to regicide: an application of Davis's model
If historians focus on what is, without doubt, the most important politico-religious event in sixteenth-century French history, the regicide of Henry III, and attempt to apply Davis's formalized reading to it, they might highlight several aspects.

The first of these is the resurgence of theories of tyrannicide from the period of the Armagnac-Burgundian quarrel, remodelled in a discourse with sacral overtones by the members of the Catholic League. This was without doubt the first 'basis' of the regicide of 1589, even if the 'objective' legitimation of Jacques Clément's act only appeared after 1 August. Let us consider several examples. For the people, their original obedience to God ought not to be superseded by that owed contractually and secondarily to the king. It had to come first, for God was all. There was a contractual hierarchy which dictated that God 'when he said render unto Caesar what is Caesar's, also said render unto God what is God's'.[2] For the people, as opposed to those who were stigmatized as 'politiques', there was a sphere of conditional

---
[1] Natalie Zemon Davis, 'Les rites de violence', in *Les cultures du peuple. Rituels, savoirs et résistances au 16e siècle* (Paris, 1979), 251–307.
[2] *De la difference du Roy et du Tyran. Dedié à M. L. L. D. M.* (Paris, 1589), 29–30.

obedience and another in which obedience was absolute.³ 'This is why we can say that the subject does not owe obedience to an impious or unjust king, as his oath of fidelity is relative to that which the king himself made beforehand to conserve and maintain the Catholic religion as well as his subjects in their rights'. If this oath was violated, in effect by the disobedience of a king who refused to apply the laws of the realm, the people had to limit themselves to obedience to God. Man could not obey a king contrary to the honour of God, instead he had to 'deny his obedience', taking away power from the prince who had become a tyrant. This applied both to a prince who had ceased to obey God by acting against the church and denying the oath he had pronounced at his coronation, and to a heretic prince like Henry of Navarre who, being outside the faithful, had no obedience to God.⁴ So much so, he could be put to death, whether by human or divine right, as was proclaimed in *L'Arpocrate ou rabais du caquet des politiques et jebusiens de nostre aage*.⁵ This was because the realm was not a 'patrimony' of the king.⁶ The king who did not obey divine commands obliged himself not only to have to account in the next world for the souls of his subjects, but he could no longer be obeyed.⁷ He even had to be avenged for the double murder at Blois, it was declared to the Parisians. The vengeance that the people appropriated to themselves expressed an appropriation of obedience. The libellist, author of *Le Faux-Visage descouvert du fin Renard de la France*, while telling the Parisians that the God of armies was on their side, underlining that their 'quarrel' was just, insisted on one point: God's commandments legitimate the action. If they are not followed, and if the disobedient and bloody king is not

---

³ For example in the *Lamentation ou petit sermon funebre, prononcé en l'eglise Nostre Dame de Rheims, aux funerailles de feu Monseigneur Illustrissime et Reverendissime Loys Cardinal de Guyse Archevesque de ladite Eglise, et premier Pair de France, cruellement massacré aux Estats de Blois le XXIIII de Decembre* (s.l., 1589), F.

⁴ *De la difference du Roy*, 53–4. Jean de Caumont, *Advertissement des avertissements au peuple tres-crestien* (s.l., 1587), 28; 26, that a heretic on the throne of France, 'Ce seroit contracter tout apertement avec le diable. Ce seroit estre à la fin du monde, et à la veille du jugement dernier'.

⁵ *L'Arpocrate ou rabais du caquet des politiques et jebusiens de nostre aage. Dedié aux Agens catholiques associez du Roy de Navarre* (Paris, 1589) [Approbation of 28 Sept.], 10.

⁶ *Apologie ou deffence des Catholiques unis les uns avec les autres, contre les impostures des catholiques associez à ceux de la pretendue Religion* (1586), 19.

⁷ *Response à un livre de Belloy plein de faulsetez et calomnies, deguisé souz cet excellent et beau titre de l'autorité du Roy* (Paris, 1588), 49. This is with reference to Henry of Navarre, but foresees the style of speech that followed the double murder at Blois: 'il n y a loy soit Salique, soit divine, ou humaine, qui nous commande d'obeyr à celuy qui n'obeyt, ny à Dieu, ny à son Eglise'.

punished, divine wrath will be provoked: 'if one does not (take re)venge for the injuries done to Him, given that he said, *nolite tangere christos meos,* dare ye not to touch my priests, be assured that He will avenge himself well, we will have to pay the price for our timidity and cowardice'.[8] The duty to obey was thus transferred, mechanically, from king to people.

Secondly, it is necessary to isolate a regicidal tension, which often manifested itself symbolically, and which ran through the first Wars of Religion. Jacques Clément did not come out of nowhere, he existed at the end of a complex chain and, moreover, the fact that he was 'a zealous' Catholic, who had received signs and divine revelations, said even more than his act appeared to signify. Immediately after the death of Henry II, the Calvinists, through the pen of minister-poets such as Antoine de La Roche Chandieu, established a link between the death of the king and the persecution that they, the followers of the gospel, endured during his reign, above all since the establishment of the *Chambre ardente* in 1547.[9] The king was a persecutor, they affirmed, like those God had punished in the Bible. The right of the sword that he claimed to exercise against the Huguenots was contrary to divine will. In opposition to this, from 1561 onwards, Catholic preachers and polemicists argued that, like Ahab and Jezebel, governments which tolerated heresy in a realm would incur divine justice. They emphasized that the sacral *virtus* of the king came from his capacity to exterminate the Huguenots. Thus, on either side, a destabilization of the ideology of royal absolutism was underway. There are several spectacular witnesses to this: as early as 1558, a clerk in the chancery called Caboche threw himself knife-in-hand on the king, crying 'Coward! I must kill you!'[10] He appears to have acted out of religious motives, as his two brothers were subsequently imprisoned for heresy at Meaux. Thus, the king, from distributor of violence by the force of his God-given sword, had rapidly become the object of violence.

On the Huguenot side, iconoclastic acts multiplied just as the occupation of religious buildings was transforming them into temples. The violence was never explicitly said to be directed against royal authority. Simultaneously,

---

[8] *Le Faux-Visage descouvert du fin Renard de la France. A tous Catholicques unis, et sainctement liguez pour la defense, et tuition de l'Eglise Apostolique et Romaine, contre l'ennemy de Dieu ouvert et couvert. Ensemble quelques Anagrammes et Sonnets propres pour la saison du jourd'huy* (Paris?, 1589) 15 Jan., 16.

[9] Antoine de La Roche-Chandieu, 'Ode ... sur les misères des Eglises françaises qui ont esté si longtemps persécutées', *Bulletin de la Société de l'Histoire du Protestantisme français,* 33 (1884), 185–203.

[10] *Mémoires de Claude Haton. Edition intégrale,* ed. Laurent Bourquin (Paris, 2001), I (1553–1565), 124–5.

for the Catholics, the same contestation of the preservation of civil peace took place: groups of militants, sometimes organized into confraternities, attacked the Huguenots gathered for the Lord's Supper, massacring some amongst them according to rituals which represented the victory of divine justice over the demonic forces sustained by Satan. There was, therefore, a loss of the monopoly of violence.[11] On the other hand, even if in the official discourses produced by each side violence was never directed towards the royal person, preserved from attack by denunciation of his 'evil councillors', yet, on a symbolic level, their words could be interpreted more radically. In 1562, at the same time as they were smashing stone and wooden images in the churches of the towns where they had seized control, the Calvinists sometimes went further. For instance, at Orléans, the busts of kings adorning the town-hall were thrown to the ground and smashed; at Notre-Dame de Cléry the statue of Louis XI was dismembered; and the heart of the young king Francis II was exhumed before being bitten into pieces by soldiers. Furthermore, there were the words reported to Blaise de Monluc, launched by an iconoclast who denied royal law, speaking of Charles IX as a 'little king of shit' who should be put to work like all of his subjects. There were further examples at Angoulême, where the tombs of Francis I's ancestors were opened up and the skeletons burned.[12]

It appears that, occasionally and symbolically, there was at work a violence which denied all royal sacrality and tended towards the idea that the royal person was only human. It is evident, too, that there was a parallel unconscious regicidal tendency amongst militant Catholics as early as 1562. And, above all, in the explosion of violence during the St Bartholomew's Day massacre in Paris can be identified a form of symbolic regicide, in the sense that the slide towards collective massacre expressed the power of a collective desire to see the king of concord substituted by the biblical king who eschatologically exterminated heretics. This would be the second 'basis' for the regicide of 1589, putting into relief the negation of the royal oversacralization which had been taking place in the realm of France since 1515, and which saw the sovereign not only claim to be an image of God on Earth, but to be a living Christ capturing in his own person the relationship to the divine. Such a *christomimésis* doubtless reached its climax during the reign of Henry III, the king of three crowns.

Thirdly, the search for the 'basis' for the murder at the Pont de Saint-Cloud requires us to go even further. The events of 1 August 1589 did not limit

[11] See Denis Crouzet, *Les Guerriers de Dieu. La violence au temps des troubles de religion (vers 1525 –vers 1610)*, 2 vols (Paris, 1990), I, 595–626.
[12] Ibid., 756–62.

themselves to the resurgence of a tyrannicidal 'right', and a symbolic tension translated into a desire for the death of a king who appropriated God unto himself. To apply Davis's 'model' necessitates that we dig deeper into this archaeology of conflict, to uncover its original source at the beginning of the reign of Francis I. At this time, royal power began its struggle with a satirical culture which did not hesitate to denounce the slide of royal authority towards tyranny, to self-regulatory ends.

It is not the aim, in the discussion which follows, to cover all the problematic elements of satire or its variants and targets in the early years of the reign of Francis I. This is for several reasons. First, the extreme fragility of printed material which means that only a fragment of these works has survived. Furthermore, we have to suppose that an important part, even most, of the satirical expression was in oral or manuscript form. Secondly, the fact is that political satire suffered, as will be shown, a sharp check and strict control from the first months of the reign of the son of Louise of Savoy. Consequently, in studying satire and the violent forms it took under these restrictions, and in analyzing its rare outbursts, we are seeking less to reconstruct the art or techniques of political criticism, but rather the will to change the presentation of royal majesty, in all its complexity, and especially to appreciate the reactions that this change inspired. The Christ-like king that Francis I wanted to present himself as to the English ambassadors in 1518 in the courtyard of the Bastille, dressed in a white robe and with dishevelled hair, was by the start of the 1520s the object of a contested discourse. Through drama, in order to legitimate itself, this discourse used the register of playful rituals like those of Mother Fool and, thus, the language of 'popular culture'. Contrary to what was perceived as a rupture in relations between the king and his people and with God, the word engaged in a struggle in which certain expressions could provoke radical temptation. Before the 'tyrant' of Blois, there was a stigmatized Francis I. Stigmatized, above all, because he was no longer the king who laughed.

The king who laughed

It was during the reign of Louis XII—historians are agreed upon this point, as were contemporaries at the time of the Wars of Religion—when the myth of a golden period of monarchy was first elaborated. And it was during this period that royal virtue was felt to move principally, and with the greatest force, around the concept of 'counsel'. The king possessed the virtue of making himself readily available to listen to his subjects, and reigned in the same participatory way. Or at least that was the image that he wanted to convey and project, using the same skills with which he communicated and managed his authority.

The work of Nicole Hochner clearly demonstrates the existence of a true idealization of monarchy which began to disappear during the first years of the reign of Francis I. A series of short works by Pierre Gringore allows us to appreciate a specific political vision, which called upon princes to take counsel from the 'sages' at the risk of otherwise committing 'errors, horrors and vile evils'. Beginning with the reign of Louis XII, debate raged between 'an opinion which preached the concentration of the king's powers and led directly to a totally absolutist ideology, and an affirmation that the council was the guarantor of judicial order'.[13] The isolation of the king was to be condemned since fools could endlessly manipulate him just as they pleased, because Mother Fool reigned at his court. Pierre Gringore suggested Saint Louis as the model king, because he governed according to the law and justice, relying on 'Good Counsel', an allegory of free speech able to express itself in an open, public and pluralistic manner. He insisted that no virtue could maintain itself without deliberation, without the presence of a supporting minister or of an institution that permitted the sovereign to be aware of popular 'appeals' and 'grievances'. Through the mask of madness, satire was important in giving voice to the popular will, to which it was propitious for the king to listen so that he could get to know the wishes, problems, and desires of his people. This is the image of a monarchy moderated by a discourse to which the king agreed to listen, even if this same discourse did not hesitate to criticize those who were at the monarchy's side, advising it daily.

There were, therefore, two parallel systems of courtly advice: the counsel of those courtiers chosen by the king, and the advice of fools (also courtiers) who used satirical inversion to confess that they were duping the king. Thus, with ruses of their own devising and for their own pleasure, they diverted him from the expectations of his people. The good prince was a watchful prince, who lent his ear to what fools said, to those who without knowing it possessed through their foolery as much as their words the means to denounce the evil councillors with which the prince surrounded himself. Among the fools there was, of course, Mother Fool who Gringore used to denounce courtly abuse. She accomplished her given role in a playful manner, because she was apparently unaware of the consequences of her words by which she swore that she ruled by absolutely dominating the court.

Thus, what is important here is the existence of a 'verbal space' which permitted, by the means of a ritualized discourse founded on the madness of its own commendations and the insistence upon courtly perversion, a language of correction to which the king could listen. Furthermore, he

---

[13] Nicole Hochner, 'Pierre Gringore: une satire à la solde du pouvoir?', *Fifteenth-Century Studies*, 26 (2001), 102–20.

could draw on the consequences in order to represent an essential royal virtue, the virtue of *humilitas* or of moderation. And Gringore, drawing on some themes elucidated in Jehan Meschinot, never ceased to reiterate that the prince should be able to personally combine four virtues. The first was justice which should allow him to correct those who within his realm 'are committing vice'. But forgiveness and truth should not be kept too distant, as without them, peace could not reign.[14] And then, there was humility, which must never allow him to abandon himself to pride. The king and madness thus formed an indissoluble couple. The allegorical figure of Mother Fool, who 'grumbles' constantly and at cross purposes, was encouraged, according to Jehan Bouchet, by the king himself, who wanted each to 'play freely and that the young should declare abuses... because confessors and other learned men do not want to say anything'. Satire was accepted as the spur which made those who governed see themselves as if in an inverse mirror image, and take stock of themselves when there was the risk of a screen being placed between them and their people. It inclined them to not let themselves be trapped in a form of political hubris. Laughter and power stimulated each other in an accepted exchange as regenerators of an ever-present corruption around the royal person.

But this verbal space did not function only in a single direction at the start of the sixteenth century. It was, according to the words of Mother Fool, part of the image of royal power that the sovereign possessed in his own person, a form of self-control which could manifest itself in two ways. This spontaneous ability to self-correction was used, at first, by Louis XII in the duchy of Milan, in the course of the great ritual of mutual 'seduction' embodied in his entry of 1509. It appears that there 'the lords of Milan' intended to offer the king an imperial triumph on the days after his victorious expedition against the Venetians. Four arches were built through which three triumphal chariots paraded before the king. The first carried the allegories of Strength, Prudence, and Renown—or Victory, Happiness, and Renown—supporting a throne on which it was envisaged Louis XII would sit. When the sovereign was invited to place himself on the 'seat of victory', he refused, according to Hochner, to 'play the game'.[15] This refusal of the assimilation of royal authority into an

---

[14] Jean-Claude Aubailly, 'L'image du Prince dans le théâtre de Gringore', in *Le pouvoir monarchique et ses supports idéologiques aux XIV –XVIIe siècles*, eds Jean Dufournet, Adelin Fiorato, Augustin Redondo (Paris, s.d.), 175–83, which draws on *Les Folles Entreprises de 1505 et sur leur croisement avec la Vie de Monseigneur saint Loys par personnaiges, de 1511 –1512.*

[15] Nicole Hochner, 'Le trône vacant du roi Louis XII ou les significations politiques de la mise en scène royale en Milanais', in *Louis XII en Milanais, XLIe colloque international*

imperial system was accentuated when Louis XII, by means of letters sent to the Lyonnais, forbade any formal entry on his return from Italy although triumphalist preparations had already begun. The king renounced the celebration of his glory; he did not want to embrace 'the theme of royal dignity in imperial glory'. He delivered indirectly, in this gesture, a political treatise of monarchical moderation, in which humility, faced with itself, remained a cardinal virtue and, above all, illustrated the continuity of the idea that 'the true glory of the king is the love and unity of his people, the material and moral prosperity of his subjects, and not his victories or his conquests'. Espousing the vision of Claude de Seyssel, he refused to take on an imperial identity which would merge with an absolutist vision of his authority. In contrast, Guillaume Budé would say to Francis I that the king who maintained his realm in a territorial *status quo* would not be worthy of remembrance. This is quite another concept of glory and significantly different. 'Louis XII wanted to be a warrior and a victor, but not an absolute emperor'. Above all, he wanted to show that he could maintain a reflective, critical distance from his own actions.

On the other hand, this tension was very much integrated into the representations which the sovereign himself practised as a means of correction. Therefore, he did not accept it only as a regulatory discursive procedure directed towards himself and his government, but also as itself a tool of his authority, allowing him to neutralize tensions. An image of Louis XII can be extracted from the sources, the image of a king who, first of all, gave his favour entirely to those with 'military experience', who preferred men of war to men of learning.[16] Above all, he had a manner of speaking which did not come from the rhetoric of *gravitas*. To articulate his reprobation with regard to the behaviour of certain of his subjects, the king expressed himself through an allegorical mode of discourse which allowed him to make himself understood without the recipient feeling humiliated. The sovereign was, according to the later historian Bertrand Girard du Haillan, using 'jokes' which spread among the people and helped to create an impression of moderation: he was

---

d'études humanistes, eds Philippe Contamine and Jean Guillaume (Paris, 2003), 227–44, communication dactylographiée, 25 pp. See also 'Louis XII and the Porcupine: Transformations of a Royal Emblem', *Renaissance Studies*, 15 (2001), 17–36.

[16] Bernard de Girard, seigneur du Haillan, *Histoire generale des roys de France contenant les choses mémorables advenues tant au royaume de France qu'és Provinces estrangeres sous la domination des François, durant douze cens ans... et continuée de la chronique de Louys XI. des escrits d'Arnaud le Ferron, et de quelques autres Autheurs, iusques à Louys XIII., aujourd'huy regnant*, 2 vols (Paris, 1629), 229.

thereby acting as his own fool, using irony to say what he wanted to say. For example:

> ... seeing that Queen Anne was desirous to command and was plotting several things according to her own design, he said that he could forgive much of a modest woman. Thus, she insisted and importuned him in the hope of marrying her daughter Claude to Charles of Austria, nephew of the Emperor Maximilian. I want, he answered her, to make an alliance between the mice and the cats of my realm. But, unhappily, she answered that it appeared that all the mothers-in-law had also conspired to be as awful as possible to their daughters-in-law. To which he retorted, do you consider that there is no difference if your daughter rules in Brittany under the sovereign authority of the kings of France, or is the wife of an all powerful king, enjoying with him the wealth of an all noble and flourishing realm? Would you prefer the rear end of a donkey to that of a horse? At the start, nature decorated does with horns as impressive as those of the stags. But the does came to prefer themselves to the stags and God, incensed by this, ordered that they should be born without horns. Because he [Louis XII] was used to making himself understood through fable or apologia, admonishing the queen in this way, through insolence it did not diminish the power she had.

A second example concerns the son of Louise of Savoy. Louis XII learned that the young duke of Angoulême had incurred many debts.[17] A part of these had been contracted with the royal treasurers. Louis XII thus summoned the putative heir to the crown, and told him that he was concerned to know how the money lent to him would get back to the treasury:

> the king begged him to forget about it, but gave him a lesson by this fable. I was travelling, he told him, one day with my father, both of us riding, and I thought that I was near to the town where we were going. Seeing church spires, and bored by the long journey, I turned to my father. 'Look', I told him, 'our journey is finished, we have arrived in the town'. But as we were still several leagues distant from it, turning to me, 'my child', he said, 'in future when you see the bells and towers of churches, do not say that your journey is over'. Thus, he tacitly made it understood that it is unworthy and unseemly,

---

[17] Anne-Marie Lecoq, *François Ier imaginaire. Symbolique et politique à l'aube de la Renaissance française* (Paris, 1987), on the play/game and François d'Angoulême, 80–5.

under the banner of largesse, for a prince to play with the wealth and commodities of a realm to which he has not yet succeeded.

Indeed, Louis XII used mockery as a corrective, by drawing on a contorted language that allowed him to avoid directly saying things, but allowed him to come at them in such a way as to avoid conflict or repression. He was the king of laughter. He accepted the principle of a rhetorical game, sometimes self-generated, which played around with the allegorical stories which he imagined, in order to diffuse potential conflicts, to neutralize potential postures of violence, and to heal rifts by laughter. Louis was a sovereign who played on words, who stood in opposition, as we will see, to Francis I's desire to master rhetoric, to his *gravitas*.[18] In the days after 1 January 1515, laughter and power, or rather the smile and power, were no longer intrinsically associated in the intellectual osmosis that was one of the arts of government of Louis XII.

The serious sovereign

Francis I, raised by his mother to be fascinated by the principle of his divine election, never integrated satire into the way he expressed or corrected his decisions. The sovereign, according to André de La Vigne, was capable of addressing himself to foreign ambassadors, 'without repeating himself nor changing, but in the most cold and wise manner in the world'.[19] The skilful son of Louise of Savoy imposed Ciceronian modes of address which located power in a more direct language differentiated from advice, such as expressed in the praises sung to the monarchy by Marot. 'As for me, I don't want to sing hymns/ Other than my king's: his brilliant actions/ Fill me with sufficient cause'.[20] This was a cold and immediate power, in contrast to the playful

[18] Sylvie Beguin, 'L'Ecole de Fontainebleau "Des histoires anciennes et moderns"', in *François Ier. Du château de Cognac au trône de France. Actes du Colloque du 500e anniversaire de la naissance de François Ier* (Cognac, 1996), 261–70. It also equally evokes the fact that the king was a great admirer of Cicero, the Ciceronian humanist Giulio Camillo Delminio having taught him the art of speech-making. For Delminio see, *Dizionario biographico degli italiani*, XVII (Rome, 1974), 220. The epigram of Marot can also be cited, 'Du roy et des perfections': 'Celluy qui dit ta grâce, éloquence et sçavoir N'estre plus grans qu'humains, de près ne t'a peu veoir, Et à qui ton parler ne sent divinité Des termes et propos n'entend la gravité, De l'empire du monde est ta presence digne Et ta voi ne dit chose humaine mais divine. Car combien doncques de roy l'âme pleine de grâce, Si oultre les mortelz tu as parolle et face'.

[19] André de la Vigne, *Chroniques et gestes*, cited by Lecoq, *François Ier imaginaire*, 424.

[20] Cited in Ulrich Langer, *Vertu du discours, discours de la vertu. Littérature et philosophie morale au XVIe siècle en France* (Geneva, 1999), 37.

words of Louis XII, who tolerated laughter towards his authority as being at the heart of his own expressions of his power. It was from God alone that Louise's son was certain of holding his authority; more immediately, it was only God who could recognize the merits or faults of the prince. Above all, none of his subjects had the right to comment upon or correct his authority, even if appropriating the identity of Mother Fool. Even praise, when it is sung, as Ulrich Langer writes, 'is not conceived of as an augmentation of the person and does not constitute in any way a significant event in the life of the praised person, rather it is supplementary, an opportunity to take it or leave it, subject to the pleasure of the sovereign. The glory of the sovereign is such that poetic eulogy makes no difference: "it is really true, that in praising you/ One cannot (given that it is already so great) augment it" '.[21] Furthermore, and later in the *Discours de la court* published by Claude Chappuys in 1543, the king, by the fact of his comparison to the divinity and by his submission to God alone, becomes an *imago deitatis*, raising and lowering men by his grace according to his own pleasure.[22]

One can see this clearly in the *Journal d'un bourgeois de Paris*. From his accession, Francis I curbed satire, refusing to tolerate it because to his eyes it was far from a tool to neutralize the imaginary space of violence, but was an attack on *Majestas*. Beginning on 5 January 1516, the principals and regents of the Paris university *collèges* found themselves notified of the interdiction to 'neither play, nor allow to be played in their colleges any farces or other such performances against the honour of the king, of the queen, of madame the duchess of Angoûleme, mother of the said lord, of the princes of the blood, or of other people around the king's person'. A priest, monsieur Cruche, was flogged in April 1515 by gentlemen, probably sent by the king, and just avoided being thrown into the Seine in a sack. He had staged a morality play at the place Maubert, which 'included lords who were wearing the golden cloth of the Creed and carrying their lands on their shoulders ... and in the farce, was the said monsieur Cruche with his accomplices, and all sorts of things were seen, among others a chicken which was feeding from under a salamander; this chicken was carrying a thing which was enough to kill ten men, an allusion to the passion of the king for the daughter of the councillor of the parlement, Le Coq, married to Jacques Dishomme'.[23] On 19 November 1516, a new ban on staging any farce against the honour of the king was

---

[21] Ibid., 46.
[22] Ibid., 64.
[23] *Journal d'un bourgeois de Paris sous le règne de François premier (1515–1536)*, ed. Ludovic Lalanne (Paris, 1854), 13.

promulgated.[24] It should be further noted that, during the month of December, three players in farces, Jacques le Bazochin, Jehan Seroc, and Jehan du Pontalez, were taken as prisoners to Amboise, before the king himself. The performances in which they had taken part had postulated, 'among other things that Mother Fool now governed at court, and that she was taxing, pillaging and robbing all those who had escaped from imprisonment'. The king who laughed, and who accepted the mirror of laughter, very quickly was no longer a reality. And his alter-ego, Mother Fool, was now banished far from the court. It was as though an immediate transformation in the idea of the monarchy had taken place.

In a dialogue by Ravisius Textor, master at the college of Navarre, the threat which now hovered over the biting and corrective irony of the satirists re-emerged when Mother Nature demanded of her envoy what kings do on Earth. The response shows that a lesson had been learned about the by now heavy constraints on satirical language: 'as for kings, it would be dangerous to speak of them'![25] A few years after the accession of Francis I, Pierre Gringore, although he had participated in 1515 in the staging of a rhetorical work of royal praise, left for the court of Lorraine. The Commons' Fool was silenced, who was previously expected 'to speak at cross purposes, and now declared that "I am forbidden to speak" '. The relationship to language had undergone a major transformation, showing that there were words and other things which it was now impossible to express even through laughter. 'Satire was no longer permitted. Gringore had diffused a moderate and curbed vision of royalty ... which could not have been pleasing to the eyes of a Duprat or of a Francis I'. One must conclude that, even if Francis I had not already been introduced to the ideas of Machiavelli, a parallel image was deployed in his ideal of power when he acceded to the throne by the death of Louis XII. Everything happened as if the royal majesty was unable to be anything but the staging of an invincible glory. Everything had to be done in order that this glory could no longer be rebuffed, tempered, restricted or assaulted by the use of satirical expression.

The resurgence of speech and the sudden emergence of violence

Despite all of this, and in a manner that requires interrogation, some years later political satire rediscovered its violent potential. This re-emergence occurred in the context of the political debate between the royal family and

---

[24] Ibid., 44.
[25] Michel Rousse, 'Le pouvoir royal et le théâtre des farces', in *Le pouvoir monarchique et ses supports idéologiques aux XIV –XVIIe siècles*, eds Jean Dufournet-Adelin and Fiorato-Augustin Redondo (Paris, s.d), 185–97.

the constable of Bourbon, by means of a series of provocative and reciprocal moves. Probably starting in 1521, and aggravated by the death of the Duchess Anne de Beaujeu, an offensive was launched against the constable. From 26 November 1522, with the help of the king, Louise of Savoy obtained several gifts sourced from the wealth of the late duchess, such as the county of Gien and the revenues of several salt farms. On 10 January 1523, she received the county of Haute et Basse Marche, the viscounties of Carlat and Murat and the lordship of Montaigut-en-Combrailles. It appears that the hand of the duke was forced in order to accommodate her, because by now the king had by-passed both law and procedure.

Everything happened as if a form of long-distance political dialogue had established itself in these years, based on the communication of signs defining a changing power-relationship and leading to a bidding war by each party. Bourbon did not remain passive faced with the king's capacity to reply. And it is perhaps then that he would have supported the intervention of certain satirists to attack the claims of royal power, a power which razed all satirical expression and would not tolerate the existence of a critical or corrective space.

One correlation, even though undeniably problematic, is worth exploring. It was probably at the end of 1522 or in the first months of 1523 that a short text entitled *Le Monde qui est crucifié* began to circulate in Paris. It is impossible to know whether this manuscript originated from a hand-written copy of a printed play, or if it only ever circulated in its original form. It is also impossible to know if it was ever staged, which often happened with this type of text. The margin of the manuscript shows a church and a character who, holding a falcon and a sword, represents nobility.[26] The text starts with a lamentation from the church, sad and desolate, because everywhere in the world she had met with adversity, but 'God encouraged/ Kings and princes to build me'. For three years, she had suffered from taxation and first tenths, especially since her tithes had been confiscated. Without doubt, she adds, the day would soon arrive when she would have to offer up her jewels, crosses, chalices, and reliquaries. It is as though she had been crucified and her speech was an indictment of the fiscal policy of the crown.

But *Le Monde qui est crucifié* did not limit itself to a lament for the church. A voice was given to the second estate, Nobility, who immediately asserted that she had been 'diminished'. This is a time of words, rather than deeds, she declares. Hearts have lost their daring, their weapons dispossessed of their glorious shine. Warriors, who should protect the poor subjects of the realm of

---

[26] Anatole de Montaiglon, *Recueil de poésies françaises des XVe et XVIe siècles morales, facétieuses, historiques*, 14 vols (Paris, 1855–1876), XII, 219–26.

France, are 'more rapacious than the savage wolf'. The *francs-archers* have devastated Picardy. They have also participated in a crucifixion of the world. And above all Nobility has to contrast the Italian victories of the past, which bring to mind the good times of King Louis XII and gave the nobility renown, with the present confusion. Towns and castles have been lost; Milan has been abandoned. The drama recounted implies systematic accusations against the reigning king, above all when Nobility complains that, 'Since the time that kings have reigned [here]/ There was never such evil disarray/ As I am of abased honour'. Honour is said to have been lost by the fact that the Genovese who, after the defeat at Bicocca on 29 April 1522, were left to their own devices by the French and, having opened their doors to the imperial troops, had seen their city pillaged. To explain this catastrophe which was shameful to Nobility and, moreover, meant that everywhere her enemies ranged themselves against her, with their lances, their pikes, or their swords, *Le Monde qui est crucifié* launched an invective against the 'petticoat government', behind which the influence and actions of Louise of Savoy were identified. The possible influence of the constable can be guessed at. It presses the circulating accusations, according to which the mother of the king would not have advanced the promised subsidies to Lautrec and would have instead diverted them to her own coffers and in favour of certain of her familiars. The events of the year 1522, disastrous and calamitous for France, were next to be listed with the most brutal realism: English military operations and the intervention of the Hennins in Picardy, which lasted until September; the cost of the artillery lost 'on the other side of the mountains'; badly commanded armies.

A third character appears in this context to incarnate another estate of the realm. Labour reminds us that there was a time in the near past when he lived happily, in peace, 'a time of plenty'. This time is over because now he knows only misfortune. It is he who embodies the world crucified only half-alive, suffering. He has to nourish the men of war, all the rascals and 'those that deserve to be hanged', who know only how to blaspheme God, liars, thieves, and robbers. And he must suffer and pay tax after tax. Furthering his misery were plague, famine, and war. Labour bears the cross of poverty and does not hesitate to hurl his malediction against those who are responsible for all these miseries. In this 'present time' where he is crucified, in this 'bad weather' which threatens to endure, 'who can restrain himself from grumbling?' Labour thus evokes a saturation point which can also be understood as a veiled threat: 'Beneath this burden my spine fails me/ In such state I cannot last;/ I can go no further, nor work any more'.

Le Monde qui est crucifié is symptomatic of the tensions which were brewing in these months: the policy of Francis I since his accession had been to reduce the corrective function which was offered by the Parisian satirists. It appears that they had re-launched their offensive and that their target was the conduct of the affairs of state, fiscal as much as military. With their spirits lifted they proceeded to repeat the arguments already developed by the constable of Bourbon. They made comparison between former times, when all went well for the three estates of society, and the new, in which the lives of all had worsened. However, according to the criteria which traditionally presided over satirical language, the king was kept at a distance from the defamatory complaint. But only in appearance, of course.

Despite the disappearance of pieces printed by the booksellers, other examples of such texts have been conserved which may appear to have been composed intending allusions 'against the honour of the king', or at least against his desire for glory which excluded all correction.[27] A sort of war of words was doubtless at work, of great violence if one takes into account the fact that Francis I had precisely expressed the exaltation of his sacrality as Christian king by the prohibition of the corrective speech of the satirists. The authors of the libels were arrested at an unknown date, and only liberated on 20 March 1525. But all of them had targeted their attacks on the monarchy, to the point that (as shown by Anatole de Montaiglion) it published a refutation entitled, *La defence contre les Emulateurs, Ennemys et Mesdisans de France*. The piece entitled *Le Monde sans croix* is more explicitly radical than its predecessor; among the miniatures which are displayed in the margins of the manuscript, one depicts a woman wearing a red dress and a black, blue-lined mantle, as well as a red hat topped off with red, yellow, and blue feathers. She holds a sceptre in her right hand, fitted with a shattered cross, which symbolizes the rupture between the political order and the divine will; she leans to the left against a weapon, a sign that she only wants war and that she feeds on it. Above her head, most significantly, flutters a pennant on which is marked the inscription *Tirannye*. The other images show a sphere sown with tears, an allegory of the suffering of a world which knows only war and hunger, a churl called Commons, a richly dressed woman named Rapine, and another elegantly clad woman. This is Avarice holding sacks full of gold coins, from one of which a cross is falling, a symbol of the oppression undergone by the Church; at her feet is depicted an ill-closed coffer full of gold. These three women, evoking the monarchical tax system, have put an end to all equity, justice, and law, and have inverted a harmonious order of virtues.[28]

Another critical method is enacted in *Le Monde qu'on achève de paindre*. Several groups of animals incarnate the people who seize power in order to

---

[27] On the liberation see, *Journal d'un bourgeois de Paris*, 234.
[28] Montaiglon, *Recueil de poésies françaises*, XII, 193–201.

satisfy themselves contrary to the common good.[29] First of all, there are the asses, who raised to high office dispose of their 'authority' without having merited it, to the detriment of men of learning. Their flattery and their bribes have permitted their rise. It is possible to recognize Chancellor Duprat amongst them! The satirist does not hesitate to say that the world nowadays is a mad world, a world turned upside down by courtly ambitions. Then come the foxes, using their tricks and pretences to further their own ends, wearing all possible disguises and thus embodying hypocrisy and untruth: 'If one sells, the other costs;/ If one is cunning, the other is perverse;/ If one is drunk, the other is tasteful;/ The Foxes are far too diverse'. They take the realm for all it is worth, thanks to the offices that they occupy: they are the robbers who oppress the commons. At their side, one notes again, also en route to repaint the world, are the ravenous wolves who are today in 'favour', great gorgers of gold. All these animals should be 'reproved', but the upside-down World complains that nothing is undertaken against them; again, this highlights the topic of a past time when the world was ruled with moderation and everyone received their rights. Now excess rules and the World prays Christ to return in order that all these asses, wolves, and foxes will be finally defeated by 'he' who Christ has 'placed Above the people', by his grace alone: the king.

All these texts are thus constructed around the image of inversion: the people are compared to a being who is nothing more than skin and bones because he is subject to continual exactions to the point of collapse, such is the damage done by greed and abuse. Named World, this being speaks of that which once was by paraphrasing the *Lamentations* of Jeremiah: 'God made me once by his grace/ So very perfect, so well proportioned/ That one sees me flower everywhere/ Without going/ Against what he ordained me to do'. Then, peace reigned between sovereigns and princes.[30] Everything had

---

[29] *Le Monde qu'on achève de paindre*, in ibid., XII, 201–8.

[30] In Montaiglon, *Recueil de poésies françaises*, XIII, 129–35. Another text, from perhaps a little later, takes up again this motif: 'Il s'agit de La Complainte du Temps passé/ Par le Commun du Temps present,/ Lequel a tout dueil amassé/ pour faire à Fortune present'. The author opposes here the time when Mars dominated men to that when the people 'était sans douleur ne martire', before the price of wine sextupled. Everything was subordinated to worldly pleasure and Good law slept. Personal interest was primary, such that formerly 'un chacun son prochain aimoit'. Pride dominated. At the end of the text, Fortune enters into the debate to tell the Communal Present that no man can resist her when she turns her wheel and extends her hand. Then she lets her sister Hope speak. The text demands interrogation: to the extent that Hope is the device of the House of Bourbon, and that the Communal Present says that he will let himself henceforth be guided by Hope, knowing well 'qu'après ce règne humain/ Nous parviendrons où est

changed, and the satirist, very much implicated in this essentially political critique, returns to the image of dogs biting the people and sucking their blood. 'Mad pleasure' governed thanks to a 'mass of evil fools'. Virtues were extinguished because 'false reports', 'treason', and 'false turns' had taken the lead over truth and wisdom. The weak were left defenceless against the strong, and only those who had enriched themselves were appreciated. None of the estates were immune to this corruption: in the Church, it is a 'madman' who, solicitous of a benefice, finds himself immediately provided for. Amongst the nobility, with the exception of those who are 'by virtue ennobled', the oppressors are as numerous. Men of letters who above all others should be mirrors of wisdom are also accused of only thinking of amassing worldly riches. And finally, the common people have done nothing except imitate the actions of those placed above them. The World, who is nothing more than bones, implores God that, 'by the means of the human king Francis I', all thieves should be chased away, 'a heap of treasurers' and 'ignorant braggarts' should disappear, and 'these asses of officers/ Pot-bellied and proud,/ Who from one court-case make four new ones' should be abolished.[31] It was the kingship of war which was denounced by these attacks against the men of law and nobility, a predatory and costly monarchy. *Le Monde qui n'a plus que frire* begins, for its part, with a significant quotation: *Nolite confidere in princibus, in filiis hominum in quibus non est salus* (Ps CXLV, v. 2). The body of the World is again depicted as decimated by hunger, whereas once the frying pan was always full of pieces of meat or fowl, of lamb or mutton, of pigeons or of sparrows. Everything that is fit for frying now goes to the landsknechts.[32]

---

nostre Esperance' and that he must turn away from 'tout faux espoir' in order 'avoir le règne souverain'. Should we not divine here a playfulness regarding the very action of the constable? Isn't it a question of saying that through the constable the return to the past is possible? Hope, who is 'preste de t'ouyr/ et reconfort te donner au besoin', ends the piece: 'Or sus donques, prens bonne jouyssance; Esveille-toy et t'oste de mal an, Et je t'asseure qu'en parfaite alliance La paix auras, avant qu'il soit un an, Et plus n'en peut; Paix a sur luy victoire'. The Communal Present cries: 'Jerusalem!; Tu parviendras en eternelle gloire'.

[31] '*Le Monde qui n'a plus que les os*', in ibid., XII, 209–14.
[32] '*Le Monde qui n'a plus que frire*', in ibid., XII, 215–18 which insists, perhaps, on the fact that the reign of Francis had bridled the previous freedom of speech, by which it could be heard (J'ay beau crier et monstrer ma douleur,/ Envers chascun faire mon oraison,/ Car maintenant on n'entend plus raison): Le temps passé, j'avois des advocatz; Qui se mètoient tous les jours en dangier; Par leurs sermons ilz me voulloient vangier, Mais maintenant ilz n'ont garde du cas. Je vouldrois bien aujourd'huy demander De quoy me sert le

Injustice rules. The only response that is made to the world's disarray is constituted by new taxes which are added to the old ones.[33]

At the heart of this new monarchical ideology, the fact that the king no longer engaged in dialogue negated the reason for any game-playing. There is a sense of this at the moment when the constable adopted a sharply provocative attitude with regard to Francis I, in that he was playing a game that did not exist any more. Some of the satirists themselves advocated another traditional game which attempts had been made to repress since 1516. In this game, it was possible for allegories such as Mother Fool or the Poor World crowned by a cross to speak to the sovereign to try to guide him towards correcting the political order. It is possible to imagine that pieces like those analysed here were much more numerous than these rare surviving examples, and their playful aspect suggests that they may have been performed as little 'shows' in streets or taverns. They not only reflected and catalysed a communal idea, but they were also the vector which formed or structured this strand of thought. It is possible that the constable had taken into account the meaning of this parallel game when provoking it. The reforming programme that he appeared to have formulated to justify his alliance with Henry VIII and Charles V draws explicitly and clearly on the theme of the corruption of royal counsel and of fiscal 'tyranny'.

It is certain that the defeat at Pavia led to a satirical effusion which could be seen as either internal or external to the realm because it emanated from the sphere of imperial-Bourbon propaganda. In one piece from autumn 1525, *Chanson faite à Lyon contre le chancelier de France sur sa conduite pendant la régence*, it is noted that Antoine Duprat, the 'Gilded chancellor', had taken part in the activities aimed to weaken Charles de Bourbon.

> In order to use your sorcery,
> You have made the king chase Bourbon away:
> Whose counsel was sound;
> It harmed your lies,
> Gilded chancellor.

The poetry composed during the captivity of Francis I maintained a hostile attitude towards the king. He was compared to Pharaoh holding captive the

---

renom de justice, Quant el soubstient toute faulce police, Qui ne se veult pour mes cris amender'.

[33] Ibid., 215–18.

people of God and resisting His will.[34] Charles V, for his part, was recognized as being the greatest warrior of all time, having defeated arrogance and tyranny, and the 'folly' of a prince, who having abandoned his natural territory, had rebelled against an order ordained by God and against an emperor protected by God.[35] French power was chastised because Francis I, in his pride, had ignored the fact that Fortune ruled the world, and that the emperor, the new Caesar, was Fortune's favourite. The salamander was imprisoned and his fire extinguished. Like 'sheep', he had led these French 'braggarts' to their death.[36] The poetic pieces scoff, mocking the defeat of the king and his captains with an intense, desacralizing violence. The author of a *Magnificat* was inspired in this way by the letter of the king to Louise of Savoy, putting into the mouth of the prisoner king an almost burlesque song of thanks. The captive sovereign intoned *Magnificat anima mea Dominum* to thank God for having preserved him from death and having left him his honour, his life, and his health. In counterpoint, he argued that 'not everyone has managed to escape'. The Burgundian princes, by a single blow, were avenged for the humiliations suffered at the time of Louis XI. It even evoked 'vengeance', by suggesting that Francis I would suffer the same end as Charles the Bold. The emperor, meanwhile, was the triumphant victor who would make peace reign in Christendom and depart on crusade, and the poets thus interpreted the battle in terms of signs from God confirming imperial superiority.

There is also a whole series of texts that scoff at the defeated arrogance of Francis I, mocking him for leading his troops blindly to carnage, the presumptuous king punished by God. The motive for this game is clear in an *Epistre Satiricque* which was addressed to the king of France, probably at the end of his Spanish captivity, and which was published in Antwerp by Jean Gryphius in 1527. It appeared as a parodic response to a poem written by the king to an imaginary friend; a satire on the figure of the poet-king that Francis I cultivated as much as the idea of his divinely inspired sacrality. As June E. Kane has written, the poet gave the speech to Lady Knowledge in order that a list of all the king's mistakes could be addressed, the object a process of familiarization designed to abase him. Francis I, as such, was shown as a king without reason, a king who never stopped deluding himself, a sovereign without wisdom, accumulating errors. In the first place, this was a reminder

---

[34] 'Humble requeste de la part des bons Bourguignons et loyaux à la très haulte et très puissant majesté impériale, leur bien aymé et vray seigneur', in ibid., 110.
[35] Claude Thiry, 'L'Honneur et l'Empire: à propos de poèmes de langue française sur la bataille de Pavie', in *Mélanges à la mémoire de Franco Simone. France et Italie dans la culture européenne*, 2 vols (Geneva) I, *Moyen Age et Renaissance*, 297–325: 299.
[36] Ibid., 301.

that he whom Fortune had called to the throne of France, was 'one of the least ... of the blood royal'; and she had blinded him by allowing him to abandon himself to pleasure. Then, after the success of Marignano, the reversal of fortune was accentuated when Francis I abandoned the 'experienced' to take advice from those who could be bent to his will: 'because good counsel makes you invisible'. Among these men, the admiral Bonnivet was clearly distinguished. Then came the failure of the imperial candidature, followed by the activation of hostilities on the frontier with the Low Countries. Now when he should have been able to seize Valenciennes, 'Reason' abandoned the king (and it was in this context that he refused Bourbon the command of the *avant-garde* of the French army!). Knowledge's speech pivoted on a precise point, regarding the responsibility of Francis I for his own failures: it was his biased policies and his military incompetence which caused him to lose 'a servant. This loss created real misfortune for you'. And, now, once Bourbon was exiled from the realm of France, catastrophes followed rapidly, one after another, up until Pavia. The poet plays upon the idea of the helplessness of the captive and sick king, delivered by Fortune at the price of the captivity of his sons, but not having learned the lessons of the story:

> Less than ever deliberating to follow me,
> Forgetting the promise that you have made
> And your blood that you have left hostage,
> You are always a subject to your pleasure.

France was made ill by the dishonour of its king, who only valued himself and did not hesitate to ally with a bad pope or create contacts with the Turk Suleiman. What one must remember, added the poet, was that when a prince finds himself deprived of Knowledge, it was because he was under the curse of a punishment from God. This malediction continued, because Francis I reneged on all his promises made in Madrid, including the renunciation of his claims to Burgundy, Milan, and Naples, and did not restore the former constable to his rights. To the king without reason, faith, or honour must be added the unjust king who, when he did not disgrace the best of his servants, sent them instead to die on the battlefield. Francis I was invited to plead for the help of God who punishes the 'wicked and ungrateful'. The worst was yet to come.[37]

---

[37] June E. Kane, 'Bourbon justifié, qui fut coupable', *Bibliothèque d'humanisme et Renaissance*, 47 (1985), no.1, 147–59, which specifies that the Epistle is a response to the poem P1 by Francis I, *Œuvres Poétiques*, ed. June E. Kane (Geneva, 1984), which includes the following lines directed explicitly against Bourbon: 'Je m'advançay, defendant mon pays Des ennemis, à bon droit trop haÿs . . . En maudissant Bourbon et ses

It was at the same time as the death of the constable de Bourbon under the walls of Rome that this desacralizing violence began to quieten down. Also contributing to the silencing of satire on monarchical authority was the redeployment of the language of disqualification in the sphere of religious struggle. But what is important is to see that before the crisis of the years 1584–9, before the time of the League's stigmatization of the tyranny of the unjust prince, of a new Herod or persecuting Pharaoh, before the great pulse of eschatological angst at the end of the sixteenth century, Francis I suffered for several years the threatening assaults of ritualized laughter; a laughter which anticipated the ritual peak of collective violence: the regicide committed by one man, Jacques Clément. It was directly claimed to be an eschatological accomplishment, as the sign of a renewed alliance between God and his people, because the people of God through penitence had merited that the 'arm of God' should strike down the tyrannical antichrist. Thus, the violence of the crowd and the violence of the individual seemed to merge.

---

pratiques, Connoissant bien ses trahisons iniques...'. What is problematic is that we have no knowledge that this poem circulated in printed form. For Kane, it came from the court, but it would be better to emphasize that this type of text could easily have disappeared if it had been published. The royal epistle is a propaganda text. One must note that the unknown author invites Francis I, by game always, to read 'le livre de Bocasse', precisely *Des cas et ruyne des nobles hommes et femmes reversez par fortune depuis la création du monde jusques à nostre temps, translaté de latin en langaige françois par Laurens de Premier Fait* (Paris, 1483).

Painting Power: Antoine Caron's *Massacres of the Triumvirate*

Neil Cox and Mark Greengrass

The impact of Natalie Zemon Davis's article, 'The Rites of Violence', on historical analysis of sectarian violence and religious confrontation in all sorts of culture has been profound.[1] It has even provided a perspective for those working on the German nineteenth-century *Kulturkampf*, even though that movement never resulted in physical violence at all.[2] For historians of the *Kulturkampf* of sixteenth-century France, it has led directly to an intensive re-examination of the Genevan-based engravings of religious conflict and confrontation, the famous *Mappe-Monde Papistique* (1566) of Jean-Baptiste Trento and Pierre Eskrich, and the *Quarante Tableaux ou histoires diverses* (1569–70) prepared by Jacques Tortorel and Jean Perrissin.[3] There was, however, another tradition of 'massacre' paintings and engravings, those depicting the 'massacres of the triumvirate'. This chapter examines one of the most famous of them afresh in the light of Davis's article.[4] The argument is the result of a fortuitous collaboration between two disciplinary sensibilities: an art historian, working on surrealist responses to the twentieth-century culture of violence, and an early-modern historian trying to understand a rather different culture of violence in the sixteenth century. Bringing us

---

[1] Natalie Zemon Davis, 'The Rites of Violence: Religious Riot in Sixteenth-Century France', *Past and Present*, 59 (1973), 51-91.

[2] Oliver Zimmer, 'Beneath the "Culture War": Corpus Christi Processions and Mutual Accommodation in the Second German Empire', *The Journal of Modern History*, 82 (2010), 288–334, esp. 303.

[3] Frank Lestringant, and Alesandra Preda (eds), *Jean-Baptisto Trento et Pierre Eskrich. Mappe monde nouvelle papistique, Histoire de la mappe monde* (Geneva, 2010); Philip Benedict, *Graphic History: the 'Wars, massacres and troubles' of Tortorel and Perrissin* (Geneva, 2007).

[4] Neil Cox acknowledges the assistance of The Leverhulme Trust towards the research that he undertook for this paper. Both authors are grateful to various audiences in the UK and at the Universities of Paris-1 and Paris-IV for their response to different versions of material presented in this chapter.

together is the most remarkable and interesting of the massacre paintings in sixteenth-century France: Antoine Caron's *Massacres of the Triumvirate* (Musée du Louvre, Paris) (Figure 1). Our work has the common objective of understanding the effectiveness of the visual representation of power at a particular historical moment. Power, we argue, is manifested in a work of art at a particular point in time in a form that both reveals and masks its political currency. The nature of power is exposed with all the unmistakable visibility, entirely unambiguous, of an act of violence. At the same time, a cultural object has the power to evoke in us our hidden fears and unspoken thoughts. It unsettles and destabilizes the comfortable assumptions that we construct in order to turn the world around us into an ordered, stable, and controllable environment. A canvas has the capacity to shroud power—in this instance in a dazzling historicizing narrative and scenography; yet it can at the same time lay it bare, to expose its assumptions for all to observe, with nightmarish elegance and in repressive silence. We believe that these ambiguities, evident in Caron's painting, bear a determinate relationship to the ambiguities concerning particular acts of extreme violence in the historical record. We argue that Caron's painting is a mechanism for evoking the relationship between power and violence in Renaissance France.

One of the most important contributions of some figures associated with surrealism was to understand the nature of power in its chilling contemporary context, and this picture served as an exemplar.[5] Its modern history as a cultural object cannot be disassociated from that insight. Can we apply that understanding to the sixteenth century, and re-imagine what fears and thoughts this painting evoked in its viewers, what assumptions it challenged? Our historical imagination is a branch of our cultural imagination and it is not de-historicizing the former to deploy the insights of the latter. Indeed, the one can hardly be said to function without the other. This paper is an attempt to harness them both.

---

[5] Among the important groupings to address the question of sovereignty in modernity, particularly in the context of the rise of Fascism, were the Collège de Sociologie and Acéphale, developments in the later 1930s that emerged from conflicts within surrealism around 1930. The key figure in this story is Georges Bataille. For texts produced by the Collège and Acéphale, see Denis Hollier (ed.), *The College of Sociology* (Minnesota, MN, 1998); Georges Bataille, *Visions of Excess, Selected Writings 1927–1939*, trans. Allan Stoekl (Minnesota, MN, 1985), 178–239. It is plausible but speculative to suggest that the iconography of headlessness that in Acéphale was meant to capture the (im)possibility of a new kind of sovereignty may have owed something to Caron's painting as well as to the notionally inaugural act of the self-rule of the people in the regicide of 1793.

Figure 1. Anthoine Caron, *Les massacres du Triumvirat* (Réunion des musées nationaux, Agence Photographique)

I

The painting is very substantial (116 cm × 195 cm inside the frame), an oil on canvas, now divided into three separate panels but originally one undivided painting. It was purchased from a London antiques dealer on the eve of the First World War by Frédéric François Levisse de Montigny, marquis de Jaucourt. Descended from Charlotte Arbaleste, Philippe Du Plessis Mornay's wife, he had an impeccable sixteenth-century Protestant lineage. Somewhat unusually, perhaps, he married the daughter of a tannery proprietor in Manchester and died in Buenos Aries in 1969. His marriage no doubt explains why he was to be found in a London antique shop in 1913. The painting had been hitherto cut into three pieces and its new owner had it reassembled to hang as a painting in his Paris residence, where it remained until he donated it to the Louvre in 1939.

We know it is by Antoine Caron because it is the only painting that he acknowledged and dated, '1566'. The inscription is now so faded that it is almost illegible but, in the 1823 London catalogue of the sale of the Brackenbury collection, which is when the painting is first certainly known to have been in England, it apparently said:

'Ex arte Ant. Caron pict.
Curaque August. Lemusii.
Paris 1566'.[6]

This inscription is not only faded but ambiguous. It is not clear that Caron himself painted it in. It has always been presumed that the date gives us reliable testimony as to when it was completed, though this might not be the case. No one has ever succeeded in identifying who the mysterious 'Augustus Lemusius' might have been, and what kind of patronage is implied in the 'curaque'. Yet, if the name refers to the person who commissioned the painting, it ought not, a priori, to be impossible to find the person in question, someone of some notability. We started from the assumption that it was an individual living in Paris, and consulted the list of those contributing to the 'don gratuit' of 1572.[7] Only one name in that list has any degree of plausibility: 'Augustin Lemousse', a *marchand apothicaire* living in the rue Saint-Martin, not far from the church of St Nicolas des Champs and towards

---

[6] Catalogue of the Exhibition at the Grand Palais, Paris on the *Ecole de Fontainebleau* (1972–3), No. 32.
[7] We are very grateful to Professor Robert Descimon of the Ecole des Hautes-Etudes for allowing us permission to consult his searchable database of this source and for discussing the problems of this identification with us.

the corner with the rue des Graviers.[8] It might initially seem strange that an apothecary should have commissioned such a work, until we remember that it was Lemousse's companion, the apothecary Nicolas Houel who commissioned Caron in the early 1560s to undertake the cartoons for an illustrated history of Queen Artemis to present to Catherine de Médici as a gift, suggesting she have the designs made into tapestries.[9] The two female figures that look outwards from the canvas at either side might even be taken to imply that this painting, too, might have been conceived as a gift to the Queen Mother. Lemousse's near neighbours included (across the street) Guillaume Le Jars, *trésorier de la maison du roi*, an enthusiastic patron of the arts in his own right and the father of the remarkable Marie de Gournay, who saw the third edition of Montaigne's 'Essays' (1595) through the press.[10] The post-mortem inventory of his house on the rue Saint-Martin of 22 August 1578 provides us with a revealing glimpse of the size and eclectic taste of the picture collection of Lemousse's near neighbour.[11] The *grande salle* downstairs had ten pictures on display in it—including religious scenes ('un jugement de Michel l'Ange'; a 'Résurrection', 'l'Immolation de l'Agneau' and a 'Jugement de Jésus Christ fait par Pilate'), landscapes (three paintings), classical mythology ('Sacrifice de Policène'), the moral virtues ('Charité') and two contemporary paintings ('feu Sr de Guise' and 'une courtisane'). Upstairs in his study, Guillaume Le Jars had forty other paintings, mostly landscapes and portraits, but including one of 'le feu Roy François II' and a sequence of small paintings of the months of the year.[12] So much of the artwork of the French sixteenth century has been

---

[8] Bibliothèque nationale de France, Paris, [hereafter BnF] MS français 11692, fo. 131v [emprunt de 1572]. He paid 15 *livres*, below the average for the Parisian notability, but *c.*150 grams of silver was nonetheless an appreciable amount of precious metal to have around the house.

[9] Jules Guiffrey, 'Nicolas Houel, apothicaire parisien fondateur de la maison de la Charité chrétienne et premier auteur de la tenture d'Artémise', *Mémoires de la société de l'histoire de Paris et de l'Ile de France*, 25 (1898), 170–270; Valérie Auclair, 'De l'exemple antique à la chronique contemporaine. L'Histoire de la Royne Arthemise de l'invention de Nicolas Houel', *Journal de la Renaissance*, 1 (2000), 155–88.

[10] BnF, MS Français 11692, fo. 132.

[11] Archives Nationales, Paris, Minutier Central IX/281 (Inventaire après décès du Guillaume Le Jars, 22 August 1578). See Michèle Fogel, *Itinéraires d'une femme savante* (Paris, 2004), ch. 2. The authors are very grateful to Michèle Fogel for generously providing her notes on this fascinating inventory, and for allowing us to cite them.

[12] Other paintings around the house included an 'image de Saint François' in the downstairs reception room, three paintings in the 'petite chambre' upstairs (including a 'Reine de Navarre', an Adoration, and a painting of 'deux homes et deux femmes riant, tenant un chat') and four in M. De Jars' upstairs chamber (including three of 'drôleries façon de

lost subsequently that it is not now so apparent to us that there was an important market for it, even during the Wars of Religion.

Caron's *Massacres* was a twentieth-century discovery, first reproduced in December 1929 in the pages of the heterodox journal of so-called 'dissident' surrealists, *Documents*; the remarkable black and white photographs of the painting, possibly taken by Jacques-André Boiffard, being accompanied by a disturbing interpretative essay by French critic and ethnographer Michel Leiris.[13] We do not know how the discovery came about, though *Documents* was funded by art dealer Georges Wildenstein, owner since 1928 of *La Gazette des Beaux-Arts*, and thus a well-connected figure in the Paris art world. Leiris encountered Caron's painting in the autumn of 1929, presumably in Jaucourt's Paris residence though not inconceivably merely in the form of the photographs, around the time that he began a course of psychoanalysis with the Freudian-trained Docteur Borel. In some surviving notes on one of his sessions on Borel's couch he jotted down in his diary the involuntary memories that had emerged: 'childhood—nightmares, games, masturbation, childish mawkishness, tears, strange battles', explicitly linking these memories to the painting that was currently on his mind.[14] He alluded to those moments as tearing away the thin veneer of civilization.[15] Edited by the librarian, philosopher, and part-time pornographer Georges Bataille and

---

Flandres' and a landscape) as well as two further paintings in the 'Grand Chambre' where he died.

[13] Michel Leiris, 'Une peinture d'Antoine Caron', reprinted in Michel Leiris, *Zébrage* (Paris, 1992), 13–20 from *Documents* (1ère année) No. 7 (décembre 1929), 348–55. The importance of Leiris' essay has already been explored in Neil Cox, 'A painting by Antoine Caron', *Papers of Surrealism*, Issue 7 (2007), available online from the UK Surrealism Centre archive at http://www.surrealismcentre.ac.uk/papersofsurrealism/journal7/acrobat%20files/articles/Coxfinal.pdf [accessed 16 September 2011].

[14] Jean Jamin (ed.), *Michel Leiris. Journal (1922–1989)* (Paris, 1992), 203–5 (cited at 205), 'enfance—cauchemars, jeux, onanisme, sentimentalité infantile, pleurs, rares batailles'.

[15] 'La civilisation peu être comparée sans trop d'inexactitude à la mince couche verdâtre—magma vivant et détritus variés—qui se forme à la surface des eaux calmes et se solidifie parfois en croûte, jusqu'à ce qu'un remous soit venu tout bouleverser. Toutes nos habitudes morales et nos usages de politesse, tout ce manteau de couleur fraîche qui voile la crudité de nos instincts dangereux, toutes ces belles formes de culture dont nous sommes si fiers ... sont prêtes à s'évanouir au moindre tourbillon ... laissant apparaître dans les interstices l'effrayante sauvagerie, révélée par les fissures, comme l'enfer devrait l'être par les tremblements de terre, quand ses révolutions d'ordre cosmique font éclater la fragile pellicule de la périphérie terrestre et dénudent momentanément le feu central'. Michel Leiris, *Brisées* (Paris, 1966), 32, reprinted from 'Civilisation', originally published in *Documents* 4 (September 1929), 221–2 (cited at 221).

with strong input from radical art historian Carl Einstein, *Documents* lasted for only fifteen issues in 1929–30. Its subtitles changed; alongside constants such as 'Archéologie, Beaux-Arts, Ethnographie', others came and went, 'Doctrines' being replaced by 'Variétés'. According to Leiris, the secretary of the magazine, *Documents* was a 'war machine against received ideas'.[16] In the December 1929 issue Leiris's Caron article was juxtaposed incongruously with chilling images from Gaston-Louis Roux's paintings, especially '*l'Arracheur de Dents*' ('The toothdrawer'), specimens of the marquis de Sade's handwriting seeking to prove that it reveals the human psyche, a diagram of Salvador Dalí's nightmarish painting *Le Jeu Lugubre* ('The Lugubrious Game'), and hyper-realistic representations of human violence in the twenty-six eleventh-century bronze bas-reliefs on the doors of San-Zeno at Verona.[17] The 'Critical Dictionary' that was a regular feature of the magazine carried entries on '*crachat*' ('spitting'), '*débâcle*' ('collapse') and '*informe*' ('shapeless').

Leiris had no time for the historical context of the painting in question. Putting works of art safely away in the past rendered them impotent. Speaking for the whole surrealist project, he wrote: 'this is why we so much want to transport ourselves back more completely to our savage ancestry, and why we can hardly bear to do otherwise than to eliminate in one fell swoop the intervening centuries and to place ourselves, with all our vulnerability and nakedness, before a world that is more immediate and novel'.[18] Its cultural power lay in its capacity to stir up the political psychology of the present (in the immediate wake of the Great Crash of 29 October 1929), the potential and dangers of revolution, the capacities of state power for good and evil, and the terrifying possibilities of religious or ideological (fascist) violence. Leiris's article on the painting is a triptych, like the painting itself. We move from autobiographical reminiscence through an exploration of the artist's psychological motivation to a poetic evocation of the experience of massacre. In a Proustian moment of involuntary memory inspired by the painting, Leiris recalls childhood obsessions of immolation, of being swallowed up by wolves

---

[16] For more on *Documents* see Dawn Ades and Simon Baker (eds), *Undercover Surrealism: Georges Bataille and DOCUMENTS* (London, 2006). The journal was reissued in a two volume fascsimile by Paris publisher Jean-Michel Place in 1991.

[17] Articles by Roger Vitrac (356–8); Pierre Ménard (365–8); Georges Bataille (369–72), and (?)Robert Desnos (373–6); dictionary entries, 381–3.

[18] Leiris, 'Civilisation', 221 ('c'est pourquoi nous aimerions tant nous rapprocher plus complètement de notre ancestralité sauvage, et n'apprécions plus guère que ce qui, anéantissant d'un seul coup la succession des siècles, nous place, tout à fait nus et dépouillés, devant un monde plus proche et plus neuf').

and horses. He evokes his preoccupations with extreme violence: his elder brother threatening to remove his appendix with a bottle-opener: playground taunts that the father of a class-mate would smash his head in with an axe: the bandage covering a large gash on the hand of another. For Leiris, however, these are just particular instances of what is a typical childhood experience, which our 'civilization' conveniently cloaks for us as we grow up. The cultural power of Caron's painting is its capacity to enable us to access uncomfortable but profoundly rooted human experience. 'My childhood seems to me analogous to that of a people perpetually in the grip of irrational fears, living under the shadow of sombre and cruel mysteries. Mankind becomes a wolf, preying on its own kind, and animals exist to eat, or to eat you'.[19] To unlock the psychological world of the painter, Leiris deliberately eschews any biographical detail or historical precision in favour of an anecdote from the nineteenth-century compilation on magic by abbé Alphonse-Louis Constant [pseudonym: Eliphas Lévi], *Le Dogme et ritual de la haute-magie* (1856).[20] The gruesome story, set at the French court in 1574 as Charles IX lay on his death-bed, involved the evisceration and decapitation of a young child undertaking its first communion, its body parts being then deployed in a black mass to summon the devil for an oracular pronouncement through the mouth of the decapitated child. In response to the king's interrogation, a voice is heard to respond in Latin: 'Vim Patior' ('I suffer violence'), interpreted by the king as an augury of the eternal torment which awaited him for having permitted the massacre of St Bartholomew. Constant borrowed the story from Bodin's *De la démonomamie des sorciers* (1580), who in turn had acquired it from the diplomatic gossip-mill.[21] But, for Leiris, it was not its historical veracity that mattered ('Il y a toutes les chances pour que cette histoire soit fausse') but the imaginative truth that it liberated: Caron's apparent obsession with

---

[19] Leiris, 'Une peinture d'Antoine Caron', 350 ('Mon enfance m'apparaît analogue à celle d'un people perpétuellement en proie à des terreurs superstitieuses, et placé sous la coupe de mystères sombres et cruels. L'homme est un loup pour l'homme, et les animaux ne sont bons qu'à vous manger ou à être mangés').

[20] Eliphas Lévi [Alphonse-Louis Constant], *Dogme et ritual de la haute magie*, 2nd edn, 2 vols (Paris, 1861), 235–8.

[21] Jean Bodin, *De la demonomanie des sorciers* (Lyon, 1597), 155. Bodin's source was 'Pruinski' (Pruvinski ?), a Lithuanian in the legation which came to Paris in September 1573 to offer the kingship of Poland to Henri duc d'Anjou (Bodin refers to him as the source on the ability of those in northern latitudes to see better in the dark in Jean Bodin, *Les Six Livres de la République*, 6 vols, *Corpus des Oeuvres de Philosophie en langue française* (Paris, 1986), V, 14). The same story, however, had circulated about Francis II at the very beginning of the civil wars and it was probably picked up by Bodin's source on his way through Germany to Paris.

decapitation. Leiris's own compulsive fascination with the latter re-emerged within months of the Caron publication, when he discovered photographs of Lucas Cranach the Elder's paintings (two of them now lost) of three famous female heroines, Lucretia, Judith, and Salomé, these last two themselves decapitators.[22] In the opening essay of his autobiographical collection *L'âge d'homme* (1939), probably written a decade previously, Leiris admits to his own feelings of castration, a masochistic eroticism which Holofernes' decapitation at the hands of Judith evokes in him. Those are the emotions he attributes to Caron ('d'ordre sadique ou masochiste'), ending the article with a verse evocation of its power:

'... whilst inescapably they spill,
As spills the rubbish on the morning streets,
The severed heads that lick the shadows and the statues' feet'.[23]

II

Seven years after Leiris's publication, the art historian Gustave Lebel returned home excitedly from an auction at the Hôtel Drouot to announce: 'I am the first to have seen a painting by Antoine Caron'.[24] The work in question was Caron's *Augustus and the Sibyl* which featured the following year at the Paris Universal Exhibition in 1937 as a 'masterpiece of French art'. Lebel went on to assign a number of other paintings to Caron and to re-evaluate the 'Massacres of the Triumvirate', placing it in its historical context in a way that Leiris had dismissed. The majority of what we know about the painting was therefore already discovered by the time of its deposit in the Louvre in 1939.[25] And the belief that it was Lebel's discovery that had triggered the renaissance of the entire oeuvre of Caron (thereby entirely sidelining Leiris) was perpetuated by Lebel's disciple Jean Ehrmann.

In one important respect, Ehrmann provided the wherewithal for us to contextualize the picture more accurately. To understand Caron's painting we have to place it in relation to others depicting the same subject. For it was far from the only picture of the Triumvirate massacres to be painted. From

---

[22] Cox, 'A painting by Antoine Caron'.
[23] Leiris, 'Une peinture d'Antoine Caron', 355 ('tandis que tombent inéluctablement / comme tombent les détritus le matin dans les rues / les têtes coupées qui lèchent l'ombre et les pieds des statues').
[24] Gustave Lebel, 'Antoine Caron', *L'Amour de l'Art*, 18 (1937), 317–25; cf Jean Ehrmann, *Antoine Caron. Peintre des fêtes et des massacres* (Paris, 1986), 7.
[25] Gustave Lebel, 'Nouvelles précisions sur Antoine Caron', *L'Amour de l'Art* 19 (1938), 271–80; Gustave Lebel, 'Notes sur Antoine Caron et son oeuvre', *Bulletin de la société nationale des antiquaires de France* (1940), 7–34.

1945 to his death in 1984, Ehrmann diligently tracked down Triumvirate massacre paintings in public and private collections the world over, releasing his results in successive publications, including his monograph on Caron published posthumously in 1986.[26] Unfortunately, he did not deposit (as he evidently intended) the detailed dossier of his findings in the library of the Société de l'Histoire du Protestantisme Français in Paris. The majority of the extant canvases were (and remain) in private hands and are therefore not readily accessible. They quite often moved from one owner to another during Ehrmann's lifetime, and have no doubt continued to do so thereafter. Ehrmann's task was not assisted by the fact that many of the works are close copies of one another. We deduce from the evidence he published that he identified twenty-three oil paintings on wood or canvas (including that of Caron) and some further woodcut and engraved prints, which we shall allude to shortly. Photographic reproduction is available in print for only fifteen of the paintings.[27] For the remainder, the details are more fragmentary.[28] Only two of them have an artist's attribution and date. They vary widely in size, from the very substantial painting that hung in the church at Belle-Eglise in the Oise until it was damaged by vandals in 1953 (135 × 216 cm) to the modest fragment which Ehrmann located in the hands of an art-dealer in Rome and which subsequently been sold on to other private hands (20 × 20 cm—he subsequently noted it as 20 × 30 cm).

Ehrmann attempted to categorize what he had found, first by size (1955), and then (1972 onwards) by a more ambitious mapping of stylistic variation onto possible social and political appeal. One 'family' of paintings emphasized the 'antique' in terms of costume and décor—paintings aimed at the taste of the court and aristocracy. A second 'family' was more 'politicized'—pictures that included a fleur-de-lys motif over a doorway to the left, and a Latin inscription, on a wall to the right or running across the bottom of the picture: 'Cum tribus infaelix serviret Roma tyrannis, haec rerum facies quam

---

[26] Jean Ehrmann, 'Massacre and Persecution Pictures in Sixteenth-Century France', *The Journal of the Warburg and Courtauld Institute*, 8 (1945), 195–9; Jean Ehrmann, *Antoine Caron peintre à la Cour des Valois, 1521–1599* (Geneva and Lille, 1955), 48–9; J. Ehrmann, 'Tableaux de massacres au XVIe siècle', *Bulletin de la société de l'histoire du Protestantisme français*, 118 (1972), 445–555; Jean Ehrmann, 'Artistes franco-flamands de l'Ecole de Fontainebleau (Simon de Myle)', *Bulletin de la société de l'histoire de l'art français* [New Series] 3 (1972), 63–77; Jean Ehrmann, 'Hans Vredeman de Vries (Leeuwarden 1527–Anvers 1606)', *Gazette des Beaux-Arts*, 121 (1979), 13–26; Ehrmann *Antoine Caron. Peintre des fêtes et des massacres*, esp. 221–2.

[27] See Appendix I.

[28] See Appendix I, Part 2.

modo cernis erat' ['When unfortunate Rome was governed by three tyrants, events such as you see here depicted took place']. Among these, he detected a further 'Protestant' sub-group in which an individual is very clearly being forcibly restrained by the centurions whilst his tongue is cut out and a '*sacoche*' ('satchel') of trial papers is being attached behind him, the reference clearly being to contemporary judicial practice in the burning of heretics. These typographies are not, however, very watertight, even among the paintings for which we have reproductions. And Ehrmann's proposition, made first in 1955 and sustained through to his publication in 1986, that they were mainly dependant on a missing prototype tableau by the Flemish artist Hans Vredeman de Vries, was implicitly called into question in 1977 when one of these paintings (now in the Collection Massey, Tarbes) was restored, revealing unambiguously both the signature of the artist ('VRI'—Hans Vredeman de Vries) and also a date ('1570'). This is very late for an artist who is credited with having painted the prototype, even though it is possible that he had treated the subject before.[29]

Rather than searching for a prototype or archetype, we should perhaps be looking rather for a coalescence of interest in the subject and ways of treating it. Here, we are on surer ground. The interest in the history of the Roman triumvirate seems to have begun with Nicolò dell'Abate (*c*.1509–71), who was commissioned to paint a set of narrative frescoes on the subject in a contract with the city fathers of Modena to adorn three walls of their Sala dei Conservatori (known as the 'Sala del Fuoco' from the logs that were said to be kept constantly alight in the fireplace of the chamber so that merchants in the piazza could light their stoves from it in winter) in the Palazzo Comunale.[30] The work was undertaken in 1546. The choice of subject was particularly appropriate for the populist-inclined duchy because 'Mutina' (i.e. Modena) was the site of the siege in which Decimus Brutus defended the city against the combined forces of Octavian and Anthony in 43 BC. Dell'Abate stayed remarkably close to the events as recorded in Appian's

---

[29] David Kunzle, *From Criminal to Courtier. The Soldier in Netherlandish Art, 1550–1672* (Leiden, 2002), 158–9, accepts the Ehrman prototype proposition. Cf David Kunzle, 'Hans Vredeman de Vries's Massacre by the Roman Triumvirate and Propaganda during the French Religious Wars', in *Hans Vredeman de Vries und die Folgen*, ed. by Heiner Borggrefe and Vera Lüpkes (Marburg, 2005), 161–70.

[30] Francesca Piccinini, 'Nicolo e la magnifica comunità Modenese', in Sylvie Béguin and Francesca Piccinini (eds), *Nicolo dell'Abate. Storie dipinte nella pittura del cinquecento tra Moderna e Fontainebleau* (Milan and Modena, 2005), 77–91; Erika Langmuir, 'The triumvirate of Brutus and Cassius: Nicolo dell'Abate's Appian Cycle in the Palazzo Comunale of Modena', *The Art Bulletin*, 59 (1977), 188–96.

narrative of them (we shall return to that text shortly). He painted the beginning and progress of its resourceful defence against a determined siege in two frescoes that stand before you at eye-level as you enter the chamber. Once inside the room, you turn back to find the continuation of the narrative above the doorway, recording the raising of the siege and the tense meeting of Brutus, Octavian, and Anthony outside the city. Almost immediately, however, your eye is drawn to the long wall of the chamber opposite the fireplace, under which the city fathers met in solemn deliberation. There dell'Abate chose to depict the triumvirate, Octavian in the centre, in earnest discussion about the next phase of their operations: the entry into Rome and its purge. Dell'Abate did not need to make Octavian resemble the Emperor Charles V too closely (or Lepidus to look like Pope Paul III—though some likeness has been asserted—let alone for Antony to have the appearance of the French king Francis I) for all sorts of contemporary associations to come flooding in. There was more than enough in the frescoes of the room to remind people of the recent imperial sack of Rome (1527) after a failed defence against a siege, or of the contemporary meetings of the French king and emperor at Aiguesmortes and Nice (1538). Still more, however, the frescoes expressed the *non-dits*, the things too sensitive to say around the council chamber of the city fathers. In the shadow of the d'Este ducal family, they could hardly express the extent to which they felt that civic republicanism was being overshadowed by heavy princely presences and larger imperial forces. Once more, a picture spoke across the century from the past to the present. The city fathers clearly knew about the power of an image to express their deeper anxieties, and dell'Abate knew very well how to invest a picture with multiple meanings. What more natural than that he should bring the subject with him when he made his way to the court of Fontainebleau in 1552?

We have a strong indication that he probably did, in one of the larger and more elaborate massacre of the triumvirate paintings inventoried by Jean Ehrmann (that deposited from the national collection at the Musée départemental de l'Oise in 1964).[31] Ehrmann somewhat over-enthusiastically attributed it also to Antoine Caron, his second painting of that subject he thought, albeit with a strangely different scenography. Expert opinion has not followed him in that attribution, however. It is now firmly regarded as belonging to the school of Nicolò dell'Abate, perhaps to the master himself or possibly to his son Giulio Camillo.[32] In which case, there is not a great deal to prevent us hypothesizing that it was precisely this painting which graced the chamber

[31] Appendix I, No. 12.
[32] Most recently, Béguin, and Piccinini (eds), *Nicoló Dell'abate*, 452–3 and refs; see, Ehrmann, *Antoine Caron. Peintre des fêtes et des massacres*, 26–28, figs 13–16.

reserved for the king in the *hôtel* of the Constable Anne de Montmorency in Paris on the rue Sainte-Avoye. The inventory of its contents in 1556 provides us with a description of it ('A une place d'honneur dans la chambre du Roy un grand tableau où est peint le triumvirat') with its elaborate frame in line with contemporary Parisian taste.[33] Dell'Abate served almost as the *chef de chantier* for the internal decoration of that property, especially in the 'Gallery of the Virtues' linking the chambers on the first floor, as we know from surviving drawings of various panels.[34] He knew well how to satisfy Anne de Montmorency's taste for dressing up the present through the history of the Roman past. The Constable eagerly collected manuscript copies of Roman history for his library and decorated his *châteaux* at Ecouen and Chantilly with antiquities that he acquired with an enthusiasm bordering on kleptomania.[35] Some eyebrows had been raised, according to Brantôme, when he had asked the humanist and erstwhile grammar reformer Louis Meigret to translate Sallust's Catiline conspiracy and Jugurtha into French.[36] Five years later, the Genevan-based *Histoire ecclésiastique* (1580) furnishes us with further evidence about the growing significance accorded to the massacres of the

---

[33] L. Mirot, 'L'hôtel et les collections du connétable de Montmorency', *Bibliothèque de l'école des chartes*, 79 (1918), 311–413, esp. 365 and 402; it reappeared in the 1568 inventory as 'Ung grand tableau du Triumvirat peint à l'huille et enrichy avecque son rideau de taffetas verd'. Parisian tastes in pictures and their frames are evoked in Catherine Grodecki (ed.), *Histoire de l'art au XVIe siècle. 2, sculpture, peinture, broderie, émail et faïence, orfèvrerie, armures, 1540–1600* (Paris, 1986), 21–35.

[34] See Béguin, and Piccinini (eds), *Nicoló Dell'abate*, 419 (No. 197: 'Victory' and 'Fame') and 420–1 (Nos 199–202: 'Temperance', 'Faith', 'Prudence' and 'Truth') with a complementary drawing of François de Montmorency 419–20 (No.198), the Constable's eldest son, probably commissioned for inclusion in the 'Gallery of Virtues' after his ransom from Spanish Habsburg captivity at the truce of Vaucelles in 1556.

[35] Margaret M. McGowan, *The Vision of Rome in Late Renaissance France* (New Haven and London, 2000), 56.

[36] 'Il fut un peu blâmé de s'être fait traduite du latin de Salluste en français la guerre de Catilina' (Brantôme, *Vie du Connétable Anne de Montmorency*). The work in question was *C. Crispe Saluste de la Conjuration de L. Serge Catilin, avec la premiere Harengue de Marc Tulle Cicéron contre icelui: ensemble de la guerre Jugurthine, avec l'invective de Porcius Larro contre ledit Catilin: le tout traduit par Louis Meigret Lionnais* (Lyon, 1556). The first edition was published a decade before in 1547, only days before the death of Francis I. On Louis Meigret, see Franz Josef Hausmann, *Louis Meigret: humaniste et linguiste* (Narr, 1980), esp. ch. 1. As it happened, Montmorency's *hôtel* on the rue Sainte-Avoye had belonged to Louis Meigret's relative (perhaps his step-brother) Lambert Meigret. The Constable acquired it when the latter's munitioneering activities for the French expeditionary forces in Milan led to his disgrace.

triumvirate as a subject in French political circles when it reported (in a passage relating to November 1561): 'It was then that were brought to the Court three large paintings, superbly done, which depicted the bloody and more than inhumane executions carried out at Rome between Octavius, Antony and Lepidus. These canvases were purchased for high prices by the grandees, and one of them hung in the chamber of the Prince of Condé, where it was seen by all those of the Religion'.[37] Aristocrats knew very well how to use picture power. The portraits of their ancestors were an active and present reminder of their lineage and a permanent education in the particular values of family and tradition. They could be used to make an exquisite political point, as when the Elector Palatine led the unsuspecting Louis, duke of Nevers and Henri, duke of Anjou into his gallery on their visit to Heidelberg in 1573 to show them life-size portraits of the recently deceased Admiral Coligny and his two brothers.[38] Even the knowledge, apparently widely disseminated, that a massacre picture hung in Condé's chamber at court towards the end of 1561 made a powerful point, evoking the very-present fears of a *conjuration* (to which we shall return) through the experience of the past.

III

The woodcut illustrations will take us a step closer to understanding the implicit power of Caron's painting. Ehrmann was apparently only aware of one illustration of the 'Massacres of the Triumvirate' theme, a woodcut of exceptionally large dimensions (50 × 76 cm). He located three examples of it in different collections.[39] In reality, there was also a separate, very different

---

[37] G. Baum, and Ed. Cunitz (eds), *Histoire ecclésiastique des églises réformées du royaume de France*, 3 vols (Paris, 1883–9), I, 743 ('C'est qu'alors furent apportés à la Cour trois grands tableaux excellemment peints, où étaient représentées les sanglantes & plus qu'inhumaines executions jadis faites à Rome entre Octavius, Antonius et Lepidus. Ces tableaux furent bien cherement achetés par les grands, l'un desquels était en la chambre du Prince de Condé à la veue d'un chacun de ceux de la religion'). The passage in question was first highlighted in Jean Adhémar, 'Antoine Caron's Massacre Paintings', *Journal of the Warburg and Courtauld Institutes*, 12 (1949), 199–200.

[38] Pierre Champion, *Henri III, roi de Pologne*. 2 vols (Paris, 1951), I, 19. In this particular instance, however, the Elector Palatine could not let the painting do the talking. According to the testimony of Michel de La Hugueraie, who was probably present at the time, he added for good measure: 'C'est ce bon seigneur, monsieur l'amiral, qu'on a si dignement traité à Paris, et ses deux frères qu'on a empoisonnés, l'ung en Poitou, l'autre en Angleterre'. The dukes of Nevers and Anjou chose to make no reply, and retained a frosty silence before moving on.

[39] BnF Cabinet des Estampes AA 3 ('œuvre de Gourmont', 3); BnF Arsenal Cabinet des Estampes (portefeuille 27–171 fos 24–6); and an example, probably in his own private

and much smaller (32.7 × 41.7 cm) treatment of the subject in an engraving, designed by Hans Vredeman de Vries, and executed in two separate prints signed by Jérôme Cock and Jan Galle, and produced probably in the late 1560s.[40] The legend underneath reinforces the prevailing political and moral lens through which the episode was viewed in this period, a composite of two Ciceronian quotations.[41] The larger woodcut on which Ehrmann concentrates his attention is undated and carries no identification. Variously dated (from '1561' to 'towards 1575') and sometimes ascribed to Jean II de Gourmont, it could almost certainly have been produced by any one of several engravers working out of the rue Montorgueil, the centre of Parisian woodcut illustration, or indeed by their counterparts in Lyon.[42] The woodcut is of particular interest because it carries numbers (1–38) with which to identify various parts of the scene (1 is for the triumvirs themselves; 2 for the horsemen carrying the news of the first proscriptions, etc). The most likely reason for this was that it was designed as an illustration to the text which was the *locus classicus* for the triumvirate massacre narrative, the one to which dell'Abate had turned for his frescoes: Appian of Alexandria's

---

collection, which he says 'enrichera plus tard les archives de la société de l'histoire du protestantisme français'. The latter have confirmed, however, that they have no such woodcut in their collections. The size of the print is much larger than the normal production of the engravers of the rue Montorgueil (36 × 48 cm). See the introduction to Bernard Portheault, and Achille Jean Gilliard [experts] (eds), *Images parisiennes du XVIe siècle, rue de Montorgueil: collection de 114 planches dont 112 couleurs d'époque* (Paris, 2004).

[40] Described and inventoried in Peter Fuhring, and Ger Luijten (eds), *Hollstein's Dutch and Flemish etchings, engravings and woodcuts, 1450–1700, vol. 47 (Vredeman De Vries, Part 1. 1555–1571* (Rotterdam and Amsterdam, 1997), 253.

[41] 'Quidquid est huiusmodi, in quo non possunt plures excellere, in eo fit plerumque tanta contentio ut difficillimum fit sanctum servare societatem: difficile est enim cum prestare ceteris concupieris servare equitatem. M.T.C. off. 1'—in reality a combination of two separate phrases from Cicero's *De officiis* to the effect that 'When more than one person wants to be first, it provokes such a violent rivalry that it is very difficult to preserve what is sacred in society [. . .] for it is difficult, when one person has the passionate ambition to be above everyone else to conserve equity'.

[42] See Jean Ehrmann, 'Massacre and Persecution Pictures in Sixteenth-Century France', *The Journal of the Warburg and Courtauld Institute*, 8 (1945), plate 46B; Jean Ehrmann, *Antoine Caron peintre à la Cour des Valois, 1521–1599* (Geneva and Lille, 1955), plate V; Ehrmann, *Antoine Caron. Peintre des fêtes et des massacres*, fig 3E for photographic reproductions of it. Ehrmann was convinced that it should be dated to 1561. In *La Gravure en France au XVIe siècle* (Paris, 1957), No. 137, a catalogue to an exhibition of that year, it is dated to 'towards 1575'.

'History of the Roman Wars'. Folded in the normal way, it would have made an impressive pasted-in and pull-out illustration to a folio edition of the text. However the only folio editions of the French text of which we are aware were produced in Lyon in 1544 and Paris in 1580, and there is no sign of any accompanying table or accompanying signatures in the text of either of them.[43] It is conceivable that there was another folio edition of which no copy has survived, or that there was an accompanying brochure which served the same purpose, of which no example now exists. The significance of Appian's histories (of which the five books on the 'civil wars' form the centrepiece) in sixteenth-century France has yet to be fully appreciated.[44] Whereas there was only one translation published in England in the sixteenth century (and that very late—1578), there were five French editions to 1558.[45] In the years of deepening political crisis in 1559 and 1560 there were no less than fourteen French re-editions of the work published in Paris. A further seventeen re-editions in French followed from Paris before the end of the century, clustering around the Third Civil War (1569–70), the aftermath of St Bartholomew (1570) and again in 1580.[46] With Lucan's verse epic *Pharsalia* (more generally known in sixteenth-century France as 'De Bello Civile'), covering roughly the same chronological period, Appian's Roman histories defined for France's elites what a 'civil war' was.[47]

It helped that the Latin and French translations of Appian most commonly available to French readers were classics in their own right. Published at the Froben press in Basel, the Latin translation of 1554 was a collaboration between Sigismund Jelensky ('Sigmund Gelenius'), a Czech humanist and philologist who made a living from translations and worked for the Froben press, and Celio Secondo Curione, Professor of Rhetoric at the University of Basel.[48] The French translation of 1544 was from a manuscript carrying the

---

[43] *Appian Alexandrin, historien grec, Des Guerres des Rommains, Livres XI* (Lyon, 1544) [No. 1 of Appendix II]; *Appian Alexandrin, Historien Grec, des Guerres des Romains, Livres XI* (Paris : Guillaume Iullian, 1580) [No. 35 of Appendix II].

[44] In reality, Appian's five books of the *Wars of the Romans* was the centrepiece of twelve 'books' of Roman history translated under Seyssel's direction, of which six more were by Appian (entitled 'Le Libyque'; 'Le Syrien'; 'Le Parthique'; 'Le Mithridatique'; 'Le Illyrien'; and 'Le Celtique'), the final book consisting of a translation of Plutarch's Life of Marc Antony.

[45] *An auncient historie and exquisite chronicle of the Romanes warres, both ciuile and foren* (1578).

[46] The French-language editions of the work are listed in Appendix II.

[47] McGowan, *The Vision of Rome*, 264–7.

[48] Sigismund Jelensky and Celio Secondo Curione, *Appiani Alexandrini Romanarum historiarum de bellis punicis liber, de bellis syriacis liber, de bellis parthicis liber, de bellis*

name of the great Claude de Seyssel. In between his busy schedule of letter-writing for Louis XII, attending council affairs, and administering his diocese, Seyssel found the time to oversee a lot of translation. He seems no sooner to have finished with Xenophon's *Anabasis* than he started on Appian in around 1505 before moving on to Plutarch, Justinus, Diodorus Siculus, Eusebius, and Thucydides.[49] He certainly did not do it all unaided and, in the Appian preface, he specifically acknowledged the help of Janus Lascaris, who had served as a fellow diplomat with him and who knew Greek (Seyssel did not). He had apparently found a manuscript translation of the Appian text in the royal library – probably that of Pope Nicolas V – although he readily admitted that it was so defective that it was often incomprehensible. Later on, Seyssel also discovered and translated Appian's Hispanic and Hannibalic Wars, although that manuscript was subsequently lost, and has only recently been rediscovered in the British Library.[50] All these manuscripts were worked up into manuscript presentation copies for the king—that for Appian's Civil Wars still survives, very badly damaged by fire in 1904, in the National Library of Turin. Seyssel was reluctant to publish any of them on the grounds that they contained a precious, rare wisdom which was suitable only for the ears of princes.[51] He would no doubt have disapproved, therefore, of the publication in 1544, complete with his long preface. It began with a classic exposition of the strengths and weaknesses of democracy, aristocracy, and monarchy. Everyone was agreed, he went on, that monarchy was (all things considered) the best form of government. Yet, because of the 'idiocy and imperfection' of the human condition it can become corrupted.[52] Fortunately, there were ways of preventing that happening, by building in protective mechanisms of 'good laws and civil customs'. It was a simple step for Seyssel then to praise

---

mithridaticis liber, de bellis civilibus libri V, de bellis gallicis . . . epitome (Basel, 1554). For Celio Secondo Curione (1503–1569), see Markus Kutter, *Celio Secondo Curione. Sein Leben und Werk (1503–1569.* Basler Beiträge zur Geschichtswissenschaft No. 54. (Basel, 1955); and, for Sigmund Jelensky (c.1497–1554), the entry in Christian Gottlieb Jöcher, and Johann Christian Adelung (eds), *Allgemeines Gelehrten-Lexicon* (Leipzig, 1784–1897).

[49] Rebecca Boone, 'Claude de Seyssel's Translations of Ancient Historians', *Journal of the History of Ideas*, 61 (2000), 561–75, esp. 575.

[50] British Library, London, Harleian MS 4939.

[51] Boone, 'Claude de Seyssel's Translations', 567–70; cf. Rebecca Art Boone, *War, Domination, and the Monarchy of France: Claude Seyssel and the Language of Politics in the Renaissance* (Leiden, 2007).

[52] Appian, *Appian Alexandrin, Historien Grec, des Guerres des Romains, livres XI* (Paris: Guillaume Iullian, 1580), preface sig. Aaij.

the constitution of the French monarchy. The latter was so girded with officials ('in such large numbers ... both as leaders, and subordinates [...] and in such good and notable personages that it was truly a Roman Senate').[53] Its nobility was 'so honoured and revered of the people, and having such authority over the lower orders, and nevertheless in such awe of justice that it did not have the effrontery to take law into its own hands and irrationally mistreat its own subjects'.[54] Therefore, 'it happened that hardly any, not even those who had nothing to lose, had the effrontery to carry out something worthy of punishment at the behest and whim of a prince, because the fact that they had acted under his orders would not prevent them, sooner or later, from being punished for it'.[55] So, 'evaluating this French imperium overall, it embraces the three sorts of political governance', and it does so in 'a harmony and consonance which is the cause of the preservation and increase of this Monarchy'. We can already hear the characteristic leitmotifs of the *Grande Monarchie*, written over a decade later, making their appearance. Seyssel's dream of a monarchical republic was one that was shared by a whole generation of France's Renaissance elite. They *wanted* to believe that they were part of a strong monarchy that was no tyranny because it had laws which prevented rulers doing just as they pleased. The lessons of Appian's history were, Seyssel's preface concludes, that Rome experienced terrible problems when it was governed by more than one person. It was 'continuellement vexé & trauaillé par dissensions intestines, & par seditions ciuiles, tandis qu'il a esté regy & gouuerné par plusieurs'. It is in the context of that preface, Seyssel's contextualizing of Appian's historical account as a warning piece for what happens to a political monarchy when it is governed by more than one person that we should look again at Caron's painting.

IV

It is immediately apparent how different the composition of Caron's painting is from the other surviving triumvirate paintings. The triumvirate generals, Octavian, Marc Antony, and Lepidus are a distant, threatening, impersonal authority, tucked in the far distance under a protective baldachin,

---

[53] Ibid., sig. Aaiij ('à si grand nombre ... tant en chef, que subalterns [...] de bons & notables personages, que c'est un vray Senat Romain').

[54] Ibid., verso ('qui tant est honoré & revere du people, & à si grande auctorité sur les gens de bas estat, est neantmoins en telle crainte de la iustice, qu'il n'ha loy ne hardiesse de mesfaire, contre raison, à ses propres sujets').

[55] Ibid., sig. Aaiij ('il aduient que bien peu de gens, mesmes ayans à perdre, soient si osez de faire, par le commandement precipité d'vn Prince volontaire, chose digne de punition; par ce que le commandement ne les excuseroit pas d'estre apres, tost, ou tard, punis ...').

surrounded by security guards patrolling the vast empty spaces of Flavian's Amphitheatre, the Coliseum, itself portrayed not as it would have been in 43 BC (for it had not yet been built) but as it was in Caron's own day.[56] The archaeological ruin became a cut-away view into the entrails of the building, a glimpse into a world of assumed, *de facto* authority. Here, as elsewhere in the painting, Caron drew upon a sequence of engravings sold by the Rome shop of Antoine Lafréry for visitors to the Eternal City and marketed under an album cover as the *Speculum Romae Magnificentiae* in the 1550s.[57] Directly behind the Coliseum Caron portrays the Pantheon, with imperial lions on either side and an obelisk to the left. Elsewhere in the canvas is the Castel San'Angelo in the background on the left, the Septizonium, the Forum, the arches of Emperor Constantine and Septimus Serverus, the Campidoglio with the equestrian statue of Marcus Aurelius, Trajan's column, Cestius' pyramid and the three columns of the temple of Castor and Pollux. It is as though all Rome has been assembled into a canvas equivalent of a cabinet of rarities.[58] The images are of the consolidated weight and concentrated power of the state, distant but omnipresent.

That distance is enhanced in the picture in all sorts of ways: by the steps up to the Pantheon, and around the Coliseum, by the sequence of balustrades that run laterally across the middle distance, by the strong contrasts of light and shade to the left and right of the painting, reinforced by the skyscape, and by the monumental column to the left and the obelisk to the right that rise from the central foreground and block out an implied triptych in the painting. Between them and in the centre is an elliptical reflected marble and stone staircase, itself a direct borrowing from Book 5 of Serlio's *Architecture*, published in Lyon in 1547. That staircase orchestrates an important feature of the scenography of the painting, a division between the city on the one hand, and the world 'sub urbe' and 'ex urbe' that lies in the immediate foreground. That enables Caron to give the viewer a cut-away view into the sewers and basements beneath the streets and to reinforce the message that, from the perspective of power, what went on outside the city was as important as what went on within it. The killing of those proscribed *ex urbe* is a literal mapping

---

[56] Marie-Domitille Porcheron, 'La mort romaine représentée. Les "massacres du Triumvirat" par Antoine Caron', in *La mort, les morts et l'au-delà dans le monde romain*, ed. by François Hinard (Caen, 1987), 365–70 provides a detailed analysis of the relationship of the painting to the architecture of ancient Rome.

[57] Ehrmann, *Antoine Caron. Peintre des fêtes et des massacres*, 26 (fig. 11); see, McGowan, *The Vision of Rome*, 149–50.

[58] McGowan, *The Vision of Rome*, esp. 155–9 for Caron's painting in the context of the 'image of Rome' in the imagination of late Renaissance France.

of absolute authority. As Giorgio Agamben has shown, authority is instituted and made visible with a defensible border, the world *sub urbe* ordered through the rule of law guaranteed by absolute power in contrast to the chaotic and violent world outside the city walls. Under the proscription, the rule of law is suspended and those formerly protected by the law are rendered stateless and already dead. Their purging from the city constitutes a brutal reestablishment of state order.[59]

The painting is programmatic. Various elements of the Appian narrative are presented as taking place in an implied sequence that has to be read into the picture, beginning from the moment that the triumvirate moved their forces into Rome. They ordered Publius Titius to proclaim the new magistracy ('*nouveau magistrat*' says Seyssel's translation) of the triumvirate as '*réformateurs*' (Seyssel's rendition of the Greek 'harmostes/harmostoi', or provincial governor/s), 'chosen to reform and restore to a better state the commonweal').[60] To the left of the painting, Caron clearly depicts all this, whilst the city speedily filled with arms and military standards, disposed in the most advantageous places. At the same time, Appian emphasizes that the triumvirate arrogated powers in perpetuity to themselves, without any legal basis, and that they did so explicitly as revenge for the assassination of Julius Caesar under the guise of reform.[61] Insofar as we can speak of artistic intentions, it seems that Caron was particularly concerned to represent the attempts of governments that proclaimed themselves as 'reforming', and about '*réformateurs*' (with all the ambiguous resonance of that term in the France of the 1560s), about assassinations and revenge killing, and about blatant disregard for law and constitutional authority—even if the meanings of his painting in its reception exceeded such de facto monarchist politics.

The triumvirs had already begun the process of rounding-up and selective elimination of Roman senators and nobles, the famous 'proscription' for which they had prepared lists of the potential victims before entering the city. They ordered the heads of the victims to be used as the means for rewarding those who carried out the proscriptions. Caron uses the balustrades to depict the head-count, whilst centurions carry off decapitated bodies or bring more trophies for their rewards. There is a grim juxtaposition of headless bodies, bodiless heads and lifeless statues in the painting. To the left of the painting is a statue of Apollo, Caron drawing directly on the *Belvedere Apollo*

---

[59] See Giorgio Agamben, *Homo Sacer: Sovereign Power and Bare Life*, trans. Daniel Heller-Roazen, (Stanford, CA, 1995) esp. 15–38.
[60] Appian, *Appian Alexandrin, Historien Grec*, (Paris, 1580), fo. 332 ('éleu pour reformer & remettre en meilleur estat la chose publique').
[61] Ibid., fo. 335.

from the engraving by Antoine Lafréry (adding the hands, however, as Primaticcio had done, to the bronze copy of the statue in the gardens at Fontainebleau).[62] Above it, however, there is a headless figure down a well, about to be massacred. To the right is the statue of Emperor Commodus, painted as Hercules, with the child Telephus in his arms, looking up and beyond to another head of a decapitated victim. Again it was a copy of a Lafréry engraving, this time reversed.[63] Are we not to read into the painting something about what happens to political authority when it is headless, decapitated of its integrity and legitimacy?

In the central foreground, Caron depicts the first victim of the proscription in Appian's account, the tribune Salvius. Caron has used some artistic licence in depicting the precise circumstances, but Appian certainly mentions the centurion's grabbing him by the hair. The technicoloured assassin, richly caparisoned, is wielding a distinctive and unusual curved, single-bladed sword with a gold hilt, S-shaped quillon and decorated pommel. In his left hand he brandishes the severed head.[64] The eye is unerringly drawn towards this head and this sword. It is probably already present, albeit in a much less demonstrative fashion, to the bottom left of the 'Massacre' painting now ascribed to the school of Nicolò dell'Abate, to which we have already referred. Where did artists find the inspiration for this unusual object? Like almost all the décor in this highly staged painting, there is, no doubt, a point of reference. Designs for highly decorated swords '*à l'antique*' were part of the fashion for exquisitely fashioned antique armour among the French court aristocracy in the first half of the sixteenth century. There are surviving pattern-books for Pierre Woeriot, a swordsmith in Lyon in around 1555, who evidently served a substantial clientele.[65] Two others exist for the Mantuan armourer Filippo Orsoni, dating from the 1540s and 1550s, one in the Victoria and Albert Museum and the other in the Herzog August Bibliothek in Wolfenbüttel.[66] Orsoni and Woeriot evidently distributed

[62] Ehrmann, *Antoine Caron. Peintre des fêtes et des massacres*, 31 [fig. 9].
[63] Ibid., [fig 10].
[64] Valérie Auclair interestingly suggests that this may derive from Benvenuto Cellini's sculpture of Perseus, completed a decade or so previously in Florence, though how Caron would have known of it in this amount of detail is unclear. See Valerie Auclair, 'Une vision tragique de Rome: les "Massacres du Triumvirat" d'Antoine Caron', in Michel Cassan and Susanna Caviglia (eds), *L'événement tragique au cours des périodes moderne et contemporaine*, *Temporalités* No. 5, (Limoges, 2009), 36–7.
[65] J. F. Hayward, 'Mannerist Sword Hilt Designs', *Livrustkammeren*, 8 (1959), 79–109.
[66] Victoria and Albert Museum, London, P&D Murray codex 7A; Herzog-August Bibliothek, Wolfenbüttel, Codex Guelf 1.5.3.Aug2. We have not had the opportunity to study the Wolfenbüttel codex in relation to this painting. Our information comes from

copies of their pattern-books around selected European courts so that aristocrats could choose their exquisitely ornamented armour at their leisure. The fashion for decorated sallets (fr: 'salades') and mannerist shoulder-guards, breast-plates and shields is clearly reflected in Caron's painting.[67] Among the thirty-nine sword hilt designs in the London Orsoni codex (there are a further forty-four apparently in that of Wolfenbüttel), it is possible to identify some similarities with that depicted in the centre of Caron's picture (though precise comparison is impossible because the hilt is masked by the soldier's hand).[68] There are other similarities, too, with the other ornamental armour depicted in Caron's painting. It may be significant, too, that wealthy merchant-bankers from Brescia (like Mucio) might have acted as commissioning agents for its flourishing arms industry, second only to that of Milan, with factors acting for them in Lyon and Paris.[69] The real point, however, is that Caron was inviting his aristocratic audience into his painting. Its power was not merely that it invited them to be spectators, but actors, dressed for the part.

To the right, in the immediate foreground, there is another centurion with an identical sword, about to massacre another Roman notable. It is tempting (though Caron would have been stepping outside the 'canon' of triumvirate massacre representation in doing so) to imagine that this is Laena about to kill the most famous victim of the triumvirate massacres, Marcus Tullius Cicero, former consul, the one who (emphasized Appian) had written the famous speeches against Marc Antony, accusing him of tyranny. These were the Philippics, modelled on the speeches of Demosthenes. Appian describes his murder, taking place well outside the city, but it is possible that Caron took the foreground as being the space 'ex-urbe'. Laena then reappears in Caron's painting before the triumvirs, precisely following Appian's description: 'Marc

---

J. F. Hayward, 'Filippo Orsoni, designer, and Caremolo Modrone, armourer, of Mantua (I and II)', in *Waffen- und Kostumkunde* 24.2 (1982), 87–102 and Alexandra Jackson, 'The First Renaissance Centurion', *Apollo* 510 (2004), 42–9.

[67] Stuart W. Pyhrr, and José A. Godoym (eds), *Heroic Armour of the Italian Renaissance. Filippo Negroli and his Contemporaries* (New York, 1998).

[68] E.g. fo. 1 of the Victoria and Albert codex, in which Orsoni illustrates the sword's use as a horseman's sabre or a foot-soldier's cutlass.

[69] Silvio Leydio, 'Milan and the arms industry in the sixteenth century' in Pyrrh and Godym (eds), *Heroic Armour of the Italian Renaissance*, 25–33; also, ibid., 52–3; Pascale Brioist, Hervé Drévillon, and Pierre Serna (eds), *Croiser le fer. Violence et culture de l'épée dans la France moderne (XVIe–XVIIIe siècles)* (Paris, 2002), 59; Catherine Grodecki (ed.), *Histoire de l'art au XVIe siècle. 2, sculpture, peinture, broderie, émail et faîence, orfèvrerie, armures, 1540–1600* (Paris, 1986), 284 (No. 972), 292 (No. 997), 293 (No. 999), etc.

Antony was sitting in front of the tribunal in the forum when Laena, a long distance off, showed him the head and hand by lifting them up and shaking them. Antony was delighted beyond measure [. . .] the head and hand [. . .] were suspended for a long time from the rostra in the forum where formerly he had been accustomed to make public speeches, and more people came together to behold this spectacle than had previously come to listen to him'. If so, Caron is emphasizing a point that emerges elsewhere in the painting. It is about the potential impact of massacres upon the political elites themselves, and about eloquence, its potential for good and the circumstances of its impotence.

Caron follows Appian's account in all sorts of incidental details. As the woodcut print suggests, one has to study the picture, text in hand, to pick up all the allusions. To the right is the house of the recently elevated senator Statius, a Samnite (a *nouveau riche* in Roman parlance). Realizing that he was one of the proscribed, Statius rapidly emptied his house of its belongings, ordering his slaves to give it all away before closing the doors and setting fire to it, and himself, within. To the foreground right or left are the widows, led by Hortensia. To the normally politically powerless Appian ascribes at the end of his account of the massacre, the politically most charged petition against the triumvirs. 'You have already deprived us of our father, our sons, our husbands, and our brothers, whom you accused of having wronged you; if you take away our property also, you reduce us to a condition unbecoming our birth, our manners, our sex. If we have done you wrong, as you say our husbands have, proscribe us as you do them. But if we women have not voted any of you public enemies, have not torn down your houses, destroyed your army, or led any one against you; if we have not hindered you in obtaining offices and honours, why do we share the penalty when we did not share the guilt?' Elsewhere, to the right of the picture is Salassus, whom we are told was betrayed by his wife. He led the centurions onto the rooftops, from where he jumped to his death. From the earliest Appian French translation, the glosses left the reader in no doubt how to read the text: 'Le loyer des souldars cruel & tyrannique'; 'Cruel accord'; 'Lexcuse de leur cruaulté'; 'Grande cruauté soubz espece de pitié'; 'merueilleuse pitié & cruaulté', etc.[70] And, at every point, Caron reinforces the message. The triumvirs are pictured seated in the Coliseum, the amphitheatre for gruesome gladiatorial combats and animal spectacles. The triumphal arches to left and right recall Rome's bloody victories, that on the left being surmounted by a grossly distorted (in size) statue of a man accompanied by a horse, perhaps the mythic

---

[70] Appian, *Appian Alexandrin, historien grec, Des Guerres des Rommains, Livres XI* (Lyon, 1544), 472–7.

Greek giant Diomedes with one of the Mares of Thrace, both reputed for their ferocity. The foreground statues have been chosen for a purpose too. It is not Hercules, but the Emperor Marcus Aurelius Commodus represented as Hercules that he has quite deliberately chosen to place to the right, just below that of his father, Marcus Aurelius, in the distance. Commodus' sinister reputation for brutality stained the Augustan Age (it was of his reign that Dio Cassius memorably said that it marked the descent of Rome 'from a reign of gold to one of dust and iron'). Hercules, of course, was the mythic figure who stole and slaughtered the Mares of Thrace—he is at the same eye-level with one of them, across the left-hand side of the picture. Apollo, to the left, is no figure of calm contemplation either. He has a quiverful of arrows strapped across his back and a bow flexed in his left hand, a reminder of the god who would lead his sister Artemis to slaughter the fourteen children of Niobe.[71] There is massacre, violence and cruelty, in short, everywhere in this painting.

By emphasizing the closeness with which Caron follows Appian's narrative, we should not, however, ignore the discontinuities. Somewhat surprisingly, Caron elides all the Appian references to the 'fearful portents and prodigies' which had preceded the events. Some Mannerist painters would have gone to town on the 'dogs howling continuously like wolves' the 'wolves darting through the forum' the 'new-born infant' which spoke, the 'sweat issuing from statues' which 'even sweated blood', the 'fearful signs observed around the sun' or the 'showers of stones and continuous lightning'. These elements of the narrative of that period, albeit based on other sources, left their impression on Caron's contemporary, Michel de Nostredame.[72] One of the most gruesome scenes to impress itself on the surrealist imagination of Michel Leiris was that of the beautifully dressed soldier in the foreground calmly disembowelling a corpse beneath the impassive gaze of Apollo. Appian makes no mention of disembowelling. By contrast, Appian emphasizes the social upheaval which accompanied the triumvirate massacres. 'And, over there, illustrious grandees were to be seen miserably seeking flight in disguise ... both because of their dread of the soldiers but also their trepidation before the womenfolk, children and other servants in their household, whom they knew to hate them. Furthermore, they were in fear and trembling from their slaves and freedmen, and from those who owed them money, and their neighbours who coveted their lands ... a sudden and cruel turn-around of

---

[71] All these important points are made in a valuable contribution by Auclair, 'Une vision tragique de Rome, 39–40.
[72] Denis Crouzet, *Nostradamus. Une médecine des âmes à la Renaissance* (Paris, 2011), 25–6.

all sorts of people'.⁷³ There is only one individual in Caron's tableau whom one might suppose from his tunic was low-born, dragging a semi-naked corpse behind him. That said, Caron effectively conveys the intermingling of private and public space which is an essential feature of Appian's narrative, and thereby the sense of an event that transcended social boundaries.

V

Our interpretation of the contemporary 'power' of Caron's painting has to depend upon our reading of its historical context. Every commentator, without exception, has said that it is about the so-called 'Triumvirate' in France in the spring of 1561. This refers to the conclusion of a formal pact between François Duke of Guise and his hitherto great rival at court, that hardened veteran in the arts of political survival, the Constable Anne de Montmorency, and involving a third figure, the elderly marshal and politically shrewd governor of the Lyonnais, Jacques d'Albon, sieur de St-André. The story of this pact is one of those pieces of French ancien-régime political history that survive because it helps to make sense of the often murky and confusing narrative of events rather than because it has much historical evidence to support it. Here is not the place to undertake the considerable work that still needs to be done to understand what was going on in the early months of the regency government of Catherine de Medici. Briefly, however, its authority was actively disputed by Antoine de Bourbon, the senior prince of the blood. His younger brother, Louis de Condé, had been narrowly reprieved from execution by Francis II's death in December 1560. He was newly released from incarceration, having been condemned on a charge of treason by duly convened tribunal. Actively on the agenda around the council table of the regency was how to handle the issues raised by the Estates-General of Orléans, convened in December and prorogued at the end of January. These included the spaghetti of toxic, unassigned, royal debt which threatened the stability of the monarchy, and a judicial repression of Protestant heresy that had manifestly failed to deliver the unity that it promised. The new regency government, with considerable hesitation, began to unwind the mechanisms for judicial repression, beginning with the release of prisoners awaiting trial at

---

⁷³ Appian, *Appian Alexandrin, historien grec,* (Paris, 1580), 219–20 ('Et d'autre costé lon voyoit gens illustres & grans personages fuyr miserablement en habits dissimulez ... tant pour la crainte qu'ils auoient des soldats, que de leurs femmes, enfans, & autres domestiques de leurs maisons, desquels se doutoient estre hayz. Ausurplus, en y auoit qui estoient en grande crainte de leurs esclaues & Libertins, de leurs debteurs, ou de ceux, qui auoient des terres à eux prochaines, dont ils estoient conuoiteux ... vne soudaine & cruelle mutation de toutes sortes de gens').

the end of January 1561.[74] There was something of a consensus for this measure, a continuation of what had begun in the previous year and reign. Equally, there was a wide measure of agreement for holding a national assembly of the church to resolve religious differences, a proposal that had received support from across the orders at the Estates-General, even though some people saw that simply as a bargaining counter in the seemingly endless quadrille between Rome, Madrid, and Vienna over the reconvening of the Council of Trent.[75]

This consensus began to break down in the spring of 1561. Instructions were issued to local seneschals and provosts after the court returned to Fontainebleau from Orléans in order to reconvene their assemblies and elect new delegates with sufficient mandate to resolve these questions and reconvene the Estates-General at Melun on 1 May 1561.[76] Protestants seized the opportunity afforded by these meetings to impose a common platform, a 'syndicate' upon delegates. Two copies of this 'manifesto' survive in manuscript.[77] They indicate very clearly that local Protestant-inclined deputies were invited to mask the fact that there was a concerted Protestant agenda by changing the order of the clauses and modifying the language in which they were expressed.[78] Beneath these superficial changes in the wording lay a determined consortium of pressure to wrench authority away from the regency government altogether. The monarchy would no longer be permitted to tax or to undertake offensive wars without the consent of the Estates-General. The accounts of the previous reign would be strictly investigated and excessive gifts and pensions would be retrospectively annulled. The *tailles*

---

[74] *Lettre du Roy, par laquelle est mandé que tous ceulx qui seront détenu prisonniers pour le faict de la religions soyent mis hors des prisons, car tel est le bon vouloir dudict sieur* (Orléans, 1561). Letters patent of 28 January 1561 (Orléans).

[75] Alain Tallon, *La France et le concile de Trente (1518–1563)* (Rome, 1997), 286 et seq.

[76] *Lettres missives dv Roy povr rassembler de nouueau certains personnages des trois Estatz generaulx en la ville de Paris. Plus les defences à toutes personnes de ne communiquer par escript n'autrement aucune chose des Estatz tenuz en la ville d'Orléans* (Paris). Letters patent of 14 February 1561 (Fontainebleau) [BN F 46821(8)] ; cf. Alexandre Tuetey, *Registres des délibérations du bureau de la ville de Paris, T.5 (1558–1567)* (Paris, 1892), 84 [No. 130].

[77] BnF, MS Français 20153, 71–8; BnF, MS Français 15881, fos 376–8.

[78] Ibid., fo. 376v : 'Est à noter que ces mémoires doivent estre amplifiez par raisons adjoustées ou autres articles d'abbondant, tels que chascun verra estre bon. Fault diversifier le langaige, changer l'ordre, quelquefoys en obmettre quelques-uns des non nécessaires, ou en adjouster, mesmes, où il y a certaine somme, jour ou temps spécifié, en prendre un autre approchant de là'. Cf. Noel Valois, 'Les états de Pontoise', *Revue de l'Histoire de l'Eglise de France*, 31 (1943), 239.

would be increased and the fiscal burden transferred by confiscating the wealth of religious confraternities, melting down the metal in church-bells, realizing the material value of reliquary collections, and confiscating the annates (the amount payable to Rome for the transfer of benefices) on those worth in excess of 1,000 *livres* a year. Whilst awaiting the resolutions of a national council, open to all parties and presided over by the king, there would be no prosecutions on the grounds of religious worship, the latter being the only part of the common platform that was formally agreed at the Protestant national synod of Poitiers held on 10 March 1561.[79]

In Paris, the third estate and nobility held their election meetings on the following day, Tuesday 11 March, and things did not go well. The barrack-room lawyers in attendance at the third estate argued that, since their letters of convocation had not been issued specifically to the *prévôt des marchands* they did not have to respond directly to their contents. Further, since the previous Estates-General at Orléans had been summoned by the now-deceased Francis II, it could not be resummoned into existence.[80] The nobility took up the same line of argument and pushed it several stages further, saying that since the king was a minor they could not contract any new tax subvention with him until the government of the regency was decided. They proposed to elect Antoine, King of Navarre to that post and, if he refused their nomination, to turn to his younger brother Condé, providing them with a new, purely elected royal council to which they would nominate members. It was not the Protestant programme, but it was opening the door to its adoption by another route and (from Catherine de Medici's point of view) it was a most dangerous development.[81] She responded by unilaterally annulling all the preliminary election meetings that had so far taken place and issuing new letters-patent for a new assembly, this time convoked to Melun on 1 August.[82] Rightly suspecting Antoine de Bourbon and his brother of their complicity, she confronted Navarre in her chamber at Fontainebleau

---

[79] Ibid., 242; Jean Aymon, *Tous les synodes nationaux des églises réformées de France*, 2 vols (The Hague, 1710), I, 13.

[80] *Registres des deliberations*, p. 85 [No. 132]; 'Journal de Pierre Bruslart' in *Mémoires de Condé, servant d'éclaicissement Et de Preuves à l'Histoire de M. de Thou,*. 6 vols (London and Paris, 1733), II, 25.

[81] She expressed her outrage in a letter of that same day to Jean de Brosse, later duc d'Etampes, the governor of Brittany (Hector de La Ferrière, and [Comte] Gustave Baguenault de Puchesse, (eds), *Lettres de Catherine de Médicis*, 9 vols, Collection de documents inédits sur l'histoire de France (Paris, 1880–1905), I, 173–4.

[82] *Lettres patentes dv Roy nostre Syre, à M. le Preuost de Paris pour faire nouuelle conuocation & assemblée des trois Estatz en ceste ville de Paris, au xxv. iour du moi de May, [1561]* (Paris, 1561).

in a series of tense meetings ('estant les uns et les aultres en la plus extresme contention du monde') over several days before a formal settlement was signed and sealed through the good offices of the Chancellor and the duchess of Montpensier. Navarre would be *lieutenant-général* of the kingdom, exercising the authority that the duke of Guise had formerly enjoyed in the previous reign. The duke of Guise would not, however, be asked to leave the court. Catherine would retain the 'principalle authorité', by which she meant that she retained the privy seal and, with it, the power to appoint to all the offices and benefices of the realm, to hear and respond to all despatches, and to oversee the financial affairs of the kingdom.[83] This was the agreement that was widely publicized in the succession of letters-patent streaming out of Fontainebleau just before Easter 1561 to rein in a political process that was in danger of fast unravelling.

Lent and Eastertide, however, was the season of high tension in the religious calendar. The news reaching Fontainebleau from various parts of the kingdom was of unauthorized assemblies, preaching, and provocative public demonstrations of the 'new religion'. All this provides the background to the so-called 'triumvirate', variously dated to 20 March 1561, or Easter Sunday 6 April 1561. All that we know from contemporary sources is from the seasoned court-watchers at Fontainebleau, the ambassadors.[84] Their stock-in-trade was rumour, often based on the interpretation of gesture alone: the nod of the head, the smile or the frown, the choreographed reality of the court's consummate actors. What was noticed was a more pronounced amity between the two old ducal rivals, Guise and Montmorency, culminating, on Easter Sunday, in a staged withdrawal from a court sermon, pronounced by Jean de Monluc, bishop of Valence, renowned for his unconventional indulgence towards religious pluralism and an individual whom the nuncio and Spanish ambassadors had already wanted to exclude from court altogether. It was followed, according to the best-informed Protestant source of the period, Pierre de La Place, by an evening meal, hosted by the Constable Anne de

---

[83] *Lettres de Catherine de Médicis*, I, 176–8 (Catherine de Medici to L'Aubespine [bishop of Limoges], Fontainebleau, 27 March 1561), 180 (to Jean de Brosse, 29 March 1561).

[84] These include the reports of the papal nuncio Sebastiano Gualterio (J. Lestocquoy, (ed.), *Correspondance des nonces en France. Lenzi et Gualterio, légation du cardinal Tribultio (1557–1561)*, Acta Nuntiaturae Gallicae 14 (Rome and Paris, 1977), esp. 334; Fiaschi and Alvarotti, agents of the duke of Ferrara (their despatches of 20; 24 March and 8; 18 April 1561 are analysed in Lucien Romier, *Catholiques et huguenots à la cour de Charles IX* (Paris, 1924), 103–5); for those of Thomas Perrenot de Chantonnay, Philip II's ambassador to the French court, see *Negociaciones con Francia*, 9 vols (Madrid, 1950–54), II, 85 et seq; those of the Venetian and English ambassadors have not been analysed here.

Montmorency, where the duke of Guise and the sieur de St-André were present (there were no doubt others round the table too).[85] What they talked about we can only surmise, although La Place provides some interesting incidental details. On the basis of what had happened in the previous month, there was certainly plenty to discuss and react to; above all, how best to respond to what seemed to be the looming challenge of a Bourbon ascendancy at court. Our sources refer to a pact, but only in the way that they might do so when describing contemporary diplomatic alignments—nothing to match what had just been formally concluded (i.e. signed with signet rings and publicly proclaimed) the week before between the Regent and Antoine de Bourbon.[86] The only contemporary reference to this being the formation of a 'triumvirate' was a Protestant pamphlet, now lost, of which we only know the title: *Sommaire des choses premièrement accordé [. . .] pour la conspiration d'un triumvirat*. This was clever Protestant propaganda, playing on the Constable's *penchant* for Roman history and conveniently occluding the Protestants' *syndicat* and associated machinations of March 1561 under the cover of a counter-conspiracy. At the end of October that same year, when there was a more serious plot, this time to spirit away the king's younger brother to Lorraine or Savoy (a plot with the hands of the dukes of Savoy, Lorraine and, behind them, Madrid, all over it), the propaganda acquired greater credibility. That was the moment when the massacre canvases were presented to court. How electrifying it must have been for Condé, Navarre, Coligny, d'Andelot and the other scions of the Protestant high nobility to have a picture on the walls of their court chambers, the walls that echoed to the whispers (or so it must have seemed to them) of conjuration. It was in November 1561 (and not in April) that the *Histoire ecclésiastique* tells us: 'This was the first beginning of what was *thenceforth* called the Triumvirate'.[87] These paintings, along with the run-away success of the Appian editions of 1559–60, did not 'commemorate' the formation of a triumvirate in April 1561. Rather, they helped to create the myth of its having occurred. It is that myth which became a reality in nineteenth-century liberal

---

[85] Pierre de La Place, *Commentaires de l'estat de la religion et république* ed. by J.-A.-C. Buchon, *Choix de chroniques et mémoires sur l'histoire de France* (Paris, 1836–8), 122.

[86] The Spanish ambassador wrote of a 'liga' in his despatch to Philip II of 1 May 1561 (Archives Nationales, Paris, K 1494, no. 83, *Negociaciones con Francia*, vol II, No. 293; the Italian nuncio wrote of 'cattolici forse' (Lestocquoy, *Correspondance des nonces en France*, 334). We are grateful to Eric Durot for his views on the interpretation of these two references.

[87] *Histoire ecclésiastique*, I, 743 ('Ce fut le premier commencement de ce qu'on appella *depuis* le Triumvirat').

historiography. But, if Caron's painting is to be dated to 1566, this mythic pact cannot be what it is about. There is every indication that Antoine Caron was a Catholic royalist, brought up in the conservative environments of Beauvais. What possible motive would he have had to depict something which had not happened, save in the fevered imagination of fearful Protestants, five years previously, when so much had happened so tumultuously since 1561 to change the political landscape?

In reality, we are asking the wrong question. Caron did not paint 'commemoratively'. His work is not 'about' an event as such. Rather it is a sibylline provocation, a site for religious and political reinscription that could accommodate opposing ideological positions, a fantasy space for heterogeneous perceptions, values, and versions of the recent past. The contradictory currents in the narration of the Wars of Religion, the currents that feed the sibylline message, are evident in the French élite's response to the sectarian violence of the early civil wars. Some Protestant nobles and aristocrats doubtless wanted them to be remembered as 'massacres', events that had perhaps been encouraged from on high. But in the subsequent pacifications, that was not the language that the French monarchy fostered. It preferred to cast a cloud of forgetting over the 'emotions' and 'troubles' of the recent past as part of royal pacification that celebrated (albeit with a degree of contrivance) justice, unity, and the fruits of peace. For the majority of France's court-based élite, however, 'religious riot', still less 'massacre' were not part of their vocabulary. Throughout 1561, for example, Catherine de Medici repeatedly refers in her letters to 'brigues', 'divers alarmes', 'émotions', 'insolences' and 'sédition'—the familiar language of revolt. She never uses the word 'massacre'. Indeed, the only time she *ever* referred to the massacre of St Bartholomew in her letters was seven years later, under the extreme provocation of difficult negotiations with Protestant hard-liners.[88] In this respect, her letters are entirely of a piece with others from the leading figures at the French court. They do not refer to 'massacre' in the terms that we as historians do today. Perhaps that is understandable. They could say little that might not in some way implicate them in what had happened, or possibly further exacerbate a political situation that was already potentially out of control. But did that mean that they were looking the other way? Caron's picture is a reminder that they were not. Augustin Lemousse (and he has now to be regarded as the primary candidate as the painting's patron) could take away from it the message that he wanted to hear: whether it was the disgusting reality of massacre; or what happened to the Pax Augustana when enlightened rule failed; or the need/dangers of fundamental reform (religious, or

---

[88] *Lettres de Catherine de Médicis*, VI, 245.

political); or what happened when the desire for vengeance following an assassination entered the body politic; or the perils of faction when monarchy faltered; or the dangers of tyranny. All these were, of course, the active ingredients of the politics of the moment in the year 1566.

The power of Caron's 'Massacres' for us as historians is the way in which it documents how sectarian violence troubled the political culture of Renaissance France. It was in the nature of that culture that it conceptualized things in terms of an older history which encapsulated the lessons of the past. It is a reminder that the elites did not need *necessarily* to think in terms of the rites of violence in order to explain sectarian hatred and civil war. Caron's painting is, after all, massacres with the religion almost completely excluded, in which there are no contrasts between 'cold' and 'hot' violence, or between the violence towards people as opposed to sacral objects. Yet in every way, and by implication, its power is to express a collective anxiety with all the dynamic power of an imagined reality, that 'imaginaire' which Denis Crouzet sees expressed in the 'religious riots' of Natalie Davis's wonderful article.[89]

The lessons of the past were full of terrible portents for the future, and not just of Saint Bartholomew. For Michel Leiris it was the shadow of 1793 and the triumvirate of Robespierre, Couthon, and Saint-Just. For us, it is the shadow of Nazi extermination. For the Marquis de Jaucourt it was the memory of the First World War. Leiris tells the story (which can only have come directly from the marquis de Jaucourt himself), that on Armistice Day, 11 November 1918 the painting came crashing off the wall. All good history, like this remarkable painting, has the power to evoke the past in the present.

Appendix I

'Massacre of the Triumvirate'
Part 1

The following is a list of reproductions of the 'Massacre of the Triumvirate', preceded by the summary description often given by Jean Ehrmann (those in public galleries are generally published in several other places as well and

---

[89] Denis Crouzet, *Dieu en ses royaumes. Une histoire des guerres de religion* (Seyssel, 2008), where the 'imaginaire' ('ce concept flou, fluide, mou, incernable mais recouvrant') is presented as a group dynamic ('la matrice des choix individuels') which gives historicity and significance to a particular set of events, over and beyond the 'facticité continuiste' that we might want to subscribe to them.

are well-known):[90]

1) 'ancien collection Bordier' (a painting which passed through Henri Bordier's relative Ernest Stroehlin in Geneva, sold in Paris in 1951, subsequently located in a private collection in Aix-en-Provence): Ehrmann (1972), 69 (figure 7) [48 × 77 cm].
2) 'ancien collection Vigny' (a painting which Ehrmann notes was on sale in Paris in 1951 and passed to a private collector at Aix-en-Provence: Ehrmann (1955), 50; Ehrmann, *Antoine Caron*, figure 4 [48 × 77 cm].
3) 'ancienne collection Loutsche' (a painting belonging to a private collection in Luxembourg): Ehrmann (1986), figure 6 [55 × 88 cm].
4) 'ancien collection Bardi' (a painting purchased by M. Bardi in Paris, formerly in the Galeria La Palma and now in Sao Paolo): Ehrmann (1955), planche VI; Ehrmann (1986), figure 247 [93 × 133 cm].
5) 'ancien collection Ponton-d'Amécourt' (later the Lipschitz collection, Boulogne-sur-Seine): Ehrmann (1972), figure 9; Ehrmann (1986), figure 8 [85 × 142 cm].
6) 'ancien collection Munier' (sold at Versailles and passed into the collection of M. Thesmar in Corsica): Ehrmann (1986), figure 248 [81 × 144 cm].
7) 'collection A. Cruz Eyzaguierre' (purchased in London around 1918 and moved to Santiago de Chili): Ehrmann (1986), figure 249 [91 × 146 cm].
8) 'Musée d'art, Lausanne': Ehrmann (1945) Plate 47A; Ehrmann, (1986), figure 7 [80 × 150 cm].
9) 'collection particulière, Berlin': Ehrmann (1986), figure 5 [86 × 150 cm].
10) 'collection Mazet' (sold on to other hands on 19 December 1852): Ehrmann, (1945), figure 47B [96 × 162 cm].
11) 'galerie Stein, Paris': Ehrmann, (1986), figure 250 [81 × 144 cm].
12) 'musée départemental de l'Oise, Beauvais' (from the national collection): Ehrmann (1945), plate 49 [177 × 142 cm].
13) 'collection Massey, Tarbes' (sold in Paris in 1974, having been in a private collection in the UK, and acquired by the Massey foundation in 1990): Ehrmann (1986) figure 251 [128 × 208 cm].
14) 'musée départemental de l'Oise, Beauvais' (on deposit from the église de Belle-Eglise). Cliché available from the Monuments historiques, No. 54 P-1185 [135 × 216 cm].

[90] A further oil painting has been brought to our attention by Denis Crouzet, and which was evidently not known to Ehrmann. It appeared for sale in Paris in the 1990s and is noted in the sale catalogue as: '70 × 88cms. Panneau de chêne, une planche, non parqueté'.

15) 'Caron – Louvre' Ehrmann, passim [116 × 195 cm].

Part 2

The following are the paintings of which Ehrmann also has evidence, but of which no reproduction or photographic evidence is apparently available:

16) 'commerce d'art, Rome' (apparently a fragment of the right-hand portion of No. 7, above): Ehrmann (1955); Ehrmann (1986), 221 [20 × 30 cm].
17) 'collection particulière, région Parisienne': Ehrmann (1986), 221 [48 × 76 cm].
18) 'collection Bourgeois, Versailles': Ehrmann (1986), 221 [68×99 cm].
19) 'ancien collection Oustikkel, Amsterdam': Ehrmann (1955), 49 reports that it was sold in Paris in 1954 [93 × 120 cm].
20) 'collection Maggi, Madrid': Ehrmann (1986), 221 [95 × 130 cm].
21) 'collection W. Graham, ancien dépôt chez M. Harris à Londres': Ehrmann (1945), 196 Ehrmann (1955), 49; Ehrmann (1986), 22 [86 × 143 cm].
22) 'collection particulière, Versailles': Ehrmann (1986), 221 [82.5 × 115 cm].
23) 'F-G. Pariset': Ehrmann (1986), 221 [66 × 82 cm].

Bibliography

Jean Ehrmann, 'Massacre and Persecution Pictures in Sixteenth-Century France', *The Journal of the Warburg and Courtauld Institute*, 8 (1945), 195–9

Jean Ehrmann, *Antoine Caron peintre à la Cour des Valois, 1521–1599* (Geneva and Lille, 1955), 48–9

Jean Ehrmann, 'Tableaux de massacres au XVIe siècle', *Bulletin de la société d'histoire du protestantisme français*, 118 (1972), 445–555

Jean Ehrmann, 'Artistes franco-flamands de l'Ecole de Fontainebleau (Simon de Myle)', *Bulletin de la société de l'histoire de l'art français*, (1972), 63–77

Jean Ehrmann, 'Hans Vredeman de Vries (Leeuwarden 1527–Anvers 1606)', *Gazette des Beaux-Arts*, 121 (1979)

Jean Ehrmann, *Antoine Caron. Peintre des fêtes et des massacres* (Paris, 1986).

Appendix II

French editions of Appian of Alexandria's 'Des Guerres des Rommains' (1544–1601).[91]

---

[91] Andrew Pettegree, Malcolm Walsby, and Alexander Wilkinson, *French Vernacular Books. Books published in the French Language before 1601 (Livres vernaculaires français avant 1601)* 2 vols (Leiden, 2007), I, 45–6.

1. Lyon (Antonin Constantin, 1544)
2. Paris (Galliot du Pré, 1552)
3. Paris (Guillaume Cavellat, 1552)
4. Paris (Jean Ruelle, 1552)
5. Paris (René Avril chez Etienne Groulleau, 1552)
6. Paris (René Avril et Galliot du Pré, 1554)
7. Lyon (Jean de Tournes, 1557)
8. Lyon (Jean de Tournes, 1557)
9. Paris [=Orléans] (Benoît Prévost and Eloi Gibier, 1559)
10. Paris (Jean Macé, 1559)
11. Paris (Raulin La Motte pour Etienne Groulleau, 1559)
12. Paris (Raulin La Motte pour Etienne Groulleau, 1559)
13. Paris (Raulin La Motte pour Jean Ruelle, 1559)
14. Paris (Benoît Prévost, 1560)
15. Paris (Benoît Prévost pour Guillaume Cavellat, 1560)
16. Paris (Benoît Prévost pour Vincent Sertenas, 1560)
17. Paris (Jean Caveiller, 1560)
18. Paris (Gabriel Buon, 1560)
19. Paris (Raulin La Motte pour Guillaume Julian, 1560)
20. Paris (Jean Caveiller, 1560)
21. Paris (Vincent Sartenas, 1560)
22. Paris (Pierre du Pré, 1560)
23. Paris (Fleury Prévost, 1569)
24. Paris (Gabriel Buon, 1570)
25. Paris (Olivier de Harsy, 1570)
26. Paris (Olivier de Harsy chez Michel Gadouleau, 1570)
27. Paris (Olivier de Harsy pour Claude Micard, 1570)
28. Paris (Olivier de Harsy chez Jean Ruelle, 1573)
29. Paris (Pierre Le Voirier chez Gabriel Buon, 1573)
30. Paris (Pierre Le Voirier pour Claude Gaultier, 1573)
31. Paris (Pierre Le Voirier pour Nicolas Bonfans, 1573)
32. Paris (Guillaume Auvray, 1580)
33. Paris (Lucas Breyer, 1580)
34. Paris (Michel Julian, 1580)
35. Paris (Fleury Prévost pour Abel L'Angelier et Pierre du Pré, 1580)
36. Paris (Pierre Le Voirier chez Gilles Beys, 1580)
37. Paris (Pierre Le Voirier chez Guillaume Julian, 1580)
38. Paris (Pierre Le Voirier chez Nicolas Chesneau, 1580)
39. Paris (Pierre Le Voirier chez Thomas Périer, 1580)

Afterword

Graeme Murdock and Andrew Spicer

This short conclusion will reflect on the essays in this volume and on the relationship between religion and violence in sixteenth-century France. Our point of departure is the changing historiographical context for the study of religious violence. When Natalie Zemon Davis first analysed 'the rites of violence' in the pages of *Past and Present* in 1973, she wrote of how George Rudé, Eric Hobsbawm, Charles Tilly, and E. P. Thompson among others had identified a moral economy in the collective violence of riotous crowds. Crowds were prompted by 'political and moral traditions which legitimise and even prescribe their violence'. Crowd violence was cruel, but not random, in attacking defined targets with a 'repertory of traditional punishments and forms of destruction'.[1] Davis pointed out that existing analysis of pre-industrial crowd violence had primarily involved studies of tax riots, peasant revolts, bread riots, and craft violence. Meanwhile 'the broad spectrum of religious riot' had yet to receive similar attention. In turning her focus onto the religious riots of sixteenth-century France, Davis commented that social historians found the 'seeming irrationality' of religious riots 'puzzling'. Why had so many French women and men become 'so excited about the Eucharist or saints' relics? It is hard to decipher the social meaning of such an event.' Davis was dissatisfied with those who insisted 'upon a strong linkage between religious conflict and economic issues', and with those who understood the social causes behind religious disturbances only in terms of conflict between the poor and the wealthy or between wage-earners and manufacturers. Davis wondered whether economic tensions provided the only social meanings

---

[1] Natalie Zemon Davis, 'The Rites of Violence: Religious Riot in Sixteenth-Century France', *Past and Present* 59 (1973), 53; Eric Hobsbawm, *Primitive Rebels. Studies in Archaic Forms of Social Movements in the 19th and 20th Centuries* (Manchester, 1959); George Rudé, *The Crowd in History. A Study of Popular Disturbance in France and England, 1730–1848* (New York, 1964); Charles Tilly and James Rule, *Measuring Political Upheaval* (Princeton, NJ, 1965); E. P. Thompson, 'The Moral Economy of the English Crowd in the Eighteenth Century', *Past and Present* 50 (1971), 76–113.

inherent in religious riots, and what to make of 'popular religious violence where class conflict of this type is not present?'[2] Davis therefore laid down a challenge to social historians to think more carefully about the role of religion as a pattern of meanings and performances in the lives of ordinary people.

Since the publication of 'The Rites of Violence', historians of early modern France have explored the character of different forms of violence. Not all of these examinations have reacted to Davis's clarion call to heed the influence of religion in everyday life, but they should nonetheless be considered as they have helped to develop a better understanding of early modern violence as well as to inform more recent studies of religious violence.[3] One aspect of this research has questioned the grand narrative of Norbert Elias's 'civilizing process' and the evidence for a decline in violence in the early modern period. The transformation of the duel might be regarded as indicative of this process as it changed from being a judicial and public encounter to a private means of resolving disputes which was subject to increasing anti-duelling legislation. In recent studies, however, duelling has been seen together with feuding and revenge killings as matters of honour with their own particular codes and royal recognition that legitimized this particular form of private violence and distinguished it from that of the unruly mob. The noble caste through their martial education and upbringing remained attuned to the demands of warfare. But this is a picture that was further complicated by the religious developments of the sixteenth century that established, and through royal edicts legitimized, religious difference and co-existence.[4] Affronts to family honour could spark outbreaks of religious violence, such as the Massacre of Vassy; nobles were prepared to deploy their military training and experience in the defence of not only their own families, households, and estates, but their co-religionists in general against what they regarded as an affront to their beliefs.[5]

---

[2] Davis, 'The Rites of Violence', 54.

[3] For an overview, see Julius R. Ruff, *Violence in Early Modern Europe, 1500–1800* (Cambridge, 2001).

[4] Francois Billaçois. *The Duel: Its Rise and Fall in Early Modern France* (New Haven, CT, 1990); Stuart Carroll, *Blood and Violence in Early Modern France* (Oxford, 2006); Brian Sandberg, *Warrior Pursuits. Noble Culture and Civil Conflicts in Early Modern France* (Baltimore, 2010).

[5] Stuart Carroll, *Martyrs and Murderers. The Guise Family and the Making of Europe* (Oxford, 2009), 12–19; Yves Krumenacker, 'Les nobles, protecteurs du peuple protestant en France (1598–1685)', in Ariane Boltanski and Franck Mercier (eds), *Le salut par les armes. Noblesse et défense de l'orthodoxie XIIIe–XVIIe siècle* (Rennes, 2011), 195–208.

The ritualized character of religious violence also owed something to the traditions of the lords of misrule and *charivari*, which Davis herself wrote about prior to the publication of 'The Rites of Violence'. The reversal of social norms amidst a carnival atmosphere poked fun at and embarrassed wrongdoers; it particularly claimed jurisdiction over those of marriageable age as well as those who transgressed the expected conventions of marriage, such as husbands who were dominated by their wives.[6] Not all *charivari* resulted in violence, furthermore the actions of its youthful perpetrators did not distinguish nor demonstrate any particular respect for either Catholic or Protestant adherents. Nonetheless there were instances where the distinction between religious violence and *charivari* was harder to recognize. The actions of youthful *charivari*, which were intended to right perceived wrongs in their own local community, might be regarded as being only one step away from the broader motivations of crowd violence which in the later sixteenth and seventeenth centuries could also have a religious dimension.[7] To an extent, this research has suggested that ritual assault was threatened rather than actually carried out, more often being verbal rather than physical violence. But while other factors were often present, underlying confessional tensions could also determine whether or not violence was perpetrated and in what form.

Although religious violence shared many cultural characteristics with other contemporary forms of violence, there was also something more shocking and active about it. For as Davis argued, although conflict was pervasive in early modern society, the violent forms that it could take could vary; 'religious violence is intense because it connects intimately with the fundamental values and self-definition of a community'.[8] Conscious of this wider context of developing ideas about different forms of early modern violence, the essays in this volume attempt to deepen our understanding of how murder was culturally conditioned within French society during the civil wars of the sixteenth century. In reviewing the inter-related themes that have emerged through the course of this volume, we will consider the objectives and character of violent crowds and the forms of violence that they employed. We will discuss how popular religious violence was related to elite political culture, to

---

[6] Natalie Zemon Davis, 'The Reasons of Misrule: Youth Groups and Charivari in Sixteenth-Century France', *Past and Present* 50 (1971), 41–75.

[7] John Cashmere, 'The Social Uses of Violence in Ritual: Charivari or Religious Persecution?', *European History Quarterly*, 21 (1991), 291–319; William Beik, 'The Violence of the French Crowd from Charivari to Revolution', *Past and Present* 197 (2007), 75–110.

[8] Davis, 'The Rites of Violence', 90.

the production of printed texts and images, and to the content of sermons. We will consider the frequency, location, and scale of popular religious riots, and also engage with the problem of explaining patterns of religious co-existence amid the violence of early modern France.

The essays in this volume confirm the extent to which we continue to draw on the insights provided by Natalie Zemon Davis to understand the religious riots that took place in French towns during the 1560s and 1570s. The violence perpetrated by crowds of Christians was brutal but not mindless. Many riots and massacres were communal contests over religious truth in which traditional Christian values of neighbourliness and charity were turned upside down. Crowds acted to cleanse their communities of dangerous pollution by viciously murdering those who were identified as heretics. Barbara Diefendorf stresses in her essay the powerful logic of communal restoration that inspired many rioters. She argues that Catholic crowds responded to the trauma of witnessing Reformed rituals of iconoclastic destruction of sacred objects. Catholics reacted by performing their own violent rites of repair, aiming to restore an imagined sacred community. Crowds also filled the vacuum left by inaction on the part of the legal authorities to combat the spread of heresy. As Sara Beam highlights here, popular violent rituals mimicked official use of torture to reveal truth and cleanse communities of criminals. However, popular violence failed to restore order to France, and indeed played a crucial role in exacerbating political as well as religious tensions across the kingdom.

Many murderers appear to have thought that their actions were entirely justified and took satisfaction, even pleasure, from what they had done. Rioting at times seems to have been almost recreational, with something of the carnival in rites of destruction and renewal. At Vire in 1562 Catholics performed some sort of dance as they stamped on the corpses of their victims before extracting their guts and inviting buyers for 'Huguenot tripe'.[9] At Pamiers in 1566 a Catholic youth society marched at Pentecost behind relics and a silver statue of Saint Antonin. Dancing then began to the beating of drums. When the crowd reached the Protestant district of the town the chant of 'kill, kill' went up, and three days of communal violence followed. One of the Catholic dancers proclaimed with nostalgic glee that 'it is a long time since I was up to my elbows in Huguenot blood'.[10] It is hardly accidental that many riots occurred, as at Pamiers, during important moments of the

---

[9] Denis Crouzet analyses the ritualistic and festive quality of violence in *Les Guerriers de Dieu. La violence au temps des troubles de religion vers 1525 – vers 1610* (Seyssel, 1990), (2 vols), I, 252, 297–302.

[10] Davis, 'The Rites of Violence', 75.

festive calendar when people took to the streets. Davis suggested that 'almost every type of public religious event has a disturbance associated with it'. On some occasions, the conduct of traditional Christian rituals extended directly into rites of violence. The performance of these rites dehumanized victims, which helps to explain why massacres featured such extreme acts of brutality and also the speedy return of perpetrators to their everyday lives.[11] René Girard argued that 'the function of religious ritual is to 'purify' violence; that is, to 'trick' violence into spending itself on victims whose death will provoke no reprisals'.[12] If that is correct, then it seems that in France (if only briefly and in certain specific social, political, and geographic contexts) the rules of religion seemed to break down. Performing traditional rituals no longer provided a sufficient means of symbolically enacting violent impulses. Violence against live scapegoats temporarily became incorporated into the performance of Christian ritual.

While contributors to this volume accept very much of this assessment of religious riots in France, they also raise some reservations on a number of issues. Essays test the reliability of contemporary sources about religious disturbances. In reading Catholic and Reformed accounts of massacres, as Davis put it, we have to 'do our best to sort out utter fabrication from likely fact'.[13] Penny Roberts notes the formulaic nature of recorded episodes of violence and wonders how far chroniclers may have been influenced by reports of earlier massacres. Roberts also highlights that sexual violence is under-reported in these accounts, presumably in order to defend the honour of survivors. Meanwhile spectacular acts of chaotic brutality to living and dead bodies were recorded in gruesome detail. Records of massacres were certainly shaped by what witnesses and survivors experienced and remembered. They were also affected by expectations on both sides that their opponents were barbarians who were eminently capable of extraordinary cruelty. Allan Tulchin and Stuart Carroll consider some of the implications of thinking about a learned repertoire of violent rituals. How far might rites of violence have sometimes been consciously employed as a cover for personal grievances and political ambitions in different local contexts? Could chaotic brutality be used as a deliberate tactic by those who wanted to defend their rights or to grab power from local rivals? What degree of organization can be identified behind some apparently spontaneous outbreaks of violence, and what was the role of military units within some riotous crowds?

---

[11] Davis, 'The Rites of Violence', 72, 85.
[12] René Girard, *Violence and the Sacred* (London, 2005), 37–8.
[13] Davis, 'The Rites of Violence', 55.

A number of essays take up discussion of the role and agency of nobles, magistrates, military commanders, and clergy in outbreaks of popular violence. Mark Greengrass and Neil Cox argue that rites of violence are not always obvious in noble political culture which remained preoccupied with images and ideas drawn from the Classical past. Carroll highlights examples of social solidarity between nobles across confessional boundaries. Denis Crouzet meanwhile reflects on how elite politics was far from immune from religious anxieties, and in particular emphasizes the fear of divine judgement against France if heresy was allowed to flourish unchecked. Crouzet also stresses that attacks on royal authority had a long rhetorical life in print before they were enacted during the civil wars. Mack Holt points to the role of militant clergy in propagating both the ideas and sense of mutual loathing that were necessary conditions for rites of violence. Philip Benedict directs our attention towards the role of belligerent Reformed ministers in prompting violence. He finds Reformed clergy playing an active role in political and military decision-making during the civil wars. Ministers pressed nobles, urban magistrates, and ordinary people to defend the cause of true religion.

Many of the essays in this volume discuss a range of issues relating to the location and frequency of religious riots. Given the compelling logic that lay behind outbreaks of violent sectarianism why were massacres in fact relatively infrequent, short-lived, and limited to certain geographic contexts? It is argued here that the intensity of religious riots and massacres during the 1560s and 1570s reflected the very particular social and political circumstances of those decades. Violence occurred as communities reacted to the novelty of religious division and the rapid growth in support for Reformed religion. Tulchin and Holt explore the importance of local confessional demography, highlighting the particularly dangerous environment of a religious majority fearing the challenge posed by a substantial minority community. Riots were more common in localities in which religious divisions exacerbated existing social tensions, or where religious divisions became interwoven with struggles for control over local government, or in areas with outspoken popular preachers. Violent mobs took to the streets during a national political crisis when normal patterns of obedience to royal authority were breaking down, and when royal law was faltering as an effective instrument to maintain either orthodoxy or peace. Uncertainty about royal policy towards the Reformed minority destabilized Catholic support for the crown. Popular anxiety about the consequences of being ruled by kings who failed to exterminate heretics found some resolution in direct violent action.

There is no evidence that episodes of popular violence grew more infrequent because of any decline in the mobilizing agency of religious ideology. The horrific nature of the violence did not seem to discredit Christianity in any way, nor were the cleansing rites of violence seen to have become either ineffective or unnecessary. Rather, religious riots declined in frequency as the two communities consolidated their control over distinct geographic areas. A series of formal regulations tried to provide a legal framework within which conflicts between the two religious communities could be peacefully resolved. As Roberts outlines, these laws at times caused more problems than they solved. In towns and regions shared between Catholics and Protestants the practical compromises that were needed to accommodate religious diversity often remained very grudging at best. A final settlement at the end of the civil wars provided some basis for political and social stability. A negotiated set of rights accommodated the Reformed minority but also clearly established the second-class status of Calvinists in French society.

Religious co-existence in France emerged from the military stalemate of the civil wars, and from political acceptance of the need to provide limited religious rights to Calvinists in order to secure peace. Some degree of social acceptance of religious diversity was also needed to sustain peace. Given the bitter legacy of decades of violence, how did this prove possible? We know that some ordinary people had become quickly and profoundly acculturated to confessional forms of religion which, among other things, demanded strict separation from, and violent hostility towards, those of other beliefs. The views of priests and ministers about the dangers posed by heresy seem to have struck a chord with deep-rooted and widely-held fears in French society. However, participation in rites of violence had never been the inevitable or only way in which people could demonstrate their commitment to Reformed or Catholic religion. Even during the worst of the violence, many people with firm confessional loyalties displayed degrees of ambivalence towards those who attended different churches. More porous forms of religious identity could be largely overwhelmed during intense localized conflicts. Nevertheless, ambiguous attitudes to transgressing confessional boundaries proved resilient. Individuals attended the weddings and funerals of friends and neighbours who belonged to different churches. Daily life in villages and towns was marked by any number of personal interactions across the religious divide. Individuals chose to make quiet gestures in their everyday lives that spoke of shared values of charity, hospitality, and sociability. Over time a reservoir of social knowledge could slowly build which suggested that while living peacefully with heretics was not ideal, it was at least possible. However, none of this meant that anxiety about heresy and sectarian enmities had been extinguished or had lost the power to divide families and to rupture friendships, neighbourhoods, and communities. The persistence of religious diversity provided the clear potential for future outbreaks of violence in the changing social and political environment of seventeenth-century France.

As Davis makes clear in her essay, 'The Rites of Violence' was influenced by the politics of the early 1970s and current trends in academic research. She questioned why 'present-day church historians' had failed to provide any considered analysis of religious riots. Davis argued that the reason for their silence on this subject was that for 'church historians, especially in an age of ecumenicalism, the popular violence of their Calvinist and Catholic ancestors may have been an embarrassment (as is Belfast)'.[14] Davis suggested that the private convictions of 'church historians' and their identification with co-religionist ancestors had limited the questions that they were prepared to ask of the Christian past. Calvinist historians and Catholic historians did not want to talk about popular religious violence because it might reveal a less civilized way of doing religion that they found both unpalatable and inconvenient. Such historians turned their faces away from sixteenth-century France and from Northern Ireland, where violent ways of doing religion had apparently resurfaced during the early 1970s.

Religious violence is no longer a neglected puzzle of social historians or a guilty secret of church historians. The explanation for this transformation lies partly in the impact of the work of Natalie Zemon Davis. It also reflects a broader shift in attitudes towards the history of religion. Sharp divisions between the perspectives of social historians and church historians have blurred. A shared project has slowly emerged to examine the cultural history of popular religion. The work of only a relatively small number of historians is limited in the ways suggested by Davis in 1973. Analysis of religious violence has also been significantly affected by religion's apparent come-back as a major force in global politics and international relations. Considerable energy has been devoted in the last decade to providing answers to questions of intense public interest about the causes and character of religious violence. For example, Mark Juergensmeyer has conducted interviews with supporters and perpetrators of religious violence in different parts of the world. He concluded in *Terror in the Mind of God. The Global Rise of Religious Violence* that religious violence has a distinctive and savage character. Juergensmeyer also noted that warfare has 'long had an eerie and intimate relationship with religion'. Juergensmeyer suggested that, thanks to the work of Natalie Zemon Davis and others, we know that wars have not only long been fought in the name of religion but were on occasion even fought as 'religious events'.[15] A range of authors from different disciplinary perspectives have recently discussed their perception of the negative role that religion

---

[14] Davis, 'The Rites of Violence', 54.
[15] Mark Juergensmeyer, *Terror in the Mind of God. The Global Rise of Religious Violence*, 3rd edn (Berkeley, CA, 2003), 159–60.

plays in fostering groups of fanatical murderers. According to some of this analysis, religion seems to inspire violence of a particularly brutal and relentless character. Adherents are thought to be driven to kill by motives incapable of being countered by rational argument. Suggestions have also been made about the ways in which different religions might be redeemed of their potential to foster violence among their followers. However, some writers have identified an inherent violence in the very nature of religion itself.[16]

Responding to these ideas, William Cavanaugh has raised concerns about this emerging conventional wisdom on religious violence. He suggested that there is a lack of clarity in much recent literature about how to define the categories of religious and secular and a limited understanding of the changing character of religion and its varied role in politics and society over time. Cavanaugh argued that the recent construction of a myth of religious violence also appears to be rather convenient for its consumers in the West. While religious violence is portrayed as irrational and fanatical, the secular violence of western states is presented as rational, peacemaking, and sometimes regrettably necessary to constrain the violence of those identified as religious extremists.[17] In his study of the history of tolerance, Ben Kaplan attacks a related myth that associates religious violence with allegedly 'primitive societies'. Kaplan is determined to dispel the misleading idea that 'religious conflict is a primitive form of behaviour, driven by emotion, ritualism, and tribal loyalties; the more advanced, or civilized, a society is, the greater the tolerance it will practice.'[18]

The essays in this volume do not identify any inevitable or continuous connections between religion and violence. Contributors are justifiably hesitant about identifying either any long-term trends in the history of religious violence or any direct parallels for the events of sixteenth-century France. This is not to suggest that comparative analysis of episodes of religious violence cannot prove illuminating.[19] Mack Holt is among a number of

---

[16] See for example Charles Kimball, *When Religion Becomes Evil* (San Francisco, CA, 2002); Oliver McTernan, *Violence in God's Name: Religion in an Age of Conflict* (Maryknoll, NY, 2003); Jack Nelson-Pallmeyer, *Is Religion Killing Us?: Violence in the Bible and the Quran* (Harrisburg, PA, 2003); Charles Selengut, *Sacred Fury: Understanding Religious Violence* (Lanham, MD, 2003); John Teehan, *In the Name of God. The Evolutionary Origins of Religious Ethics and Violence* (Oxford, 2010).

[17] William Cavanaugh, *The Myth of Religious Violence: Secular Ideology and the Roots of Modern Conflict* (Oxford, 2009).

[18] Ben Kaplan, *Divided by Faith. Religious Conflict and the Practice of Toleration in Early Modern Europe* (Cambridge, MA, 2007), 5.

[19] See for example Stanley Tambiah, *Leveling Crowds. Ethnonationalist Conflicts and Collective Violence in South Asia* (Berkeley, CA, 1996), 309–11. Tambiah concluded

contributors who reflect on outbreaks of violence from other periods and societies. However, as Holt makes clear, study of different communal riots confirms the complex, changing, varied, and unpredictable connections between religious affinity and violent behaviour. Natalie Zemon Davis also comments that she never sought to identify some 'timeless demonic force' through her study of religious riots. Rather, she intended to present an example of how 'murderous and destructive actions were historically and culturally conditioned' within sixteenth-century French society. At the same time Davis readily acknowledges that the ghosts of the Holocaust were very much on her mind as she thought about the massacres of Reformation France.

It is clear that the religious riots of the sixteenth century cannot be seen as some sort of forerunner of the Holocaust. While the events for example of *Kristallnacht* might be thought to share some features with earlier episodes of religious violence, the processes of dehumanization and genocide of the Holocaust were powered by that particular achievement of the modern West, bureaucracy. However, we might note a powerful question posed by Raul Hilberg, whose work Davis was reading during the 1960s. Hilberg, author of *The Destruction of the European Jews* asked: 'Wouldn't you be happier if I had been able to show you that all the perpetrators were crazy?'[20] It is precisely the 'mindedness' of violent murderers in sixteenth-century France that Davis explored. We might also consider whether the Holocaust provides further compelling evidence against drawing any straightforward trajectory in the relationship between religion and violence. The Holocaust seems rather to indicate that western modernity, contrary to its promises, has not ushered in an era of more civilized human relations or quelled ancient, murderous passions. Atheist polemicists are among those few who retain any great confidence that the answer to all our dilemmas lies in trying a little harder to be modern. Such people stridently promote their beliefs about the inherently poisonous and violent character of religion, seeming to derive great

---

that riots in South Asia provide ample evidence of 'rites of violence drawn from the repertory of religious lore and ritual, folk sanctions and punishments, and rituals of purification and exorcism'.

[20] Raul Hilberg, 'Significance of the Holocaust' in Henry Friedlander and Sybil Milton (eds), *The Holocaust: Ideology, Bureaucracy and Genocide* (Millwood, NY, 1980), 101–2; Raul Hilberg, *The Destruction of the European Jews* (Chicago, 1961); Zygmunt Bauman, 'The uniqueness and normality of the Holocaust' in Catherine Besteman (ed.), *Violence: a Reader* (Basingstoke, 2002); Davis, 'The Rites of Violence', 90.

emotional comfort from, but not see any irony in, their total war against religion.[21]

Contemporary events influenced the writing of 'The Rites of Violence' and will continue to challenge and question our assumptions when studying the violence of late sixteenth-century France. The late twentieth and early twenty-first centuries have been broadly perceived as being a period of fear and anxiety, a sense which gained added momentum in the wake of the 9/11 attacks. We should recognize that our contemporary climate of fear is very different in character from the anxieties that pervaded early modern societies.[22] At the same time recent experience might lead us to re-evaluate what place emotion should play in writing the history of violence.[23] Early modern violence was as nasty and real as contemporary violence, and we should question the assertion that 'early modern people did not have our scruples' about death and suffering.[24] We might also consider that perpetrators of brutality, then as now, intended to elicit an emotional response from eye-witnesses as well as among those who read contemporary accounts of riots or who saw depictions of violence.[25] Furthermore, both acts of violence and writing about them were and are, often as not, shaped by contemporary perceptions, expectations and fears of the enemy within.

Finally, some of the essays within this volume point towards the need to go beyond examining the extent and character of spectacular episodes of religious violence and to ask new questions relating to patterns of religious co-existence and about the rebuilding of a society torn apart by confessional conflict. In the speech that Natalie Davis gave when she accepted the Ludvig Holberg prize in June 2010, she reflected on how since the publication of 'The Rites of Violence', other scholars had refined and expanded on the approach that she had taken. They had also gone on to look at 'the popular practices of tolerance' which she described as 'the rituals of peace'. Reflecting on how the confessional conflict had 'often left a trail of bloodshed through history',

---

[21] Sam Harris, *The End of Faith: Religion, Terror, and the Future of Reason* (London, 2006).

[22] Peter Stearns, 'Fear and Contemporary History: A Review Essay', *Journal of Social History* (2006), 477–84.

[23] Sarah Apetrei, 'When Fabric Suffers More than People. A review essay on Eamon Duffy's *Fires of Faith*', *The Living Church*, 16 January 2011; Sarah Apetrei, 'Church History, Emotion and the Study of Spirituality', paper delivered at the Ecclesiastical History Conference, University of Oxford, 19 August 2011. Aspects of this paper will appear in her forthcoming *Mystical Theology and Visionary Experience in Later Stuart Britain*.

[24] Beik, 'The Violence of the French Crowd', 108.

[25] Philip Benedict, *Graphic History. The Wars, Massacres and Troubles of Tortorel and Perrissin* (Geneva, 2007); Frank Lestringant (ed.), *Le Théâtre des cruautés de Richard Verstegan (1587)* (Paris, 1995).

Davis issued a significant appeal for a new approach towards the study of divided societies:

> Within our global frame, I want to suggest a contribution historians can make in the second decade of the twenty-first century, a contribution of interest both to scholars and to wider publics. I think we can write new histories that deal with difference—those differences that people believe important in their own time and place, markers of group definition, sources of amity and sources of violence.[26]

---

[26] Natalie Zemon Davis, 'Ludvig Holberg Prize Ceremony Address', 9 June 2010, unpublished paper.

List of Contributors

Sara Beam, Associate Professor, Department of History, University of Victoria

Philip Benedict, Professor, Institut d'histoire de la Réformation, University of Geneva

Stuart Carroll, Professor of Early Modern History, University of York

Neil Cox, Professor of Art History, University of Essex

Denis Crouzet, Professor of Modern History, Université de Paris IV-Sorbonne

Natalie Zemon Davis, Henry Charles Lea Professor of History emerita, Princeton University; Adjunct Professor of History University of Toronto

Barbara B. Diefendorf, Professor of History, Boston University

Mark Greengrass, Senior Research Fellow, Albert-Ludwigs Universität Freiburg

Mack P. Holt, Professor of History, George Mason University

Graeme Murdock, Assistant Professor of European History, Trinity College Dublin

Penny Roberts, Associate Professor (Reader) in History, University of Warwick

Andrew Spicer, Professor of Early Modern European History, Oxford Brookes University

Allan A. Tulchin, Assistant Professor of History, Shippensburg University

Ritual and Violence index

abjuration 67, 68–70, 71, 122
abortion 204 n.27, 215, 260
absolutism 215, 222, 225
Adrets, baron des 193
adultery 204, 210–11, 212, 213, 215, 216, 218
Agamben, Giorgio 260
Agen 151, 155–6
Agenais, province of 148 n.67, 151, 153–6
Aiguesmortes 252
Albi massacre (1572) 108
Albon, Jacques d', sieur de St-André 265, 269
All Saint's Day (1561) 62–3
Allemagne, Baron d' 117
ambassadors 136, 153, 224, 229, 268, 269 n.86
Amboise, Bussy d' 135
Amboise, Edict of (March 1563) 45 n.47, 46, 49, 66, 189, 192
Amboise, Françoise d' 135
Amiens 86
    massacre (1562) 106
    Protestants expelled from 121–2
Amin, Shahid 26
Anabaptists 136
Angers:
    massacre (1572) 108, 110
    Protestant occupation of 175
Angoulême, duchess of 230
Angoulême, duke of 228–9
animals 82–4, 234–5
Anjou, duke of 189
Annalistes 53
anthropology 35, 127, 129
anti-Semitism 60
Antoine, King of Navarre 171, 267–8

Apollo 264
Appian of Alexandria's 'History of the Roman Wars' 252, 256–8, 260, 261, 262–3, 269, 273–4
Aquitaine 57
Aragon 59, 60
Arbaleste, Charlotte 244
Arendt, Hannah 3
aristocracy *see* nobility
armour 261–2
arson 18, 45, 111, 204
assassination 156–7, 163, 260, *see also* regicide
assemblies 51, 62, 166, 167, 169, 171, 174, 178, 180, 183, 190, 195, 266, 268
atheism 284
Aubigné, Agrippa d' 94, 194
Auclair, Valérie 261 n.64
Augsburg, Religious Peace of 22
Aumale, Claude de Lorraine, Duke of 63–4, 65
Aunis 179
Aups massacre (1574) 108, 117
Auvergne 87
Auxerre:
    looting in 111
    massacre (1568) 107, 111, 116
    relics of Saint Germain 47
Avignon 118, 119, 124
Azay-le-Rideau 93 n.87

Bakhtin, Mikhail 10
banishment 63, 198, 207, 213, 215
Bar-sur-Seine massacre (1562) 80, 88 n.62, 106, 110, 140 n.39
Barcelona 59
Bard, Jacques 202–3

Barrelles, Jean 178–9, 180
Bataille, Georges 242 n.5, 246–7
Baum, G. and Cunitz, E. 105, 109
Bayeaux, sack of (1563) 157
Beam, Sara 278
Béarn 117
Beaugency 112
Beaujeu, Anne, duchess de 232
Beaulieu, Edict of (1576) 71, 77 n.5
Bégat, Jean 66
Belle-Eglise, Oise, church at 250
Belleville, François de 179
Benedict, Philip 26–7, 39 n.26, 40, 57–8, 110, 118, 129, 280
Bercé, Y.-M. 151 n.77
Bergerac, Edict of 77 n.5
Bertrand de Girard, seigneur du Haillan 227–8
Beza, Theodore 136, 141, 144, 168, 169, 171–2, 180–4, 191, 195
Biafran war (1967-70) 159
Bicocca, battle of (1522) 233
bigamy 204 n.27, 215
Biron, Jeanne de 153 n.82
black mass 248
blasphemy 64–5, 183, 212, 213, 218
Blois 79, 86, 94, 221
Bodin, Jean 248
body social 15, 22, 30, 32, 33, 34, 36–8, 55, 64, 136
Boiffard, Jacques-André 246
Bonet, Honoré 90 n.68
Bonnivet, Admiral 239
Bordeaux massacre (1572) 108, 110
Borel, Docteur 246
Bossy, John 35–6
Bouchet, Jehan 226
Bouillon, Henri-Robert de La Marck, duke of 180 n.47, 185
boundaries, religious 21–2, 57, 61, 71, 281
Bourbon, Antoine de 265, 269
Bourbon, Antoinette de *see* Guise, dowager duchess of
Bourbon, Charles de 237
Bourbon, constable of 232, 233, 237, 239–40
Bourbons 48, 152, 165
Bourgel, Eustache de 211–12
Bourges massacre (1572) 108

Branlard, Guillaume 216
bread riots 10, 275
Brescia 262
Brewer, John 77–8
Brittany 117, 123, 228
Brulé, Renée 90–1
Brunel, minister 179
Brutus, Decimus 251, 252
Budé, Guillaume 227
Bullinger, Heinrich 193
Burgos 59
Burgundy 58, 117, 239, *see also* Dijon
burned at the stake 26, 38, 134, 145, 216, 251
butchery 80, 82

Caboche (clerk) 222
Caen, Normandy 141
Cahors massacre (1561) 27, 106, 111, 151
Cairo 28
Calvin, Jean 136, 168, 179, 195, 205, 214, 217
    biblical commentaries 181, 182
    church and state distinction 169, 170
    consultation on criminal cases 207
    on ministers bearing arms 172, 193, 195
    raising money for troops 171
    sermons 198
'Calvinist of Millau' 91, 97
Calvinists/Calvinism 55, 62, 137, 155, 156, 166, 281
cannibalism 81, 83–4
capital crimes 204–5, 207, 214, *see also* death penalty; execution
Caracciolo, bishop 140
Caraman:
    massacre (1567) 107
    massacre (1570) 112
Carcassonne 43, 80, 109
    massacre (1561) 106
    massacre (1562) 107, 121
Caron, Antoine
    Augustus and the Sibyl 249–53
    Massacres of the Triumvirate 7, 241–72
        architecture and statues in 259–60, 263–4
        Armistice Day story about 271
        artistic intention of 260
        decapitations in 260–1, 263

distinctive sword and armour in 261–2
historical context of 265–71
Leiris on 246–9, 264, 271
list of reproductions of 271–3
private and public space 265
provenance of 244–6
references to 'fearful portents and prodigies' 264
Carroll, Stuart 100, 109, 125, 279, 280
Casimir, duke of the Palatinate 183
Castelnaudary massacre (1562) 106, 111
Castile 59
castration 85, 97, 249
Castres 47, 88
  Protestant takeover of churches in 40
  religious procession in 50
Catalonia 60
Catherine de Medici, Queen Mother 18, 30, 31, 48, 63, 65, 66, 177, 245, 265–9, 270
Catholic League 68, 117, 220, 240
Catholicism 11, 13, 14, 129, 166, 232, 236
Catholics 78, 131, 156
  bishops bearing arms 173
  community 34–51, 138–9
  contrasted with Protestant rioters 14–16, 19 n.21
  emblem of the cross 30–1
  list of grievances against Protestants 64
  militant preaching 37–8, 46, 53, 222
  miracles 47
  processions 42–4, 46, 47, 50, 51, 142, 147
  response to Protestant iconoclasm 42–8
  ritual violence against Protestants 79–85
  sacred and body social 22–3
  targeting heretical persons and bodies 15, 17, 166
  tit-for-tat reprisals 79, 119–20
  urban resistance 142, *see also* massacres; priests
Caumont-La Force 153 n.82
Cavanaugh, William 283
Caylus massacre (1562) 106, 118
Céant-en-Othe 150
Cellini, Benvenuto 261 n.64
Chabot, Léonar, count of Charny 69–70
Châlons-sur-Marne 140
Chalons-sur-Saône 172
Chappuys, Claude 230

charivaris 9–10, 40, 277
Charles IV, King 66
Charles IX, King 18, 30, 31, 48–9, 51, 167 n.9, 177, 189, 190, 223, 248, 267
Charles of Austria 228
Charles the Bold 238
Charles V, King 28, 237, 238
Charny, Léonar Chabot, Count of 69–70
Chartres 46, 47
Chateauneuf 80
Châtillon, Cardinal of, abbot of Saint-Jean-les-Sens 144
children 93–4, 127, 142, 149, 248
Christin, Olivier 41, 42 n.37, 133
Christine de Pizan 24
church and state 169, 170
church synods 151, 167, 169–70, 178–80, 267
churches 41
  colloquies 27, 173, 178, 182
  mobilization of Reformed 163–4, 167, 170, 171–2, 177
  taken over and cleansed by Protestants 39–40, 44, 46, 151–2, 154, 170, 174
Cicero, Marcus Tullius 229, 255, 262
civic militias 109–10, 125–6, 141, 146–8, 150, 167 n.9
Clément, Jacques 220, 222, 240
clergy *see* ministers; priests
Cléry shrine 157
Cock, Jérôme 255
coexistence 17, 20–1, 50, 54, 57–60, 61, 72–3, 76–7, 79, 99, 117, 132–3
Coligny, Admiral, Gaspard de 18, 70, 87, 125, 126, 148, 157, 169, 181, 269
Coliseum, Rome 259
Colladon, Germain 208, 211, 216
colloquies 27, 173, 178, 182
commissioners 49–50, 51, 87, 173
Commodus, Emperor 261, 264
communalism 138
communities 34, 132–3
  bi-confessional 49–50, 160–1
  and communion 35–7
  cross-confessional co-operation 140–1
  divine protection for 36
  outsiders role in violence 150
  secular authorities and 51
Company of the Griffarins 9

Condé, Louis, Prince of 183, 184, 193, 265, 267–8
  in Beaugency 112
  Beza as advisor to 171, 177
  and Edict of January 146, 178
  massacre paintings 254, 269
  and ministers 175, 179, 180
  mobilizing the churches 146
  peace of Amboise 192, 194
  reprisal executions 119
  seizure of Orléans 170, 175
  treaty of association 177
conjuration 254, 269
consistories 37, 155, 167, 169–70, 185, 187, 189, 190, 191–2, 199, 207, 214, 216–17
Constable, Olivia Remie 60
Constans, Jean 175, 187, 191
Constant, abbé Alphonse-Louis 248
convents 46, 89, 185
Copier, Anthoine 174
Coras, Judge Jean de 25
corde 202, 203, 205, 210, 211, 212, 216 n.68
corpses:
  desecration of 14, 80, 128, 142, 149, 150, 159, 223
  eaten by animals 83–4
Corpus Christi day 25–6, 44
corruption 10, 237, 257
counsel 40, 224, 237, 239
counterfeiting 202–3, 204
Coutras, battle of (1587) 194
craft violence 275
Cranach the Elder, Lucas 249
Crespin, Jean 25, 105
Croissant, Pierre du 186
Crouzet, Denis 115, 125, 141 n.40, 166, 280
  Dieu dans ses royaumes 34
  on Fumel's murder 151, 152–3
  Les Guerriers de Dieu 16–17, 34, 55, 102, 129–30, 165, 278 n.9
  'imaginaire' 34, 271
  motives for massacres 121
  and pollution and purification model 55
  on Sens massacre 142
Crussol, count of 163, 164
Curione, Celio Secondo 256–7
Curry, Anne 90 n.68, 90 n.70

Dali, Salvador 247
dancing 207, 278
Daniel's Decree 193
Dauphiné, province of 170, 171, 172, 193
Davis, Natalie Zemon 8–29, 51, 102, 141–2, 241, 270, 275
  on academic research 282
  on assaults by butchers 82
  on 'God of paste' taunts 64
  on Holocaust and religious massacres 284
  on murder of baron of Fumel 150
  pollution and purification model 54, 55–8, 65, 71, 75, 131, 142, 166, 206–7, 216, 220, 224, 278
  on problems of analysis 84
  on religious riots 24, 25, 34, 134, 197, 271, 278, 282, 284
  on rioters as the 'people' in the streets 127, 131, 150
  on Sens massacre 142
  study of divided societies 285–6
  'The Reasons of Misrule' 10, 12, 277
  'The Rites of Violence' 72, 74, 85 n.46
    Beam on 197
    Benedict on 164, 166, 167
    Carroll on 127–8, 159
    critics of 55–8, 127–8
    Crouzet on 220
    Diefendorf on 32, 33, 45
    Holt on 53, 54
    Roberts on 75, 99
    Tulchin on 100
  'The Sacred and the Body Social' 22–3, 32 n.3, 36, 129
  Trickster Travels 28–9
De Thou, Jacques-Auguste 112–14
death penalty 26, 38, 134, 145, 198, 207, 213, 215, 216, 251
decapitation 248–9, 260–1, 263
dehumanization 16, 220, 279, 284
Deiron, minister 176
Delachenal, Jean 212–13
Dell' Abate, Nicolò 251–2, 253, 256, 261
Delminio, Guilio Camillo 229 n.18
democracy 257
Denise, Pierre 174
Desan, Suzanne 32–3, 51
desecration 14, 15, 17, 38, 44, 57

desecration of corpses 80, 128, 142, 149, 150, 159, 223
Deuteronomy, Book of 15, 53, 186 n.58
devil 209–12, 213, 217, 218
Diefendorf, Barbara 17–18, 55, 61, 65, 66, 125–6, 278
Dieulefit 164
Dijon 54, 61–71, 78, 79, 86
Dio Cassius 264
disembowelment 80, 85, 97, 264, 278
divine judgement 156, 222–3, 280
divine law 92, 99, 166, 179, 200, 208, 221
divine right 221, 229, 230, 238
Documents journal 246, 247
Doré, Pierre 135
Douglas, Mary 14, 52
Dreux, battle of (1562) 172, 175, 184
drowning 83, 94, 216
duels 25, 276
Duprat, Antoine 231, 235, 237
Durkheim, Émile 131

Edict of Amboise (March 1563) 45 n.47, 46, 49, 66, 189, 192
Edict of Beaulieu (1576) 71, 77 n.5
Edict of Bergerac 77 n.5
Edict of January (1562) 114, 127, 135, 145, 147, 166, 177, 188 n.64, 192
   Catherine of Medici and 63
   Dijon *parlement* and 66, 78
   nobility and 136–8
   prince of Condé and 146, 178
   suppression following 65
Edict of Longjumeau (1568) 68, 77 n.5
Edict of Mantes (1591) 77 n.5
Edict of Nantes (1598) 20, 33, 35, 71–2, 90, 101
Edict of Poitiers (1577) 71
Edict of Saint Germain (1570) 49, 67, 77 n.5
edicts of pacification 51, 61, 67–8, 70–1, 76, 77, 270, 281
effigies 64, 157
Ehrmann, Jean 249–51, 252, 254–5, 271, 273
Einstein, Carl 246
El Kenz, David 70
Elias, Norbert 276
eliminationist violence 103, 104 n.10, 121–3, 260

England 38, 138
engravings 259, 261
Epaula, Guillauma 212
Epistre Satiricque 238–9
Erasmus of Rotterdam 134
Estates-General 27, 144–5, 156, 158, 177, 265–6
estrapade 203 n.23, 205, 211, 212
ethics 169, 183, 188–9
ethnic cleansing 121, 161
Eucharist 35–6, 64–5, 81, 275
execution 26, 38, 134, 145, 198, 207, 213, 215, 216, 251
exhumation 223

Faget, Ambroise 179
Fallas, Etienne 205
farces 230–1
Faurin, Jean 40 n.31, 81 n.24, 89, 97
feminism 23
Fiac 88
Foa, Jérémie 49, 50, 120
Fontainebleau 252
food riots 10, 275
Forfants 9
Foucault, Michel 212
Foxe, John 157–8
France, Jehan 139
Francis I, King 42, 224, 227, 229–31, 233–40, 252, 253 n.36
Francis II, King 80–1, 155, 223, 248 n.21, 265, 267
freedom of conscience 35, 134, 138, 173, 189, 193, *see also* religious freedom
freedom of speech 236 n.32
Frégimont, châteaux of 153, 154
French law 199
French Revolution 271
Fumel, baron of 150–8
fundamentalism 73

Gaillac:
   massacre (1562) 106, 110, 111, 119
   massacre (1572) 108
   Protestants thrown from cliffs 45
   rape and murder of women (1573) 97
Galle, Jan 255
Gallican reform 136, 137
gambling 207

Gandhi, Mahatma 26
Gardet, Pierre 216
Garonne valley 117, 118, 119
Garrisson-Estèbe, Janine 33 n.6, 53–4, 85 n.46, 151
Geertz, Clifford 11, 129, 130–1
gender and violence 23–4, 85, *see also* sexual violence
Geneva 67, 69, 174
  political authority in 205–6
  torture 197–219
Geneva Company of Pastors 172, 182, *see also* ministers
Genoa 233
genocidal violence 110, 122–3, 131 n.15, 159–60, 284
German Peasants War 135–6
Germany 82 n.29, 138
Girard, René 279
Glamis, Lord 169
glory 158, 226–7, 230, 231, 234
God and the devil 199, 209–12, 217
Goldhagen, Daniel 131 n.15
Gontaut-Biron, Armand de 189
Gouberville, Gilles de 139, 141 n.40, 157
Gournay, Marie de 245
grain riots 9, 14, 18
Granada 60
Grande Rebeine of Lyon (1529) 9
Great Crash (1929) 247
Greek civil war (1946-9) 102
Greengrass, Mark 127–8, 150 n.74
Greengrass, Mark and Cox, Neil 280
Grenade massacre (1561) 106
Grenoble 172
  siege of (1562) 176 n.37
  siege of (1563) 163
Griffarins 9
Gringore, Pierre 225–6, 231
Gross, Jan 159
Gryphius, Jean 238
Guerre, Martin 25
guerrillas 102, 110
Guise, Antoinette de Bourbon, dowager duchess of 93, 134–5, 136, *137*
Guise, François, duke of 112–14, 119, 134, 136–7, 157, 163, 265, 268, 269
Guise, Henri, Duke of 125–6

Guise, Louis, Cardinal of 144 n.50, 146, 147 n.64
Guise family 135–6, 153, 156, 165

Habsburg, house of 135
Hanlon, Gregory 21, 57, 132
Harris, Sam 52
Haton, Claude 80, 91–2, 98, 142 n.46, 147, 158, 167 n.9
hatred 46, 112, 129, 139, 159–60
Heller, Henry 151
Hémard, Edme 146
Hémard, Robert, mayor of Sens 145–7
Henry II, King 68, 101, 156, 222
Henry III, King 77, 153, 220, 223
Henry of Navarre (later Henry IV of France) 18, 48, 49, 72, 183, 184 n.52, 185, 194, 221, 269
Henry VIII, King 237
Hercules 264
heresy 14, 15, 17, 18, 38, 135–6, 138, 166, 281
  hunting 145
  metaphor of disease 37–8
  in Sens 146
  torture 206
Hermesis, sieur de 141
Hilberg, Raul 3, 284
Hillgarth, Jocelyn 58–9
Histoire ecclésiastique 19 n.21, 79–80, 89, 93, 94, 109, 118, 168
  on assassination of Noel Thomas 157
  on the colloquy in Toulouse 178
  on ministers bearing arms 174
  on murder of baron of Fumel 156
  on Sens massacre 145
  on siege of Mountauban (1562-3) 185–6
  on the Triumvirate 269
  on Triumvirate massacres 253–4
Hitchens, Christopher 52
Hobsbawm, Eric 10, 275
Hochner, Nicole 225, 226
Holocaust 12–13, 123, 158–9, 284
Holofernes, general 24, 249
Holt, Mack P. 101, 113 n.26, 164, 280, 283–4
holy days and events 15, 17, 25–6, 60–1, 278–9
Holy Innocents Day (1561) 145

Hotman, François 193
Houel, Nicolas 245
Huguenots *see under* Protestants
humility 226, 227
Hurtault, Nicolas 69
Hus, Jan 136
Hutu people 159–60

Iberia 54, 58–60, 58–61, 72
iconoclasm 27, 38–9, 40, 41, 42, 43, 44, 75, 152, 156, 157, 222, 223, 278
identity politics 27–8
idolatry 39, 41, 44
incest 215, 216
India:
 Chauri Chaura riot 26
 rapes during partition 98 n.101
indiscriminate violence 102–5, 110, 116–17, 120, 121, 122, 123, 124
Indonesia 130–1
infanticide 84, 87, 90, 204
initiation rites 9
intermarriage 21, 71
Iogna-Prat, Dominique 58, 59
Ireland 93, 98
Islam 22, 28–9, 54, 58–61
Issoire massacre (1575) 108
Italy 233, 239
Jacquerie revolts 151, 152

James I, King of Aragon 59
Jarnac, Guy Chabot, baron of 179, 180 n.47
Jaucourt, Frédéric François Levisse de Montigny, marquis de 244, 246, 271
Jean II de Gourmont 255
Jeanne d'Arc 24
Jeannin, Pierre 70
Jelensky, Sigismund ('Sigmund Gelenius') 256
Jeremiah, prophet 169
Jews 22, 54
 accused of cannibalism 81
 Christian violence against 17
 Holocaust 12–13, 123, 158–9, 284
 in Iberia 54, 58–61
Jezebel 83
Joinville 134, 135
Jouanna, Arlette 192–3

Journal de Faurin sur les guerres de Castres 88
judges 25, 63, 66, 70, 90, 178, 197, 200, 201–14, 216, 217
Judith 24, 190, 249
Juergensmeyer, Mark 282
Jugurtha 253
Julius Caesar 260
just war theory 182
justice 48, 90, 183, 197–218, 226, 270

Kalyvas model 102–5, 110, 115, 116–17, 119, 121, 122, 124, 161
Kane, June E. 238, 239–40 n.37
Kaplan, Benjamin 21–2, 28, 73, 283
Kappel, battle of (1531) 167, 172
Kennedy, Hugh 59
Kenya 159
Knox, John 39, 199
Kulturkampf 241

La Charité massacre (1572) 108, 110
La Châtaigneraie massacre (1595) 108, 117
La Ferté-Milon 78–9
La Foss (lawyer) 148
La Noue, François de 189, 190, 191, 193, 194
La Place, Pierre de 268–9
La Plume 154
La Roche Chandieu, Antoine de 222
La Rochelle:
 massacre (1568) 107
 neutrality policy in 179
 refugee ministers in 192
 siege of (1572-3) 175, 176, 189–91
La Vaissière, Bertrand de, seigneur de Monbeau 148 n.67
La Vigne, André de 229
Laboria, captain 186, 187, 189
Labrousse, Elisabeth 20, 57
Laena 262–3
Lafréry, Antoine 259, 261
Langer, Ulrich 230
Langlois, Jean 144 n.51
Languedoc, province of 20, 57, 117, 170
Lascaris, Janus 257
Laugnac, châteaux of 154
Lauzerte massacre (1562) 106, 118
laws of war 90, 99

lawyers 207–8, 211, 217
Layrac, Gascony 21
Le Bazochin, Jacques 231
Le Jars, Guillaume 245–6
Le Mans:
  massacre in 87
  sacking of cathedral in 41
Le Puy 47
Le Roy, Loys 87
Lebel, Gustave 249
legal status of religious minorities 54, 59–60, 61, 71, 72, 92
Leiris, Michel 246, 247–9, 264, 271
Lemousse, Augustin 244–5, 270
Leo Africanus 28–9
Leo X, Pope 28
Leopard, Charles 179
Lepidus, Marcus Aemillius 254, 259
Léry, Jean de 81, 82, 83, 85 n.46
L'Espine, Jean de 173, 195
Libos 154
Limoges massacre (1572) 108
Limousin 179
Limoux massacre (1562) 106, 109, 116
local peace pacts (pactes d'amitié) 120, 133
Loire valley 87, 174
Longjumeau, Edict of (1568) 68, 77 n.5
Longueville, Leonor d'Orléans, duke of 180 n.47
looting 41, 111, 163
Loque, Bertrand de 185
lords of misrule 9–10, 277
Lorraine, Claude de, duke of Aumale 63–4, 65
Lorraine, duke of 269
Loudun 21
Louis XI, King 223, 238
Louis XII, King 157, 224–9, 230, 231, 233, 257
Louise of Savoy 224, 228, 229, 232, 233, 238
Louvet, Jean 174
Lucan, *Pharsalia* 256
Luria, Keith 21, 56–7
Luther, Martin 136
Lutheranism 62, 83, 136
Lyon 9, 30–1, 32, 69, 82, 178, 259
  capture of 44
  cleansing of churches in 41
  massacre (1572) 108
  Protestants in 78, 172, 193
  relics of Saint Bonaventure 47
  synod of 179
  woodcut engravers 255
Lyonnais, province of 170, 193, 227, 265

Machiavelli, Niccolò 231
Mâcon:
  expedition against (1574) 172
  fall of 179
  massacre (1562) 107
Madrid 266, 269
magistrates 49, 53, 57, 64, 67, 68, 71, 142, 169, 172, 187, 194, 280
  parlement of Paris 218
  rioters imitating 10, 14–15, 18
  Sens 146, 147, 149–50
Mamdani, Mahmoon 161
Mantes, Edict of (1591) 77 n.5
Marc Antony 251, 252, 254, 259, 262
Mardi Gras 10, 25, 26
Mares of Thrace 264
Marguerite, Princess 18
Mariéjol, Jean-Hippolyte 53
Marignano, battle of (1515) 239
Mark, James 93 n.84
Marot, Clément 229
Marr, Scott 21 n.26
marriage 10, 21, 71, 277
Marsillargues 105, 109
Martin, Bénigne, mayor of Dijon 65, 66
martyrdom 25, 96, 105, 157
Mary, Queen of Scots 113
masochism 249
Mass 36, 40, 136, 151, 166, 170
massacre paintings 241–72
massacres 45, 99, 100–26, 125–6, 263
  committed by soldiers 101, 109–14, 121, 124, 125, 140 n.39
  definition of 105–6, 109
  frequency and location of 114–20, 125, 280
  geographical distribution of perpetrators 116, 117–18
  Kalyvas model 102–5, 110, 115, 116–17, 121, 122, 124, 161
  motives for 120–4
  ordering 112–14, 125–6
  personnel 109–14

relative absence in Netherlands 119–20
and riots 110–11
social upheaval and 264–5
table of Wars of Religion 106–8
use of term 82
Mautauban 82
Mauves 57
Mazières, André de 191
Meaux massacre (1572) 108
Medici, Catherine de, *see* Catherine de Medici
Meigret, Louis 253
Melun, Estates-General of 266, 267
Mende massacre (1579) 108
Menocal, María Rosa 60
Mer 94
Meschinot, Jehan 226
Meyer, Jean 117
Mézin, consuls of 155
Michelade of Nîmes (1567) 18–20, 27, 100, 118, 128
Milan 226, 239
militias 109–10, 125–6, 141, 146–8, 150, 159, 167 n.9
Millau:
  assembly 171
  Calvinist of 91, 97
millenarian prophecy 17, 55, 121
ministers:
  bearing arms 167 n.9, 172–6, 195, 280
  in besieged cities 176, 185–93
  and local political assemblies 166, 167, 169, 171, 176, 178, 179, 180, 193, 195
  mobilization of 177–81, 195
  moral discipline of troops 184–5
  negotiations 176
  poets 222
  in political decision-making and war 169–76, 195
  prophetic politics 181–96
  raising troops 163–4, 167
  refusing to bear arms 175
  rejection of peace proposals 192, 193–4
  treatise on war 185
Miquel, Pierre 121
miracles 47, 187
miraculous visions 149 n.73, 176, 187
miscegenation 21, 71, 97
misrule 9–10, 277

mock trials 14–15, 18, 45, 53, 197
mockery 14, 81, 228–9
Modena, Sala dei Conservatori 251–2
Mombaut, captain of the Sens militia 148, 149, 150
monarchy:
  iconoclasm against 223
  idealization of 224–5
  oath of fidelity 221
  policy of limited toleration 71–2
  restrictions on authority of 266–7
  royal debt 265
  royal virtue 224–7
  Seyssel's preface on 257–8, *see also* royal authority
Moncontour, battle of (1569) 175–6
Le Monde qui est crucifié 232–3
Le Monde qui n'a plus que frire 236
Le Monde qu'on achève de paindre 234–5
Le Monde sans croix 234
Monflanquin 152, 154
monks 141, 152, 155
Monluc, Blaise de 223
Monluc, Jean de, bishop of Valence 42, 87, 268
Mons, Captain 110
Monsempron, priory of 156
Montaiglion, Anatole de 234
Montaigne, Michel de 83–4, 158, 245
Montauban 82, 174, 175, 190
  assembly 171
  delegate from 178
  siege of (1562-3) 185–9, 191–2, 195
Montbrison 27
Montélimar:
  churches 163, 164
  massacre (1567) 107
  meeting of provincial estates (1562) 193
Montmorency, Constable Anne de 147, 253, 265, 268, 269
Montmorency family 165
Montpellier 57–8
  escaped major massacre 120
  siege of (1562) 88
Montpensier, duchess of 268
Montpensier, duke of 124
Montpensier, Mademoiselle de 24
Montpezat, Antoine de 154
Montpezat, François I de 153–4

morality 37, 89, 184, 191, 195, 207, 213
morality plays 230
Morel, Petramande 210–11
Mornas massacre (1562) 106, 119
Mornay, Philippe Duplessis 194, 244
Morocco 28
Mother Fool allegory 224, 225, 226, 230, 231, 237
Mudejars 59, 60
murder 14, 45, 83, 204, 212, 213, 277
   baron of Fumel 150–8
   black mass 248
   Montpezat's use of 153
   and pardon tales 25–6
   political 156–7, 163, 260
   regicide 220–4, 240
Muslims 22, 54, 58–61
mutilation 9, 14, 15, 80, 85, 97, 141, 159, 251
nakedness 83, 86–7, 91, 93, 94, 96

Nantes:
   Edict of (1598) 20, 33, 35, 71–2, 90, 101
   limited violence in 117, 140
Naples 239
Navarre:
   Henry of (Henry IV) 18, 48, 49, 72, 183, 185, 194, 221, 269
   house of 117
   King Antoine of 171, 267–8
   Queen of 26, 192
Nazi genocide 13, 123, 131 n.15, 271
Nazi reprisals 103
neighbourliness 20, 21, 51, 71, 132–3, 139, 150, 278
Nemours, duke of 193
Nérac 171
Netherlands 38, 140, 239
   lack of religious violence in 55, 119–20, 128
   private Catholic services in 22
Nevers, François II de Cleves, duke of 140, 146, 180 n.47
Nevers, Louis, duke of 254
New Cultural History 127, 130
New Testament 188, 192
Nice 252
Nicholls, David 38
Nicodemites 69

Nicolas V, Pope 257
Nigeria 159
Nîmes 115, 116, 118, 178
   massacre (1571) 107
   Michelade of (1567) 18–20, 27, 100, 107, 118, 128
   pact with brethen in La Rochelle 190, 191
   taken by Protestant raiding party (1569) 176
Niort 57
Nirenberg, David 17, 18, 59–60
nobility 49, 180, 193–4, 269, 280
   armour 262
   clientage 164–5
   martial education and violence 276
   massacre paintings 269
   ministers' political advice to 183–4
   Protestant 135, 138, 158, 180, 269
   and regency government 267
   satirized 232–3, 236
   Seyssel's preface on 257
   use of picture power 254
Noel, Thomas 139, 157
non-violence resistance 11–12
Normand, Loys 163–4, 167, 171, 173
Normandy 117, 141
Nostredame, Michel de 264
nuns 89

Octavian 251, 252, 254, 259
O'Dowd, Mary 93, 98 n.98
Old Testament 83, 181–2, 183, 184, 191, 192–3
   analogies 195–6
   besieged cities 185, 186, 187–91
   Deuteronomy 15, 53, 186 n.58
   priests bearing arms 173
Orange:
   massacre (1562) 88, 106, 116, 119, 124
   massacre (1571) 122
   massacre (1572) 107
ordeals of fire and water 208–10, 216
Orléans 44, 80, 112, 118
   atrocities by Protestant soldiers in 96
   Estates-General of 265–6
   massacre (1569) 107
   massacre (1572) 108
   refugee ministers in 192
   reprisal killings by Protestants 119

seizure of 170, 171, 175, 177, 184
siege of 176, 192
Orsoni, Filippo 261, 262
Othe valley 150
Ottoman Empire 28
pacification, edicts of, *see* edicts of pacification; local peace pacts

Pamiers:
   massacre (1563) 107
   massacre (1566) 107, 278
pardon tales 25–6
Paris 44, 45, 69, 253
   engravers 255
   massacres south of 117, 119
   parlement of 45, 97, 145, 200, 218, *see also* Saint Bartholomew's Day Massacre
parlements 49, 197, 218
   Charles IX visiting every 49
   Dijon 63, 66, 70
   Paris 45, 97, 145, 200, 218
   Toulouse 45, 188
Paron, lord of 145–6
patron saints 36
patronage 244–5, 270
Pavia, battle of (1525) 237, 239
peace and violence 75–9
peace edicts, *see* edicts of pacification; local peace pacts
Peace Treaty (1563) 27
peasant revolts 150, 151, 152, 154, 275
Penne, Agenais 148 n.67, 152
Pentecost 178, 278
Perrissin, Jean 26, 27, 93, 94, 241
Perrussel, François 172
Persia 28
Peter the Venerable, abbot of Cluny 58, 60
Petit Conseil, Geneva 199, 202, 204–8, 211, 212, 214, 215, 217
Picardy 123
Piedmont 174
pieds-nus (peasant rioters) 150, 151, 154
Pithiviers massacre (1562) 107
Pithou, Nicolas 90, 140 n.39
Pius V, Pope 167 n.9
plague-spreading trials 204
poetry 230, 237–8, 238–9
Poissy, colloquy of (1561) 27, 173, 182

Poitiers:
   Edict of (1577) 71
   synod of (1561) 267
Poitou 57
political violence 130–1, 133, 156–7, 159–61, 163, 260, *see also* regicide
politics 165
   ministers and 166, 167, 169–71, 176, 178, 179, 180, 193, 195
   prophetic 181–96
Pollmann, Judith 55–6, 102, 119–20, 128, 134, 138
pollution and purification model 54, 65, 71, 75, 131, 142, 166
   critics of 55–8
   death penalty 216
   torture 206–7, 278
Pont-de-Camarès 185
Pontalez, Jehan du 231
Portugal 22
power 59, 242, 254, 260
predestination 37, 166
pregnant women 85, 86, 87, 88 n.62, 91, 93
priests 53, 57, 155, 230
   attacks on 89
   bearing arms in the Old Testament 173
   certificates of abjuration 68
   Dutch 55, 119
   greedy 166
   intimidation of 40
   killing 15, 19 n.21, 20, 157
   massacres of 112, 118
   sacramental authority of 36
   targeted by Protestants 75, 124
printers/printing 9, 134, 224, 278
private worship 17, 22, 62, 63, 73, 193
propaganda 91–2, 125, 148, 159, 166, 237, 269
prophetic politics 181–96
prostitution 204, 215
Protestants 11, 14, 41, 42, 43, 44, 45, 53, 57, 189, 266–7
   accused of sexual impropriety 84, 85
   and Catholic processions 42–4
   community 34–51
   contrasted with Catholic rioters 14–16, 19 n.21
   destruction of churches 46, 47
   and divine providence 47–8

exile in Geneva 205–6
'god of paste' taunts 9, 38, 64
legal status of 54, 59–60, 61, 71, 72, 92
local political assemblies 166, 167, 169, 171, 176, 178, 179, 180, 193, 195
Michelade of Nîmes (1567) 18–20, 27, 100
militancy of 35–42, 166
murder of the baron of Fumel 150–8
pacification edicts and exclusion of 50–1
political assassination 156–7, 163
propaganda 166, 269
rights of worship 154–5, 171
ritual violence 79–85
sacred and body social 22–3
shared sovereignty ideology 158
syntax of 129
targeting of defiling objects 15, 17
tit-for-tat reprisals 79, 119–20, see also iconoclasm; massacres; ministers; Edict of January
psalm-singing 9, 15, 18, 51, 64, 65, 67, 69, 115, 151, 184, 198
psychoanalysis 246, 248
public mockery 14, 228–9
Publius Titius 260
purification 14, 53, 55, 212, see also pollution and purification model

Rabastens massacre (1562) 119
Raffin, Antoine de Poton de 155–6
rape 85, 87–99, 204, 215, 216, 279
reconquista 58–61
Reformation 36–9, 132, 142, 156, 158, 166
regicide 220–3, 224, 240
relics 47, 275, 278
religious boundaries 21–2, 57, 61, 71, 281
religious coexistence 17, 20–1, 50, 54, 57–61, 72–3, 76–7, 79, 99, 281
religious conversion 39, 67, 70, 122, 135
religious freedom 59–60, 72, 73, 78, 166, 170, 177, 193
Religious Peace of Augsburg 22
religious processions 42–4, 46, 47, 50, 51, 142, 147
religious riots 31–4, 128 n.4, 149, 161, 197, 270, 271, 275–6, 278, 279, 280–2, 284
   Davis on 24, 25, 34, 134, 142, 197, 278, 282, 284

with political overtones 150–8
religious violence 9–17, 275–6
   academic research 282–3
   arbitrary nature of 55–6, 58, 139–40
   culture clash of 127, 128, 129–30
   and numbers 128
   and political violence 133
   'primitive societies' and 283
   public religious events and 15, 17, 25–6, 60–1, 278–9
   three forms of defence 14–15, see also pollution and purification model
Rennes 117, 123
reprisals 103, 118–19, 216, 217
Republicanism 155, 158
Requista massacre (1581) 108
revenge killings 18, 20, 31, 46, 109, 112, 141, 156, 260, 276
Rhône valley 117, 118, 119, 120
ritual violence 79–85, 101, 127, 149, 159, 223, 277, 279, see also torture
Roberts, Penny 20–1, 61, 71, 111 n.18, 279, 281
Rochechouart, Jean-Georges de 154
Rochefort, Thilbault de 69
Roman history 253, 269, see also Appian of Alexandria
Roman law 208, 209
Roman triumvirate 251, 260
Romans, Dauphiné 164, 171
   Carnival in 10, 109
Rome 240, 250, 266
   architecture 259–60
   sack of (1527) 252
Romier, Lucien 53, 165 n.4, 193
Rouen:
   Benedict's study of 129, 165 n.4
   massacre (1572) 108
   Protestants' capture of 44
   Protestants hanged in 119
Roux, Gaston-Louis 247
royal authority 30, 48, 51, 66, 222–3, 224, 230, 266–7, 280, see also monarchy
royal tours 30, 48–9, 51, 66
Rudé, George 10, 275
Ruff, Jacques 98
Ruffi, Jacques 172, 193
Rwanda genocide 110, 159–60, 161

Sabean, David 133
sacrilege 38–9, 43, 46, 89, *see also* desecration
Sade, marquis de 247
Safavids 28
Sainctes, Claude de 172
Saint Bartholomew's Day massacre (1572) 8, 11, 52, 56, 68, 70, 71, 107, 114, 171
  abjurations in the aftermath of 122
  Barbara Diefendorf on 17–18
  Charles IX and 248
  civic militia and 109–10, 149
  Duke of Guise's 'reckless' remark 125–6
  'form of symbolic regicide' 223
Saint Cyr, captain 175–6
Saint-Florent, abbey of 41
Saint Germain:
  Edict of (1570) 49, 67, 77 n.5
  patron saint 47
Saint Gilles massacre (1562) 107, 115
Saint Jacques 47
Saint Jean d'Angély, siege of (1569) 190
Saint Savinien, feast of (12 April 1562) 142, 147
Saintes, synod of (1562) 179, 180
Saintonage 179
saints' relics 47, 275, 278
Sallust, *The Conspiracy of Catiline* 253
salvation 36, 128, 138
Salvert, Henri 174–5
Sancerre, siege of (1573) 81 n.24
satire 224, 225, 226, 229, 230–40
Saulx, Gaspard de, sieur de Tavanes 65, 66
Saumur 21, 41
  massacre (1569) 107
  massacre (1572) 108
  massacre under military auspices 119
Sauzet, Robert 57
Savoy, duke of 174, 269
Savoy, house of 182, 205
Schwartz, Stuart 22, 28, 60
Scotland 156, 169
scribes 201
Second World War (1939–45) 12–13, 103, 123, 131 n.15, 158–9, 271
sedition 135, 204
selective violence 102–5, 117, 120, 121, 122, 123, 124, 260
Selim, Sultan 28

Sennacherib, king 163, 167
Sens massacre (1562) 27, 93–4, 106, 110 n.16, 114, 142–50, *143*, 192
Serlio's *Architecture* 259
sermons 46, 278
Seroc, Jehan 231
Seville 59
sexual deviance 84, 85, 204, 207, 214–16, 217, 218
sexual violence 85–99, 279
Seyssel, Claude de 227, 257–8, 260
Sézanne 78
Shagan, Ethan 132
Sisteron:
  killing in 109
  siege of (1562) 88
Skinner, Quentin 155
social deviance 214–15
social science 102–5, 127
social status 38, 54, 60, 67, 71, 86, 98, 138, 153, 281
sociology 35
sodomy 204, 207, 215, 216
solafideism 166
soldiers 102
  killing after surrender 109
  massacres committed by 101, 109–11, 112–14, 121, 124, 125, 140 n.39
  moral discipline of 184–5
  sexual violence committed by 88–94, 96–9
sovereignty 138, 158, 242 n.5
Spain 22, 58–60, 59, 61, 72
Spifame, Jacques de 144
storytelling 24–6, 92
Straus, Scott 161 n.101
Strozzi, Cardinal, bishop of Albi 111
structuralism 127
Suleiman, Sultan 28, 239
surrealism 242, 246, 247, 264
swords 261–2
symbolic action 9, 10, 81–2, 84
synods 151, 167, 169–70, 178, 179–80, 267

Talmud 100
Taschard, Martin 174, 186–7, 191
Taveau, Balthasar 142, 144, 147 n.63, 148
tax collectors, assassination of 156–7
tax riots 275

taxation 266–7
Textor, Ravisius 231
theft 204, 212, 213
Thompson, E. P. 10, 14, 275
Thou, Jacques-Auguste de 193
Thouars, châteaux of 153
Throckmorton, Sir Francis 136, 137
Tilh, Arnaud du 25
Tilly, Charles 275
Tingle, Elizabeth 140
Toledo 59
toleration 22, 28–9, 70–1, 77, 78, 132, 285,
    see also religious coexistence
Tortefontaine massacre (1567) 107
Tortorel, Jacques 26, 27, 93, 94, 241
torture 278
    capital crimes and 204–5
    in France 218–19
    in Geneva 197–219
    judicial procedure of 199, 201–3
    legal experts and 207–8, 211, 217
    sexual crimes 215–16, 218
    spiritual correction and 205, 206–14,
        216
    techniques of 202, 203
Toulouse 117, 148–9, 150 n.74
    Catholics resistance in 139
    colloquy of 178–9, 180
    massacre (1562) 127–8
    massacre (1572) 108
    parlement of 45
Tournon 148 n.67, 152, 154, 155
Tours:
    fall of 44, 146
    massacre (1562) 27, 94, 95, 106, 116, 124
transubstantiation 64, 81
treason 81
Treaty of Nemours (1585) 68
Trent, Council of (1545-63) 138, 266
Trento, Jean-Baptiste 241
Trexler, Richard 97
Troyes:
    attempted rape in 90
    executioner in 82 n.30
    massacre (1572) 81, 86–7, 108, 110, 116
    religious procession in 43
    well-armed Protestant minority in 140
Tulchin, Allan 18–20, 128, 279, 280
Turenne, viscount 185

Turner, Victor 9
Tutsis 159–60
tyrannicide 220–2, 224
tyranny 224, 237, 240, 262

University of Toronto 11–12
Upper Auvergne 133

Valence 27, 118, 163, 185
Valencia 59
Valognes massacre (1562) 140–1
Valois monarchs 48
Van Gennep, Arnold 9
Vassy massacre (1562) 27, 93, 106, 112–14,
    133–42, 170, 177, 192, 276
Venice 226
Verdier, Jehan du 158
Verdun 47
Vermigli, Peter Martyr 168, 172–3
Verstegan, Richard 96
Vieilleville, Marshal de la 31
Vienna 266
Vietnam War protests 11–12
Vigor, Simon 53
Villeneuve d'Agen 152
Villeneuve d'Avignon 80
Villeneuve-le-Roy 78
violation 92–3
violence 275
    carnivalesque 10, 278
    culture and 159–60
    decline in 276, 281
    eliminationist 103, 104 n.10, 121–3, 260
    genocidal 110, 122–3, 131 n.15, 159–60,
        284
    political 130–1, 133, 156–7, 159–61,
        163
    power and 242
    representations of 26–7, 93, 94, 95, 96,
        241–71
    ritual 79–85, 101, 127, 149, 159, 223, 277,
        279
    selective/indiscriminate distinction
        102–5, 124
    sexual 85–99, 279
    social friction and 134–58
    society and 276
    urban and rural 150–8, see also religious
        violence

Vire:
    massacre (1562) 107, 278
    religious coexistence 118
Viret, Pierre 168
Vivarais 171
Vredeman de Vries, Hans 251, 255

Walker, Garthine 92
Al-Wazzan al-Gharnati al-Fasi (Leo Africanus) 28–9
Weber, Max 23
Wildenstein, Georges 246
witchcraft/witchcraft trials 81, 84, 204, 206, 209, 211–12, 213, 218

Woeriot, Pierre 261
women 127
    bearing arms in besieged cities 186–7
    capacity for violence 23–4
    lack of rape narratives 85, 87–93, 96–9
    sexual slurs and degradation 85–6, 93–4, 96
woodcuts 96, 250, 254–5, 263

Xenophon's *Anabasis* 257

Zwingli, Ulrich 167, 172

PAST & PRESENT
Supplement Series

*Post-war Reconstruction in Europe:
International Perspectives, 1945–1949*
Edited by Mark Mazower, Jessica Reinisch, and David Feldman

Relics and Remains
Edited by Alexandra Walsham

The Politics of Gesture: Historical Perspectives
Edited by Michael J. Braddick

The Religion of Fools? Superstition Past and Present
Edited by S. A. Smith and Alan Knight

*Rodney Hilton's Middle Ages:
An Exploration of Historical Themes*
Edited by Christopher Dyer, Peter Coss and Chris Wickham

*The Art of Survival: Gender and History in Europe,
1450–2000. Essays in Honour of Olwen Hufton*
Edited by Ruth Harris and Lyndal Roper

Visit us online for each supplement's full
table of contents, or to order:
www.oxfordjournals.org/past/supplement.html